CHRISSIE HYNDE

ADDING THE BLUE

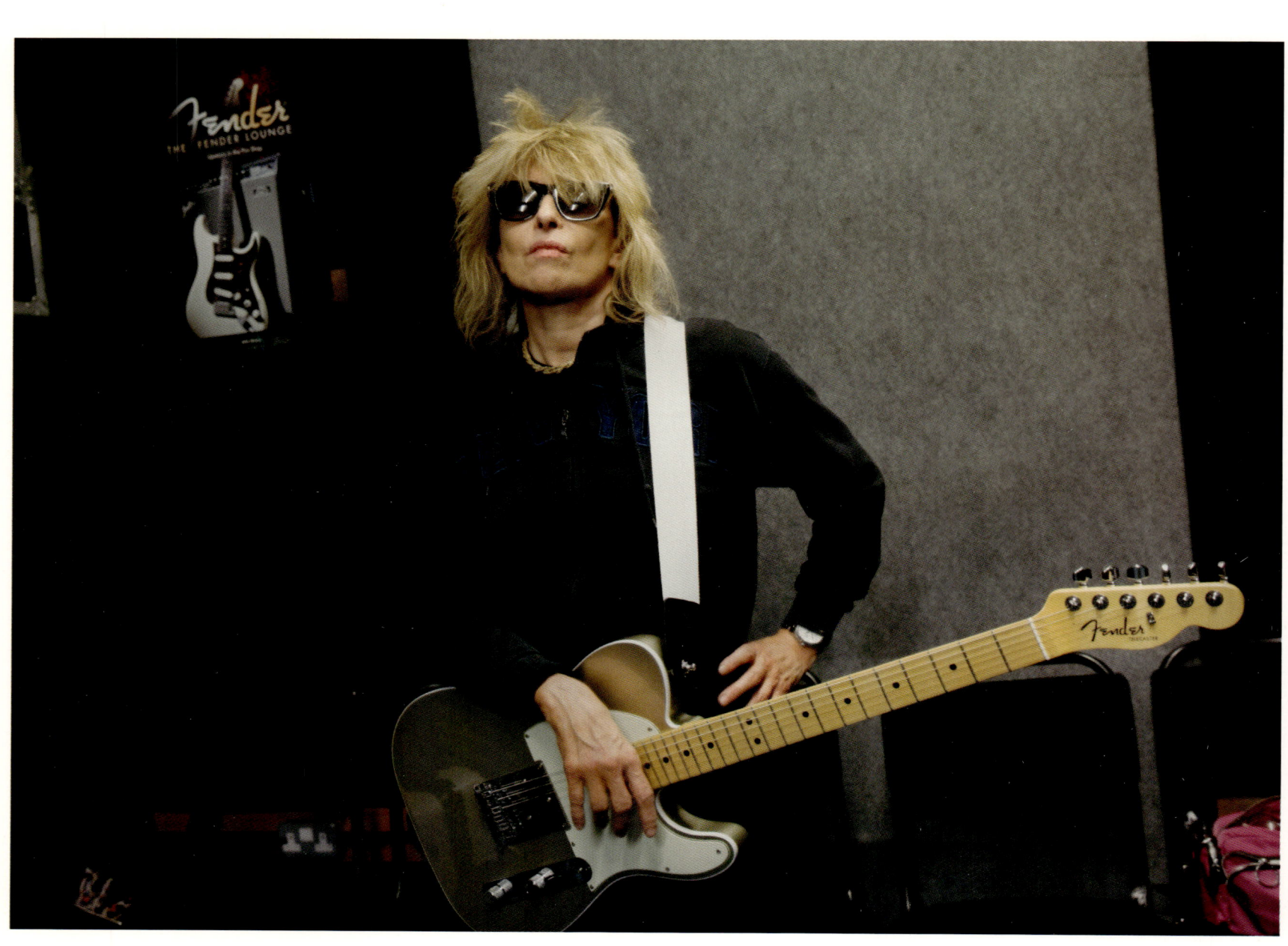

CHRISSIE HYNDE

ADDING THE BLUE

GENESIS PUBLICATIONS

SINCE 1974

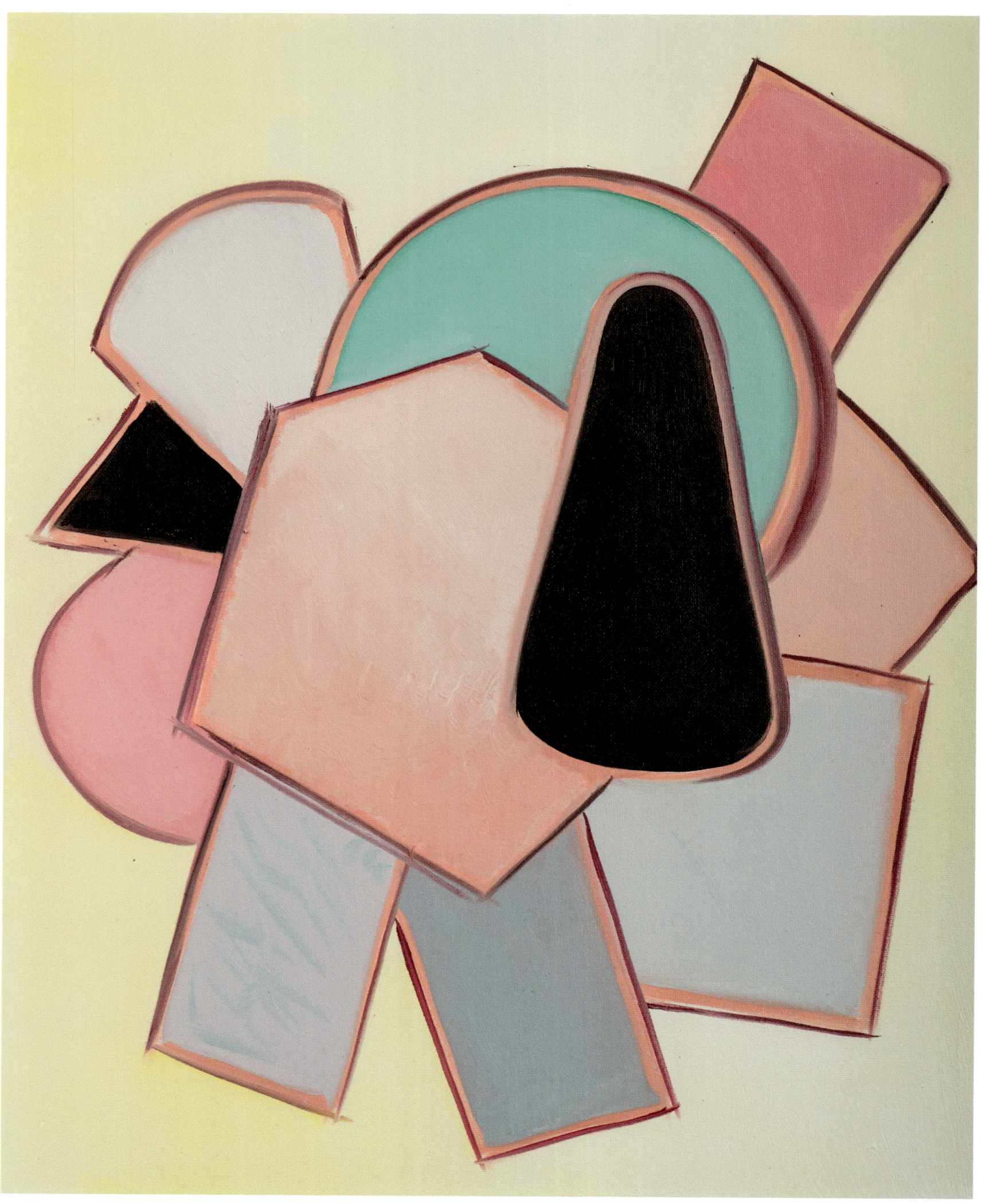

FOREWORD BY BRIAN ENO

Chrissie Hynde's paintings are full of life, love and discovery. This is a real painter. Page after page I'm thinking: this woman is really alive. Looking at somebody who's really alive makes you feel alive too.

In the art world there's a distinction made between 'outsider' artists and — actually I don't know what the others are called. 'Insider' artists maybe? Anyway, I was trying to think what the equivalent of outsider art would be in music. What is outsider music? Then it hit me: rock music. By definition. That was the whole idea. There isn't really such a thing as insider rock. If it gets inside it isn't rock any more.

So here's brilliant, fully awake Chrissie making her outsider paintings in much the same way she makes her outsider music: with no formal training but a volcano of enthusiasm and curiosity and alertness… and out come these intriguing and lovely and lively pictures. I don't know if the people who deal in 'art' will think these qualify, but for me they do the thing that art does — they wake me up, show me life, make me want to get up and do something.

WEDNESDAY APRIL
SHAPES
Oil on canvas
50 x 40 cm
(19³⁄₄ x 15³⁄₄ in)
18 April 2018

I'm always curious when creative people explore other mediums. It's often framed as a form of taboo. We have become so obsessed with categorisation in the arts that we often fail to see that those individuals doing the most interesting things really don't care about what is permitted or delineated but rather blur boundaries, cross-pollinate, follow instincts and compulsions and don't fear getting things wrong.

Chrissie Hynde has been painting in what I can only describe as a calm frenzy for nearly three years. I say calm, because the process of applying paint becomes meditative for her; but it's also paradoxically frenzied because she works so intensively and quickly, often producing a painting in a few hours, which is fast for oil and may have something to do with her intrinsic and distinctive sense of rhythm. She also seems to have no real fear of failure because although she cares deeply for the act of painting, relishes it in fact, she doesn't care at all what anyone in the art world thinks of her work.

Adding The Blue didn't come out of the blue. Chrissie's always drawn and has painted now and again. The paintings she made in 2003 started her thinking afresh but it was only when her life changed in 2015 and she had time and space that she felt compelled to have a go... and 'the floodgates opened' and she 'just couldn't stop'.

These works have a directness and immediacy that is obvious even before you know she doesn't do preparatory studies or make drawings but rather just starts 'having a stab' at the canvas. Their energy is evident across the genres. There are numerous figures and faces; still lifes with the emphasis on life not stillness or inertia (especially her flower paintings). There's the odd landscape and a growing series of abstracted forms too. Of course, the spectres of other artists inevitably hover over some of the work — Gauguin, Picasso, Georgia O'Keeffe and Van Gogh would be my first observations — but I sense little or no anxiety of influence. Rather, there is an instinctive and perceptive understanding of how certain great artists have worked and what can work for her.

When we talked about the idea of realism and representation and her shift more recently towards abstraction, Chrissie said, 'I'm not interested in realism for its own sake. I guess there are two ways of approaching it which appeal to me. There's pushing boundaries to make it more interesting, like Picasso, or there's trying to make it more beautiful, like Van Gogh.'

I'm not saying for a moment, and nor I'm sure is Chrissie, that she's a great artist, but she's an authentic one. Members of the art establishment often feel a kind of churlish resentment towards musicians who paint, but I think it enriches the cultural landscape and certainly makes the art world a more interesting place. The fact that she's a great musician doesn't undermine her painting; it underpins it. Performing and painting for her are full-on and essentially hands-on. I love the fact that in her studio, below the pots filled with brushes and under the table filled with tubes of paint, is a basket full of plectrums. Tools of her trades, old and new. She paints hands distinctively too, from the self-consciously posed arms of her sound technician David, to a series featuring her own hands, the most powerful painting in which features her daughter Yasmin's face with Chrissie's hands. There's a kind of tender visual poetry here, the daughter's face brought to life in paint by her mother's hand; there's mortality and vivacity, a labour of love and honesty.

In her searingly candid autobiography, Reckless, Chrissie wrote that 'distinctive voices in rock are trained through years of many things: frustration, fear, loneliness, anger, insecurity, arrogance, narcissism, or just sheer perseverance — anything but a teacher.' The same things forge her paintings — just look at her self-portraits if you doubt me. She learns by doing and in the process her work becomes more individual and compelling, an expression of the life force within made visible.

I always thought I would get into painting, but I got waylaid by rock 'n' roll. And then I had children, so that was game over for me. Finally, once the girls were out of the house and I was living in a place that had a room I could use as a studio, I thought, 'Now's the time.' As soon as I was in a situation where I could be alone and paint without any interruptions, I just couldn't stop.

I came from a fairly colourless background; there wasn't much music or art around at home, just a few '50s-style wire sculptures. My mother was very good with design and colour, although I didn't appreciate it at the time. She loved everything to be modern, while I longed for something old. My father was musical, but neither of them had time for artistic pursuits as they worked full time. Their generation didn't have the opportunities we had. It was all about looking after my brother and me.

When I was a little kid I liked to draw. I drew horses and I loved life drawing. At school, the art room was the place where it felt like I knew what I was doing. I was out of my depth in the more academic subjects and I probably would have gone under completely if not for my grades in art. They just about kept me from flunking out.

Then I went on to study art at Kent State University, but I didn't go to classes and I don't remember doing much painting. I did a few projects, but mainly I was a dropout. I was just biding my time until I could figure out how I could travel and see the world, which I started doing when I was 22.

When I got to England, one of my jobs was modelling for the fashion students at Saint Martin's College in London. They had a big trunk of clothes you could wear, but I just kept on my beaten-up Lewis Leathers gear. This was during the punk era. The great thing was that when I wasn't modelling I could draw the next model. No offence to those fashion students, but I think I was the only person there who could draw, so that was kind of frustrating.

I suppose I could have got into painting sooner — found a barn out in the country somewhere — but the time wasn't right for me. Rock 'n' roll seemed a lot more fun. I like a certain amount of isolation, which you need for painting, but there's a point where you start losing your sanity. But when I was proofreading my autobiography a few years ago, I noticed that I kept talking about painting, even though I didn't paint. It was like a fantasy I had. Then, when I moved to my current place a couple of years ago and I started painting, it all suddenly made sense. People worry that they've missed the boat, but it really is never too late to start doing something you love.

I thank my lucky stars every day that I can play guitar, be in a rock band, and if I want to paint, I can paint. I don't want anything else. I'm totally satisfied with that.

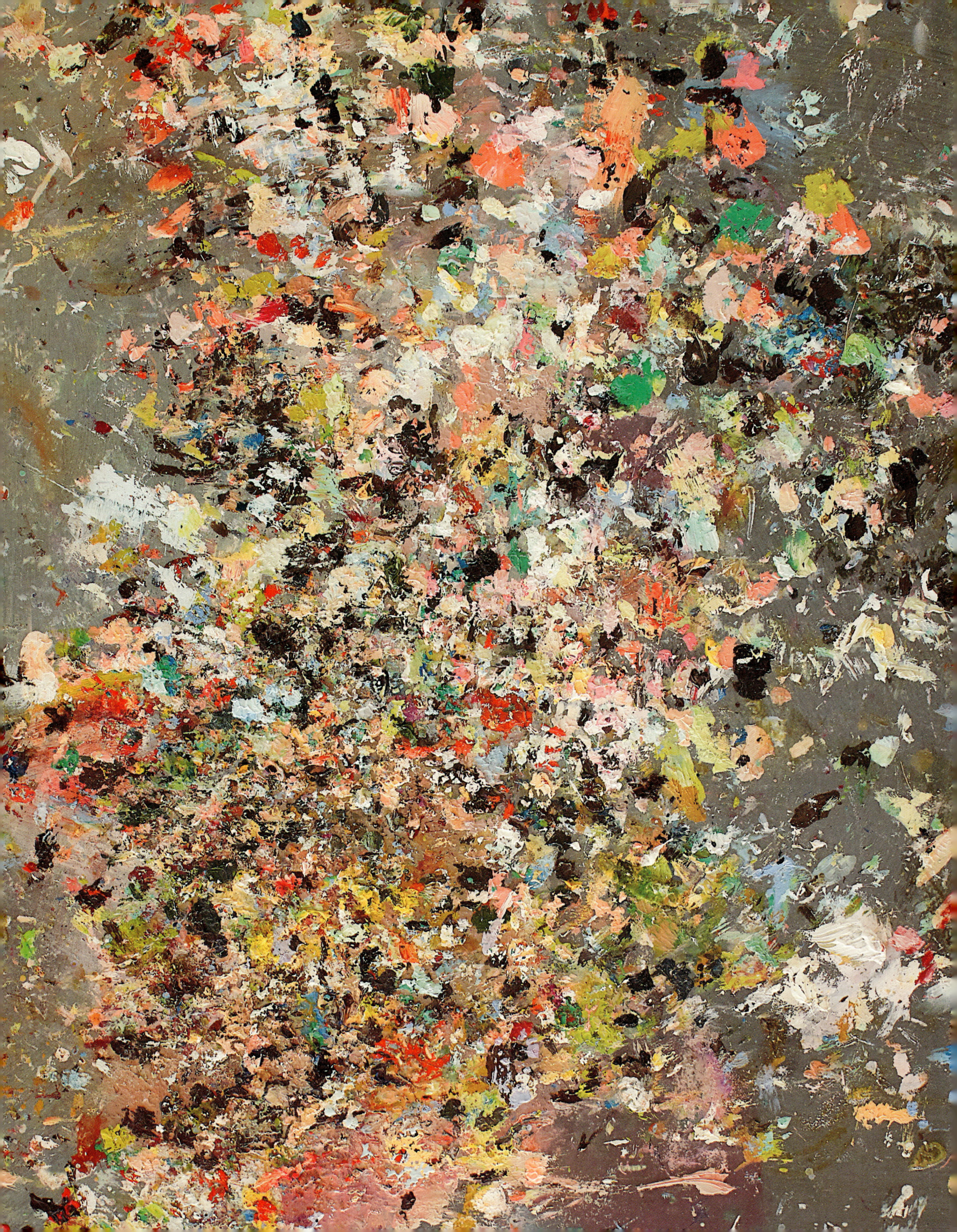

The paintings within this book are presented roughly in the order that I painted them.

OPPOSITE:
The table in
Chrissie Hynde's
painting room
in London

I don't know where painting would have gone if it had been my only serious career. I might have started with acrylics. I think when I was still a teenager, acrylics seemed the modern way to paint; it seemed fast. But I guess I just thought that oil paint is proper paint. All of the people that I love, like Van Gogh, used oil paints.

Everything about oil, the medium itself, is just so interesting: the texture of it, the way it dries, the way it looks; being able to see the brush strokes and manipulate the paint. The way the canvas bounces: you can feel it with the brush and the oil. It's very sensual and it's really exciting. Because of the way that the oil colours are, you can kind of merge them together and mix the colours on the canvas. It's a real turn-on.

Before I started I didn't know all of that yet. I wasn't part of the modern world of art, so I wasn't comparing my technique or what I was doing to what anyone else was doing. I didn't have any contemporaries or an artistic community that I was in an ongoing conversation with. I just went off and started doing it on my own, and I chose oils and I fell in love with them.

THREE DIFFERENT
KINDS OF POT I
Oil on canvas
40 x 40 cm
(15³⁄₄ x 15³⁄₄ in)
29 November 2015

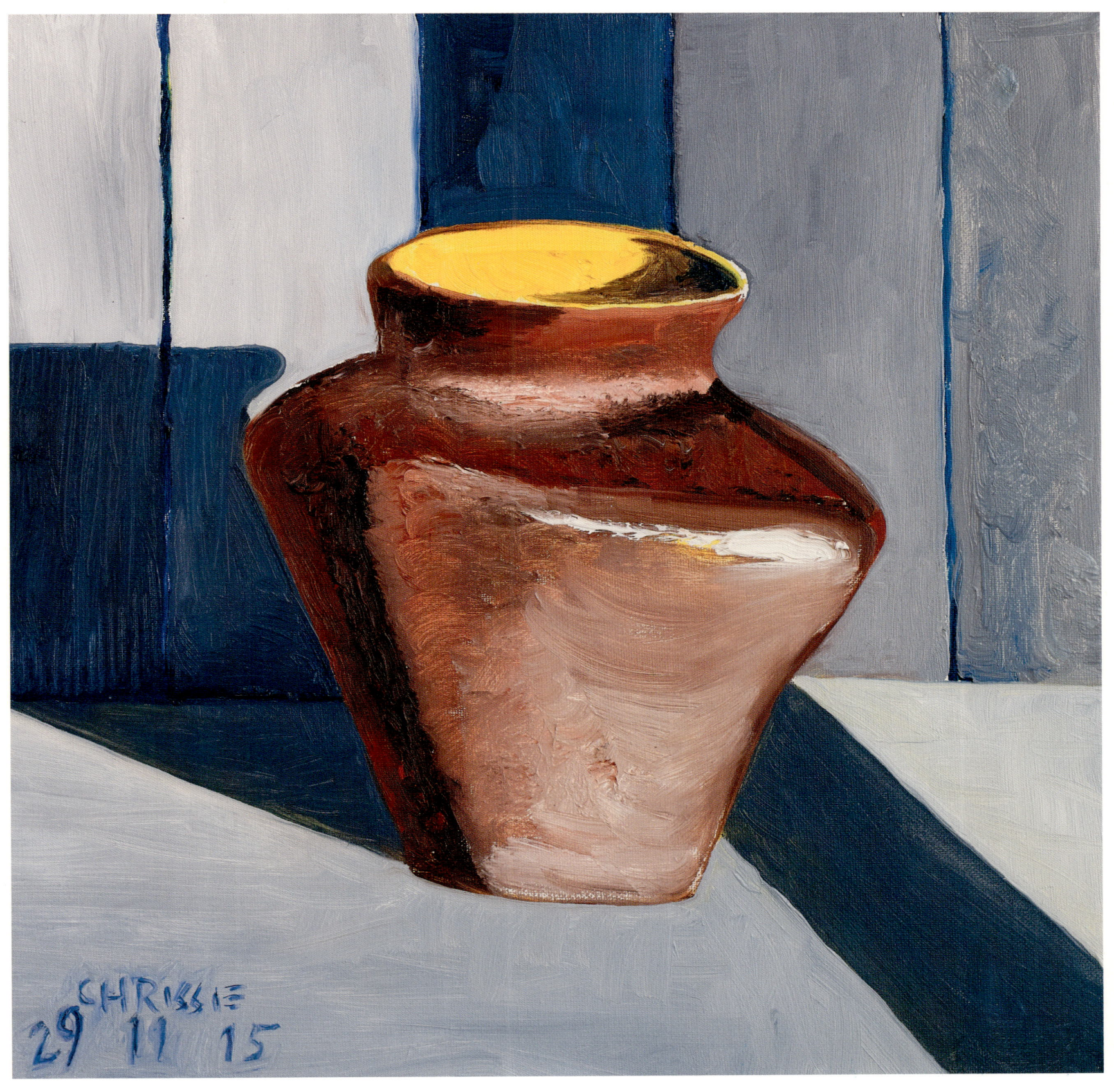

Linda McCartney's eldest daughter, Heather, was a potter and she gave me this pot years ago. It's a beautiful pot, so when I decided to have a go at painting, that's what I painted. I was so excited that I painted another one straight after.

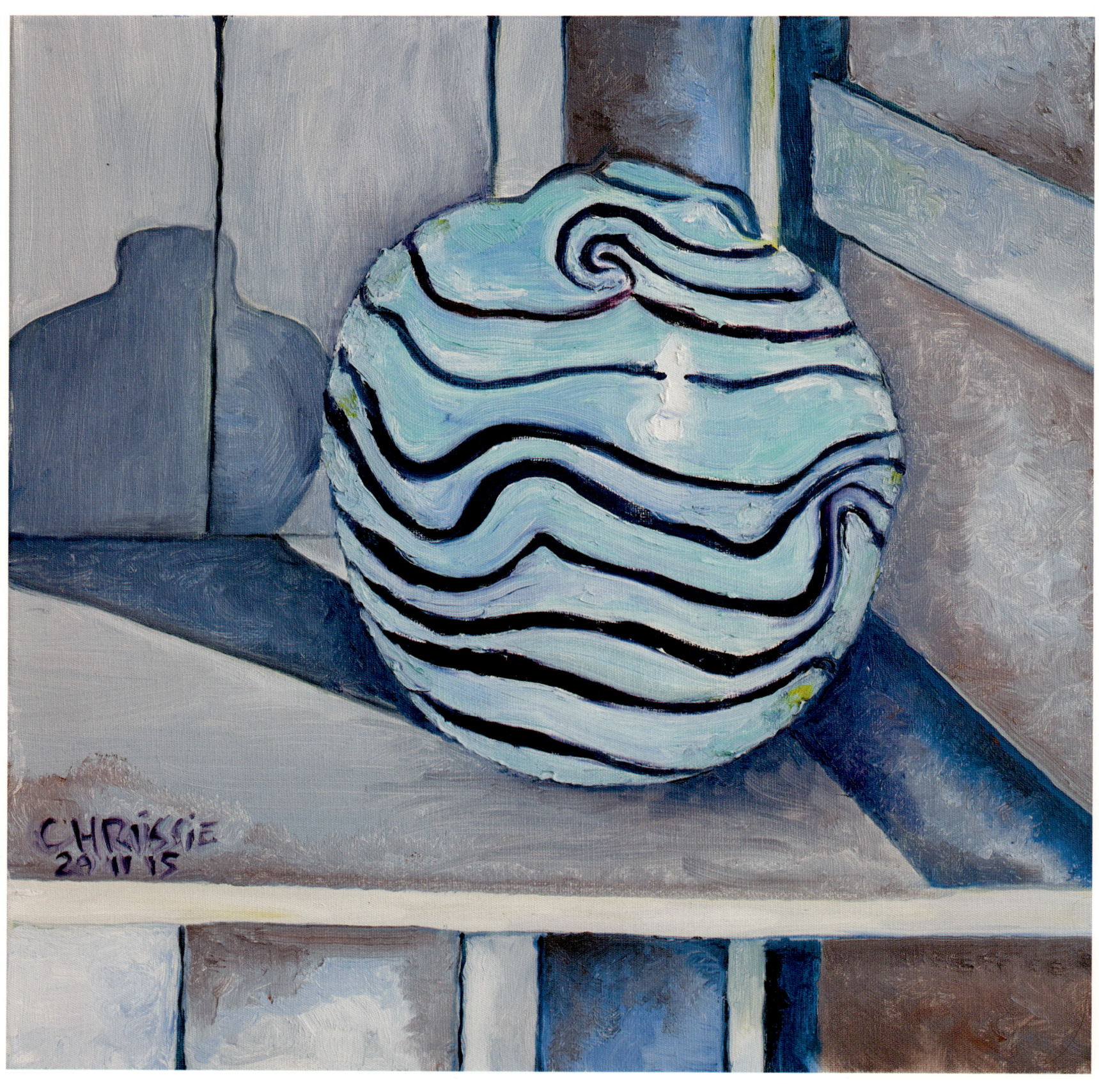

THREE DIFFERENT
KINDS OF POT II
Oil on canvas
40 x 40 cm
(15³/₄ x 15³/₄ in)
29 November 2015

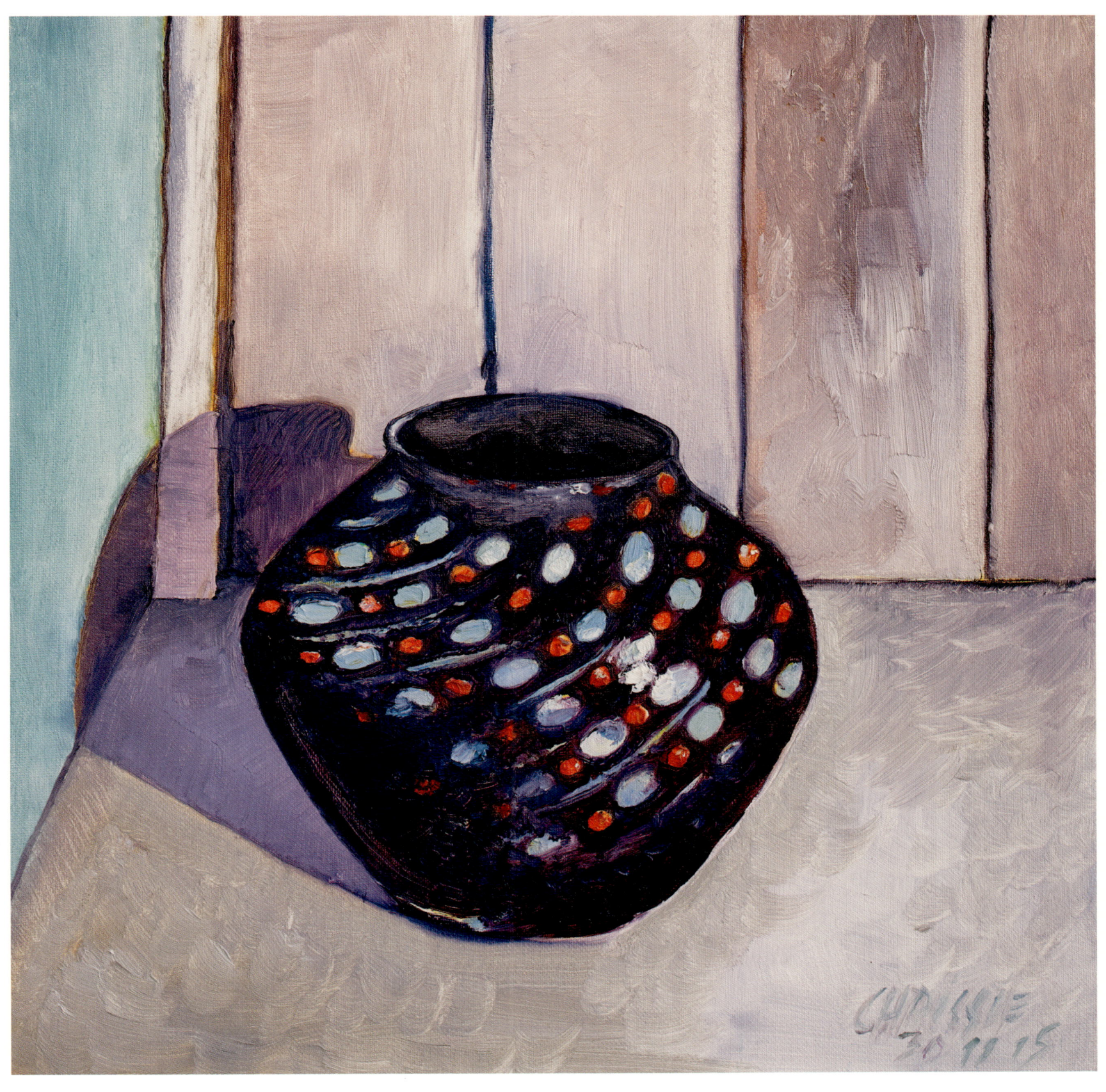

THREE DIFFERENT
KINDS OF POT III
Oil on canvas
40 x 40 cm
(15³⁄₄ x 15³⁄₄ in)
30 November 2015

I started buying flowers every day, because flowers are beautiful to look at, and if they're good enough for Van Gogh... These were my first flower paintings. And then the floodgates opened. This one is pretty much the start of my painting career in earnest.

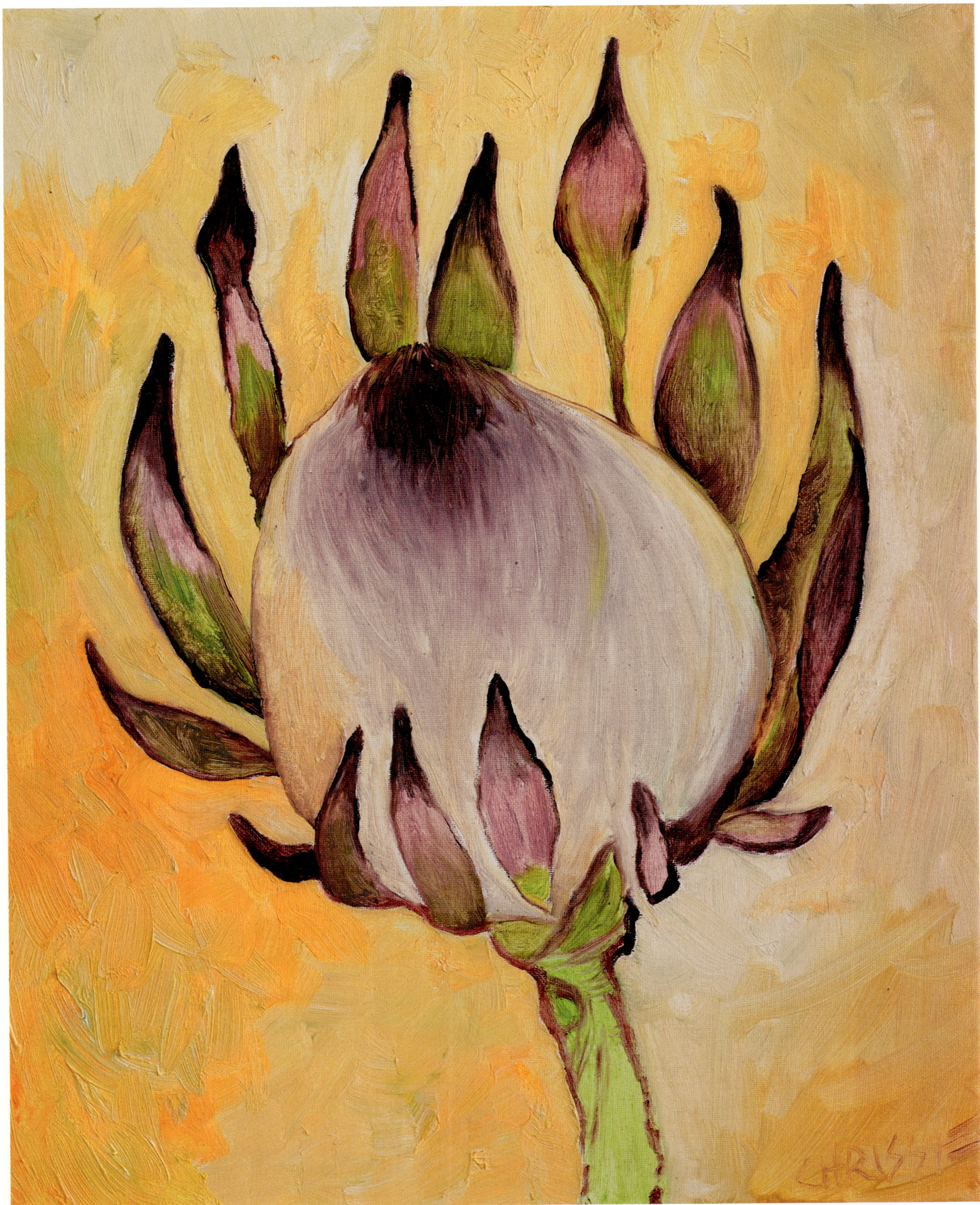

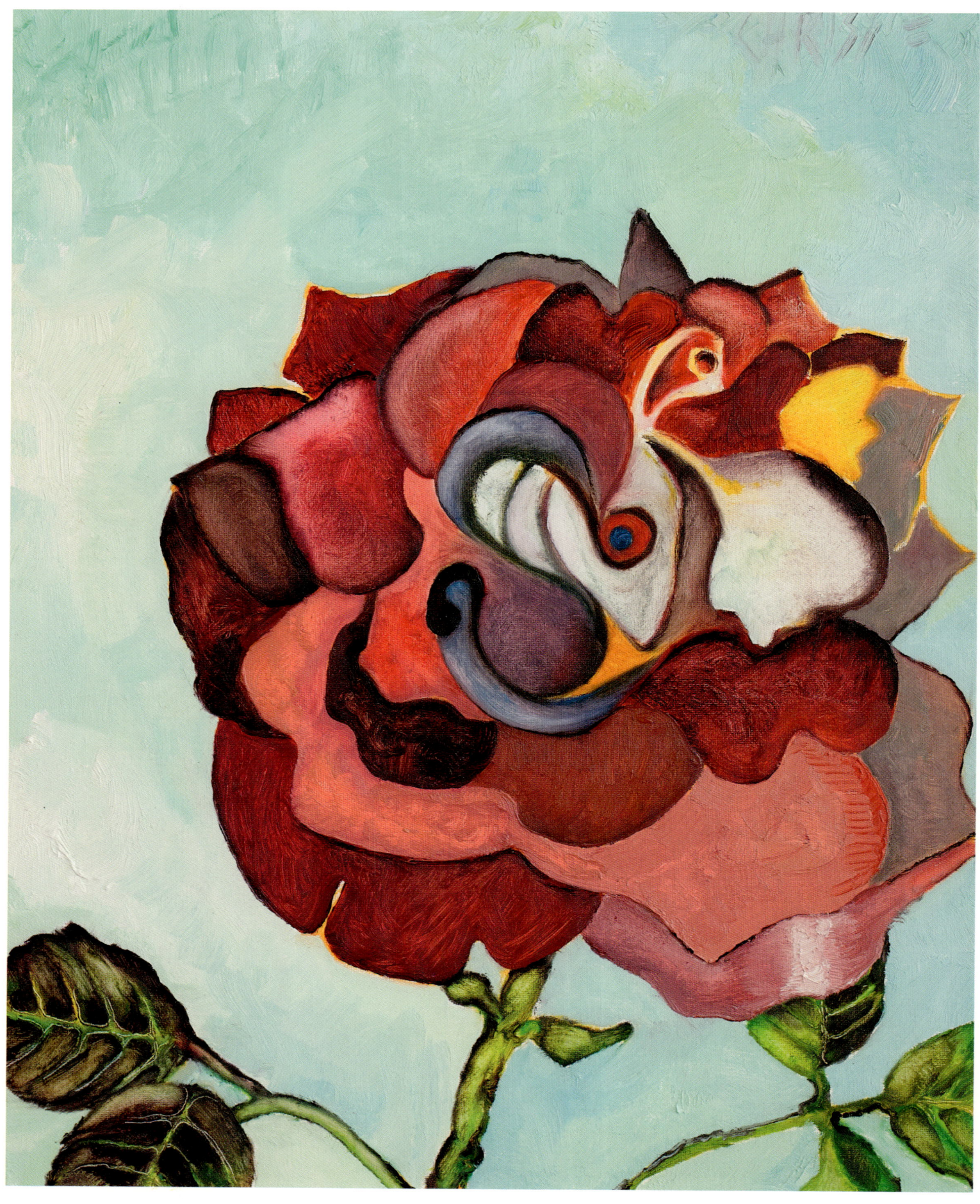

THREE FLOWERS II
Oil on canvas
50 x 40 cm
(19³⁄₄ x 15³⁄₄ in)
25 February 2016

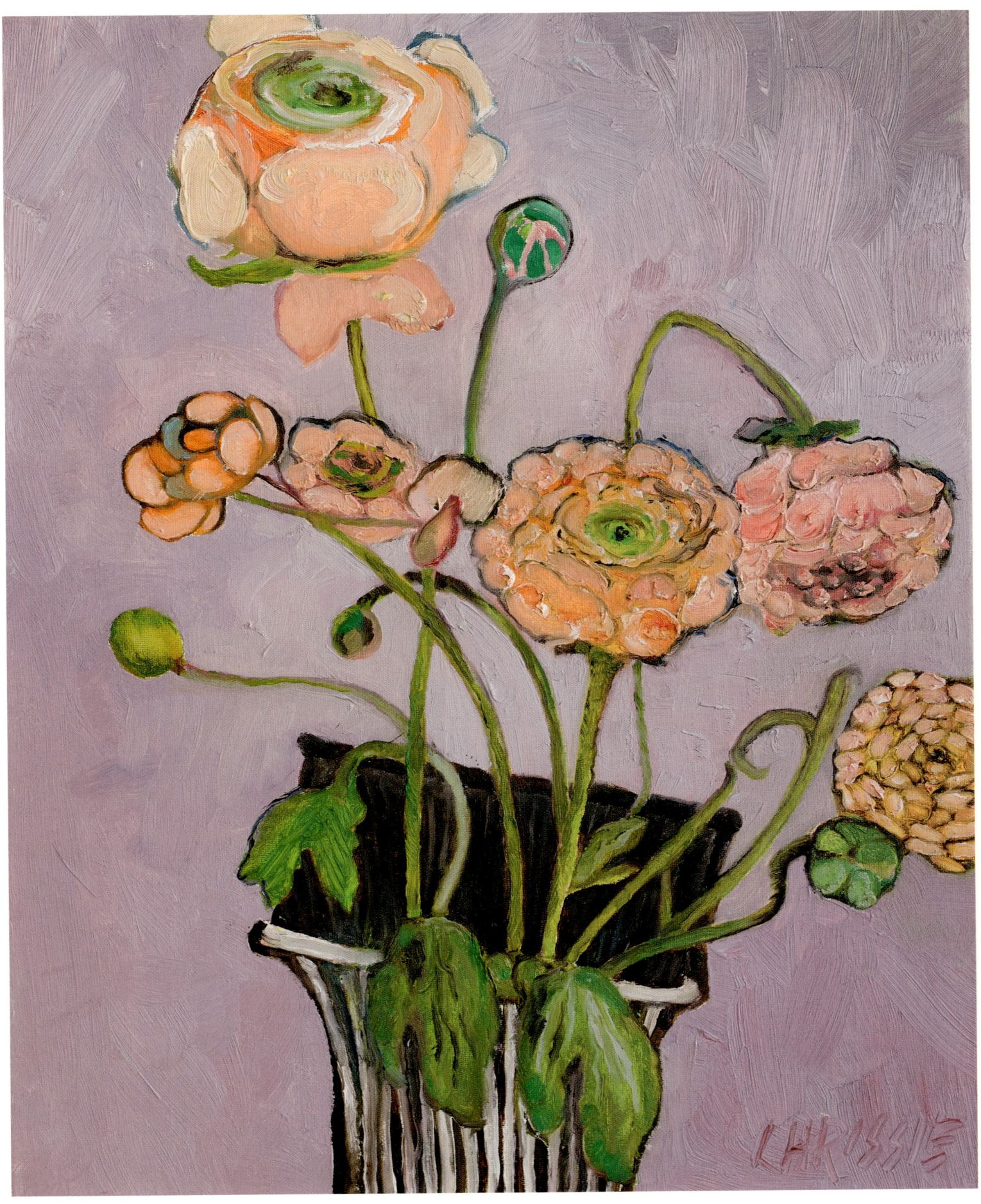

THREE FLOWERS III
Oil on canvas
50 x 40 cm
(19³⁄₄ x 15³⁄₄ in)
25 February 2016

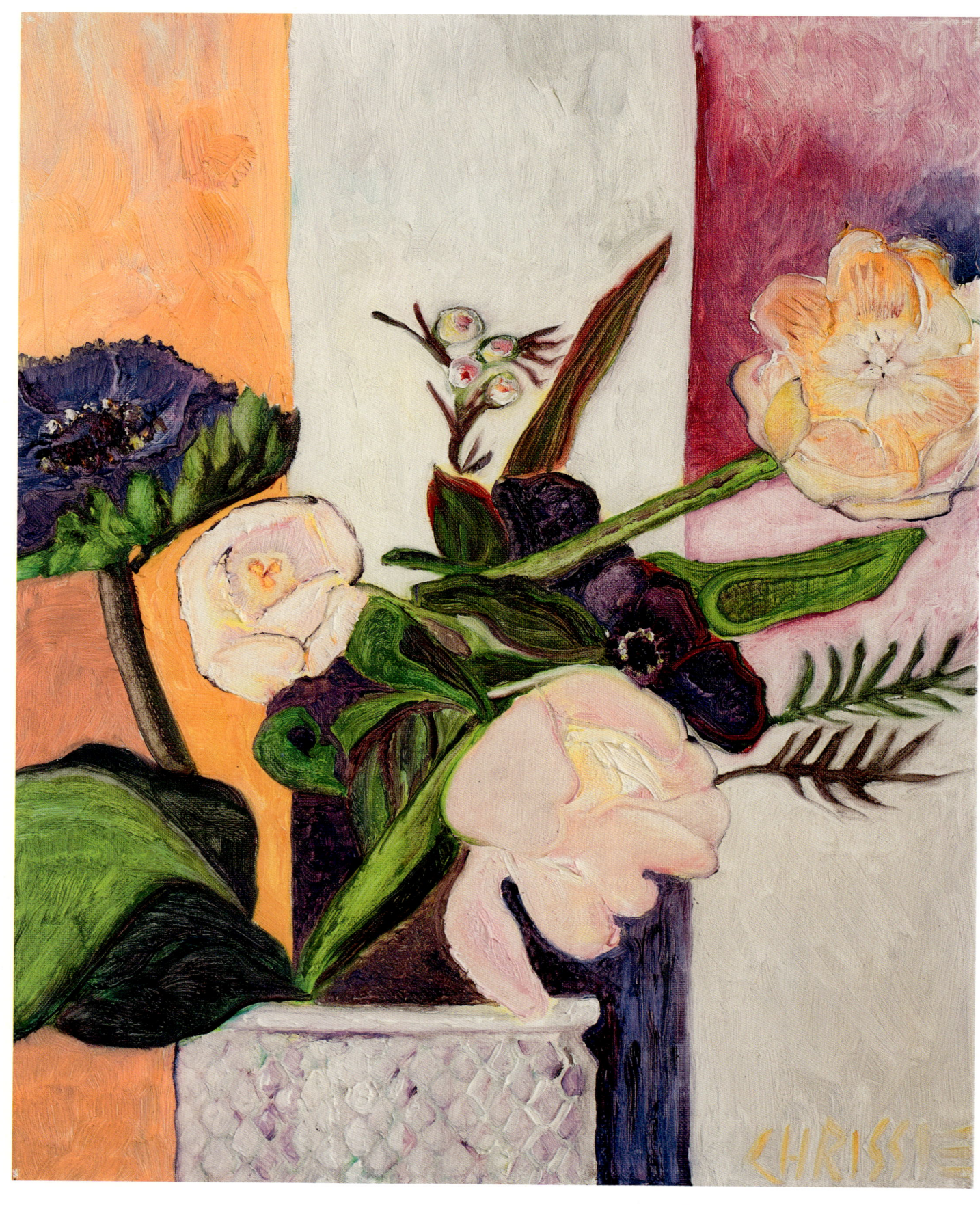

TUESDAY FLOWER
Oil on canvas
50 x 40 cm
(19³/₄ x 15³/₄ in)
8 March 2016

TUESDAY FLEUR
Oil on canvas
50 x 40 cm
(19³/₄ x 15³/₄ in)
8 March 2016

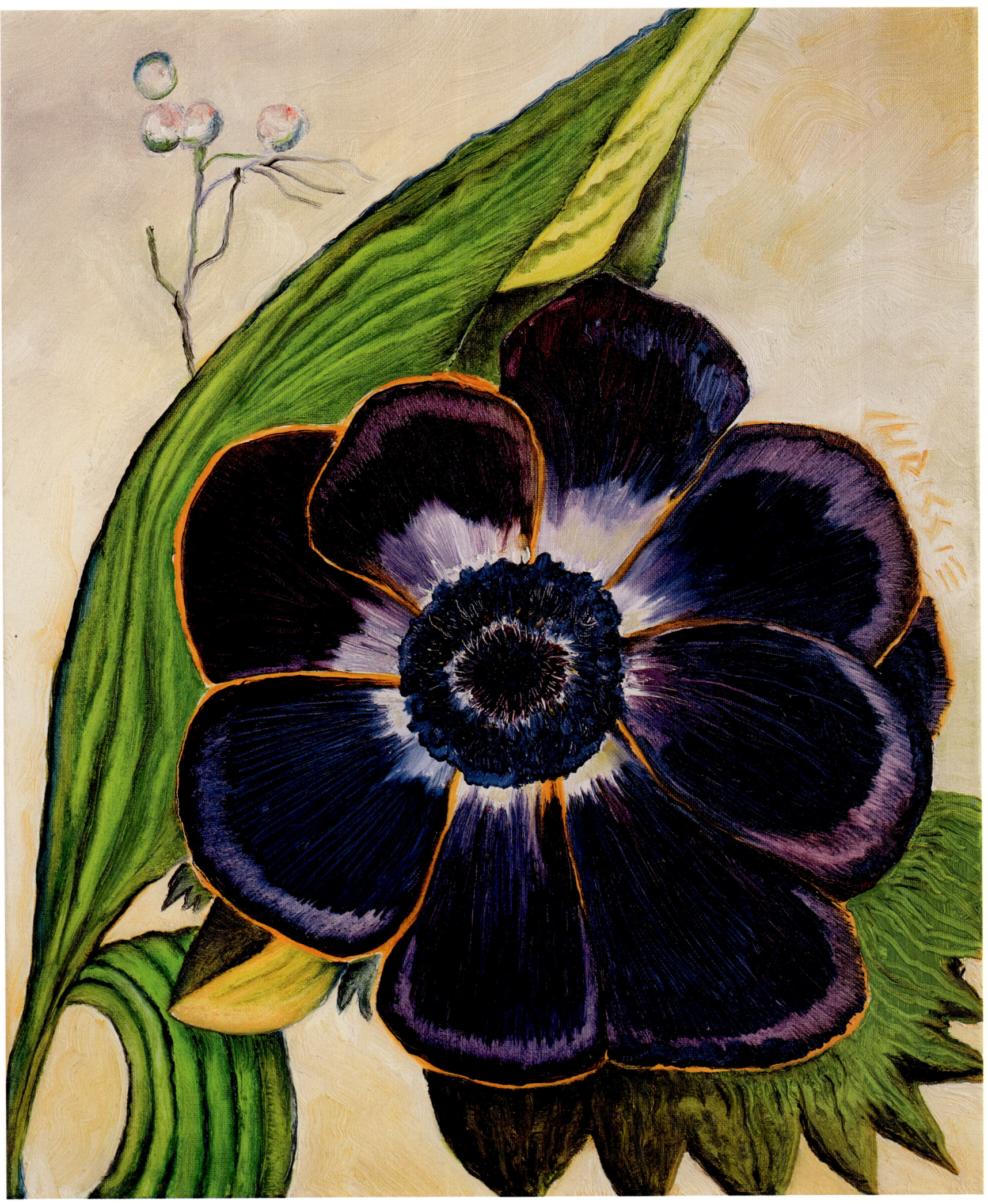

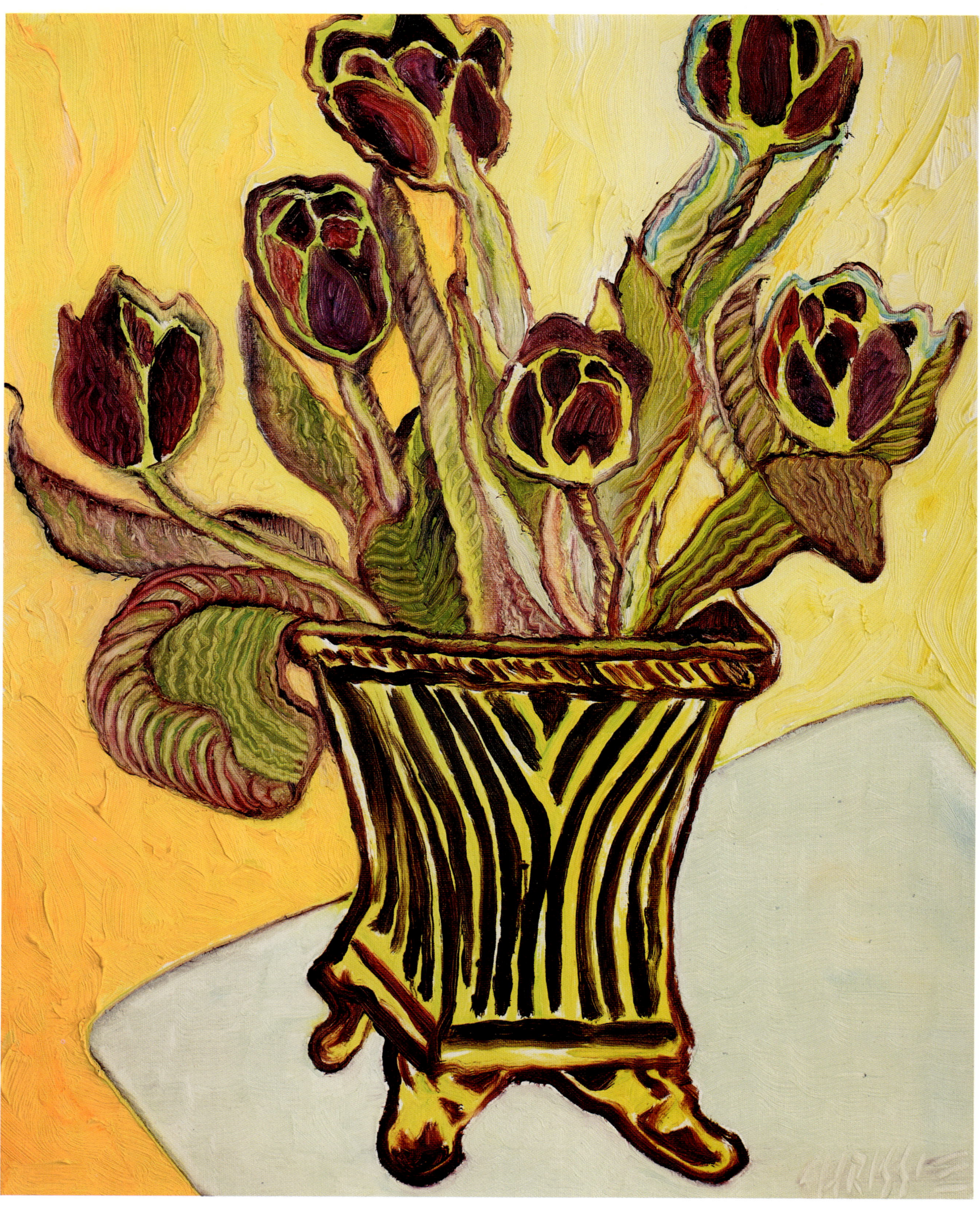

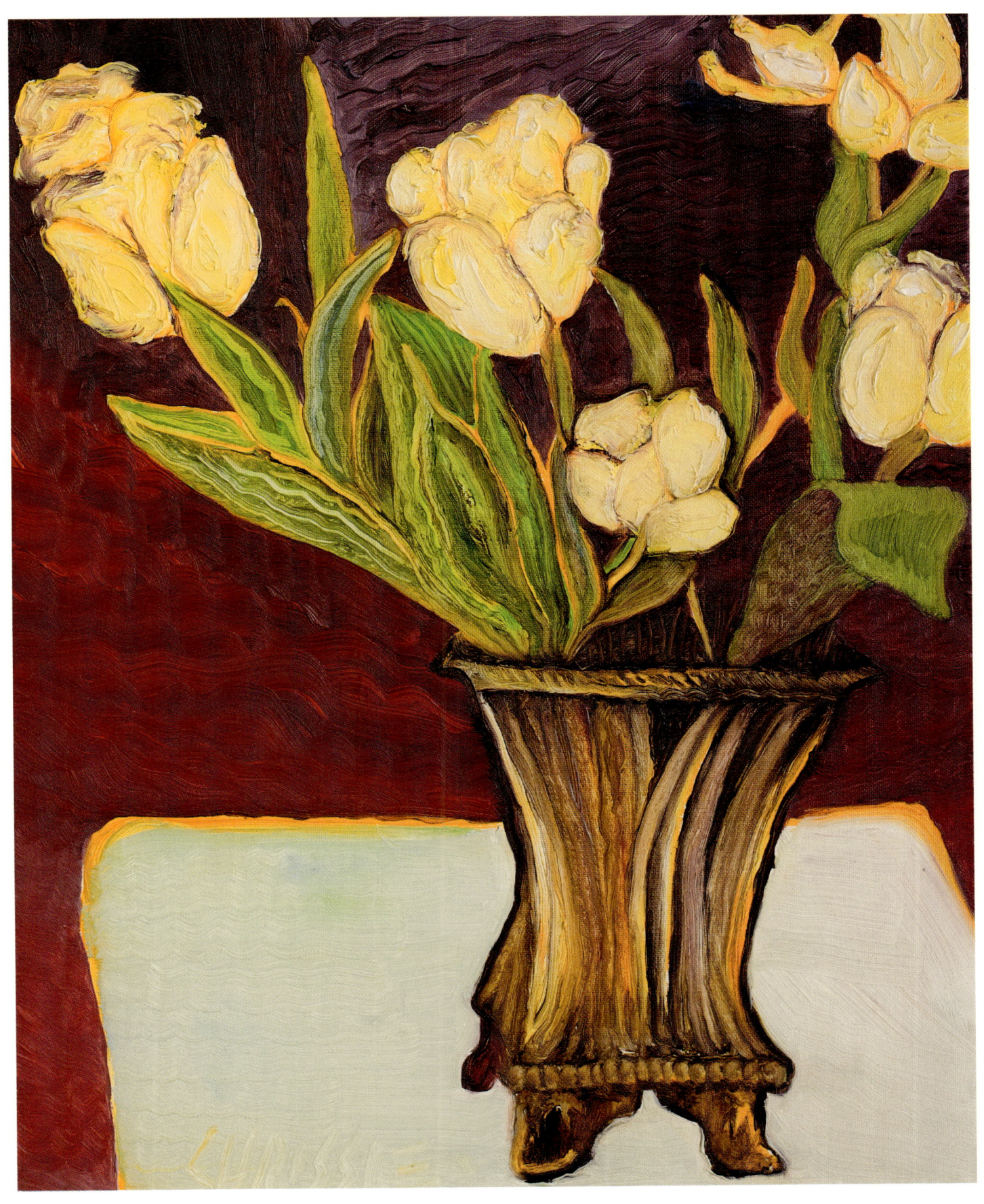

TUESDAY TULIPS
Oil on canvas
50 x 40 cm
(19³/₄ x 15³/₄ in)
15 March 2016

THURSDAY TULIPS
Oil on canvas
50 x 40 cm
(19³/₄ x 15³/₄ in)
17 March 2016

The place where I buy my canvases on the Finchley Road, North London,
had all these masks. I wasn't sure if you were supposed to paint on the mask…
or paint a picture of the mask. I didn't ask. I started painting fruit, because
I was getting a little tired of flowers, but then I thought, well, really, who wants
to look at a bowl of fruit? And so I just started dropping a mask into it. I think
I was hoping I'd learn how to do something abstract.

BOWL OF CHERRY
TOMATOES GRASS
MAT MASK
Oil on canvas
50 x 40 cm
(19³/⁴ x 15³/⁴ in)
29 February 2016

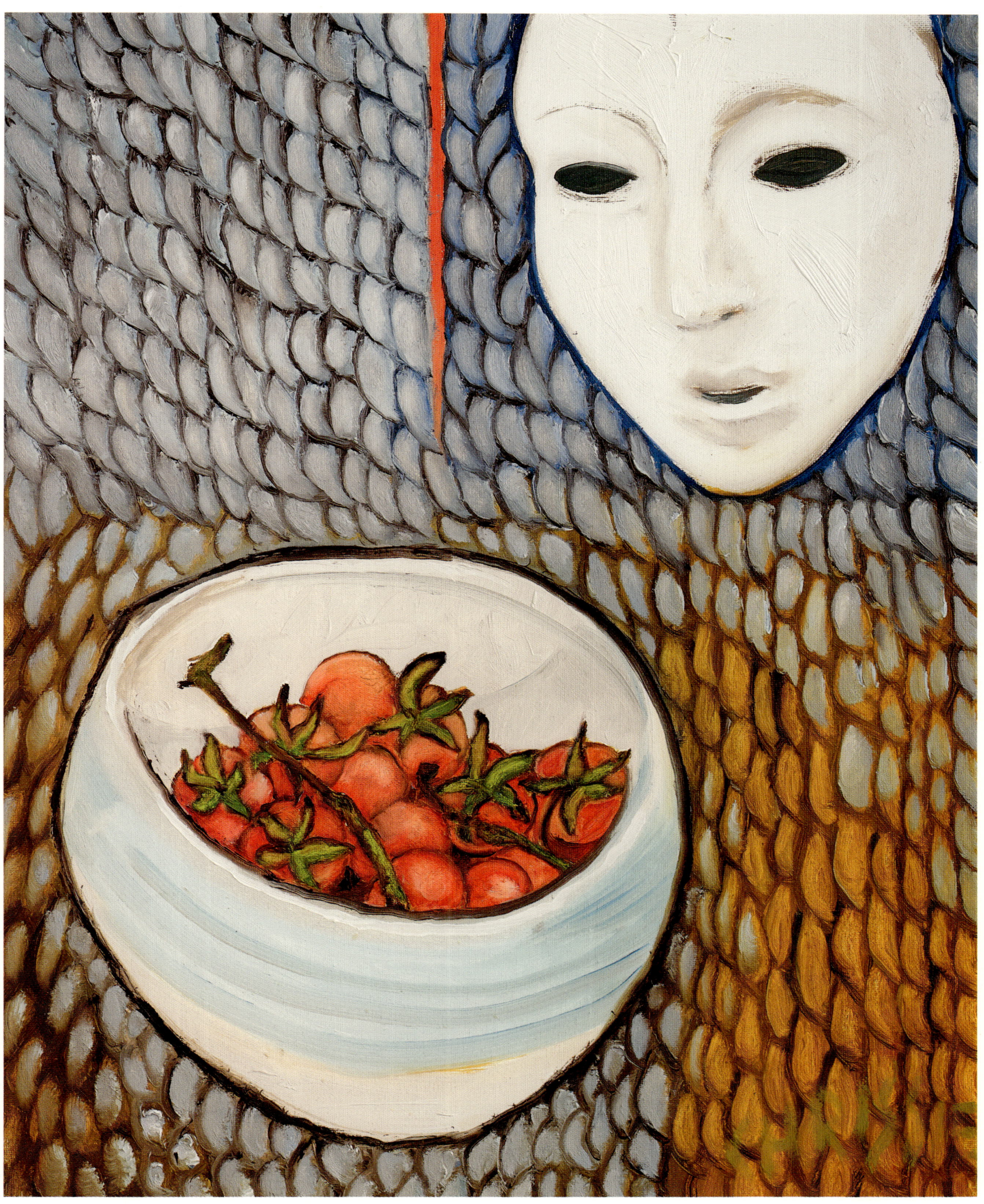

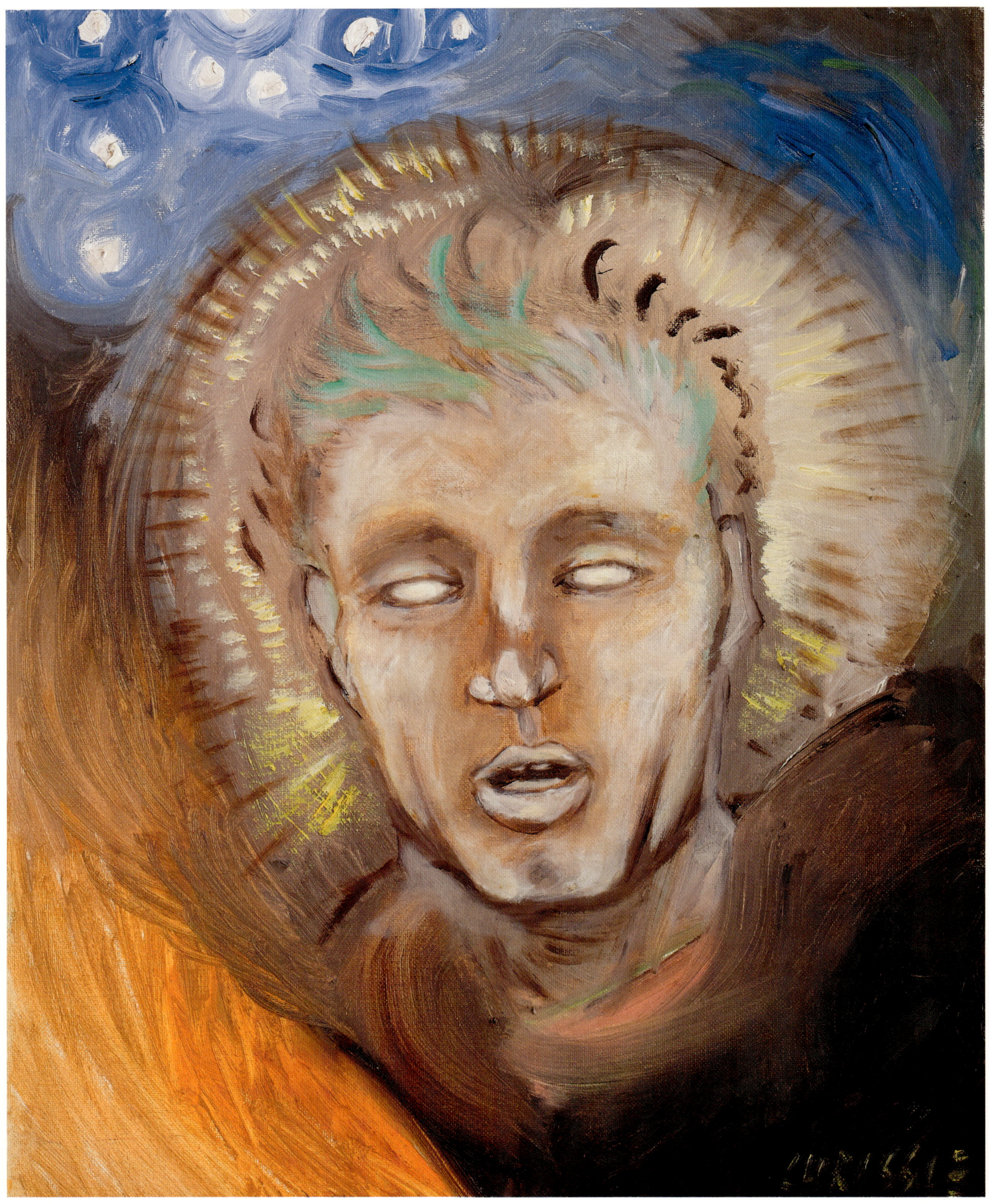

One time I was travelling long distance on a bus. We got off the bus in the middle of the night, so that everyone could relieve themselves. As I walked into the dark, I saw this motorcycle helmet stuck on a cross to mark a fallen biker, and that really made an impression on me. I named the painting after a Willie Nelson song I really love called 'Angel Flying Too Close to the Ground'.

This is my first painting of an imaginary person. I have a certain history with some bikers, so I won't say whether I had anyone in mind. Let's just say, maybe.

ANGEL FLYING TOO
CLOSE TO THE
GROUND (WILLIE
NELSON SONG)
Oil on canvas
50 x 40 cm
(19¾ x 15¾ in)
2 March 2016

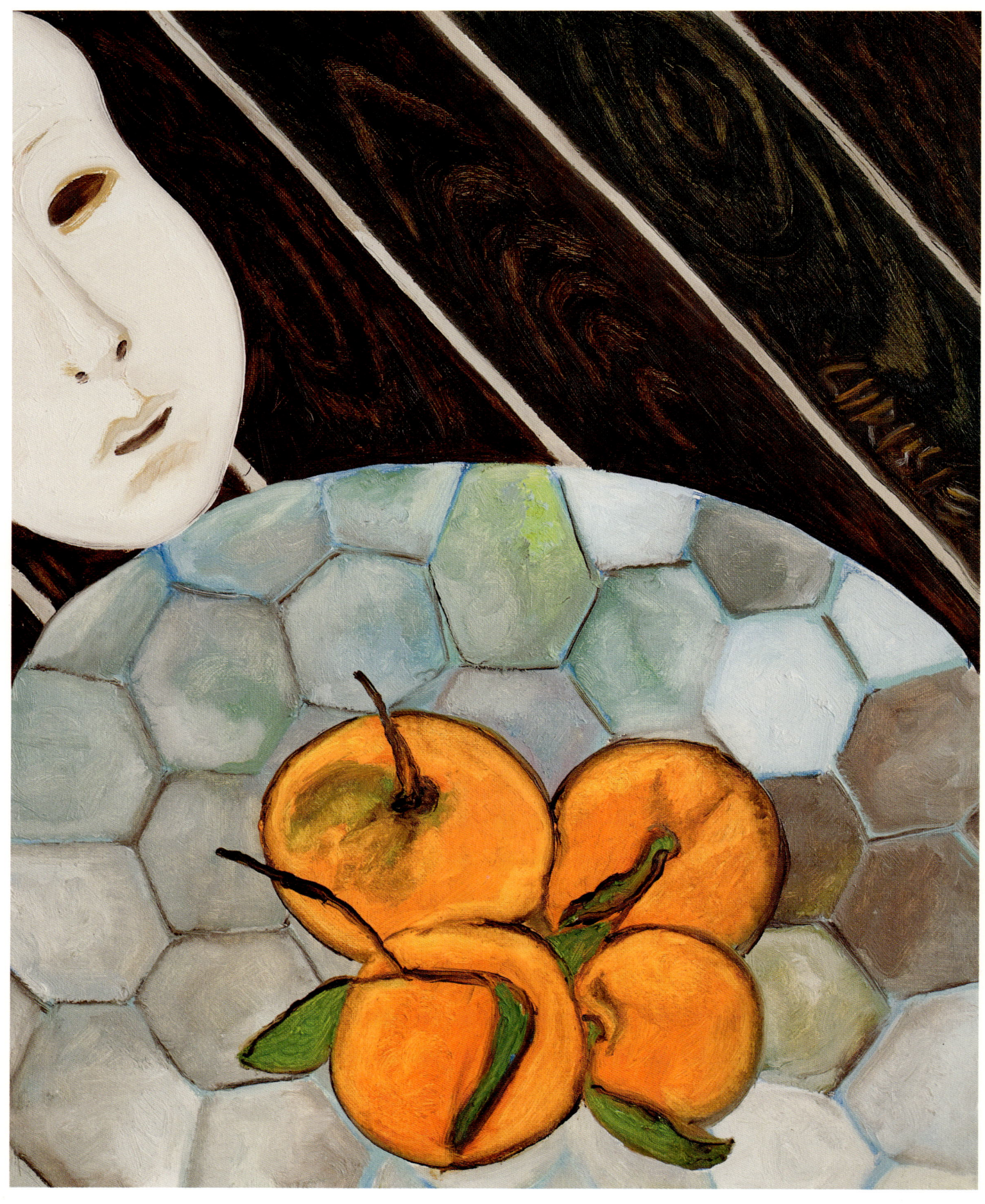

BEGINNING OF MASKS
Oil on canvas
50 x 40 cm
(19³/₄ x 15³/₄ in)
27 February 2016

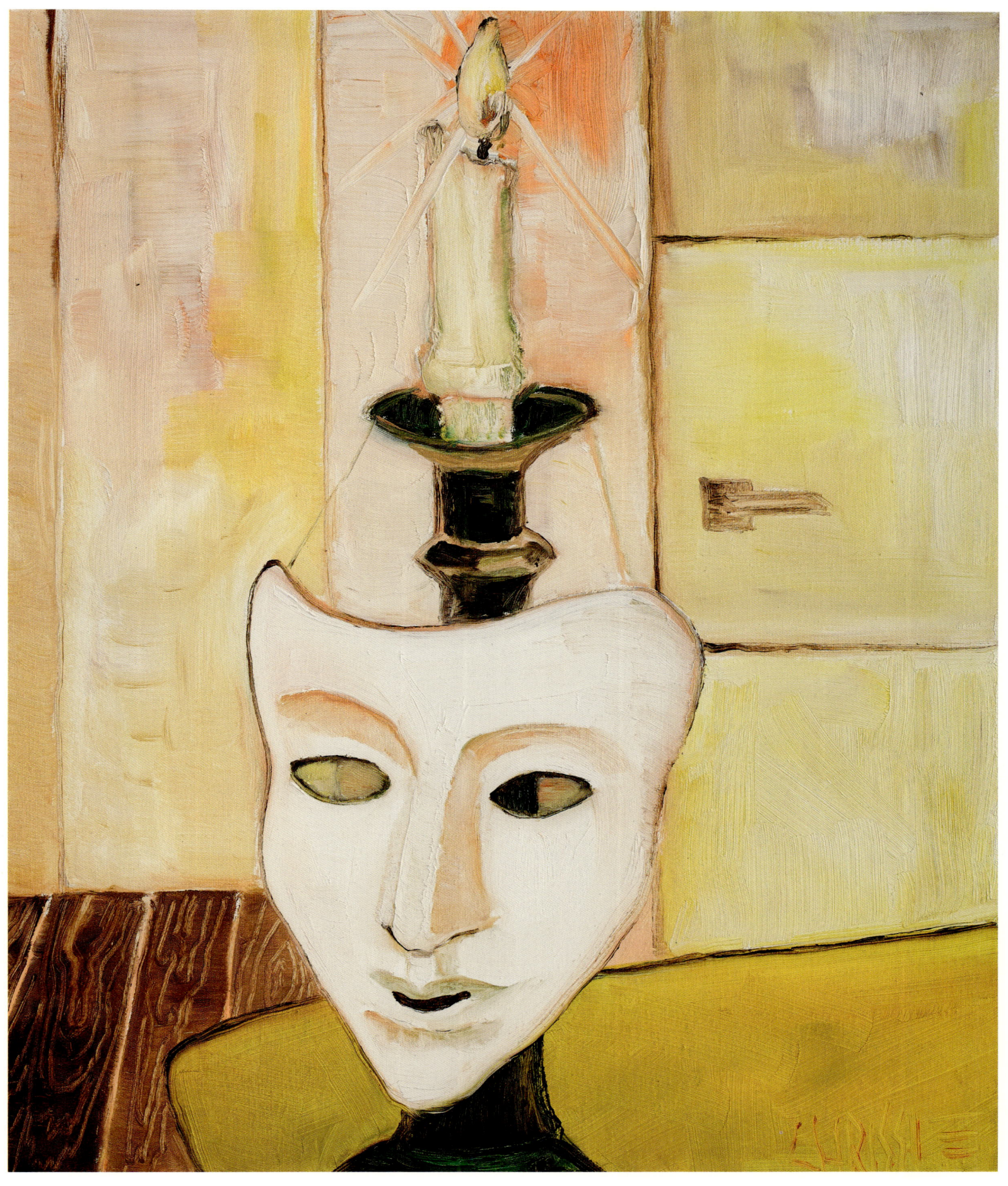

SATURDAY MASK
CANDLE
Oil on canvas
60 x 50 cm
(23$^{1/2}$ x 19$^{3/4}$ in)
13 August 2016

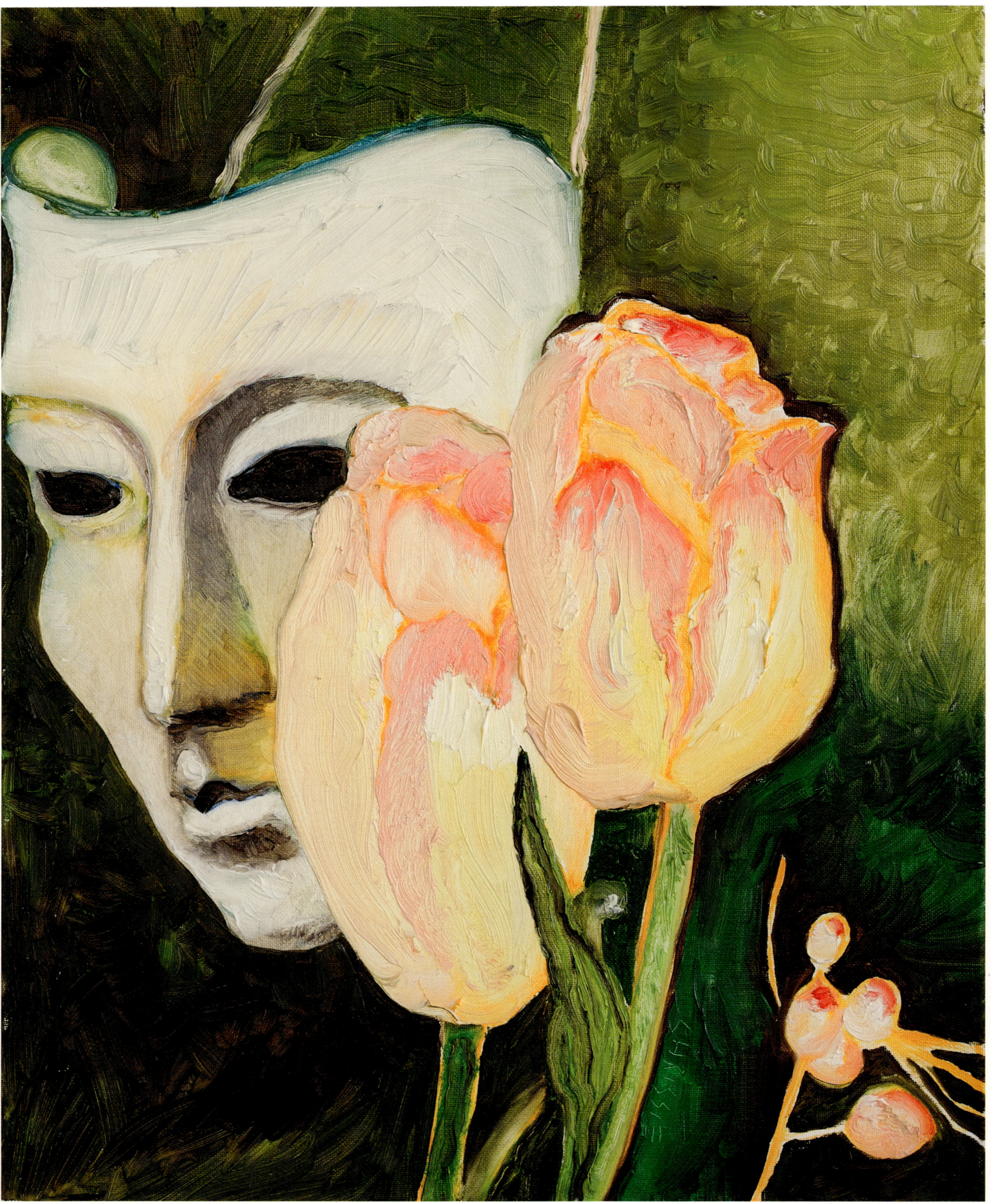

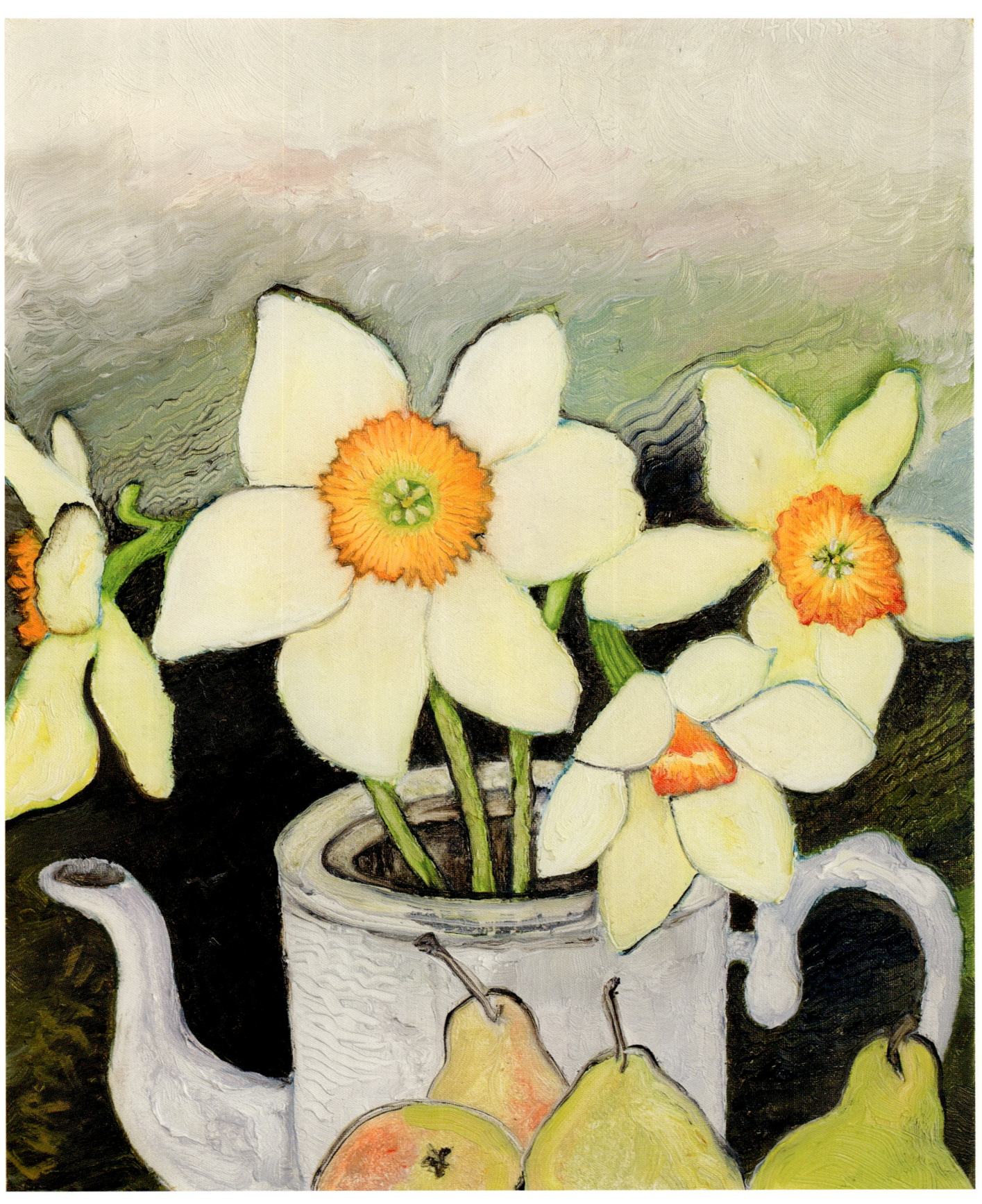

Sometimes I spend too long on a painting that I should have left alone. I get it looking pretty good and then maybe I have to go out and when I come back I have another stab. It can end up looking a little too studied.

MASK FLOWER SUNDAY
Oil on canvas
50 x 40 cm
(19¾ x 15¾ in)
13 March 2016

DAFFODILS POT PEARS
Oil on canvas
50 x 40 cm
(19¾ x 15¾ in)
14 March 2016

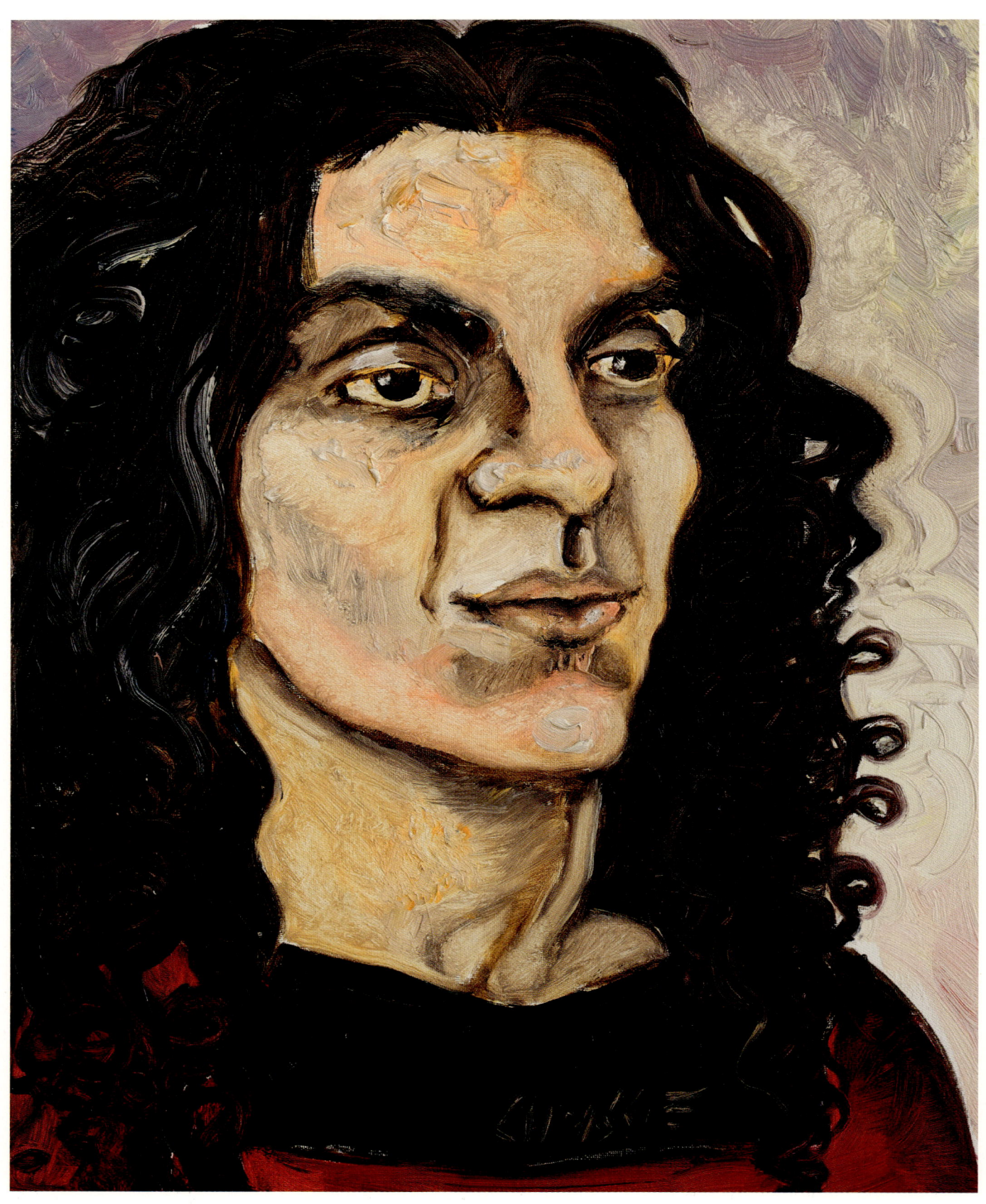

Tanya Seghatchian is a good friend of mine. She's a film producer, and she came in and sat for me. She only wears black and red. It's the first portrait I had done in a long time.

TANYA
Oil on canvas
50 x 40 cm
(19³/₄ x 15³/₄ in)
5 March 2016

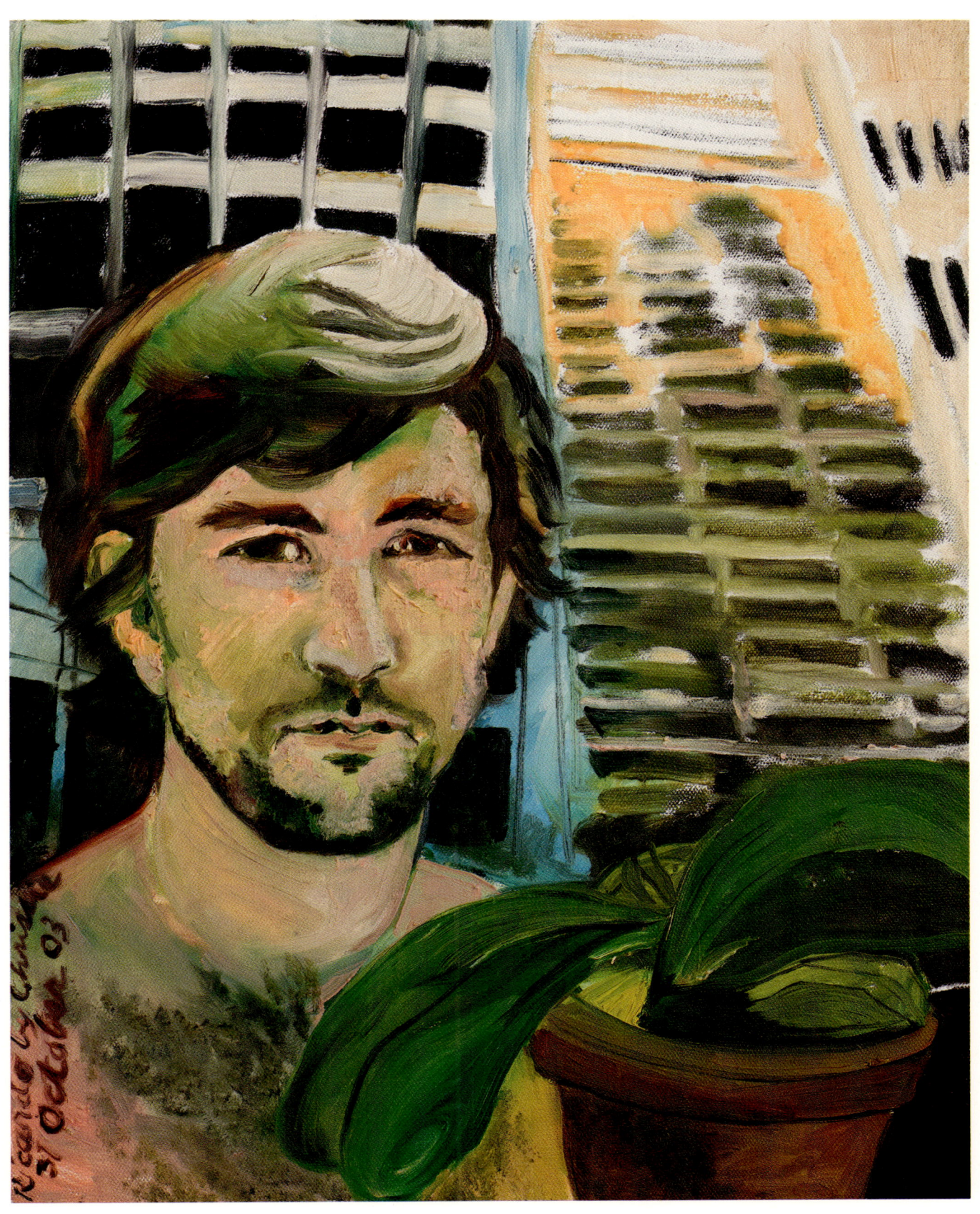

I did a couple of paintings about 15 years ago after visiting São Paulo with
my friend Ricardo Alcaide, who is an artist. This one was largely taken from
a photo, which I don't normally do, but I think it captures something of
Ricardo and São Paulo.

AVENIDA SÃO LUÍS
Oil on canvas
30 x 30 cm
(11¾ x 11¾ in)
31 October 2003

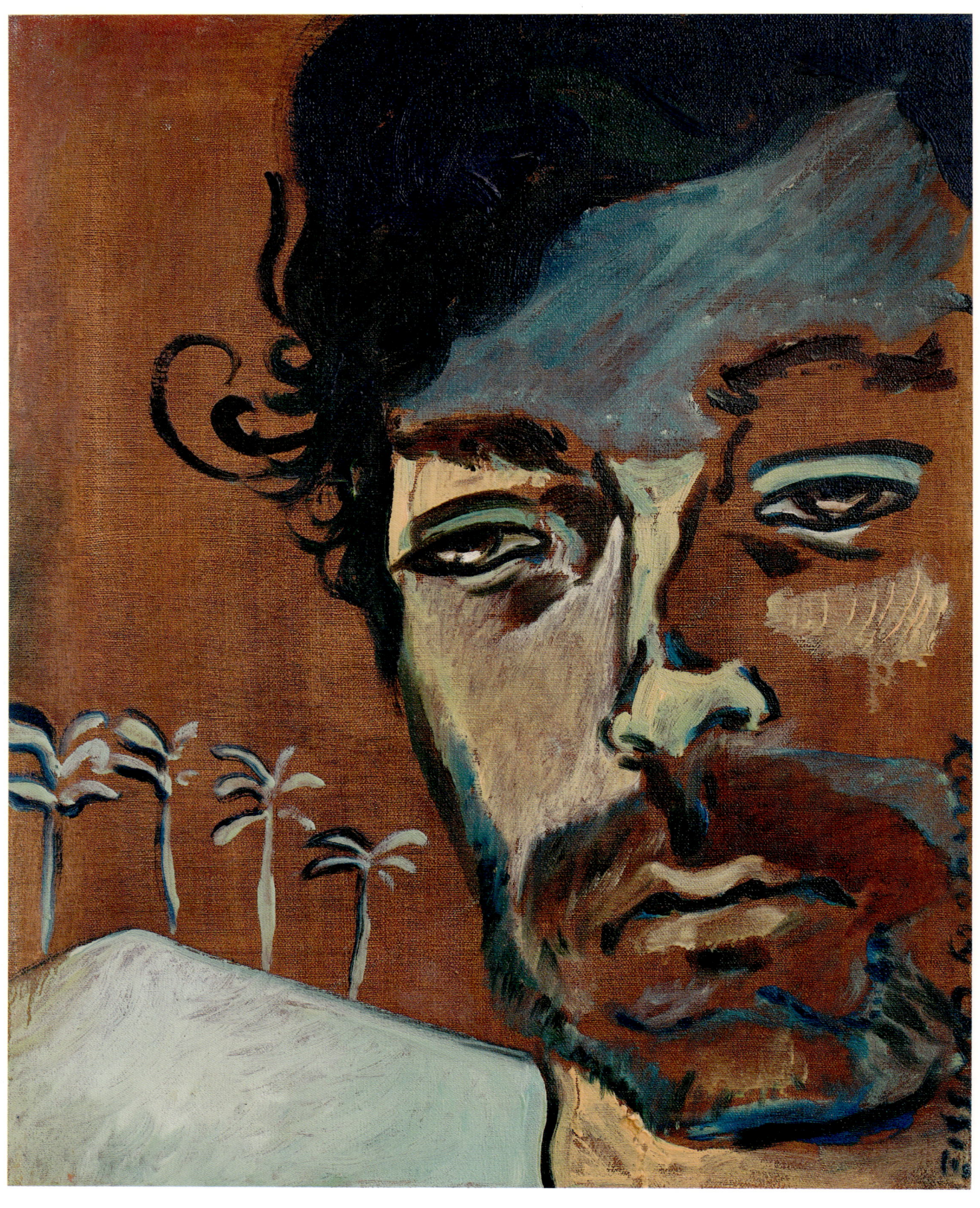

These two paintings of Ricardo are from sketches.

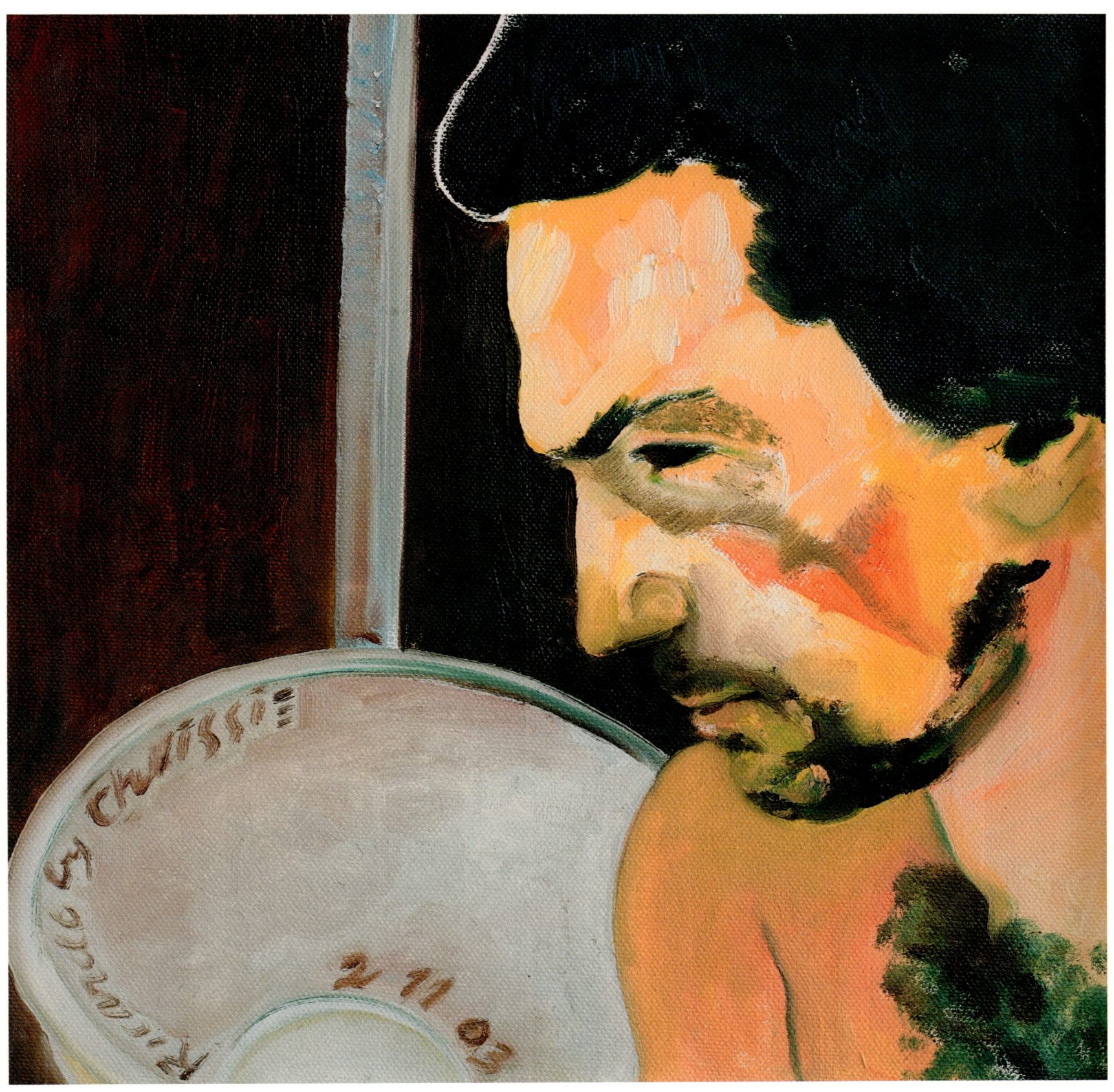

FIRST HANGOVER
BRASILIA
Oil on canvas
50 x 40 cm
(19³/₄ x 15³/₄ in)
1 November 2003

RICARDO SUMMER
SEVILLE
Oil on canvas
50 x 40 cm
(19³/₄ x 15³/₄ in)
2 November 2003

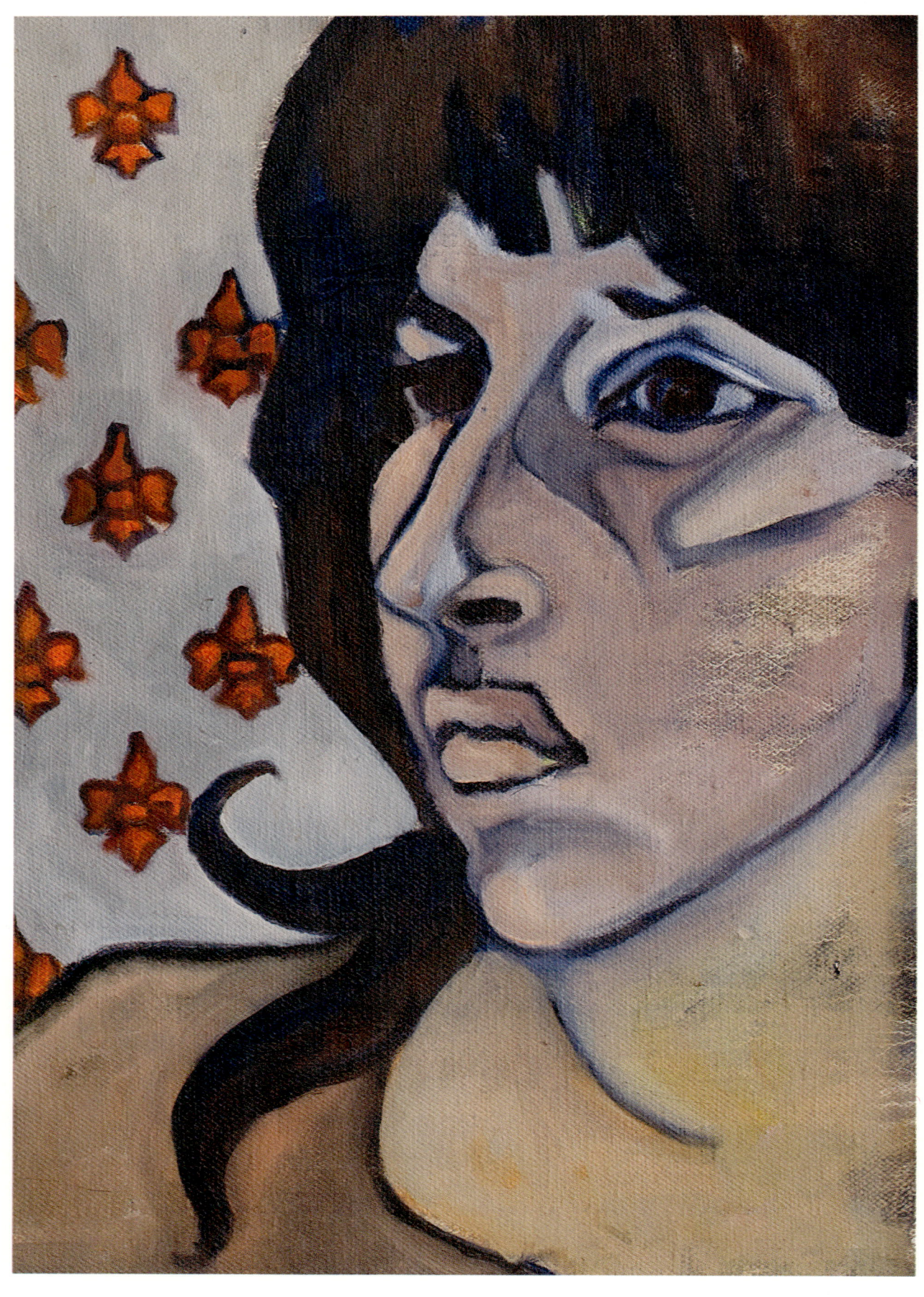

I painted this one of my elder daughter, Natalie, in 2003. I had it framed, because it was her. It does look like her, I'll say that.

TWO NATALIES I
Oil on canvas
35 x 25 cm
(13³⁄₄ x 9³⁄₄ in)
2003

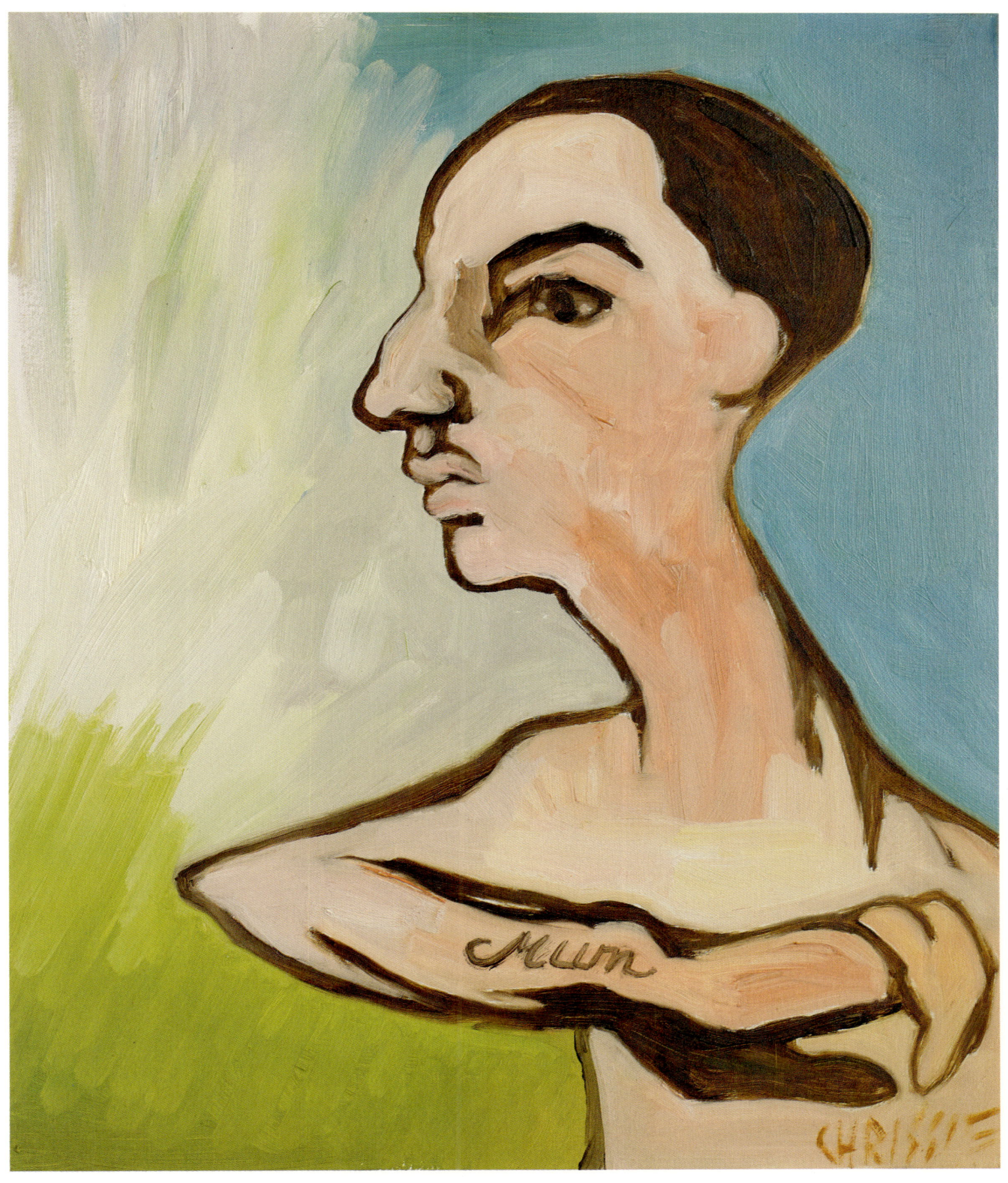

And then I painted her again more recently, with her tattoo of 'Mum'.
I love that tattoo.

TWO NATALIES II
Oil on canvas
60 x 50 cm
(23½ x 19¾ in)
24 May 2016

I felt that something was starting here and I kept going back to it for a while. These are my early abstracts.

I try not to do portraits, although that would be my natural inclination as it's a real pleasure. I suppose portraiture is not that adventurous but I still love it, if I can find someone who will sit for me.

This painting marked the beginning of me trying to get away from portraits and into abstraction, which is more challenging. It's pretty much like writing songs. I might know what I want to write about, but generally I just dive in and see what's down there.

TUESDAY FLOWER WITH
DIFFERENT LIGHT
Oil on canvas
50 x 40 cm
(19³/₄ x 15³/₄ in)
22 March 2016

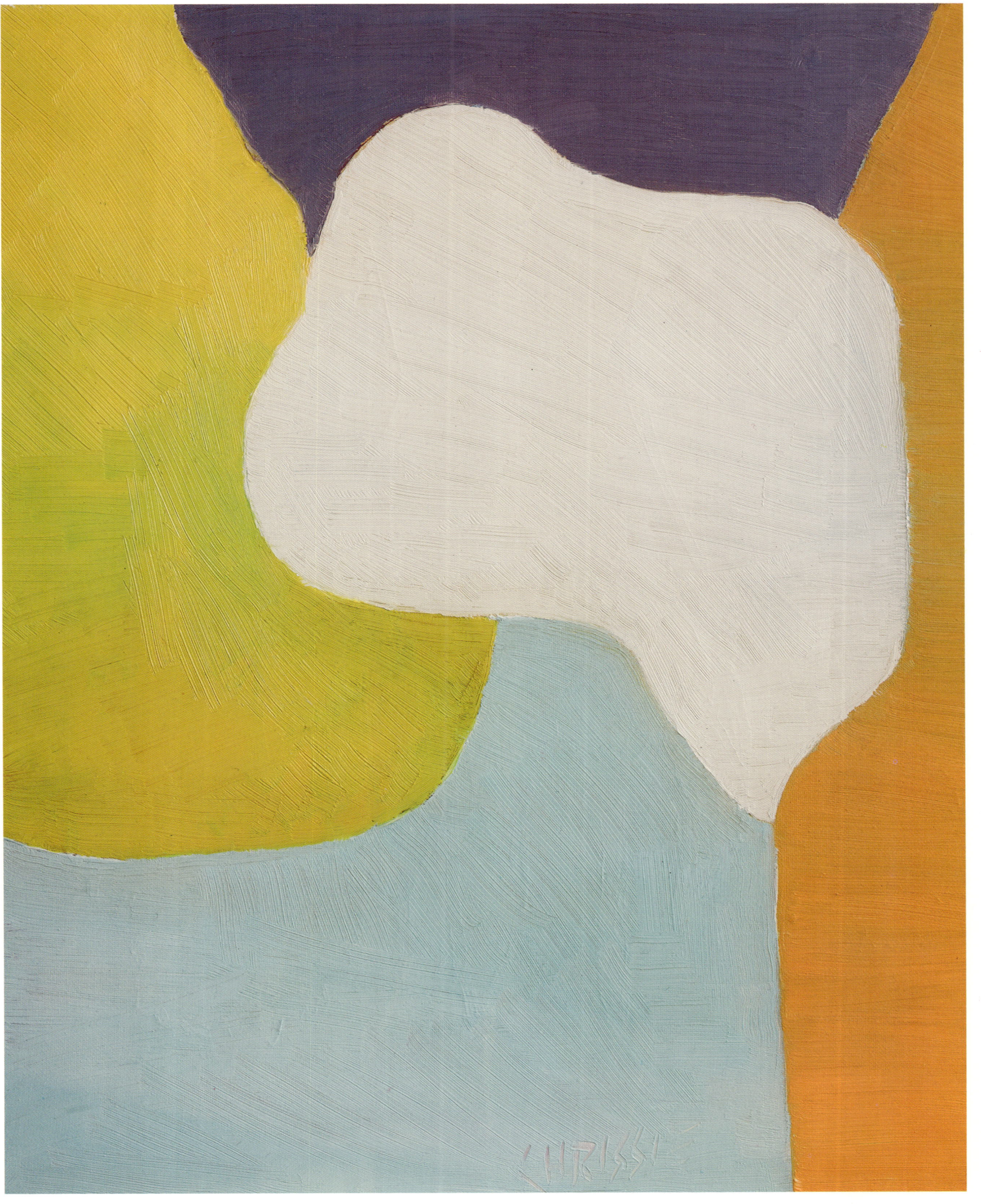

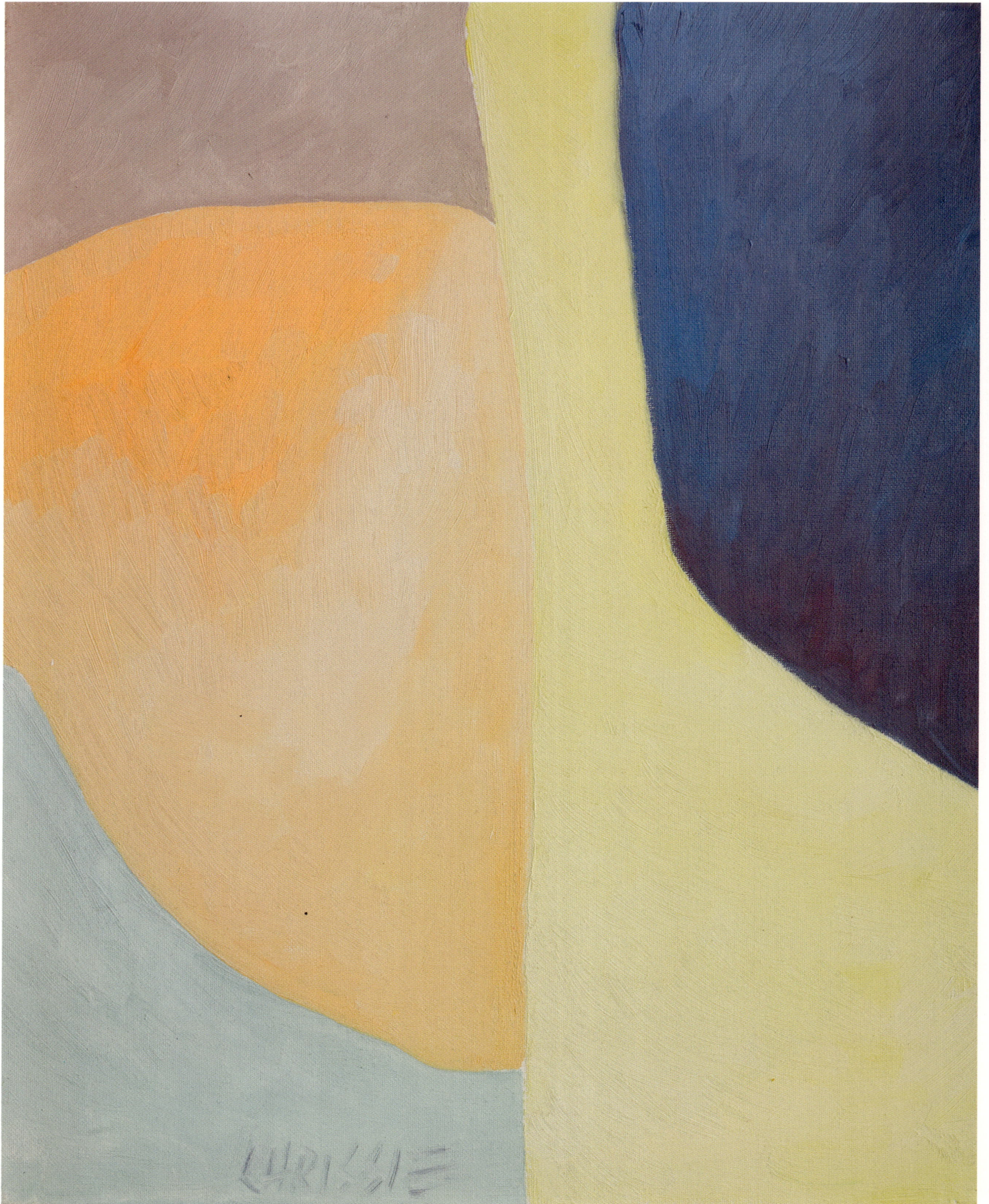

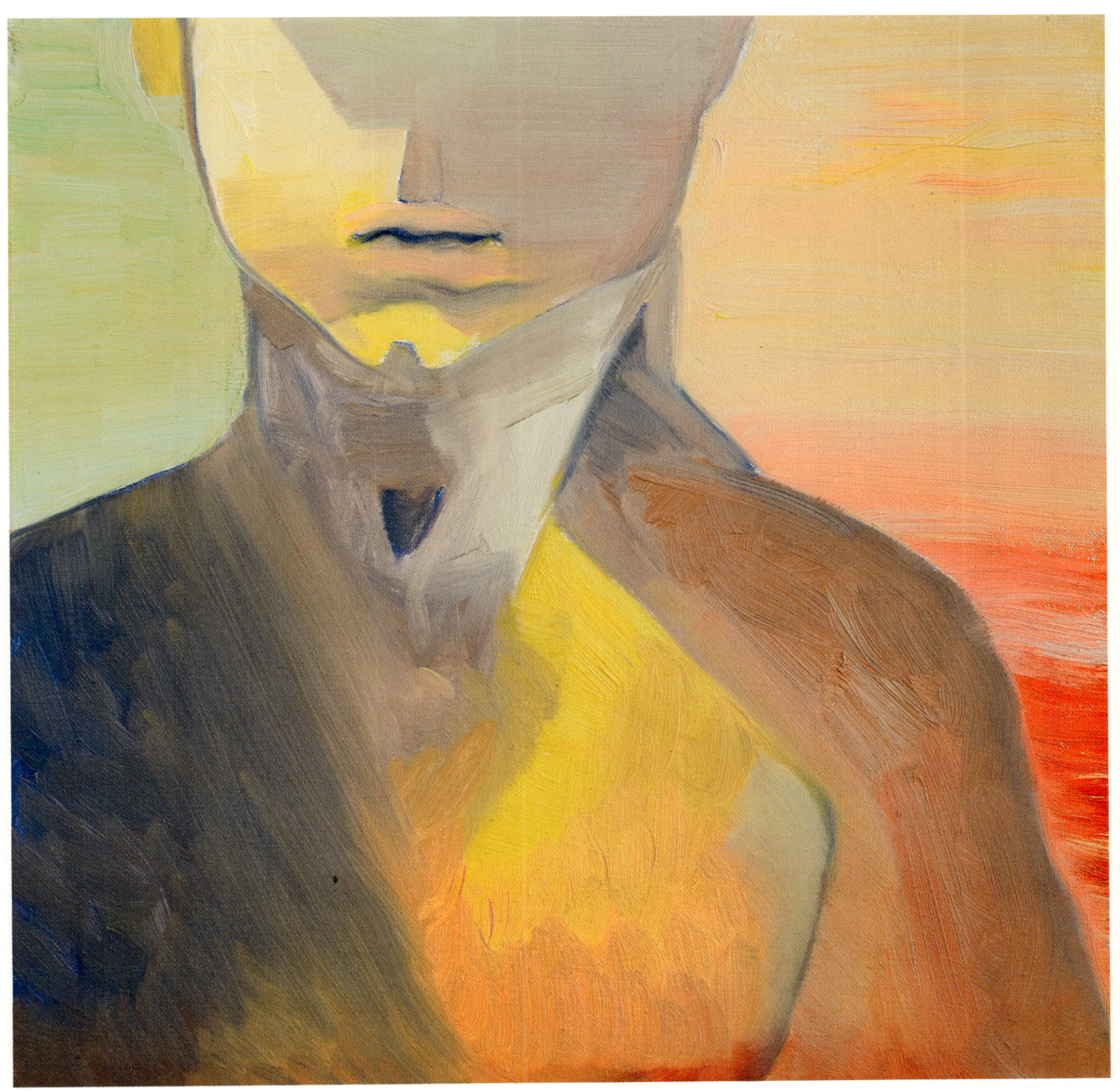

HYACINTHS WAITING
Oil on canvas
50 x 40 cm
(19³/₄ x 15³/₄ in)
23 March 2016

THURSDAY HEAT
Oil on canvas
40 x 40 cm
(15³/₄ x 15³/₄ in)
19 May 2016

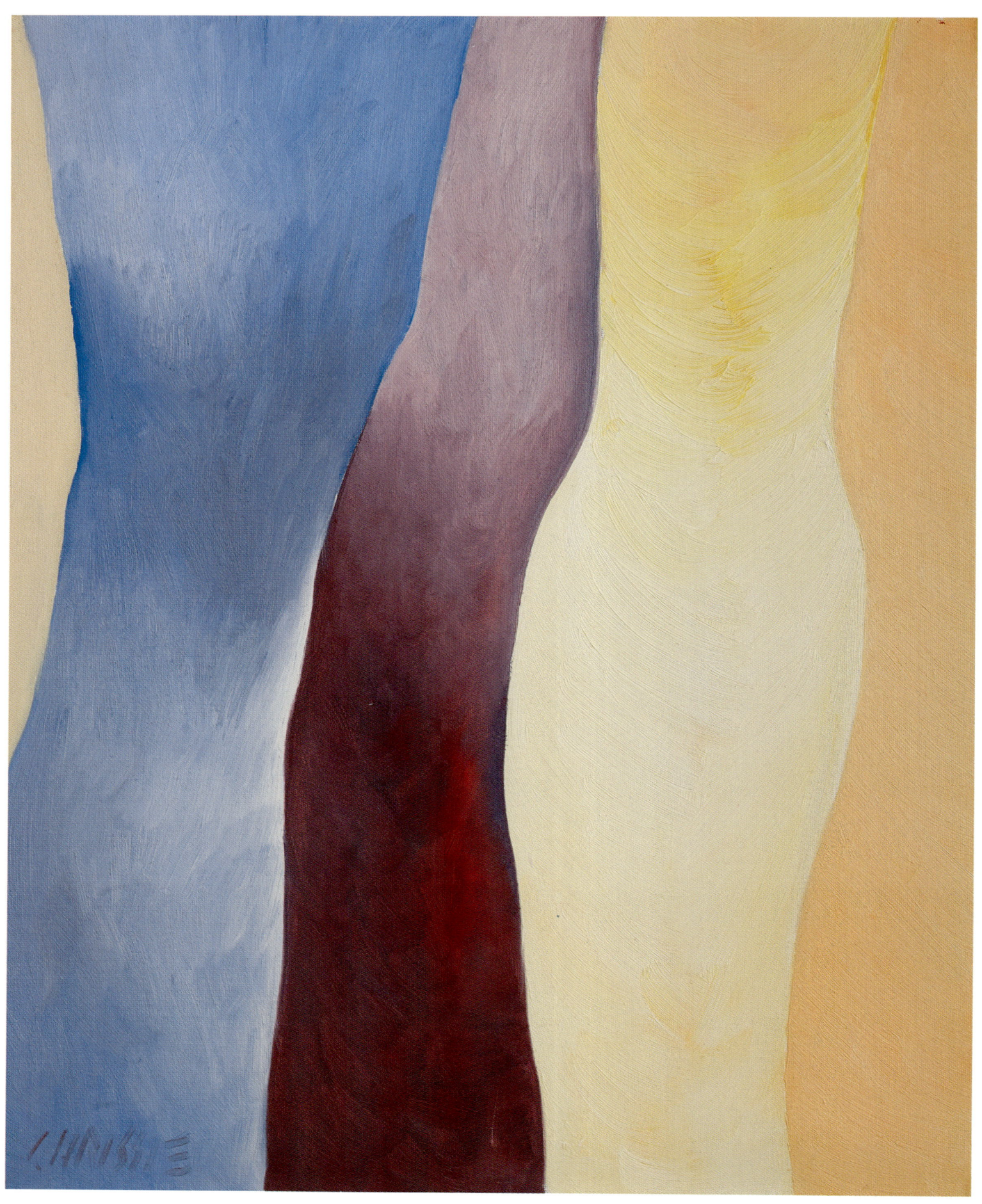

MAN WOMAN HEAT
Oil on canvas
50 x 40 cm
(19³/₄ x 15³/₄ in)
24 March 2016

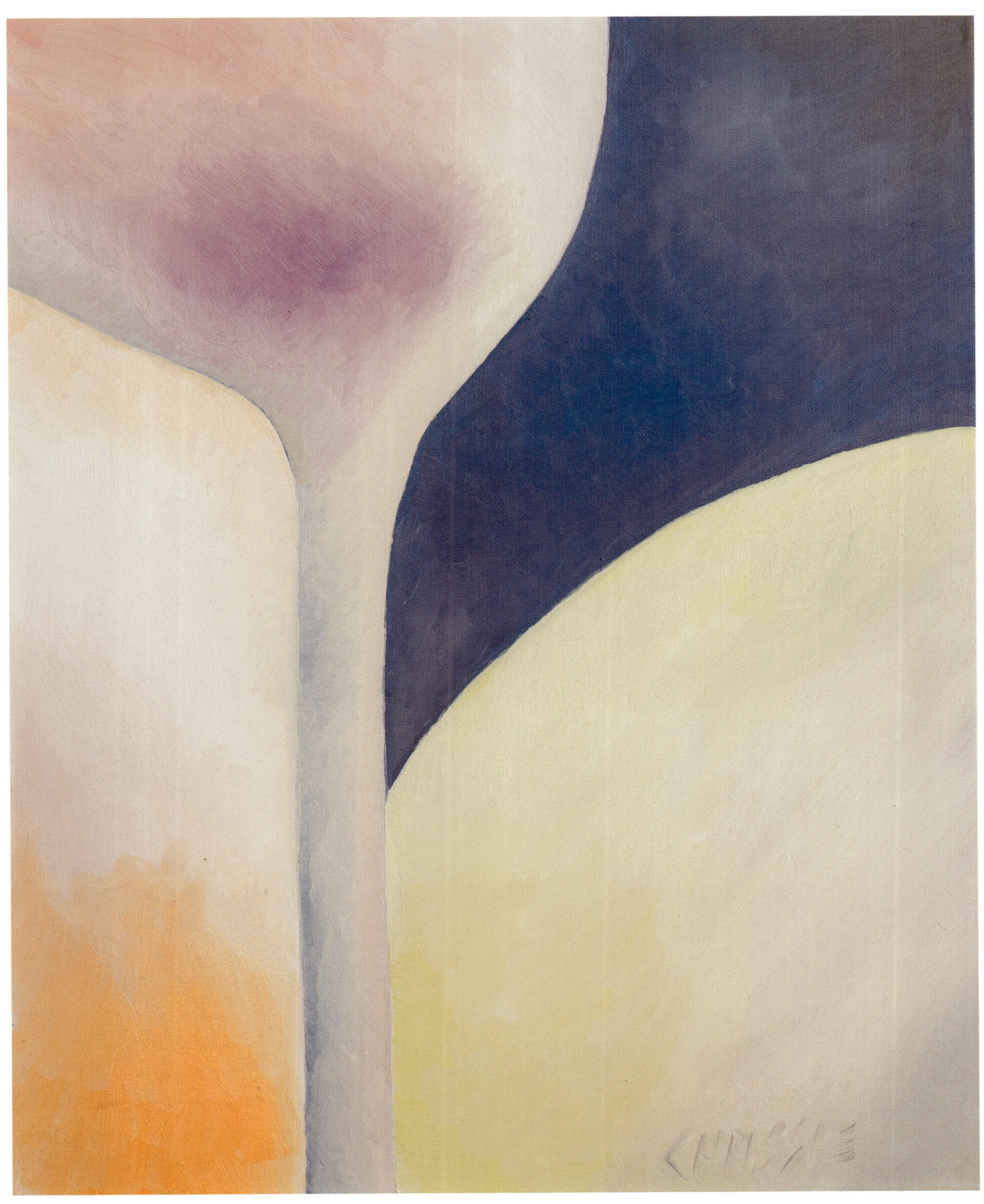

WAKE UP FLOWER
Oil on canvas
50 x 40 cm
(19¾ x 15¾ in)
24 March 2016

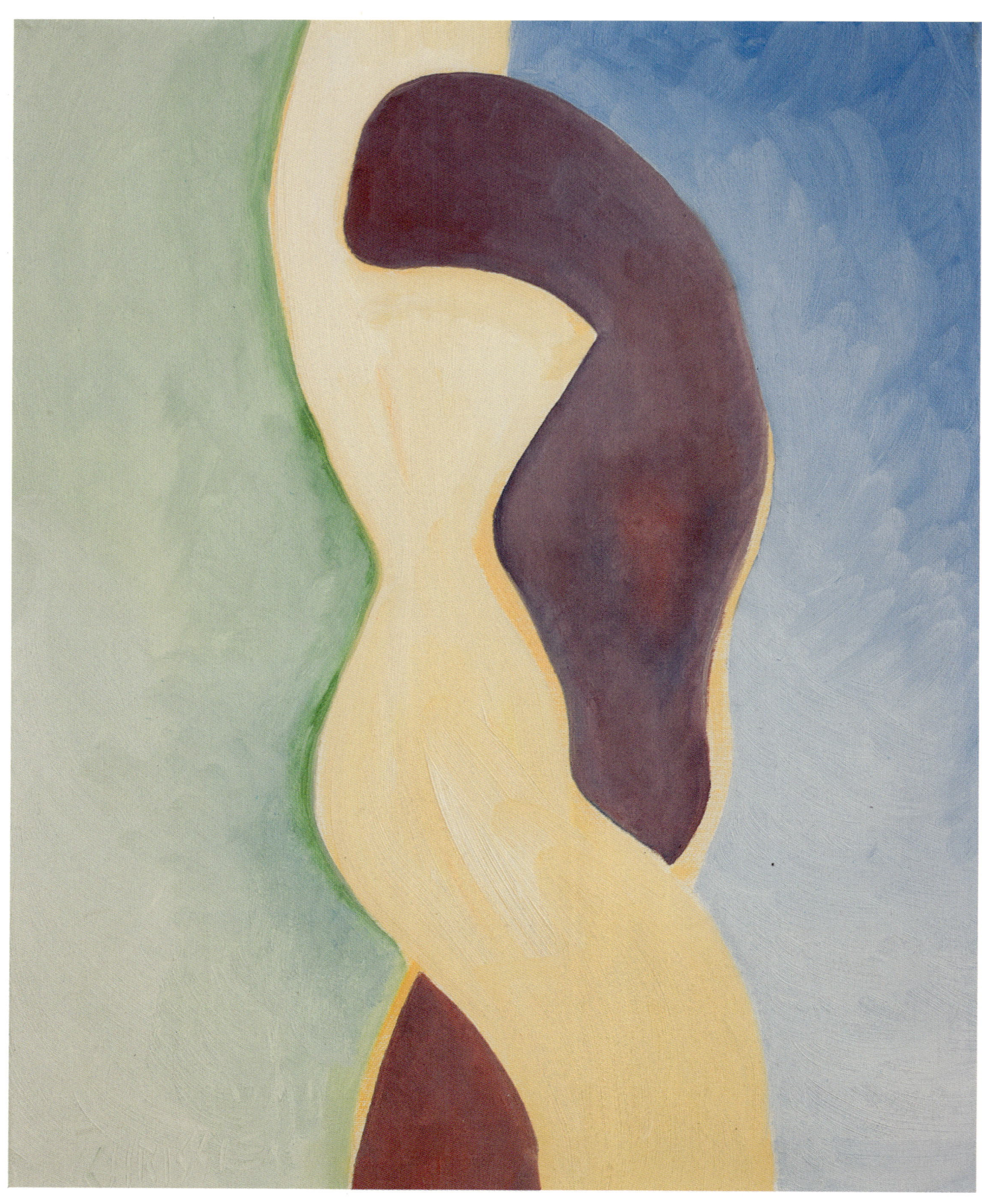

THURSDAY EMBRACE
Oil on canvas
50 x 40 cm
(19³/⁴ x 15³/⁴ in)
24 March 2016

TWO LOVERS
Oil on canvas
50 x 40 cm
(19³/⁴ x 15³/⁴ in)
28 May 2016

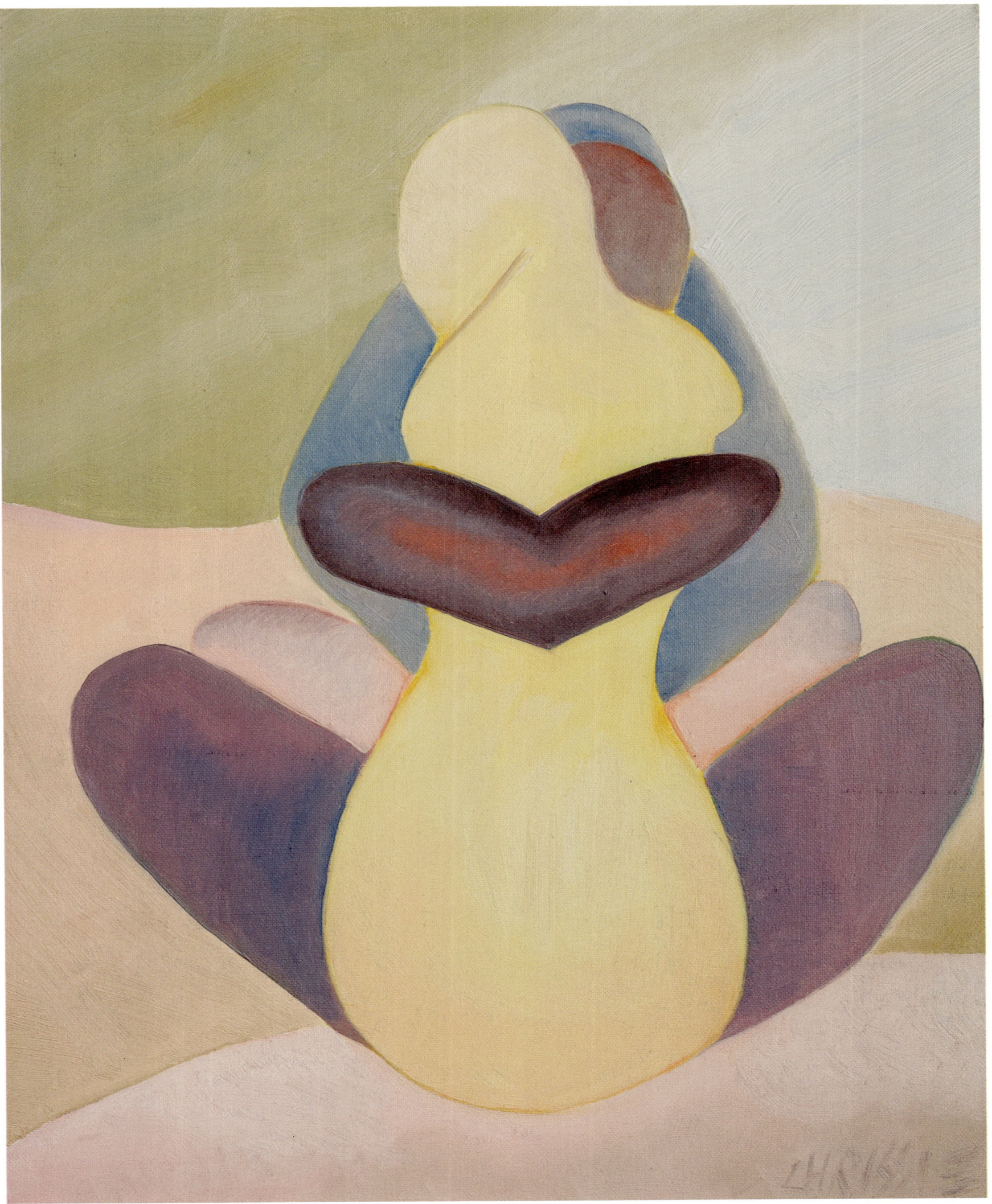

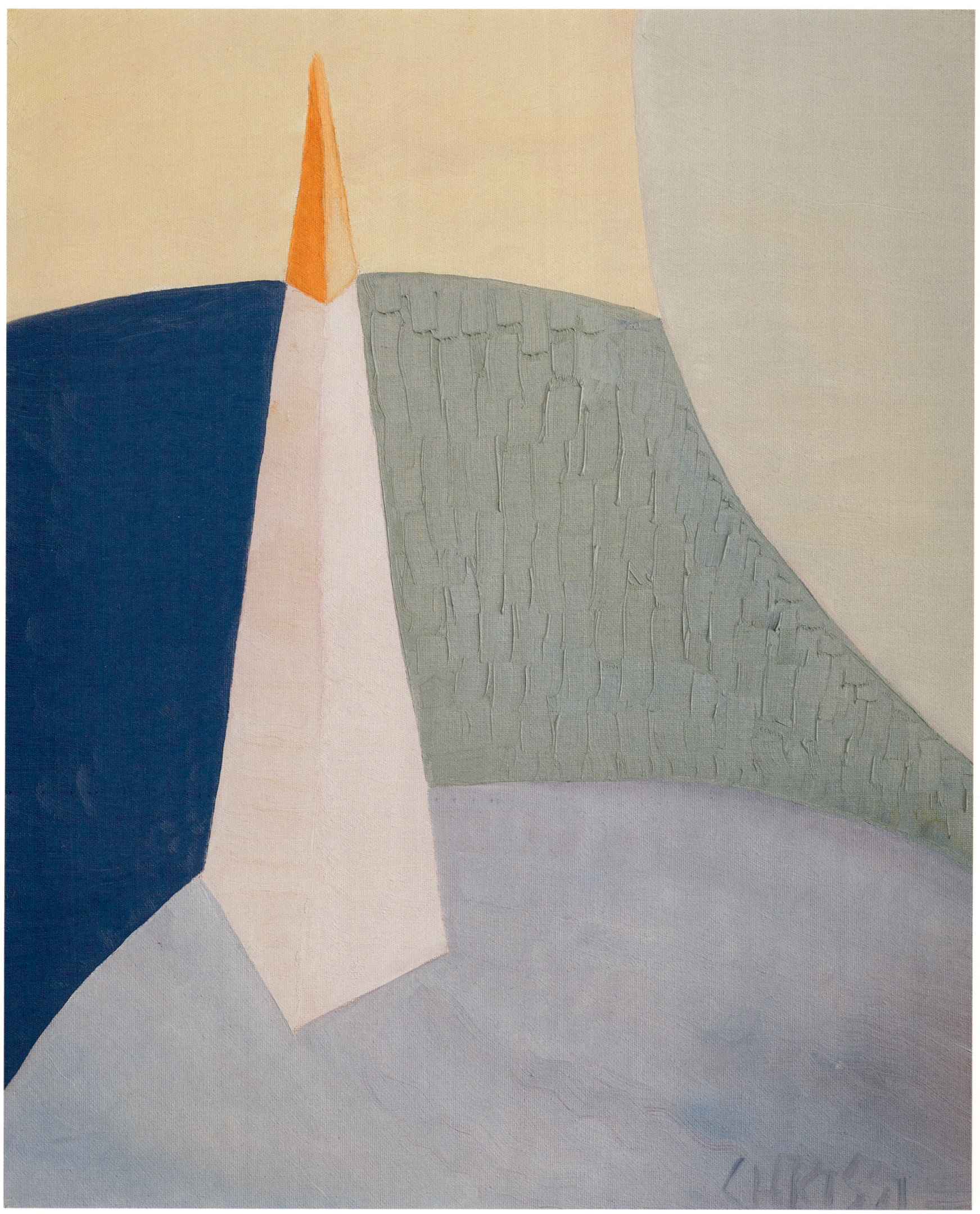

I do most of my paintings in one go, over three or four hours. It's a great meditation. I don't listen to music or anything, I just stare at the canvas and get completely absorbed in it. Then afterwards there's this enormous sense of relief that I got through it, and it just feels really good. In that way, it's like performing — the feeling I get after doing a show.

This one is called 'West London'. It's a landscape of my neighbourhood. The spire belongs to St Mary Magdalene, a striped brick church surrounded by council estates. I can see it from my roof.

WEST LONDON
Oil on canvas
50 x 40 cm
(19³ᐟ⁴ x 15³ᐟ⁴ in)
28 March 2016

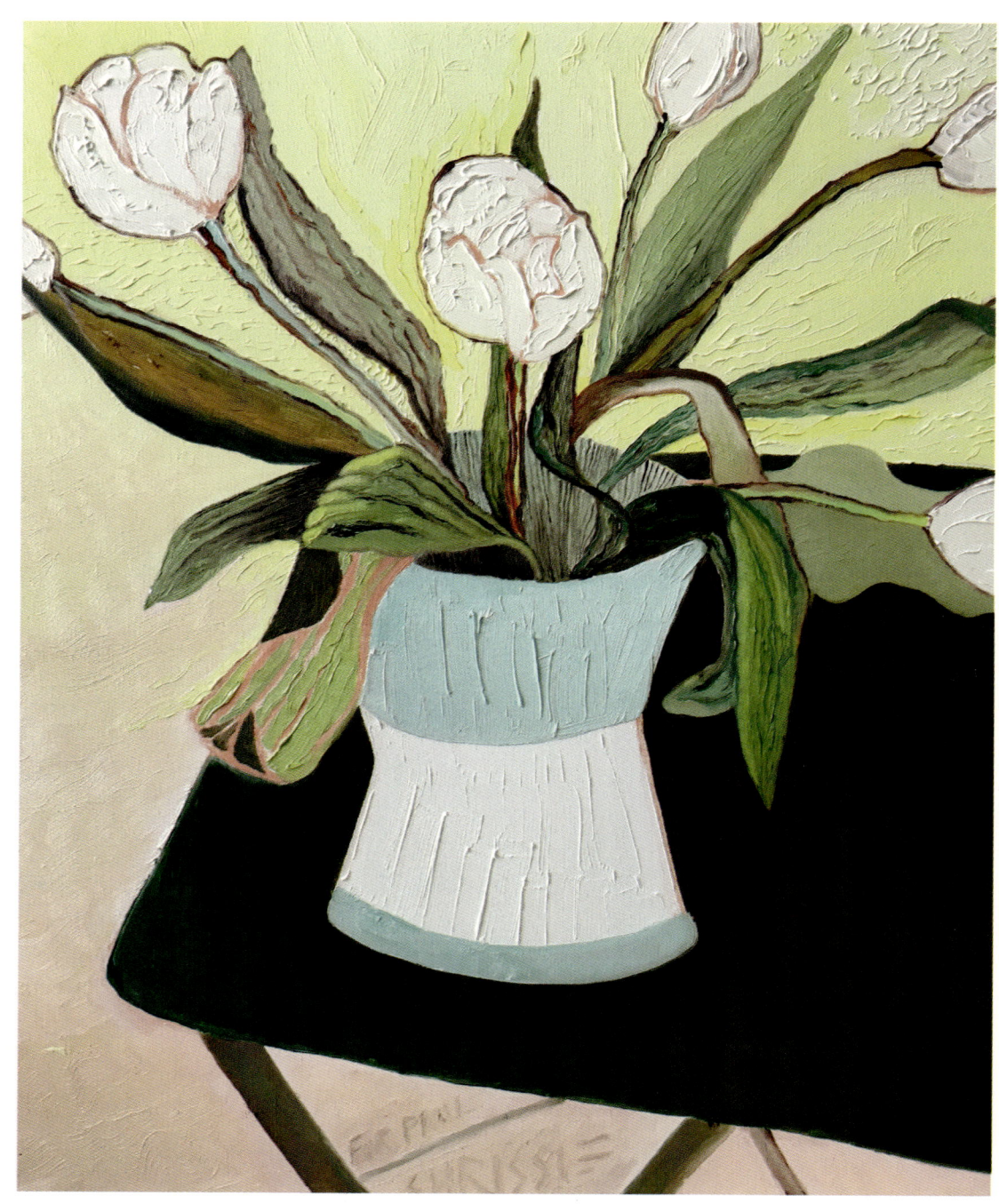

This one was a present for my friend Paul Allen. It's the only painting I've given away so far — so the only one of mine hanging somewhere in the world. This is a snap I took of it before I gave it to Paul.

JET LAG TULIPS
Oil on canvas
75 x 60 cm
(29$^{1/2}$ x 23$^{1/2}$ in)
12 April 2016

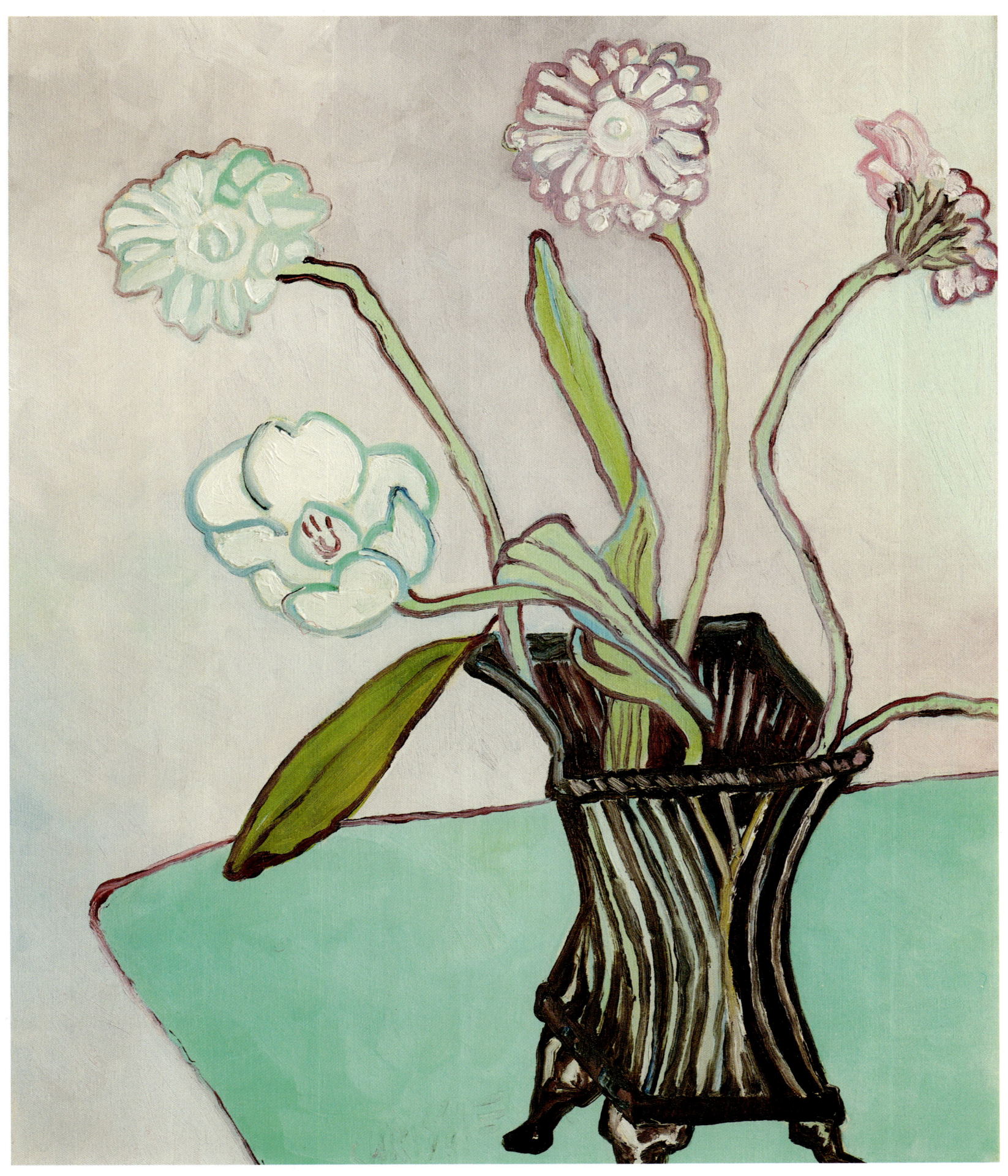

NEW DAY FLOWERS
Oil on canvas
60 x 50 cm
(23$^{1/2}$ x 19$^{3/4}$ in)
12 April 2016

I was hanging out with some new friends on a cruise that Paul invited us on. That's where I met Rina Kara, a scientist from South Sudan. She didn't pose for me, but when I came back after spending a week with them I did this painting. I didn't plan to paint her, but when I finished I thought it looked like her. That's how painting works. It's the same with songwriting. Sometimes I don't really know what it's about until it's finished.

WEDNESDAY SUN
Oil on canvas
60 x 50 cm
(23¹/² x 19³/⁴ in)
13 April 2016

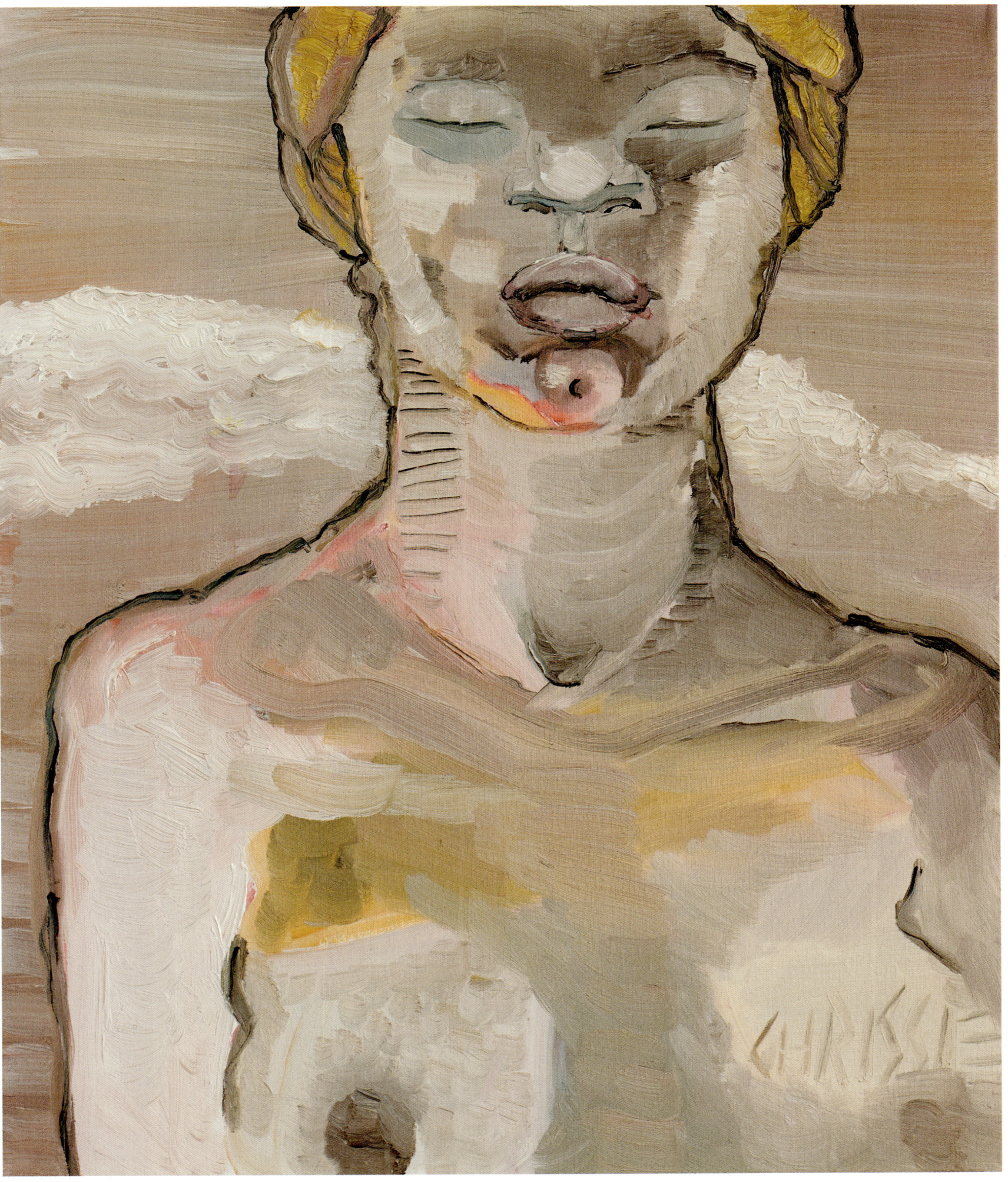

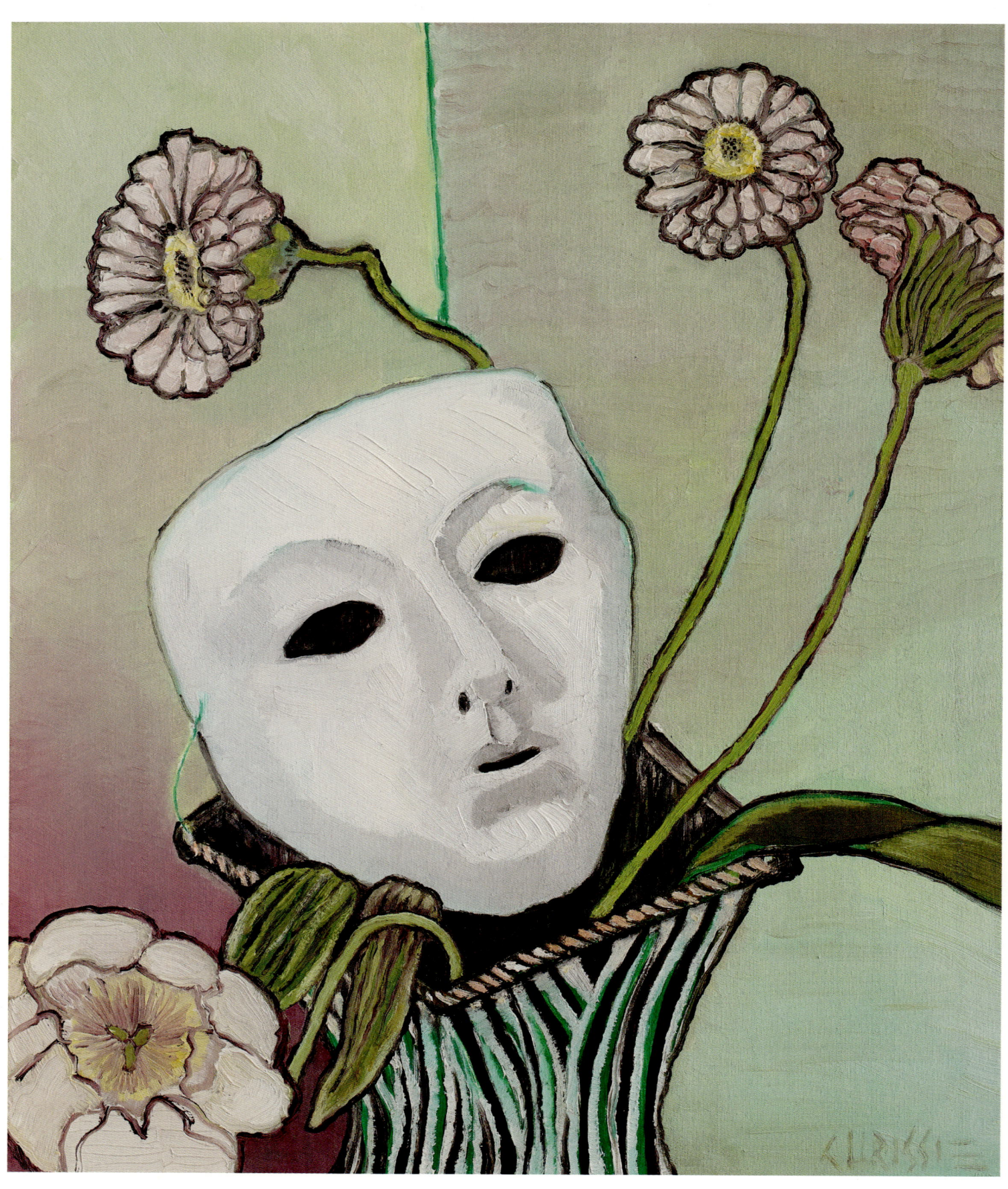

I can't get away from painting flowers. There just doesn't seem to be a better meditation. It's like getting high but cheaper. That bloody mask kept creeping in; it's just so doggone fun to paint.

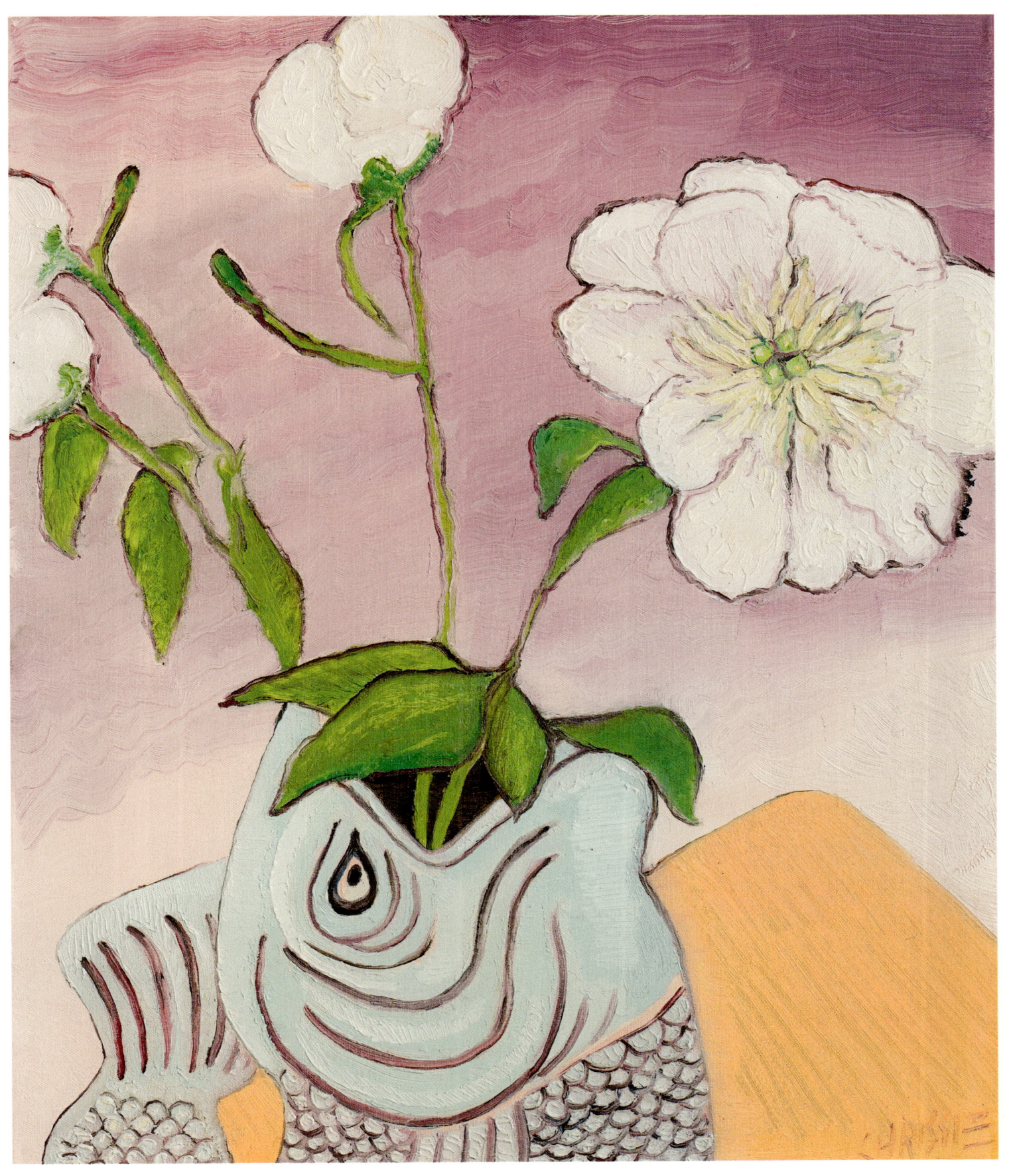

GREEN FLOWERS MASK
Oil on canvas
60 x 50 cm
(23$^{1/2}$ x 19$^{3/4}$ in)
19 April 2016

PEONY FISH VASE
Oil on canvas
60 x 50 cm
(23$^{1/2}$ x 19$^{3/4}$ in)
22 April 2016

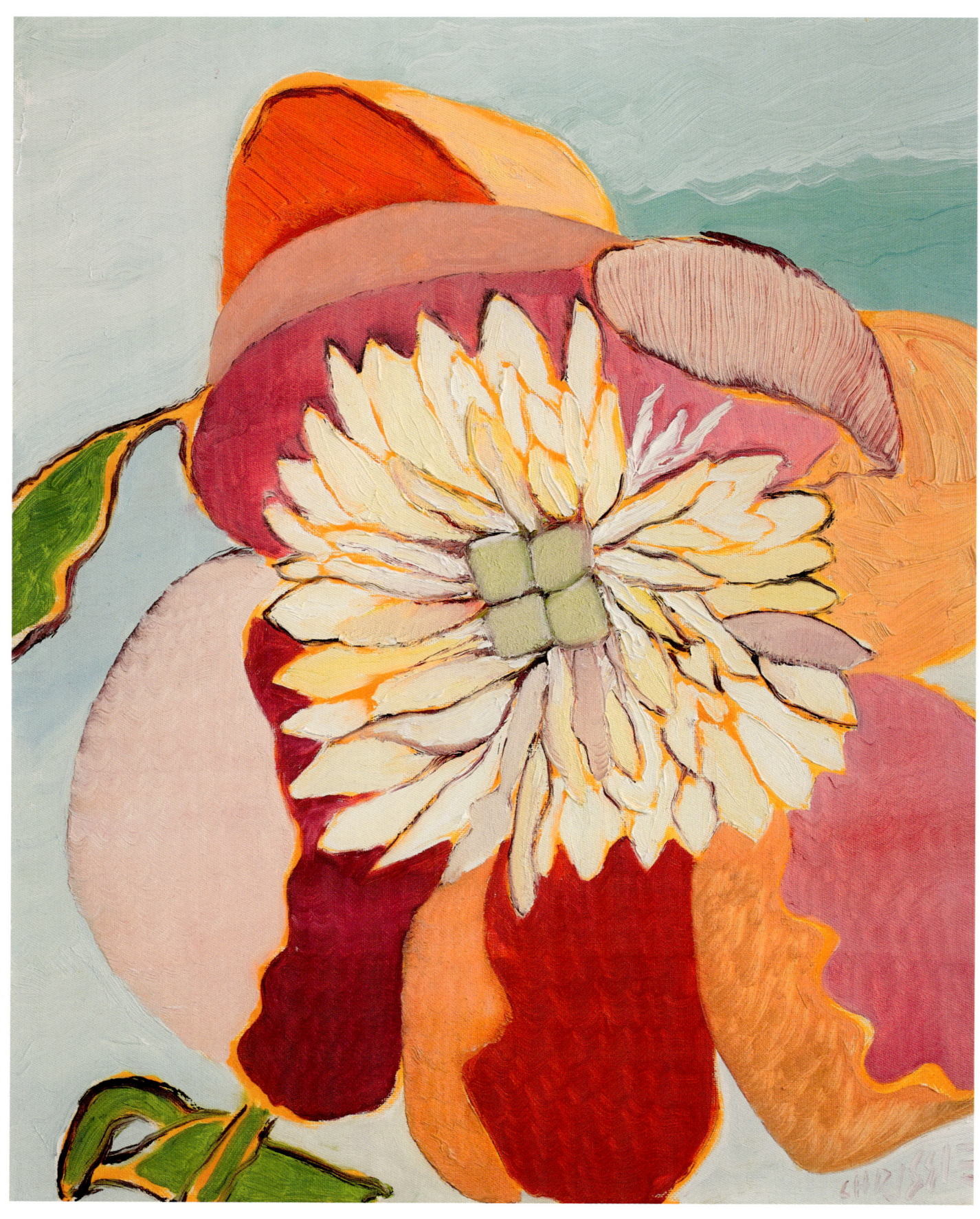

I had some leftover paint that I didn't want to waste, so I painted this really fast in colours that I wouldn't normally have gone for. It's nice to do something you didn't expect would work.

NON NON PEONY
Oil on canvas
50 x 40 cm
(19³⁄₄ x 15³⁄₄ in)
23 April 2016

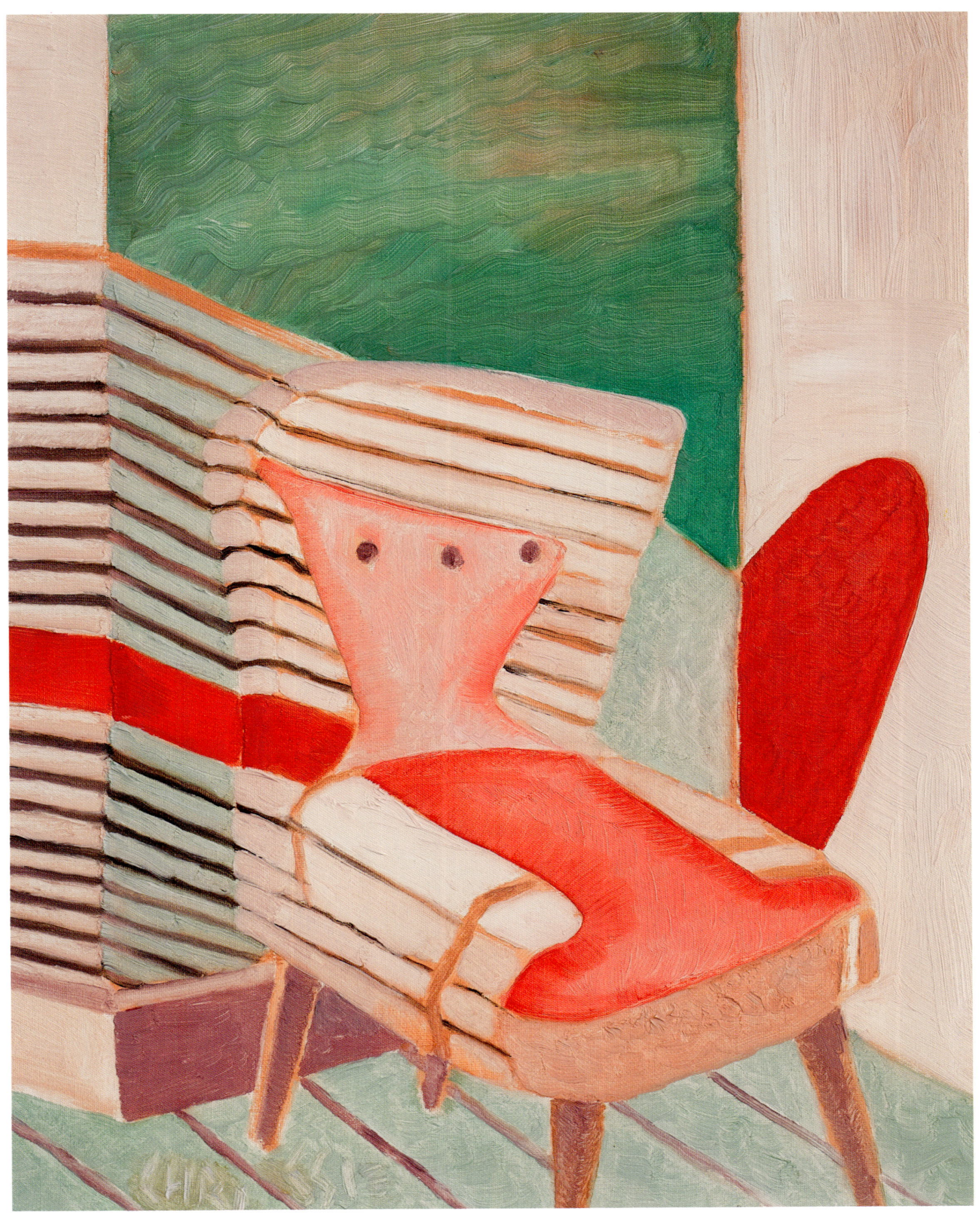

MORNING SUN CHAIR
Oil on canvas
50 x 40 cm
(19¾ x 15¾ in)
27 April 2016

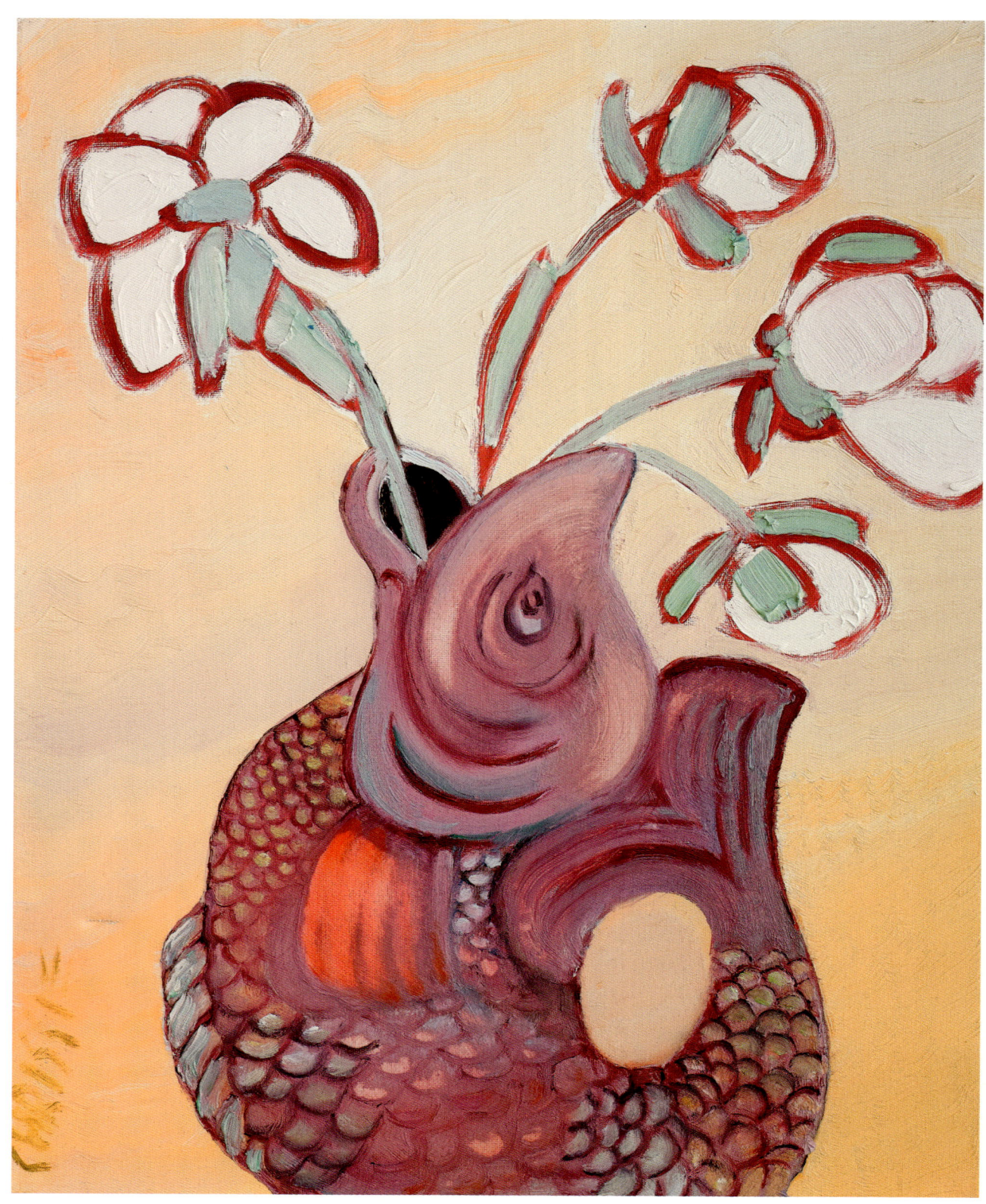

I sent a snap of this painting to my friend Michael Wincott, the actor, and by the time he replied to say how much he liked it I'd changed the colour on the vase three times. So then I had to go back and try to restore it to the one he liked. I spent more time on those bloody scales than I had on all the other paintings and it's still not as good as when it started out.

ONE AMONG MANY
VERSIONS OF THE
DREADED FISH —
RAD FISH
Oil on canvas
50 x 40 cm
(19¾ x 15¾ in)
25 April 2016

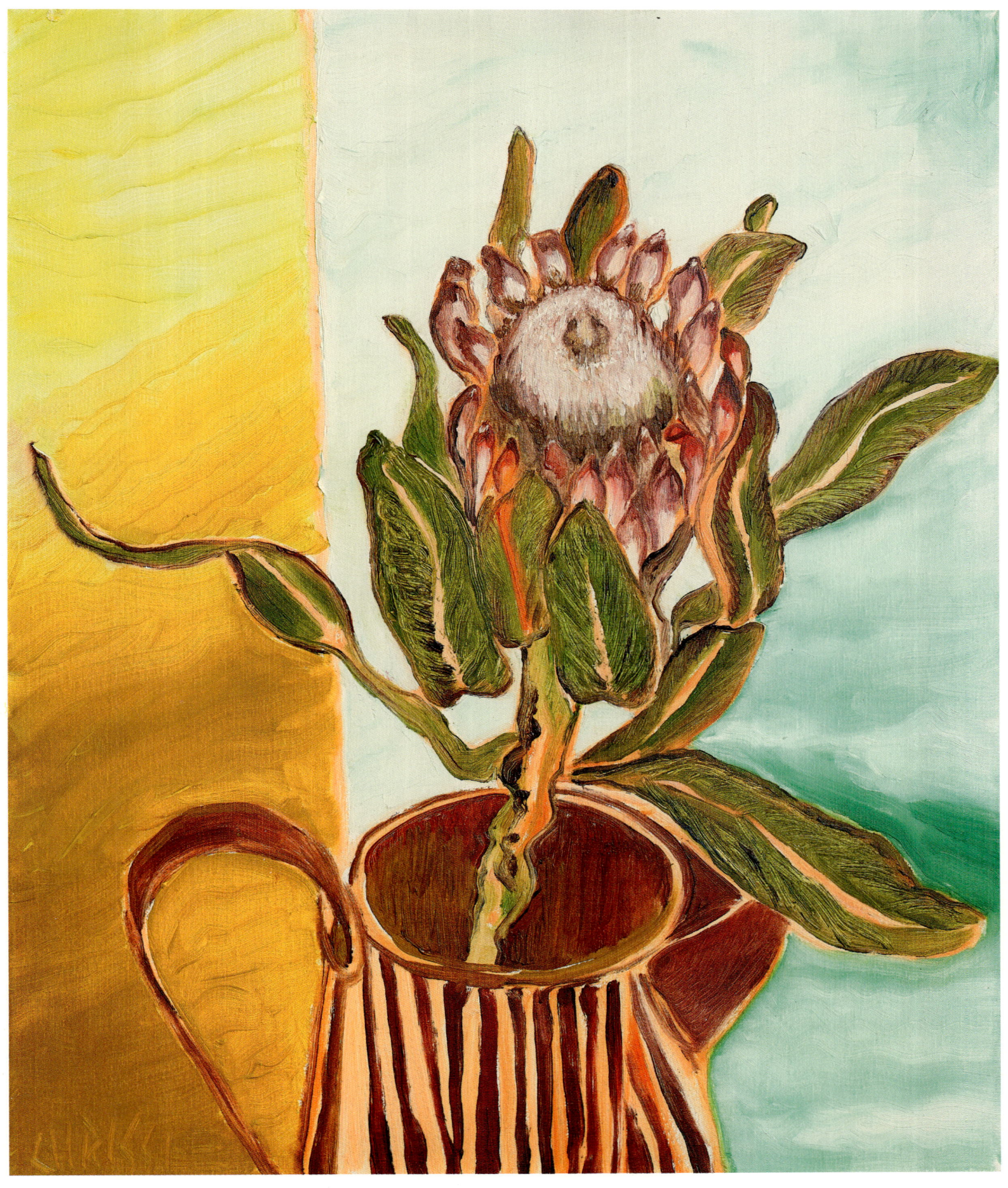

SATURDAY FLOWER
Oil on canvas
60 x 50 cm
(23¹⁄₂ x 19³⁄₄ in)
30 April 2016

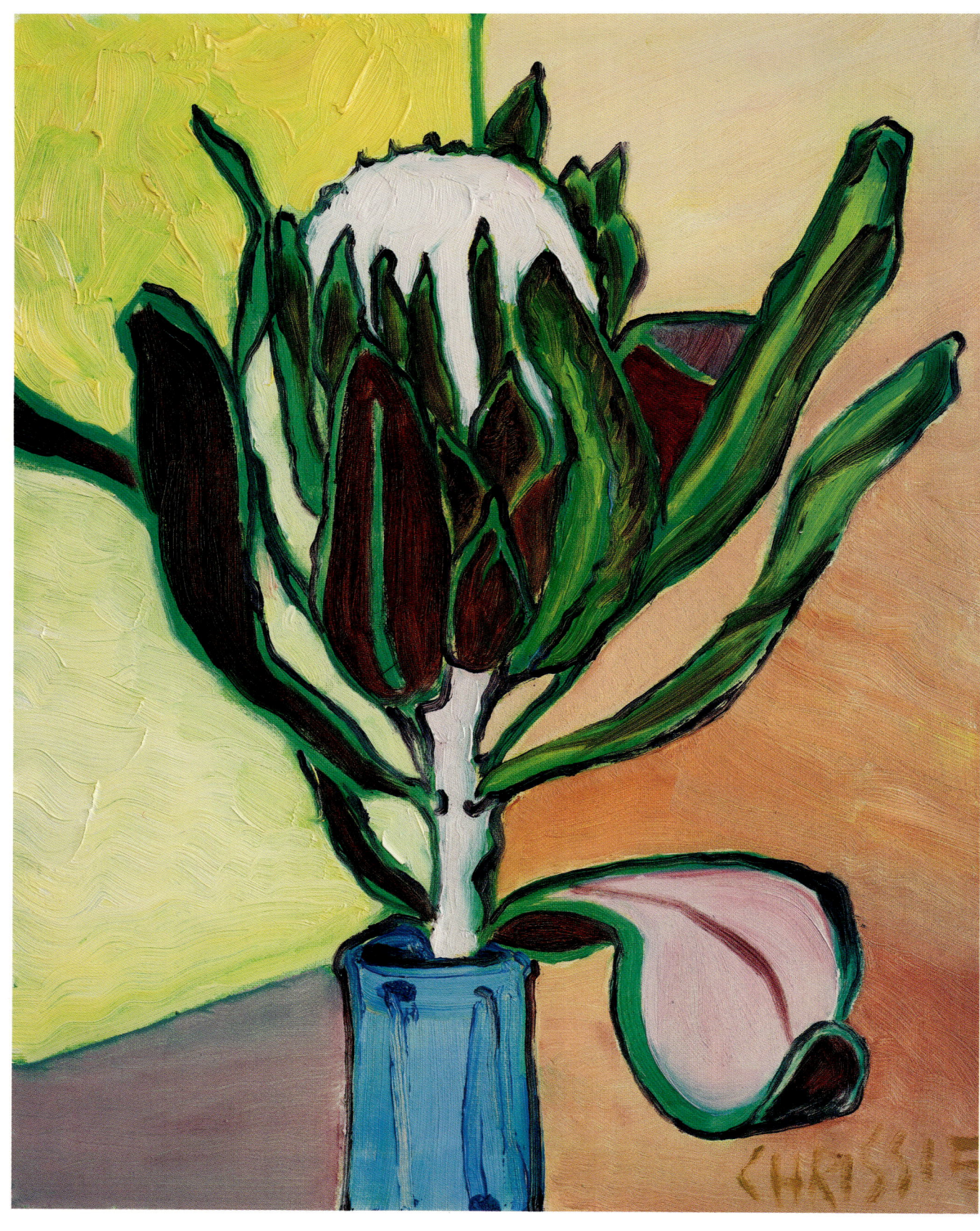

I painted this when I got back from Paris on the train and I named it after Marianne, a friend I'd been visiting there. Then later that evening I could see the flower was starting to droop, so I thought I'd better paint it again fast before it died. These are two of my favourite flower paintings.

MARIANNE FLOWER
Oil on canvas
50 x 40 cm
(19³/₄ x 15³/₄ in)
5 May 2016

DESERT FLOWER
Oil on canvas
50 x 40 cm
(19³/₄ x 15³/₄ in)
5 May 2016

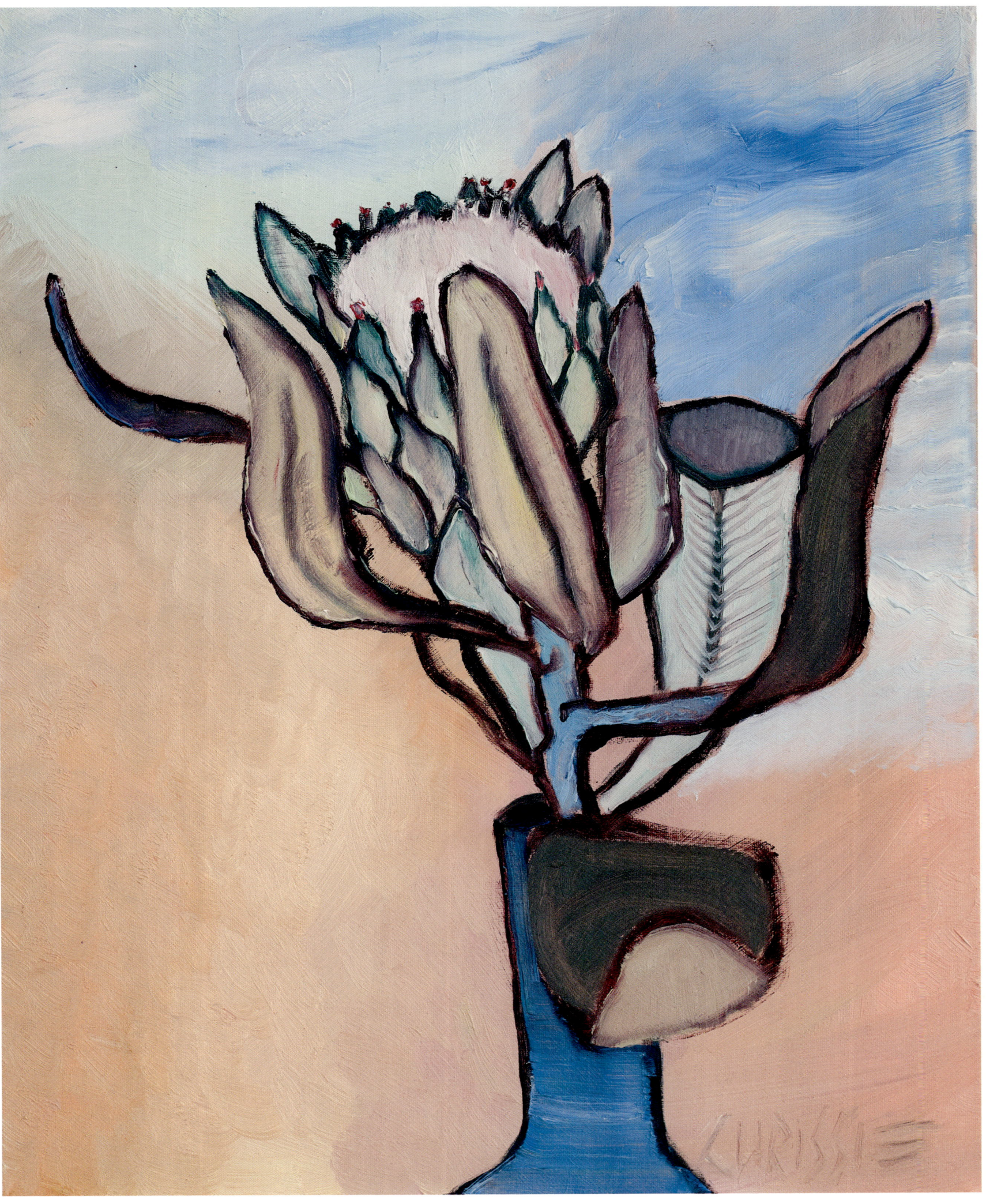

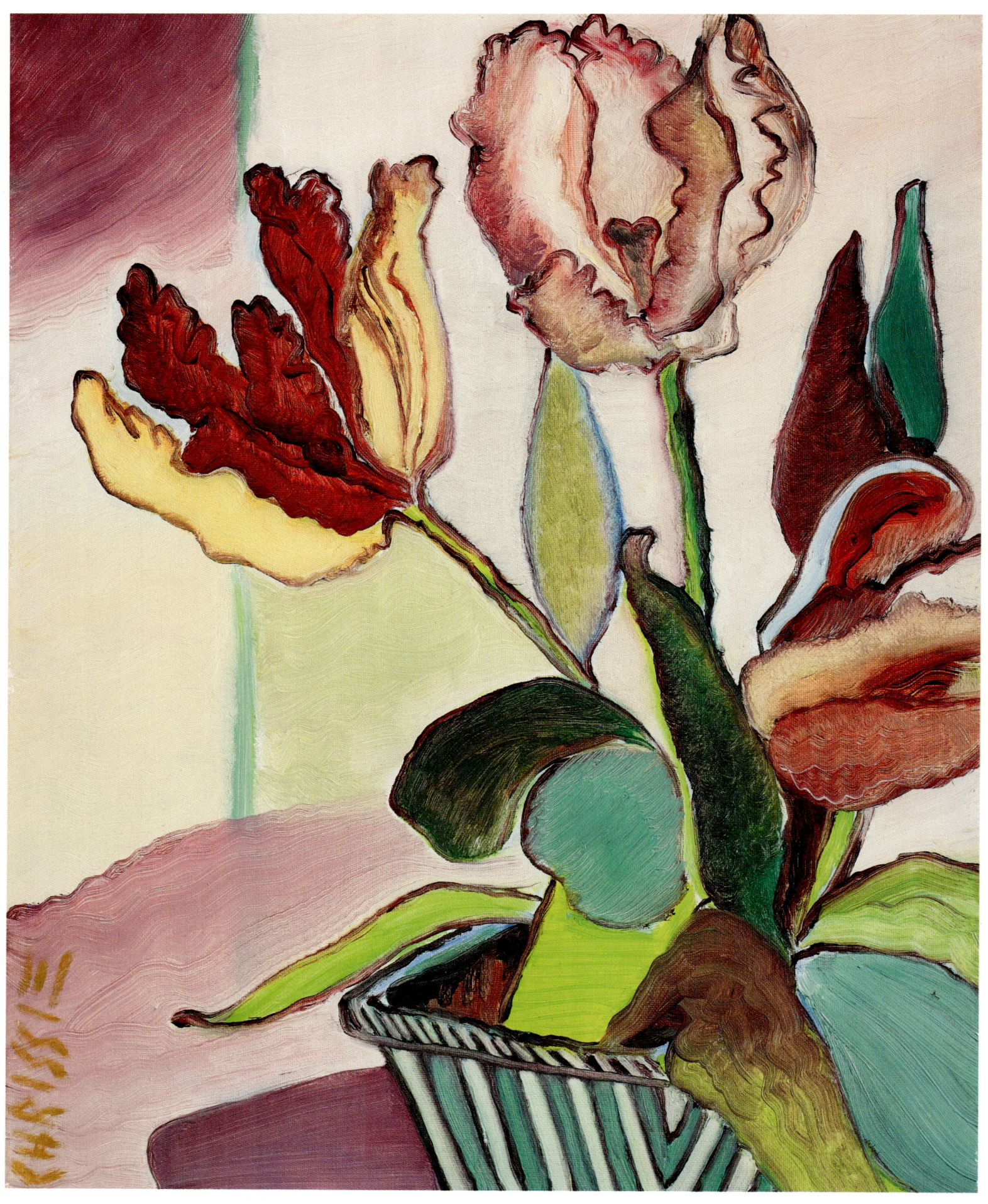

FRIDAY TULIPS
Oil on canvas
50 x 40 cm
(19³/₄ x 15³/₄ in)
6 May 2016

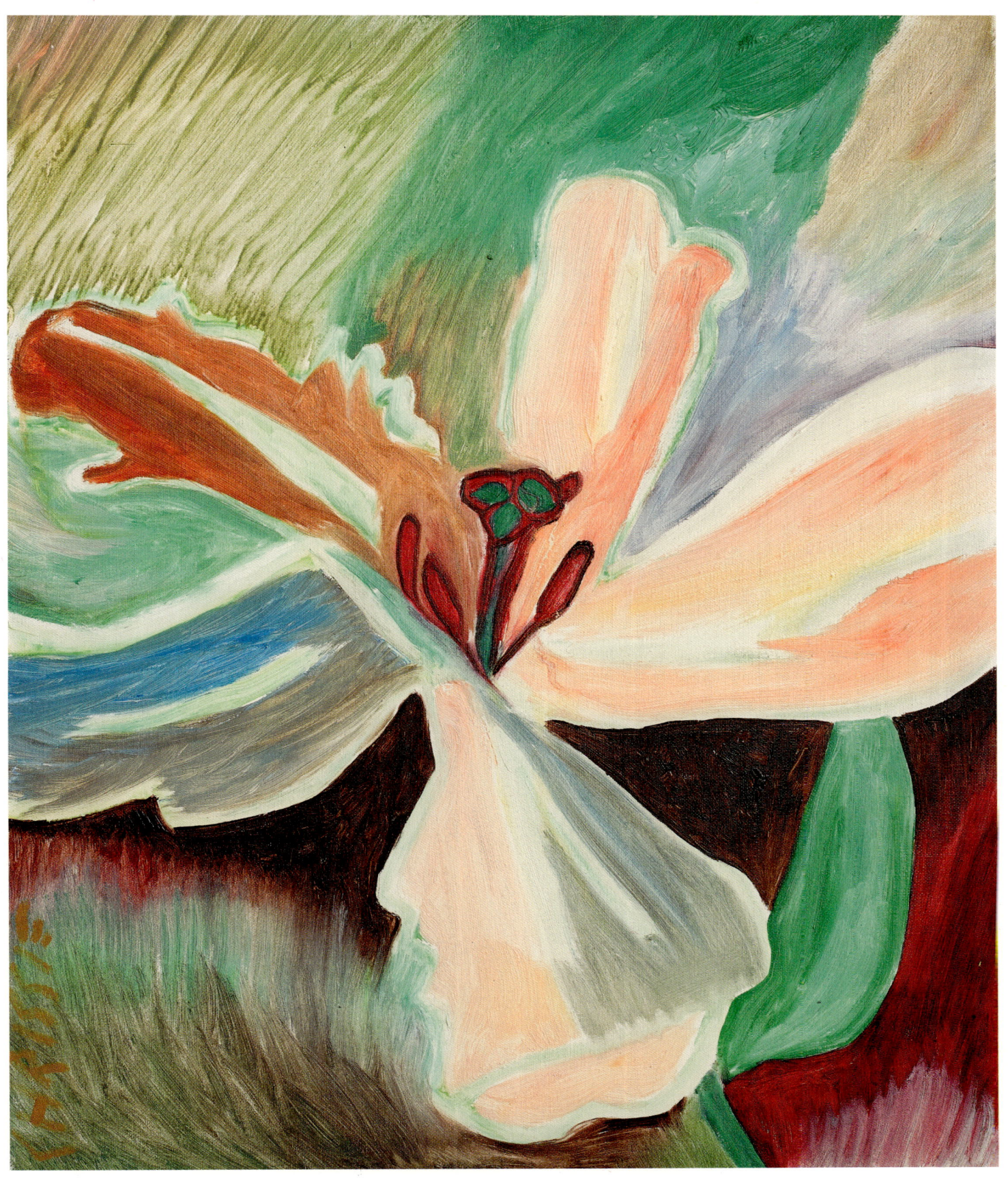

*Painting flowers was starting to make me lazy. It was making me shy away
from the challenge of abstracts. I also thought this looked like a scarf and
that jolted me into realising it was time to move on.*

HALF-HO_R FLOWER
Oil on ca_vas
60 x 50 cm
(23½ x 19¾ in)
11 May 2016

I was getting to the point where I never wanted to see another flower for the rest of my life. And I was starting to think that I couldn't really paint, because I always had to refer to something, which didn't feel very creative. So I bought some bamboo as a departure, and to try some different colours, and as a move towards abstraction.

GREEN BAMBOO
Oil on canvas
50 x 40 cm
(19³/⁴ x 15³/⁴ in)
7 May 2016

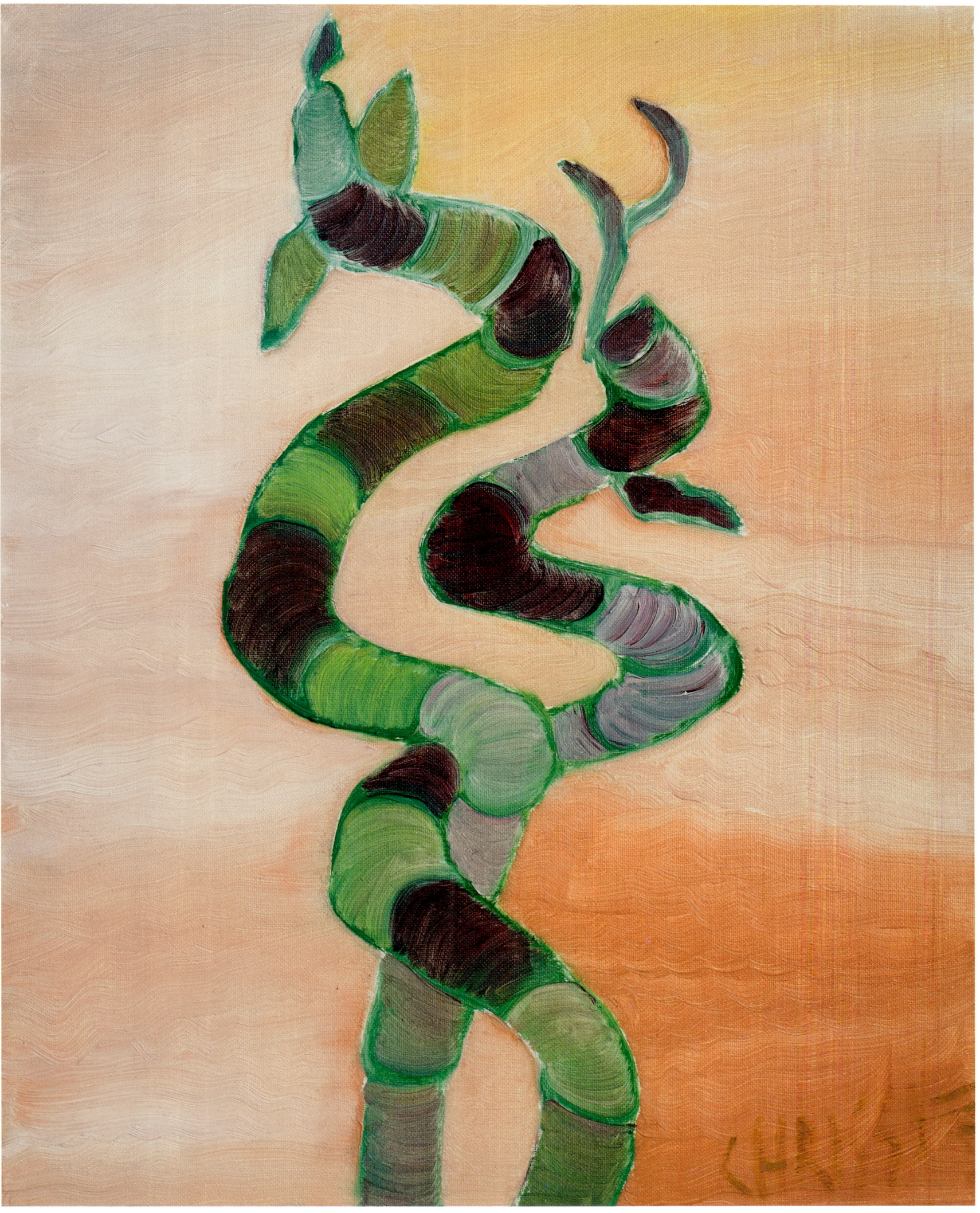

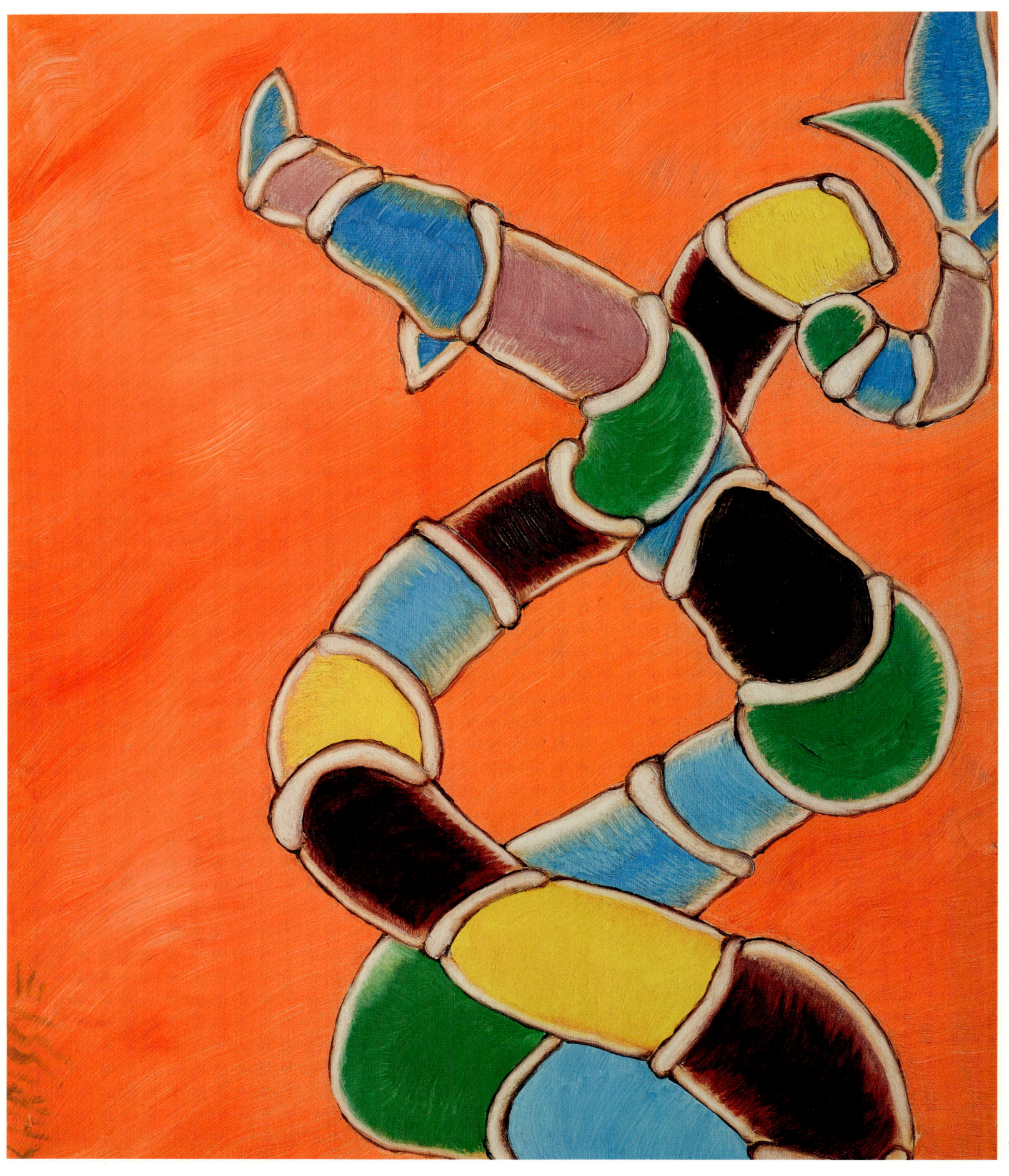

TUESDAY BAMBOO
Oil on canvas
60 x 50 cm
(23¹/² x 19³/⁴ in)
10 May 2016

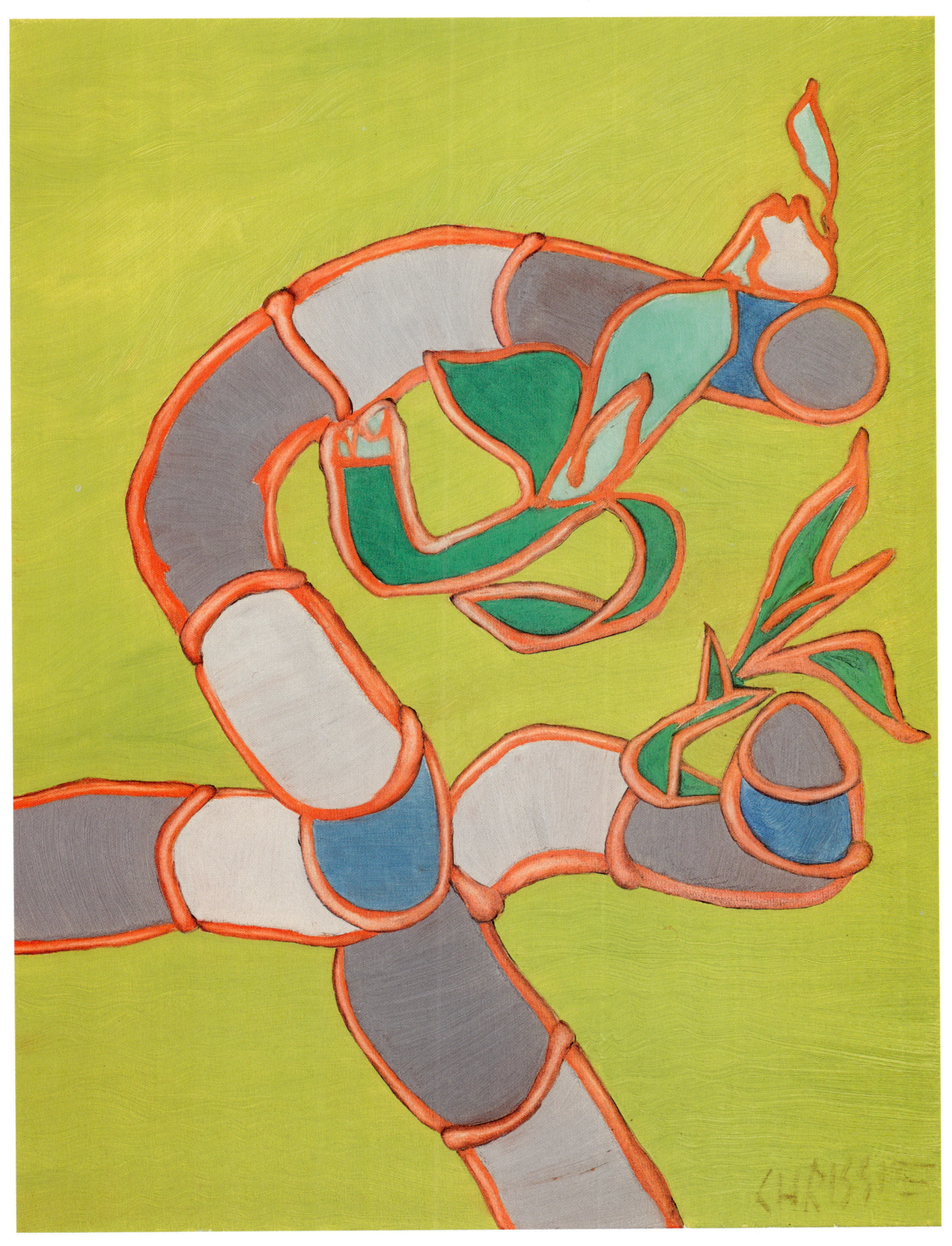

WEDNESDAY BAMBOO
Oil on canvas
80 x 60 cm
(31¹⁄² x 23¹⁄² in)
11 May 2016

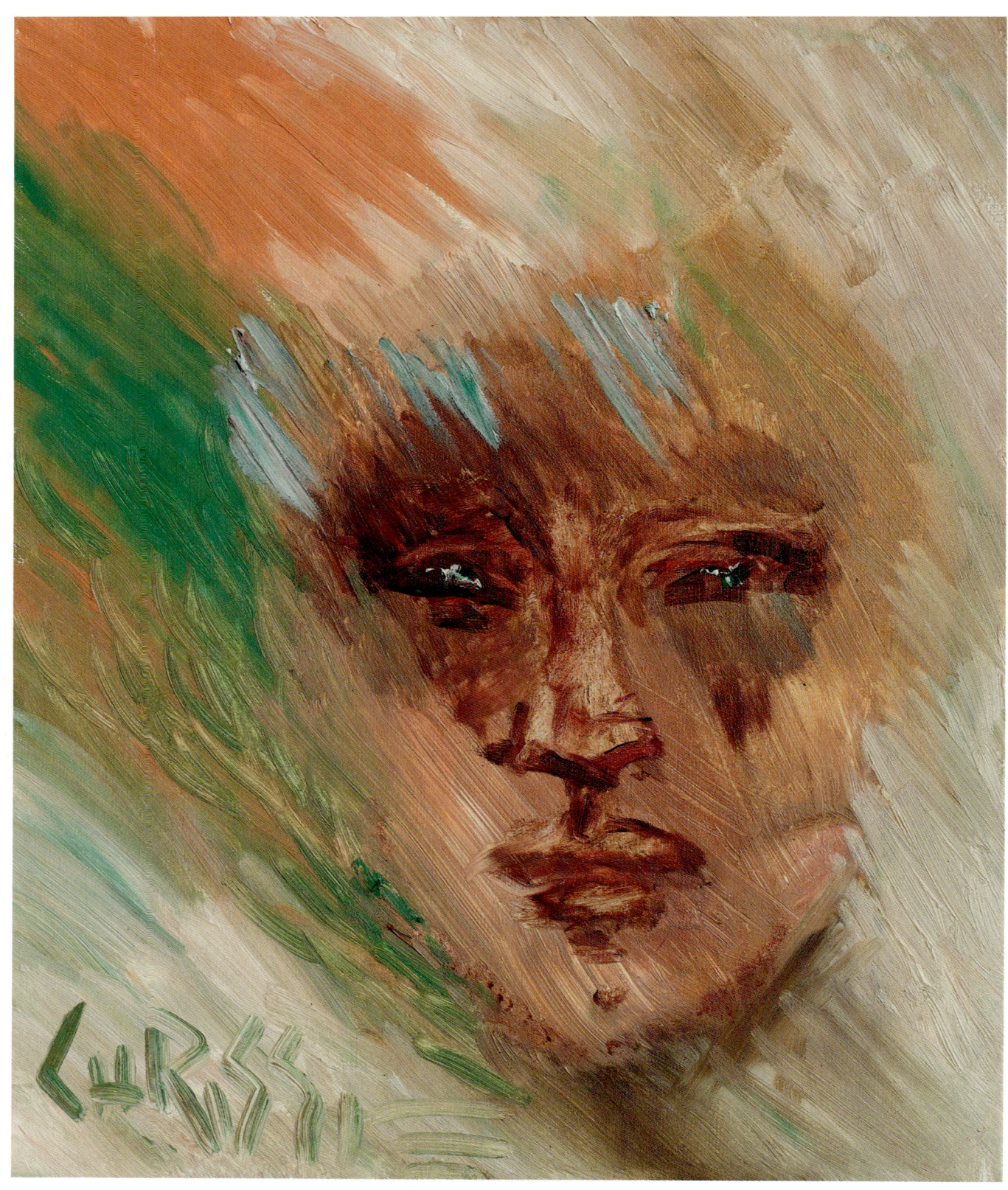

SAID I'D NEVER
DO IT AGAIN
Oil on canvas
60 x 50 cm
(23¹⁄² x 19³⁄⁴ in)
11 May 2016

VENTRILOQUIST'S
DUMMY
Oil on canvas
50 x 40 cm
(19³⁄⁴ x 15³⁄⁴ in)
27 May 2016

I swore I'd never do a self-portrait, because I was worried I'd spend too long on it, zero in and get too precise, and I think that can be quite boring to look at.

But then I was sitting there wanting to paint someone but there was no one else here. I don't have to look in the mirror to do a self-portrait, because, having been looking in the mirror to put my make-up on for 50 years, I think I get it now. I get the picture.

Frankly, self-portraits seem vain to me: 'Here's another picture of me, everyone.' If I had someone else around here, I'd paint them all the time instead.

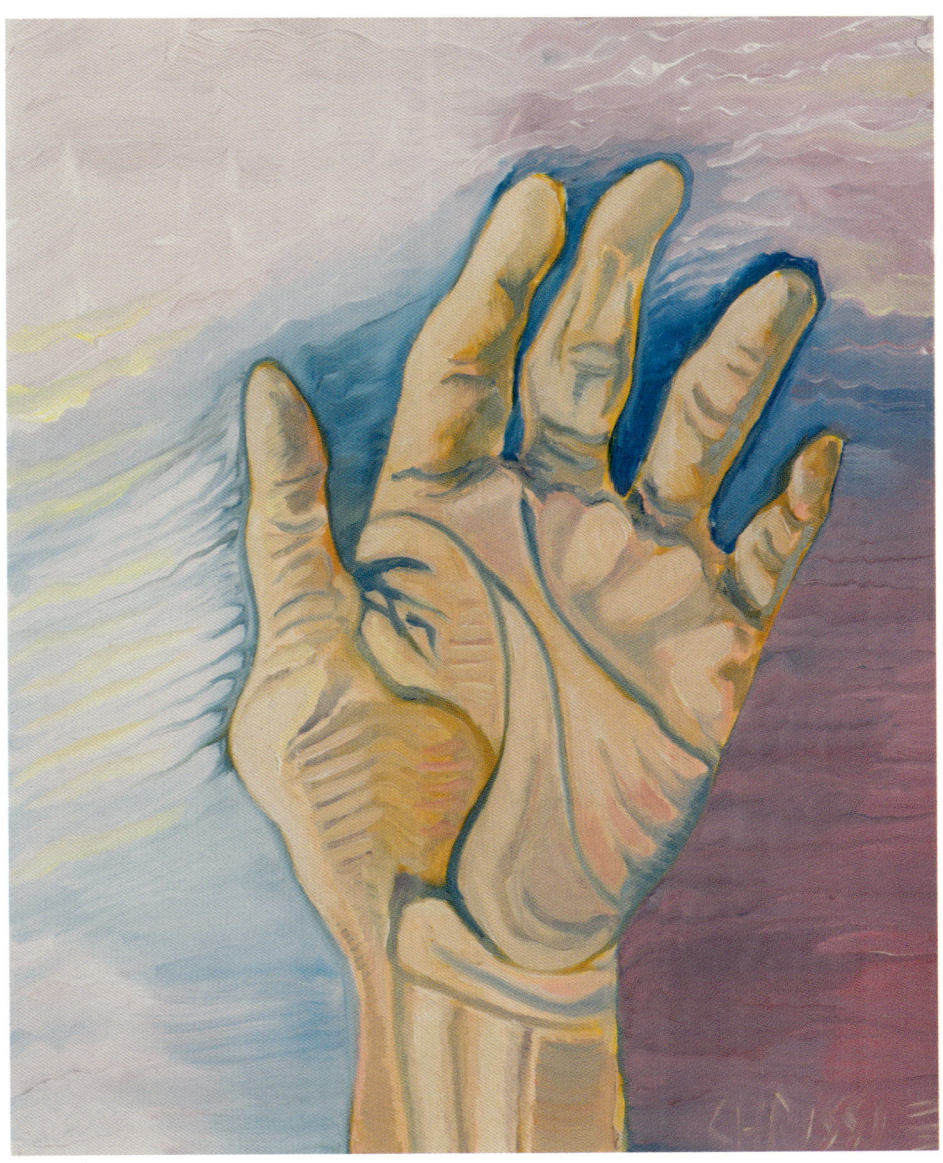

Michael Wincott has helped me a lot. He was the one who suggested I should try to go abstract.

I would send him one of my attempts and he would write back with a really in-depth critique. His reactions were often much more interesting than the paintings were. I'd read them and think, bloody hell, you put a lot more effort into that than I did!

So, for example, this hand: 'A formidable presence, dignity from anguish, signalling a desire for respite, or rescue from time. There's repeated striations of the hand and outside it. The division of left and right, the gathering storm surrounding the oasis of blue. That horizontal then vertical band, that musculature of the wrist. Very three-dimensional, a lot of movement there, a plea, a warning, an unexpected follow-up to the self-portraits. Strong surprise, what prompted this?'

He sent me an equally colourful response for almost every painting I had done, and the fact that he was seeing so much in them really encouraged me.

After bamboo came monograms, an attempt to self-nudge into abstraction.

MONOGRAM I
Oil on canvas
60 x 50 cm
(23¹/² x 19³/⁴ in)
13 May 2016

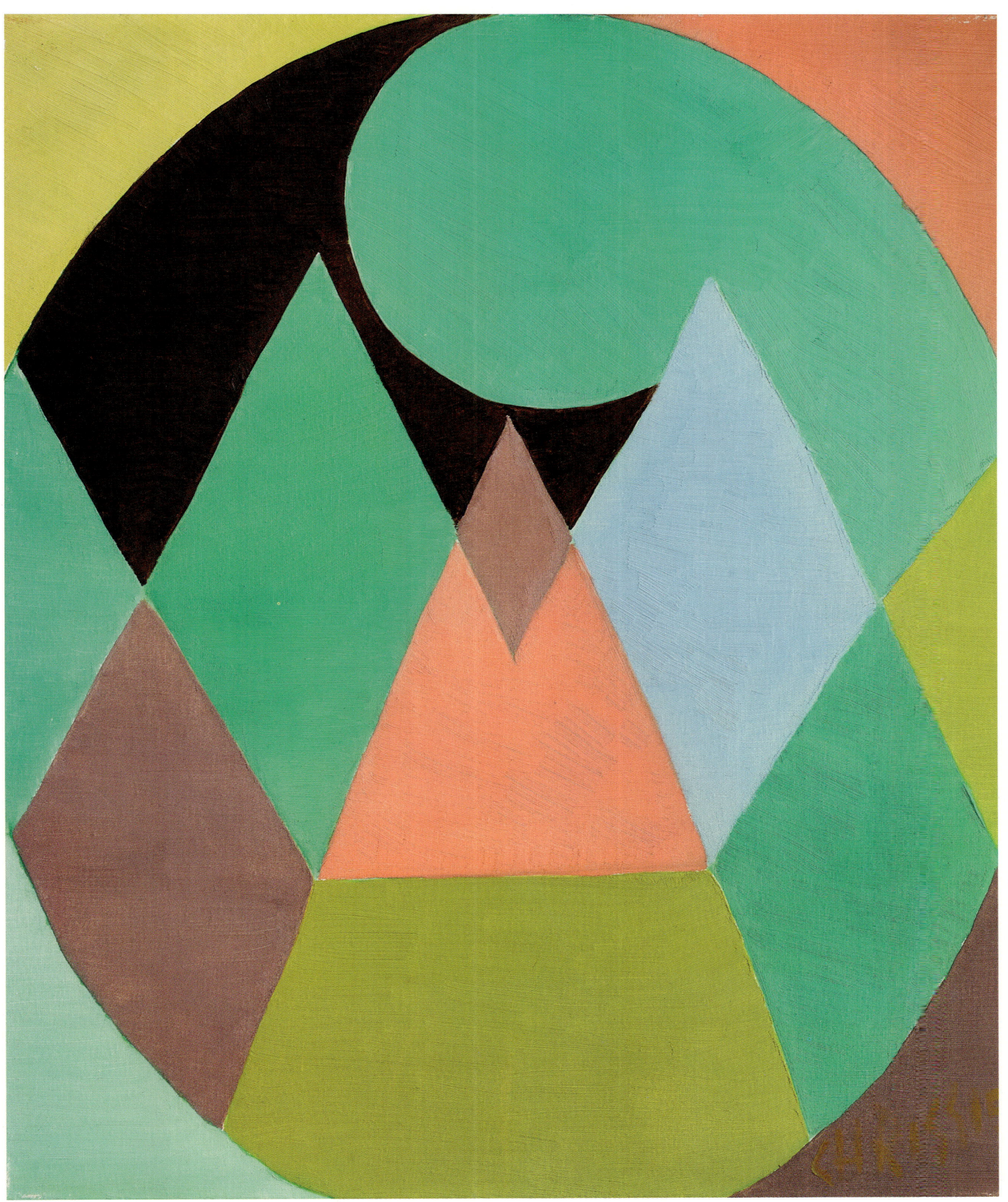

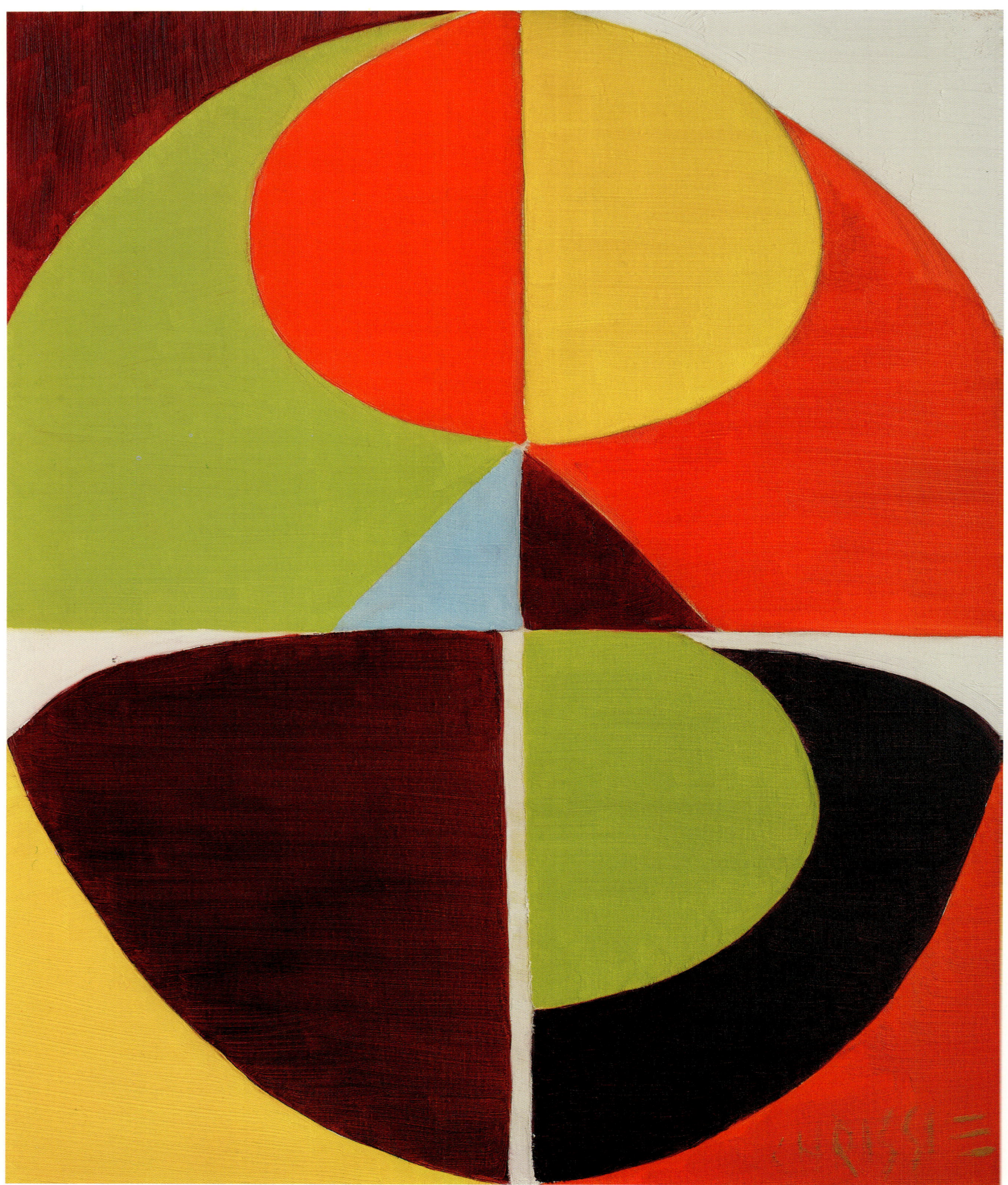

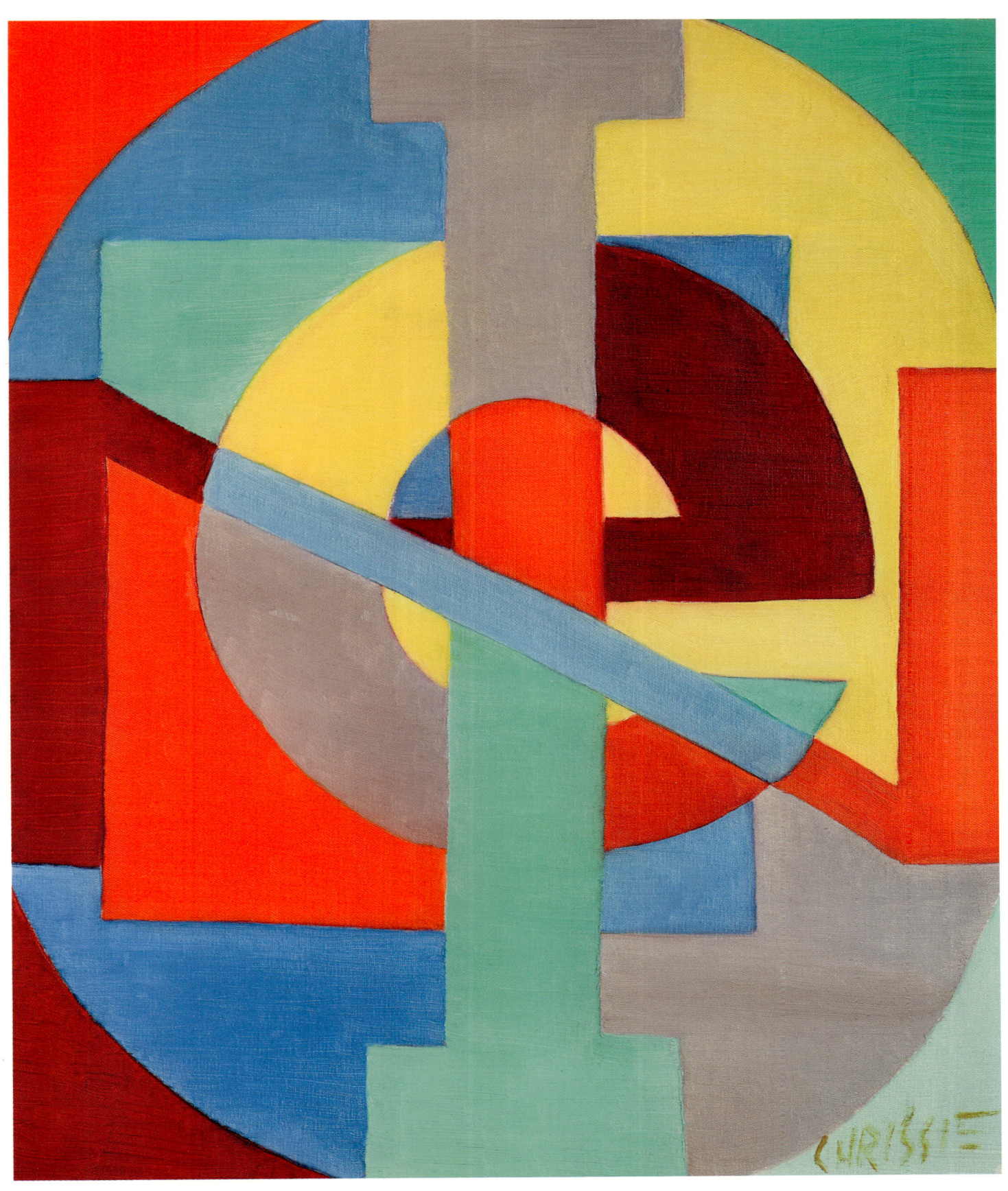

MONOGRAM II
Oil on canvas
60 x 50 cm
(23¹/² x 19³/⁴ in)
14 May 2016

MONOGRAM III
Oil on canvas
60 x 50 cm
(23¹/² x 19³/⁴ in)
15 May 2016

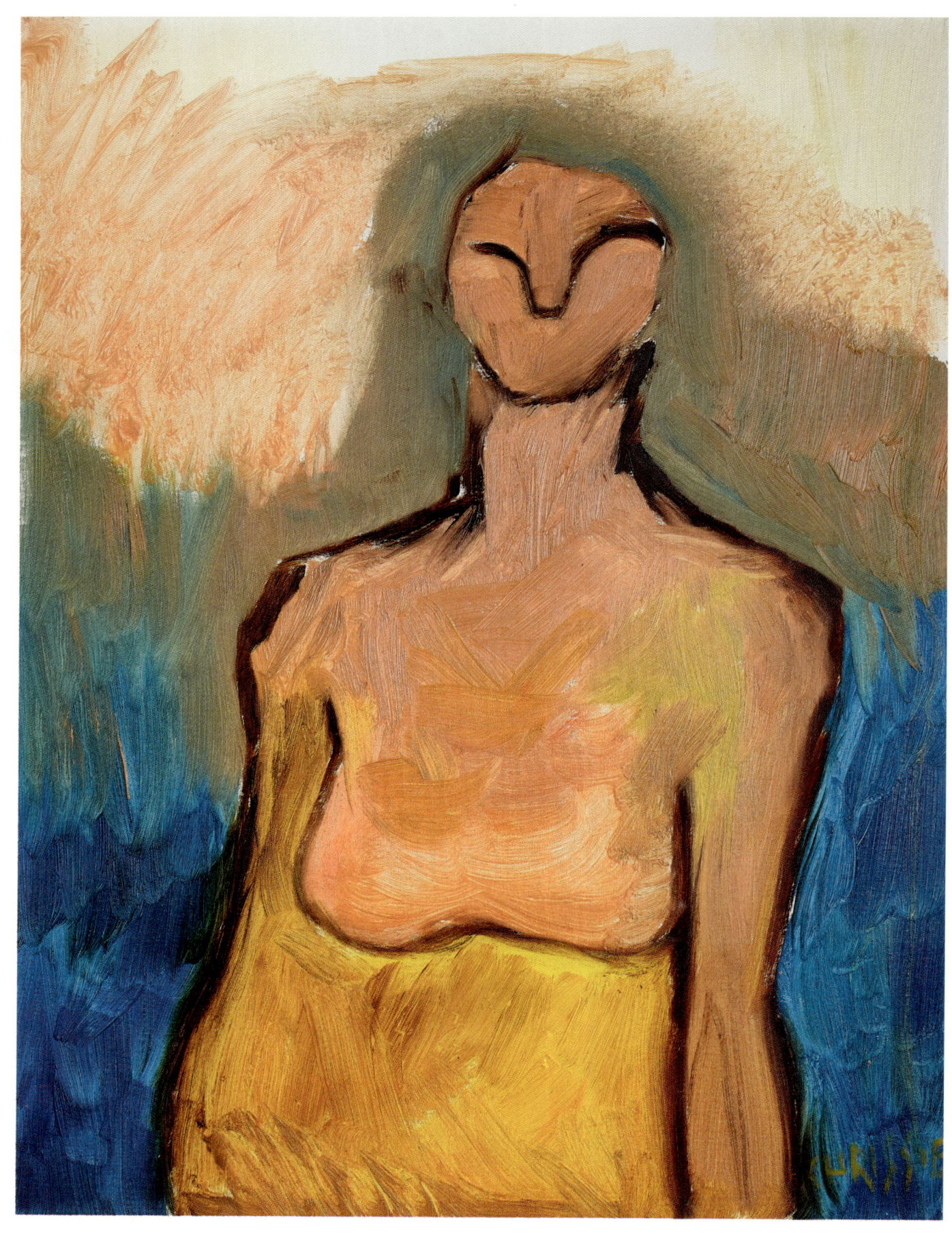

MONDAY SELF-PORTRAIT
Oil on canvas
80 x 60 cm
(31$^{1/2}$ x 23$^{1/2}$ in)
16 May 2016

TUESDAY SELF-PORTRAIT
Oil on canvas
80 x 60 cm
(31$^{1/2}$ x 23$^{1/2}$ in)
17 May 2016

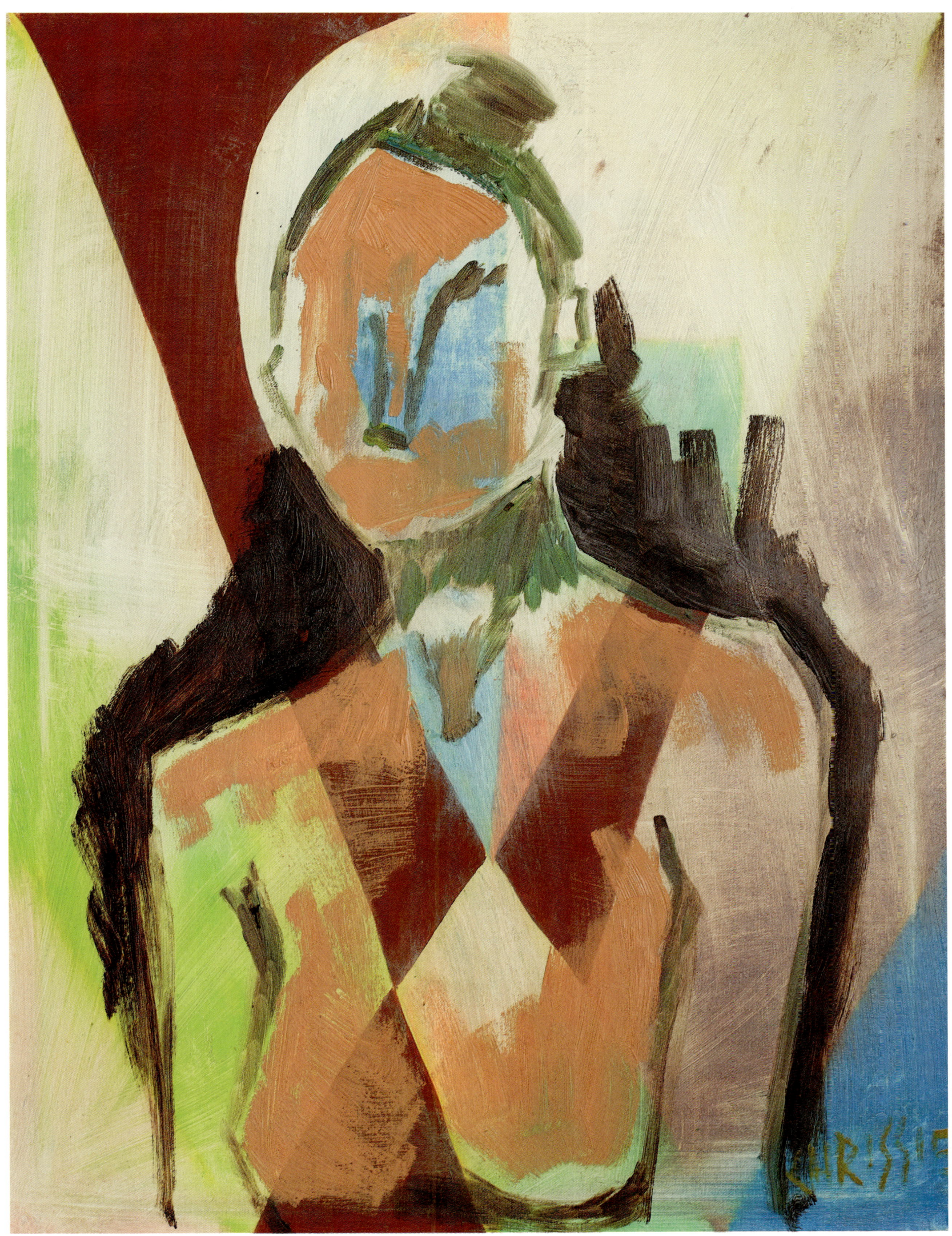

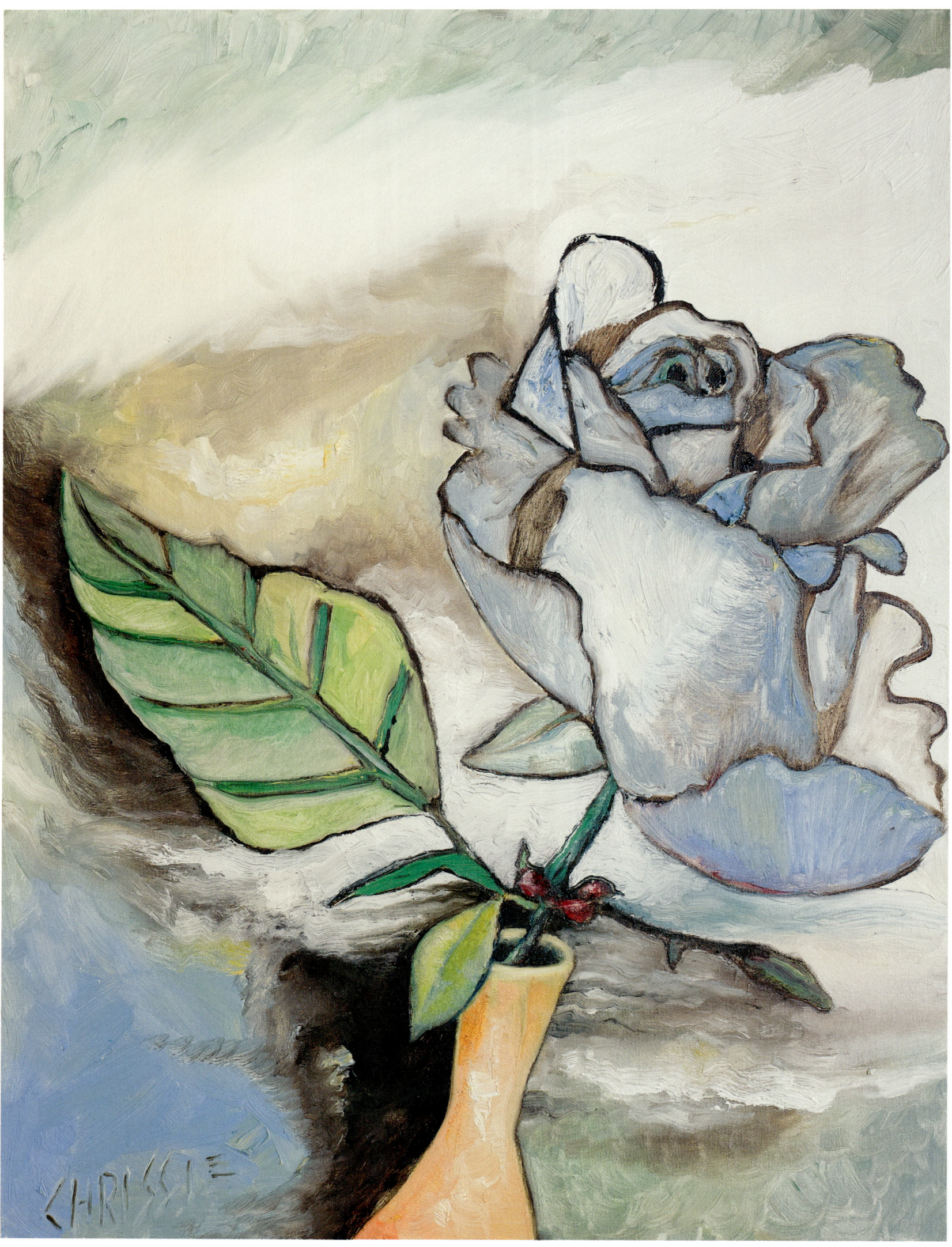

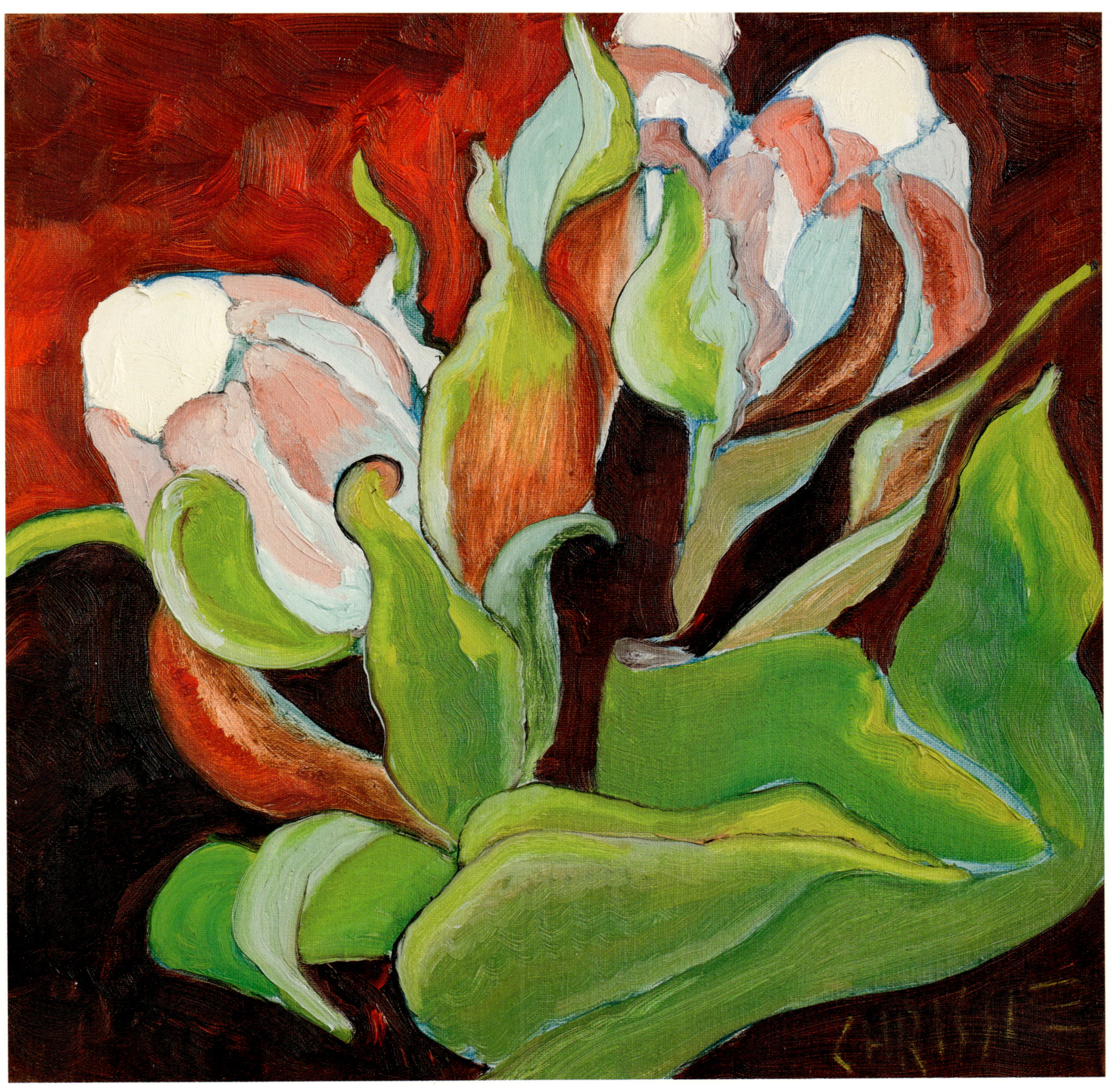

This was a little bunch of flowers I got over at my friend Clare Reihill's, who is director of the T.S. Eliot Estate. I nicked them. If I see flowers, I've got to paint them before they die. So I just asked her, 'Are you finished with those?'

BLUE ROSE STORM
Oil on canvas
80 x 60 cm
(31¹⁄₂ x 23¹⁄₂ in)
6 February 2016

THURSDAY CLARE
FLOWERS I
Oil on canvas
40 x 40 cm
(15³⁄₄ x 15³⁄₄ in)
19 May 2016

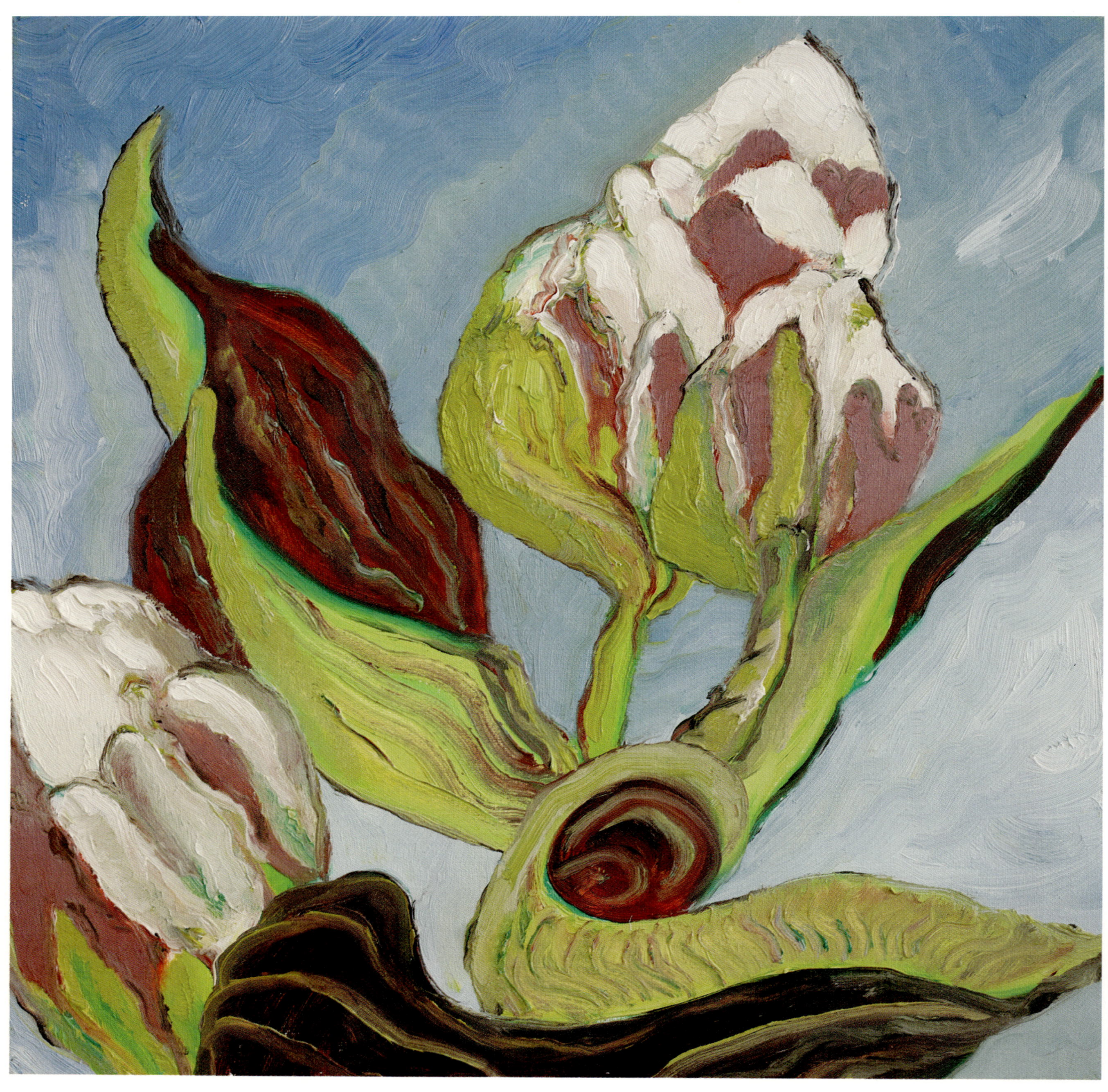

THURSDAY CLARE
FLOWERS II
Oil on canvas
40 x 40 cm
(15³⁄⁴ x 15³⁄⁴ in)
19 May 2016

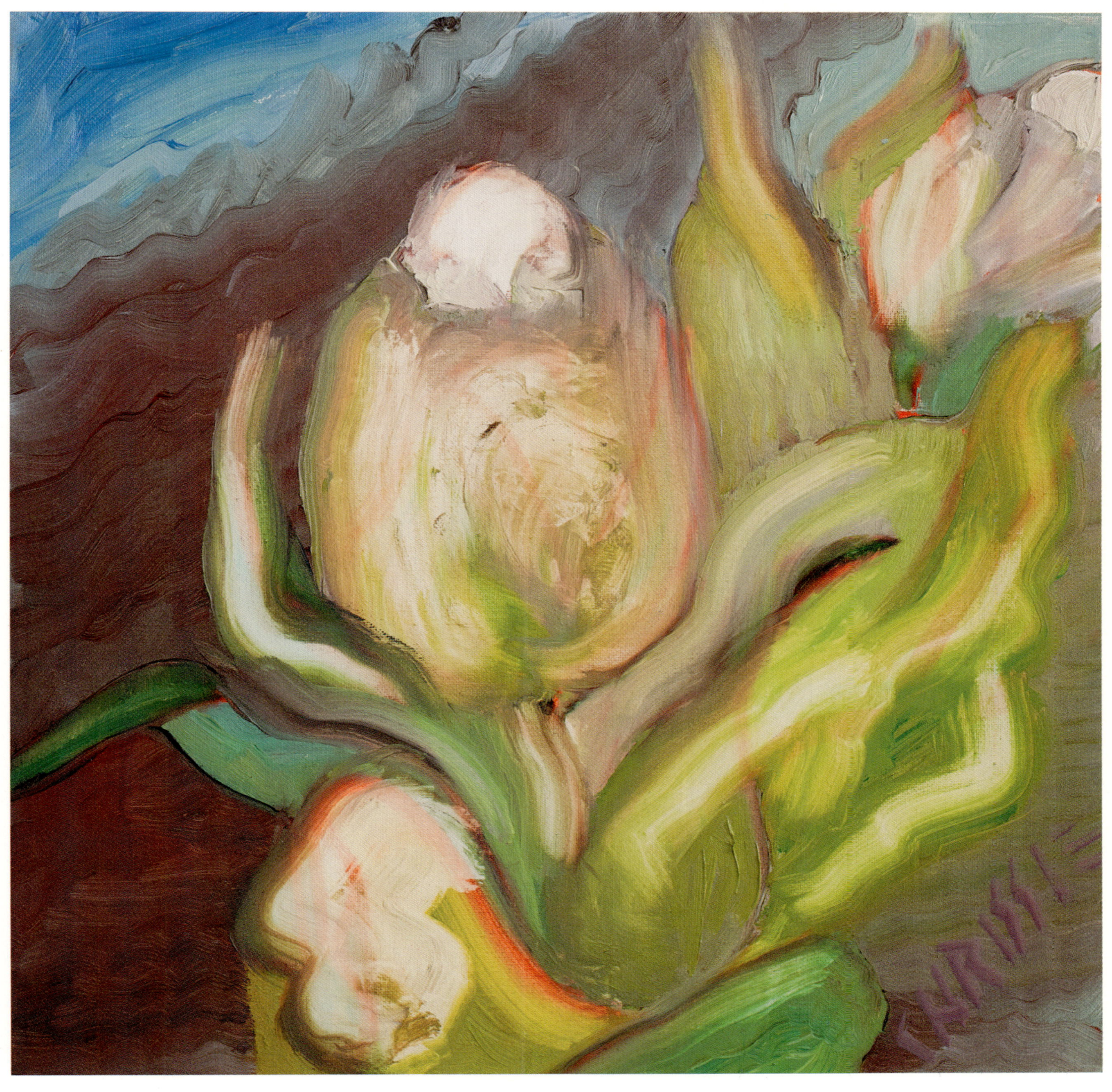

THURSDAY CLARE
FLOWERS III
Oil on canvas
40 x 40 cm
(15³/₄ x 15³/₄ in)
19 May 2016

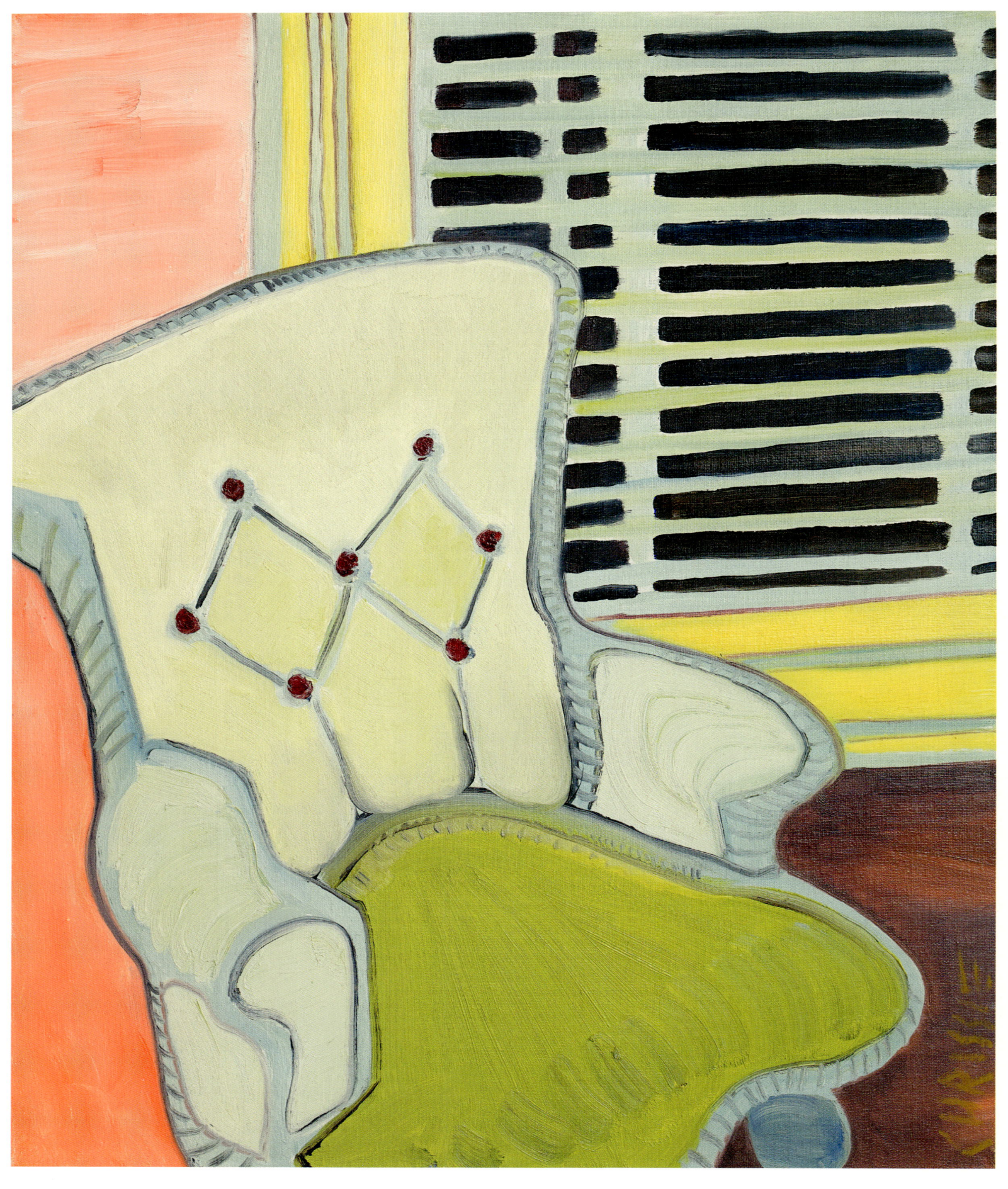

MONDAY CHAIR
Oil on canvas
60 x 50 cm
(23½ x 19¾ in)
23 May 2016

This chair was the only thing I had in my studio, so I painted it a lot.

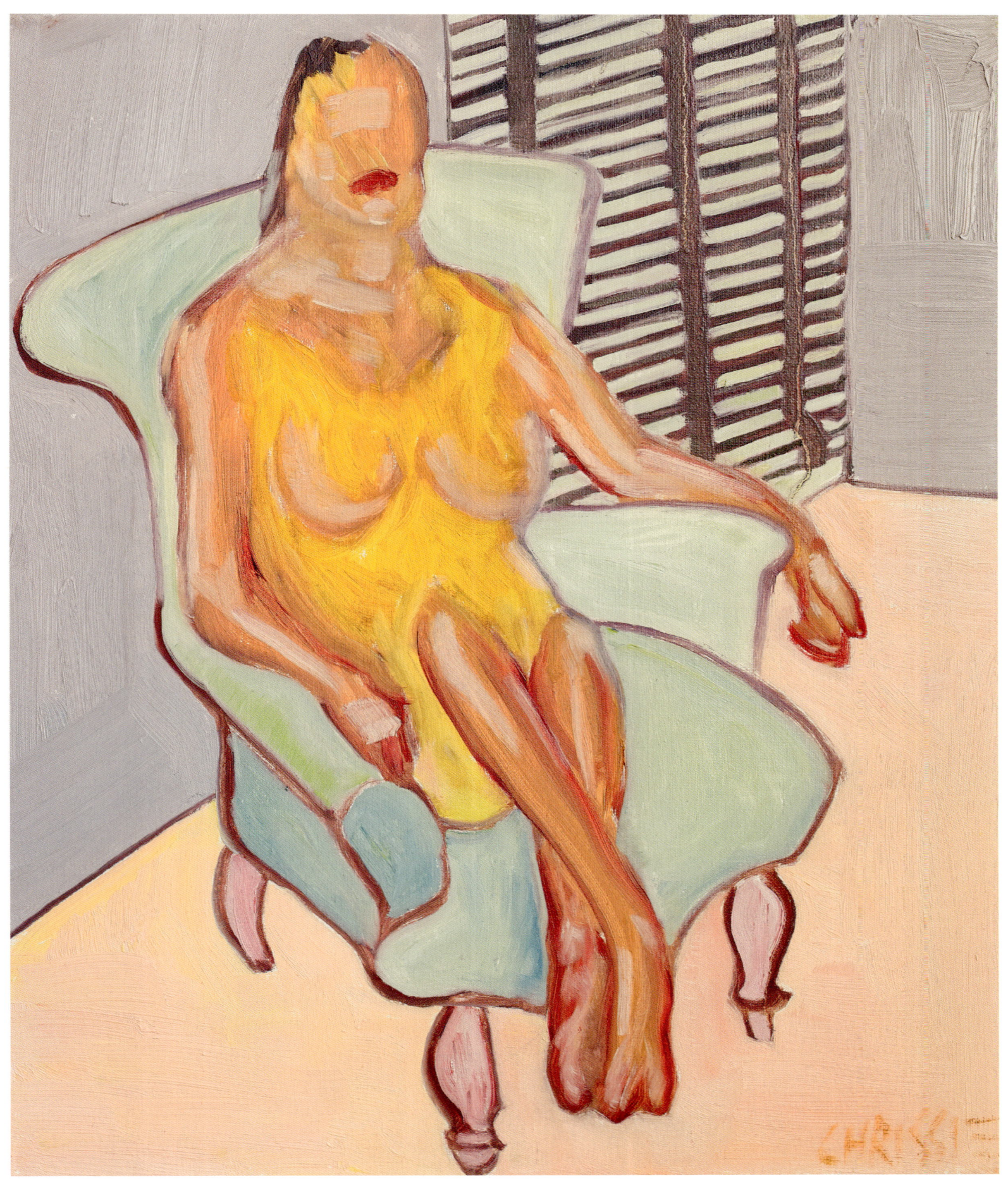

This is one of my favourites, the beginning of my imaginary people series.

WOMAN SITTING
Oil on canvas
50 x 50 cm
(23½ x 19¾ in)
24 May 2016

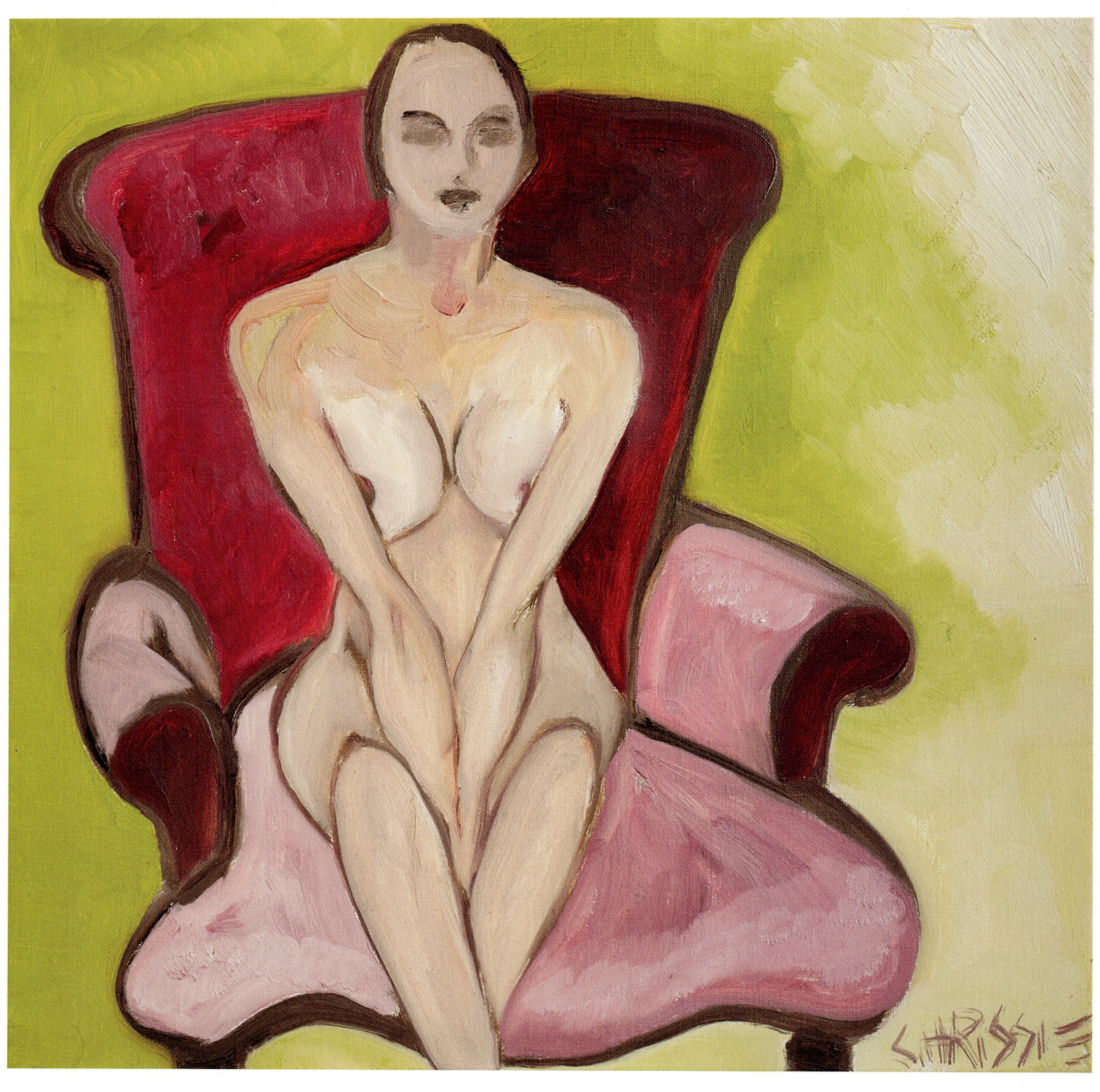

GIRL CHAIR SATURDAY
Oil on canvas
40 x 40 cm
(15³/₄ x 15³/₄ in)
28 May 2016

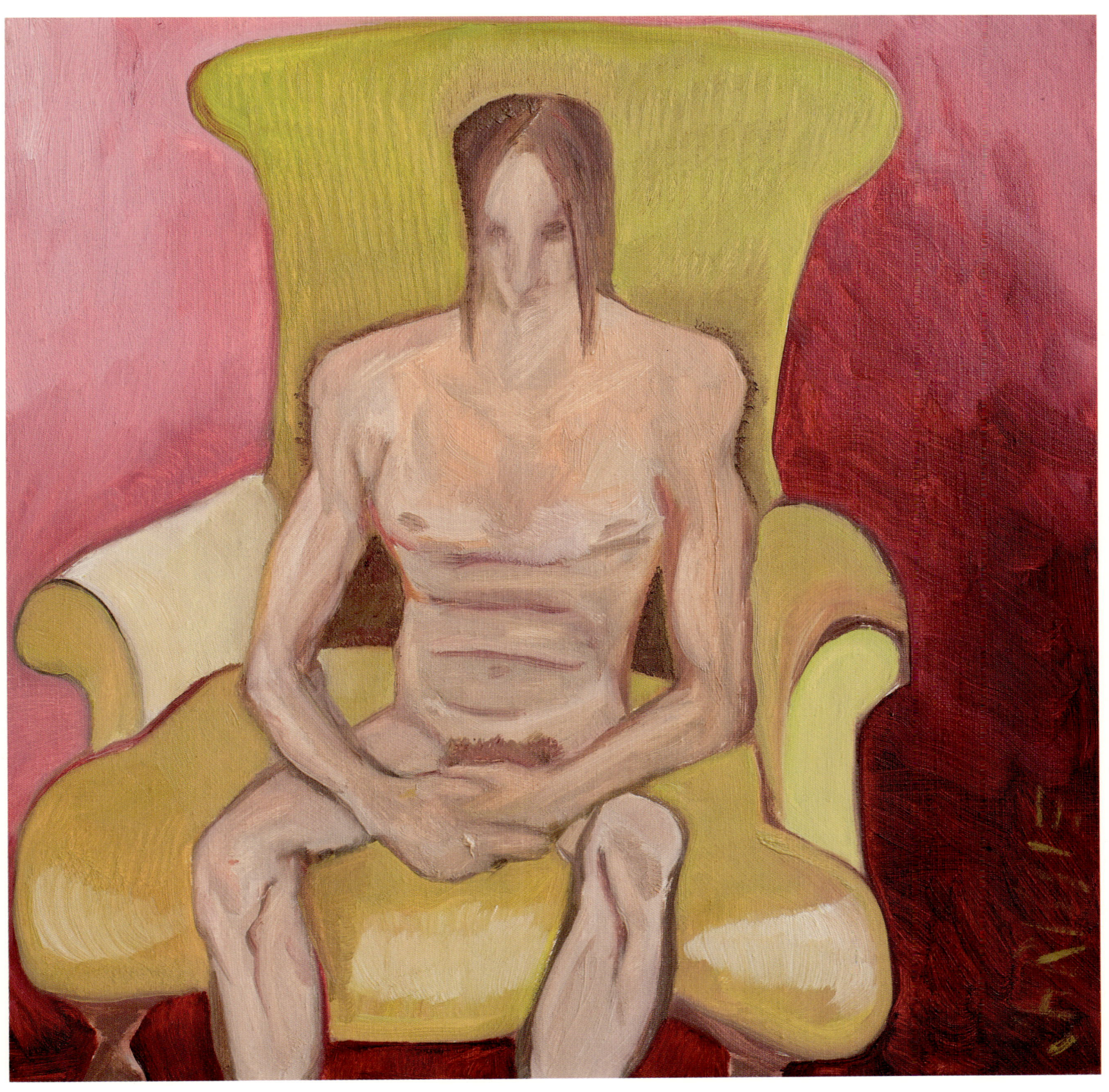

After I finished this one, I realised it looked exactly like a guy I used to go out with. I don't see him anymore, because he's on another continent. He doesn't have a phone or computer, so I can't get in touch with him. Maybe this was him trying to get in touch with me.

MAN CHAIR SUNDAY
Oil on canvas
40 x 40 cm
(15³⁄₄ x 15³⁄ in)
29 May 2016

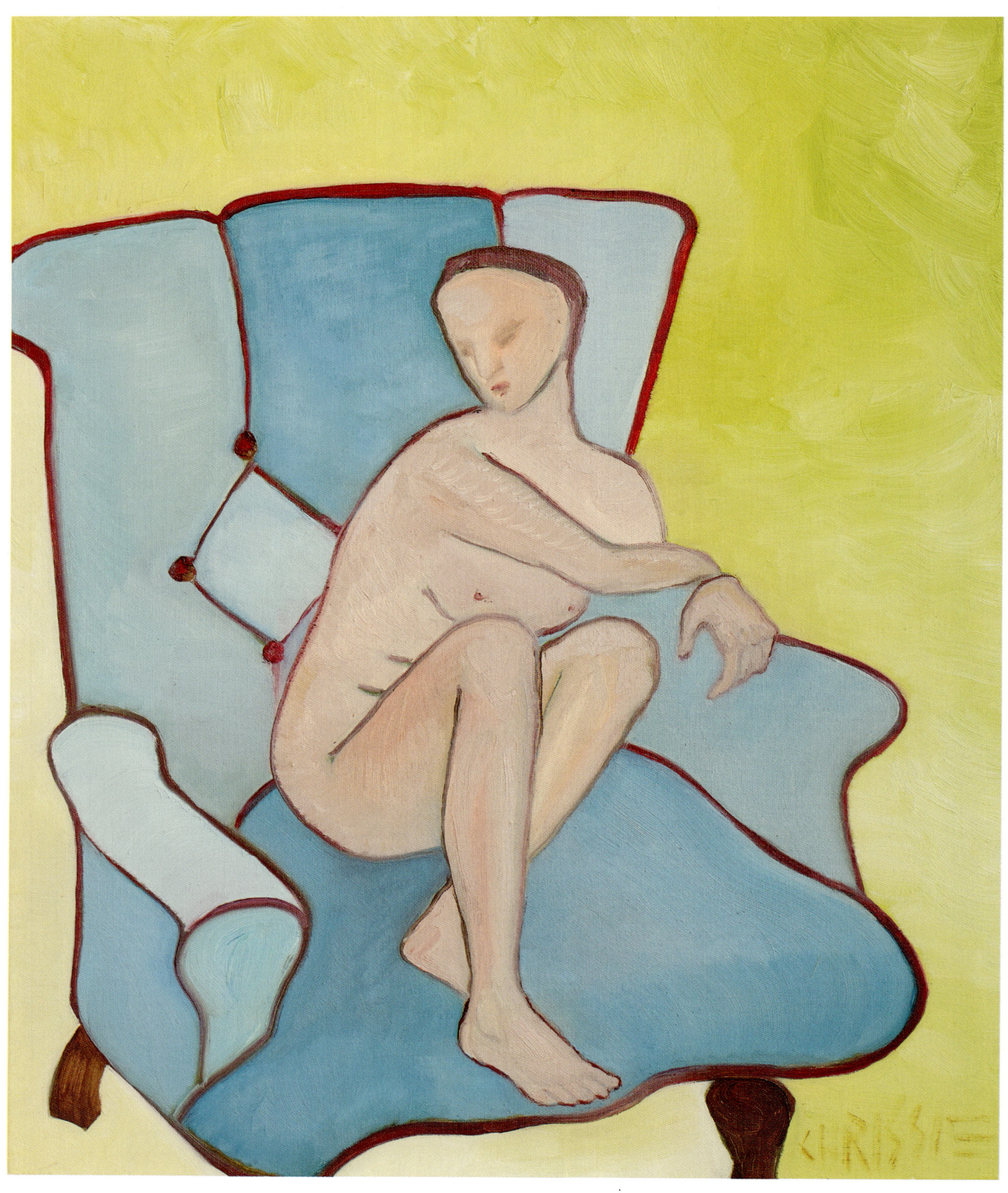

GIRL IN BLUE
Oil on canvas
60 x 50 cm
(23¹ᐟ² x 19³ᐟ⁴ in)
30 May 2016

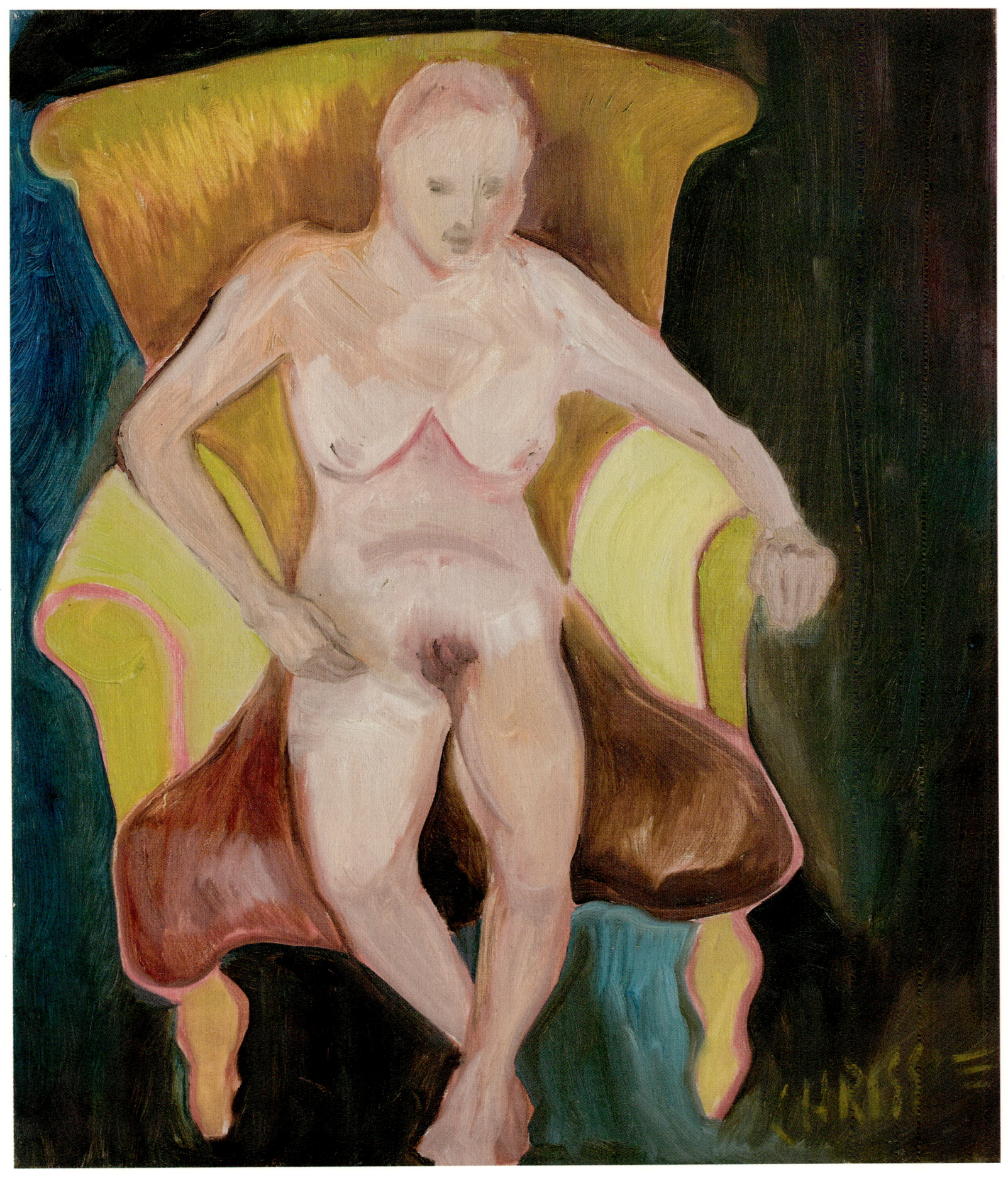

IMAGINARY FIGURE
IN CHAIR
Oil on canvas
60 x 50 cm
(23¹/² x 19³/⁴ in)
30 May 2016

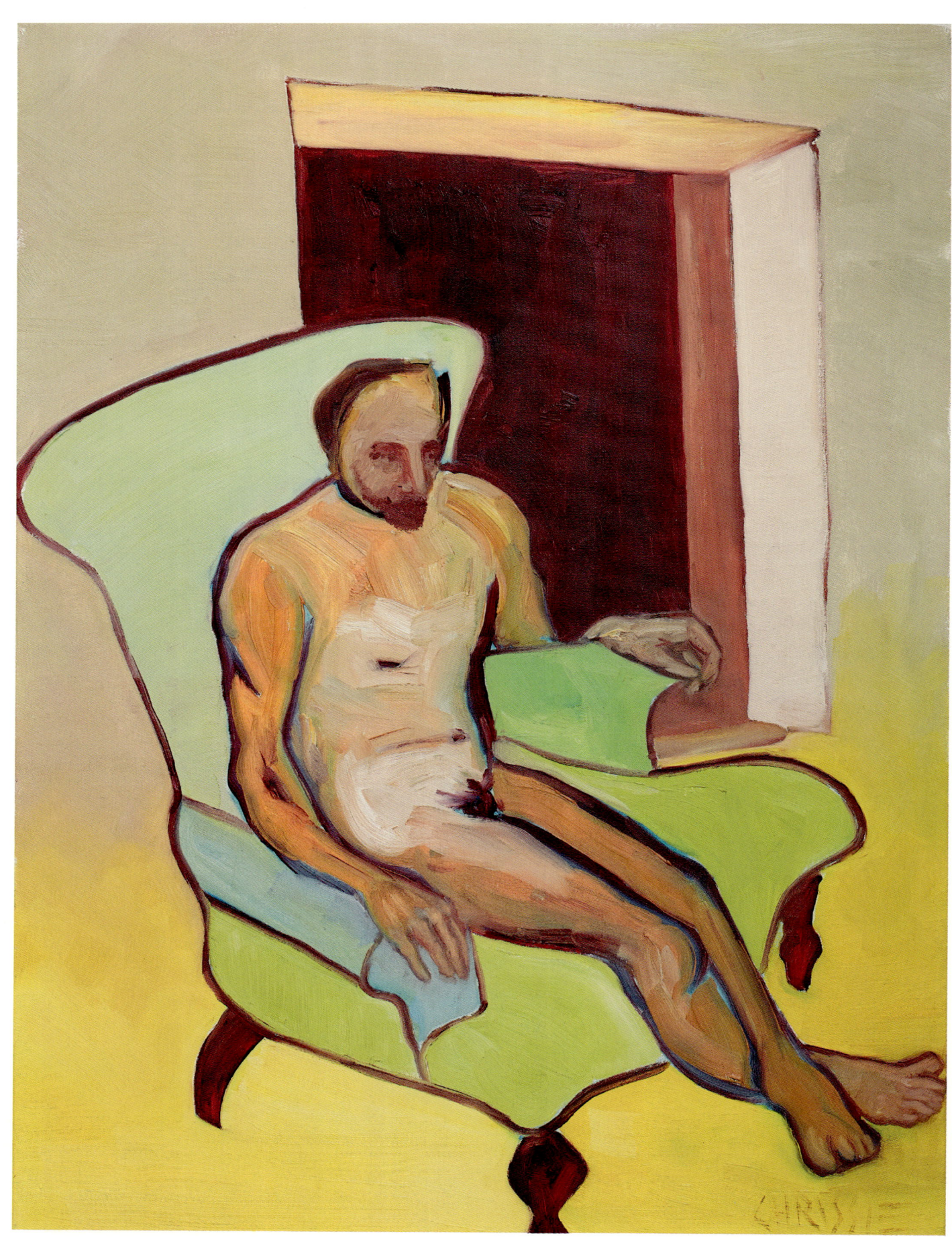

FINAL MAN IN GREEN
Oil on canvas
80 x 60 cm
($31^{1/2}$ x $23^{1/2}$ in)
30 May 2016

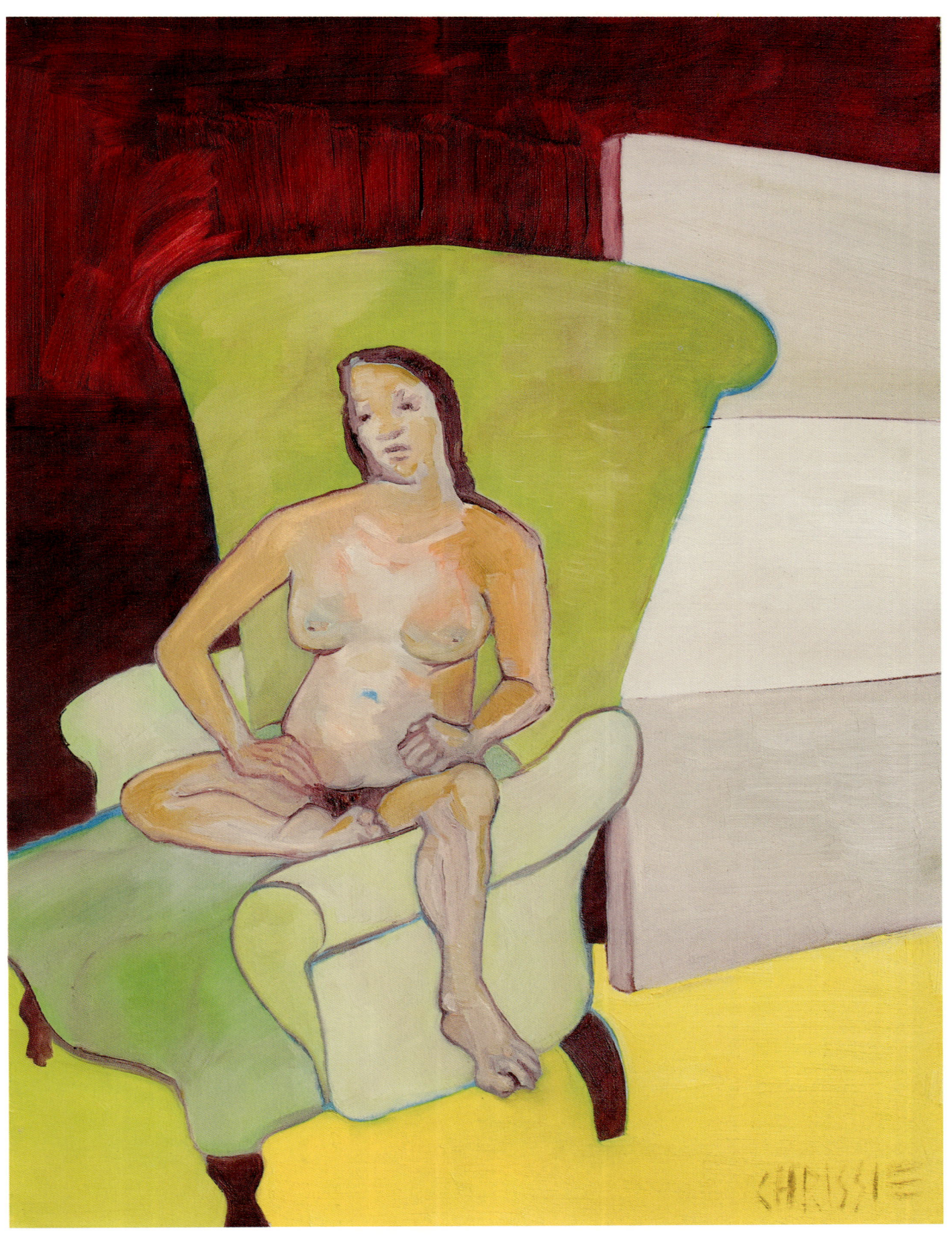

I've got a lot of mileage out of that chair. I've retired it and moved it out of the studio now.

GIRL IN GREEN
Oil on canvas
80 x 60 cm
(31½ x 23½ in)
30 May 2016

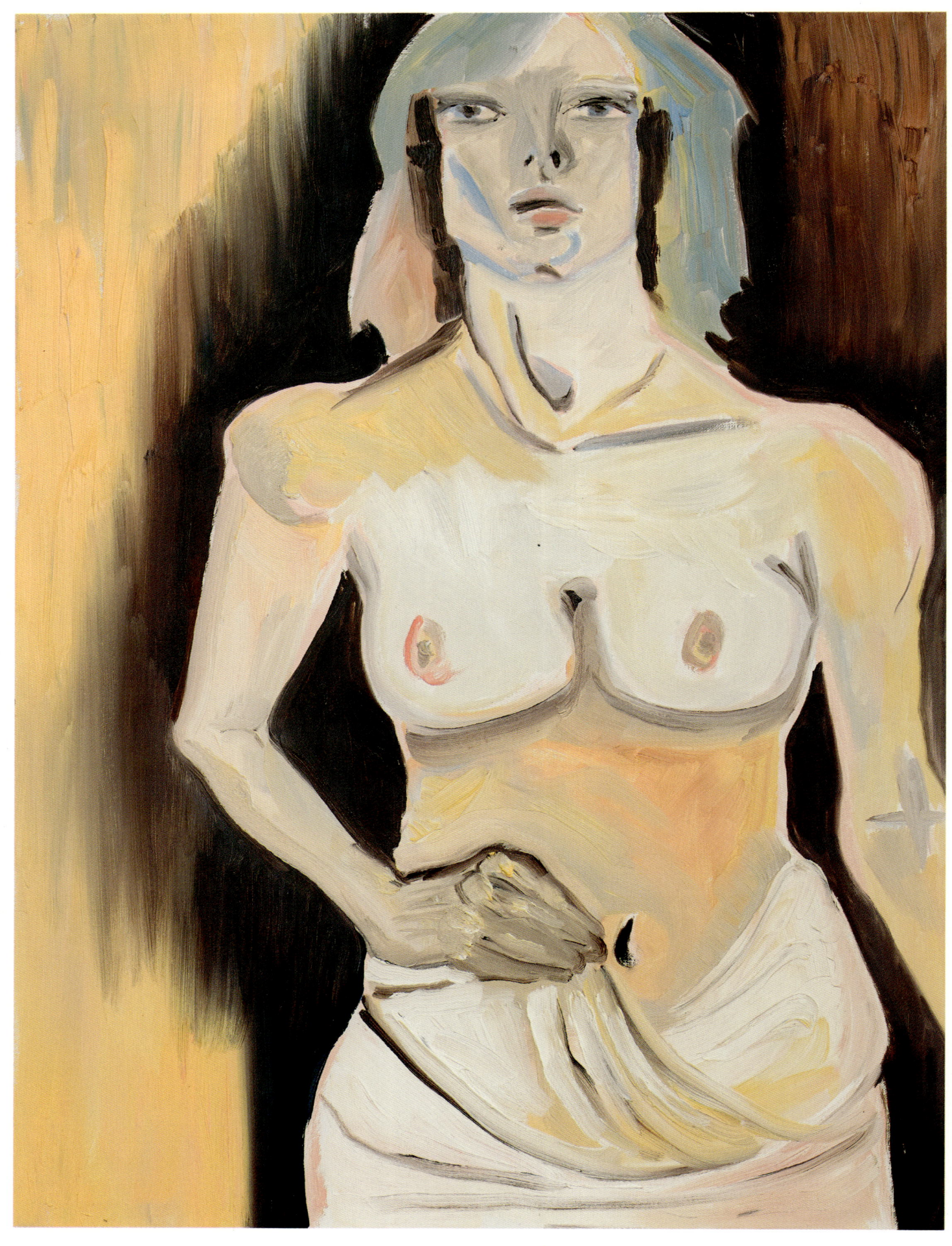

WOMAN IN WRAP
Oil on canvas
80 x 60 cm
(31¹/² x 23¹/² in)
3 July 2016

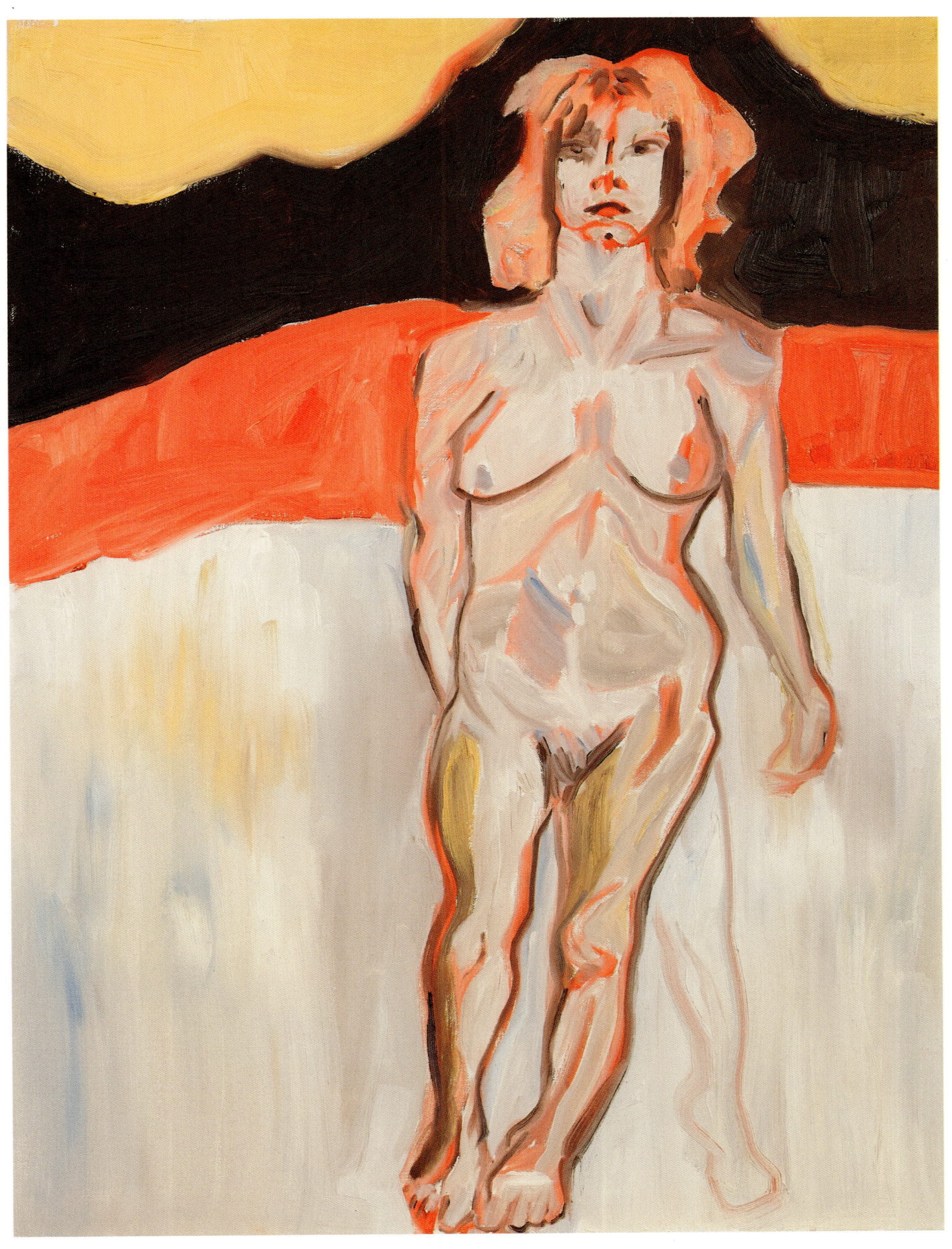

WOMAN WALKING
Oil on canvas
80 x 60 cm
(31¹/² x 23¹/² in)
3 July 2010

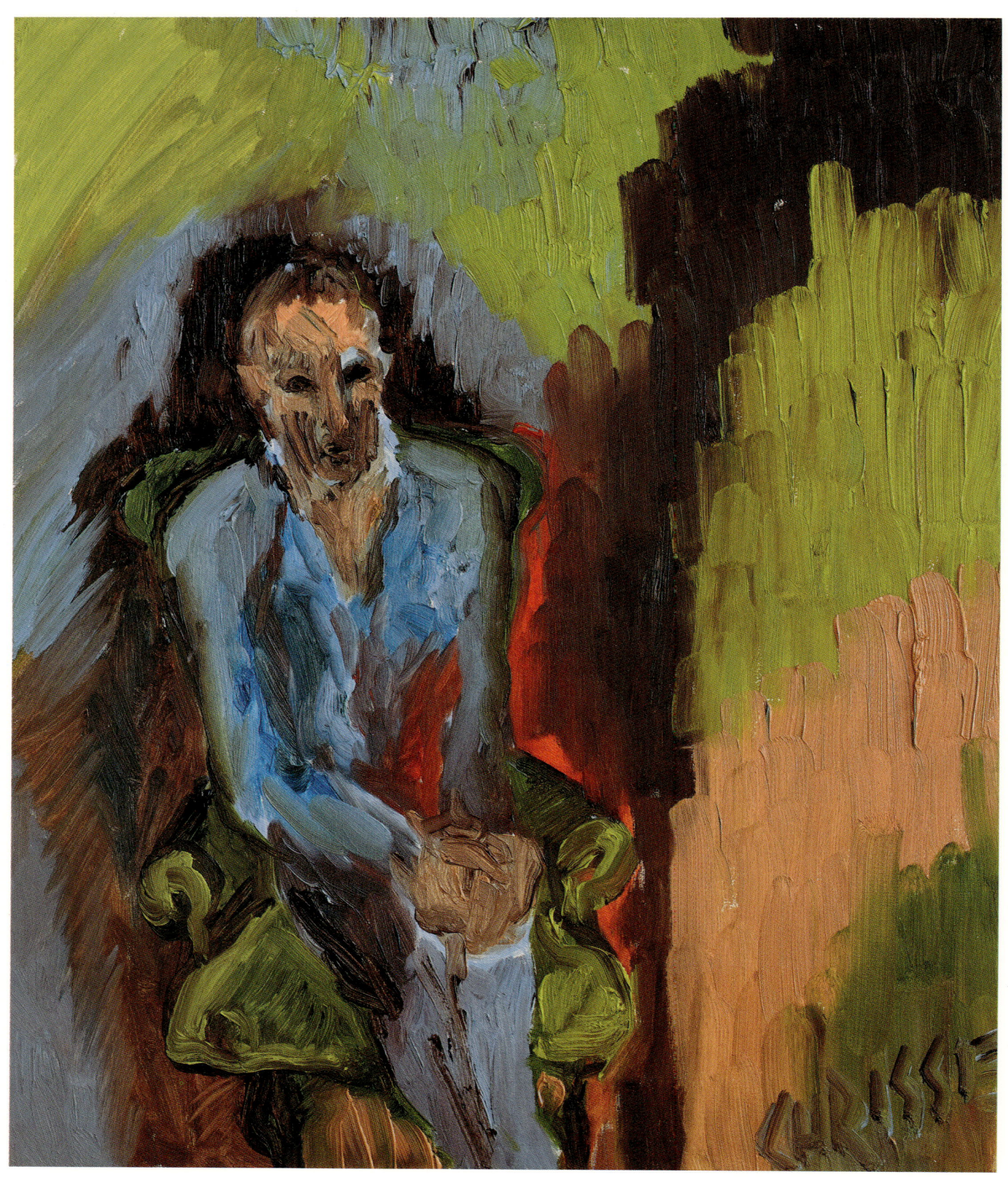

I had been on tour just before I painted this. Every time I stop painting for a while, I get worried that I won't be able to do it again. But it comes back. This was the first in my lonely man series.

MAN ALONE CHAIR
Oil on canvas
60 x 50 cm
(23¹ᐟ² x 19³ᐟ⁴ in)
26 July 2016

MAN ALONE CHAIR
SUMMER HEAT
Oil on canvas
60 x 50 cm
(23¹ᐟ² x 19³ᐟ⁴ in)
26 July 2016

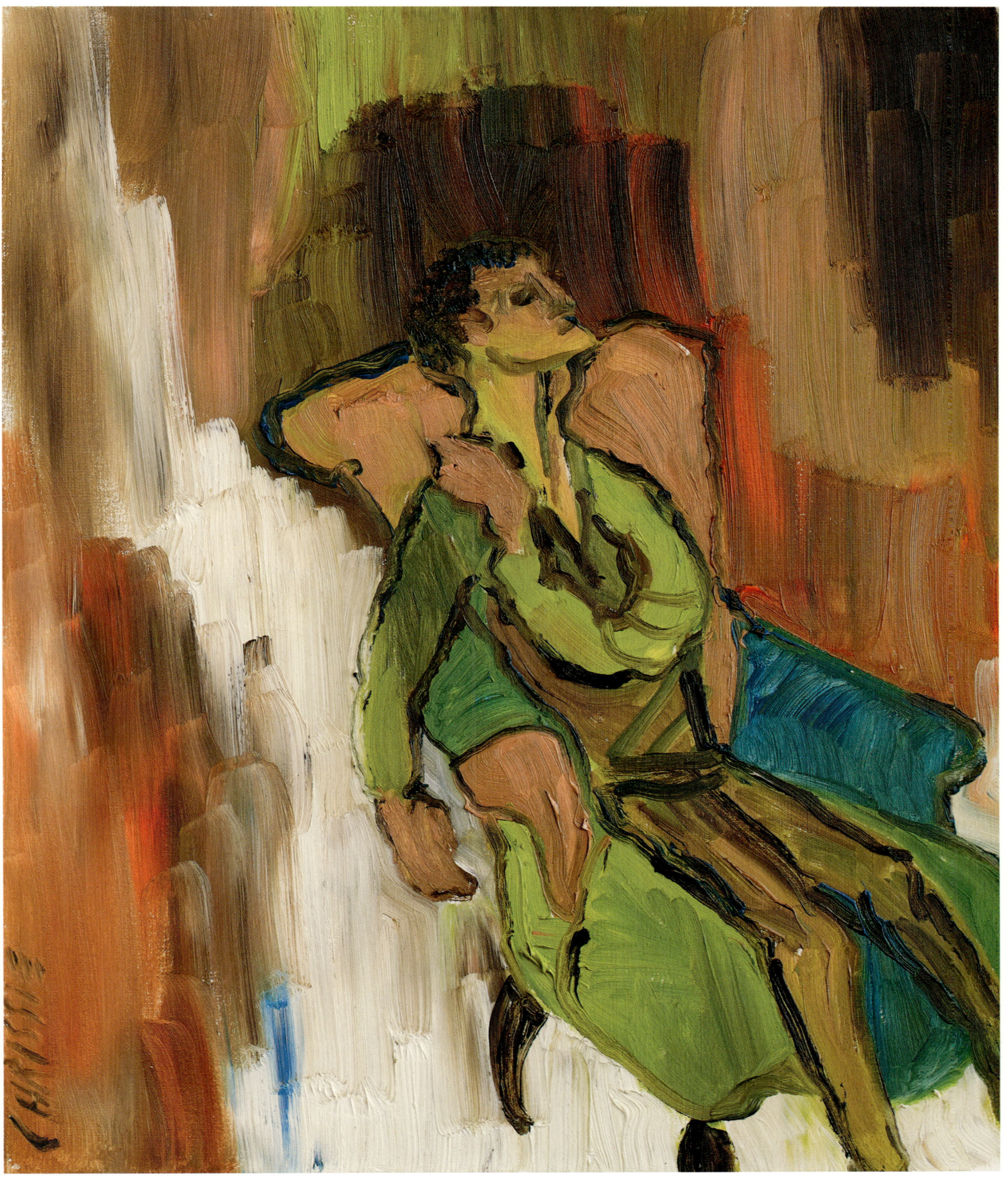

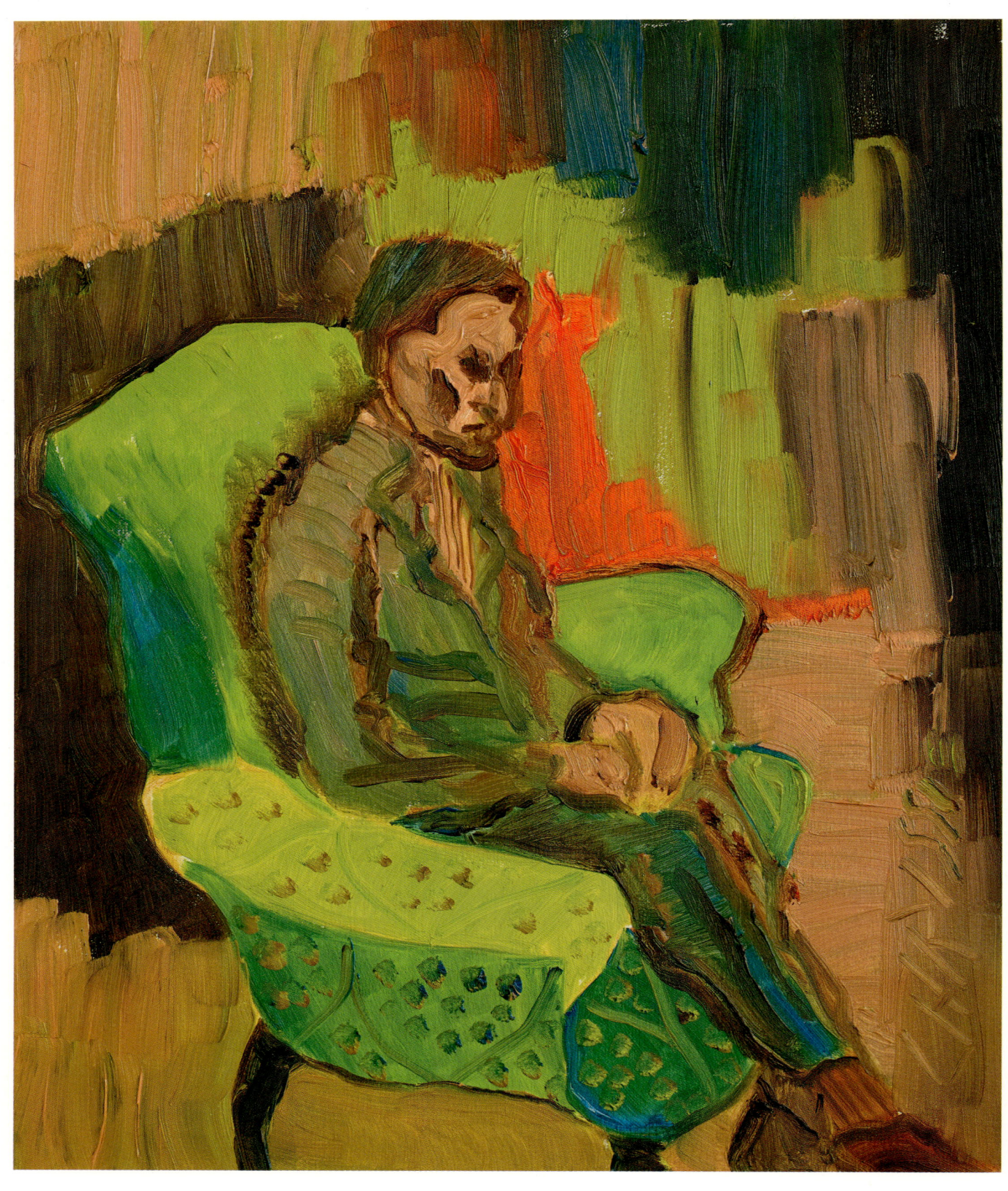

Being in a band is a team thing, but painting is absolutely a solo thing.

MAN ALONE IN REPOSE
Oil on canvas
60 x 50 cm
(23¹/² x 19³/⁴ in)
25 July 2016

MAN ALONE WAITING
Oil on canvas
60 x 50 cm
(23¹/² x 19³/⁴ in)
25 July 2016

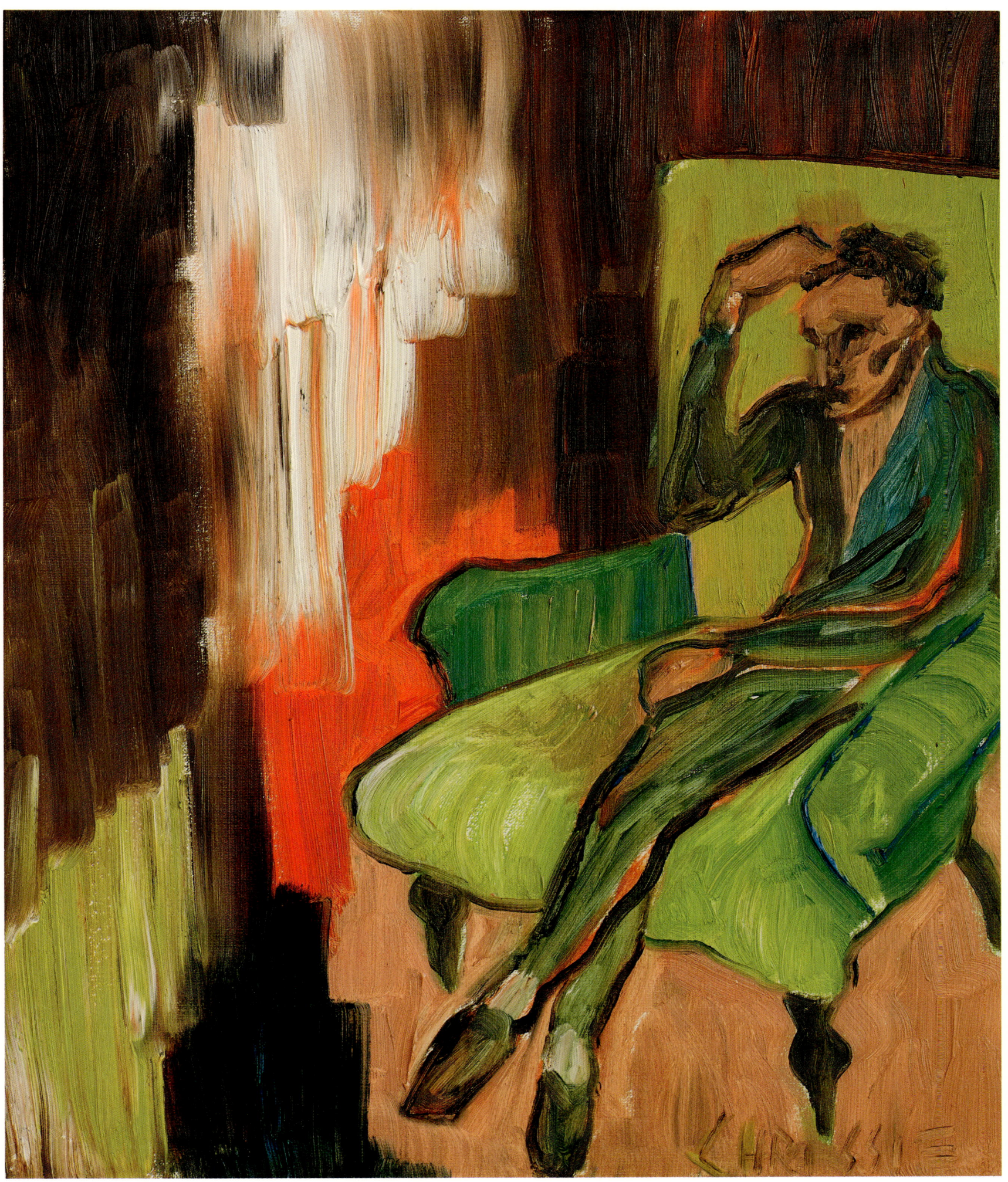

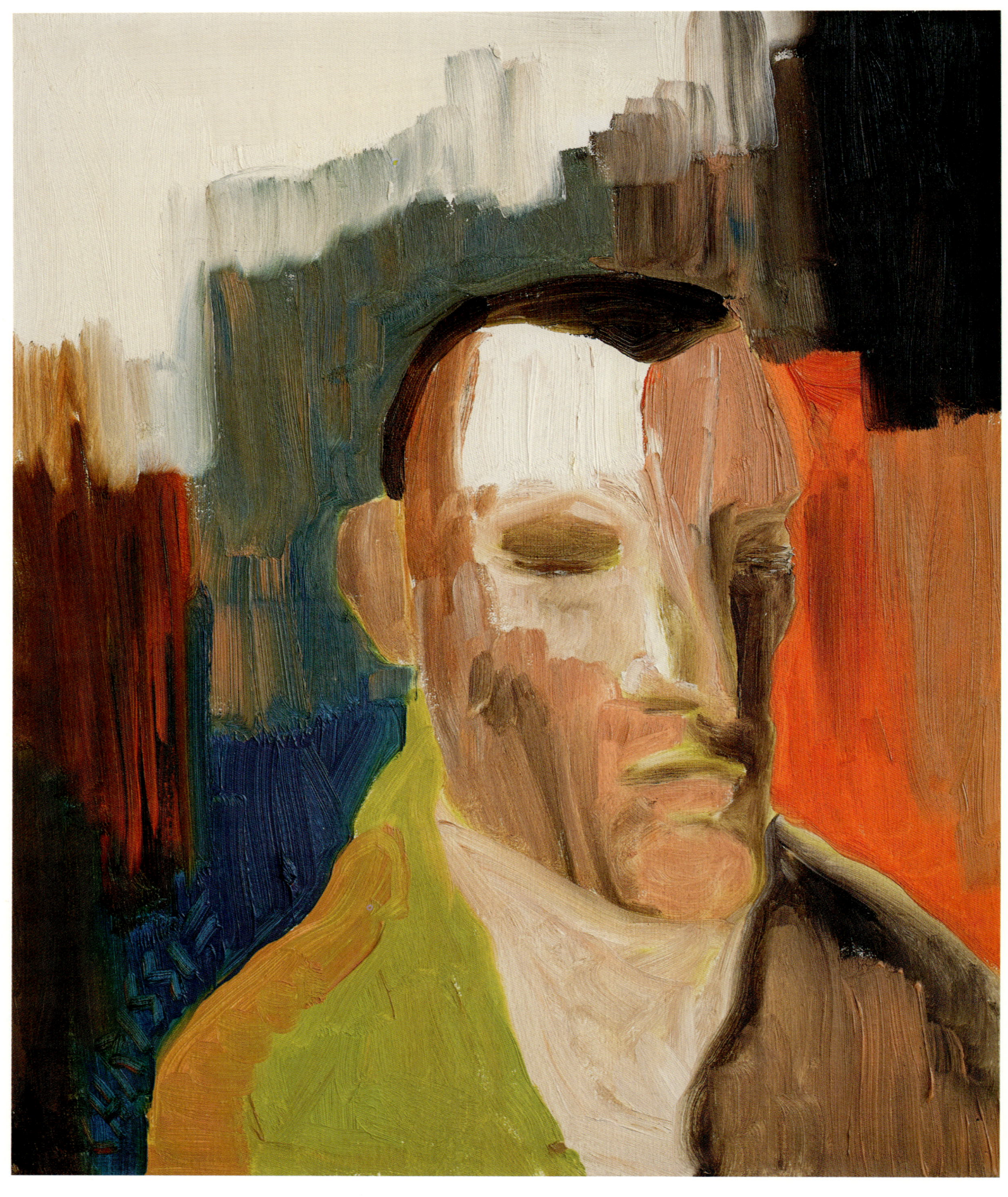

THE WAITER
Oil on canvas
60 x 50 cm
(23¹⁄₂ x 19³⁄₄ in)
27 July 2016

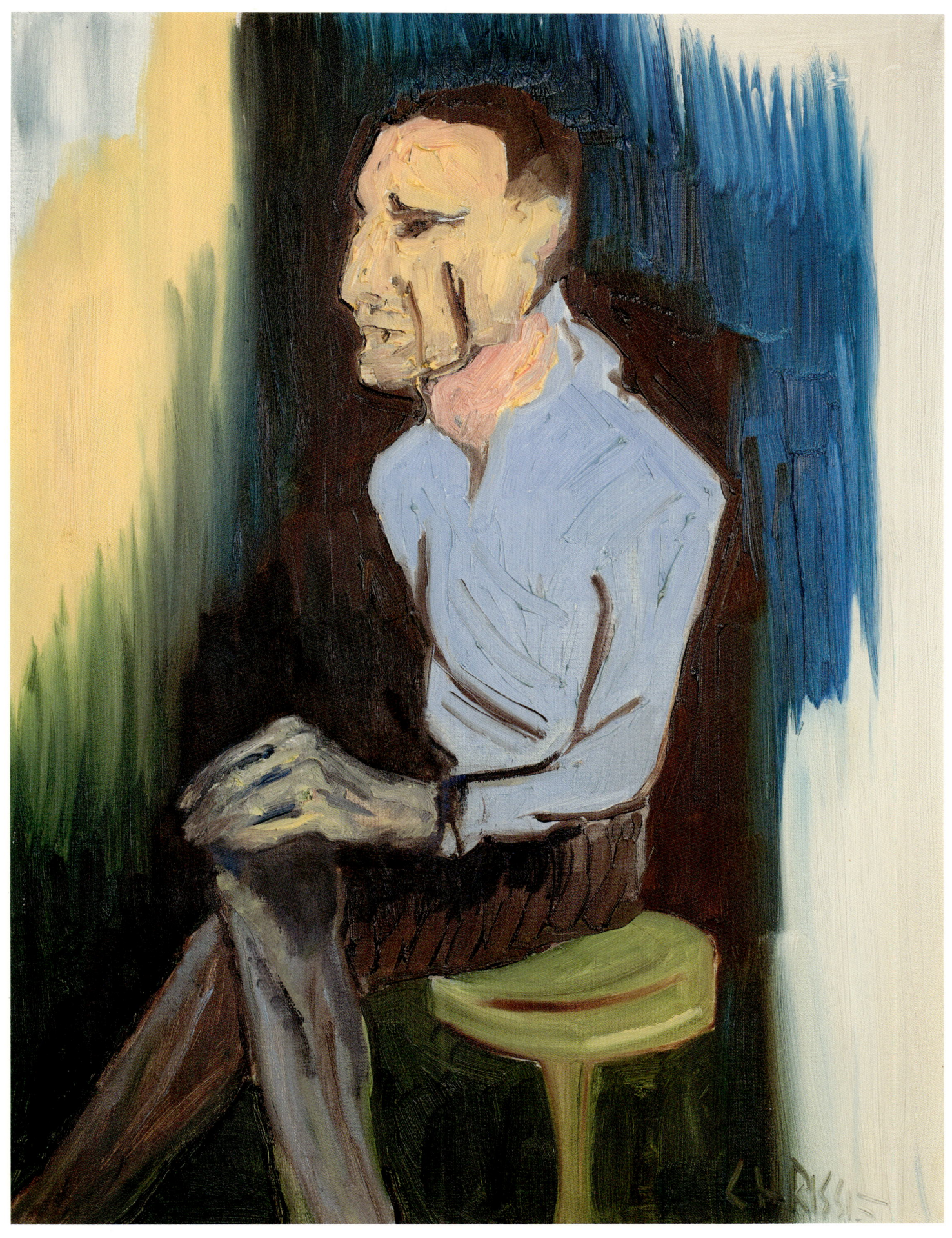

MAN ON DRUM STOOL
Oil on canvas
80 x 60 cm
(31$^{1/2}$ x 23$^{1/2}$ in)
5 October 2016

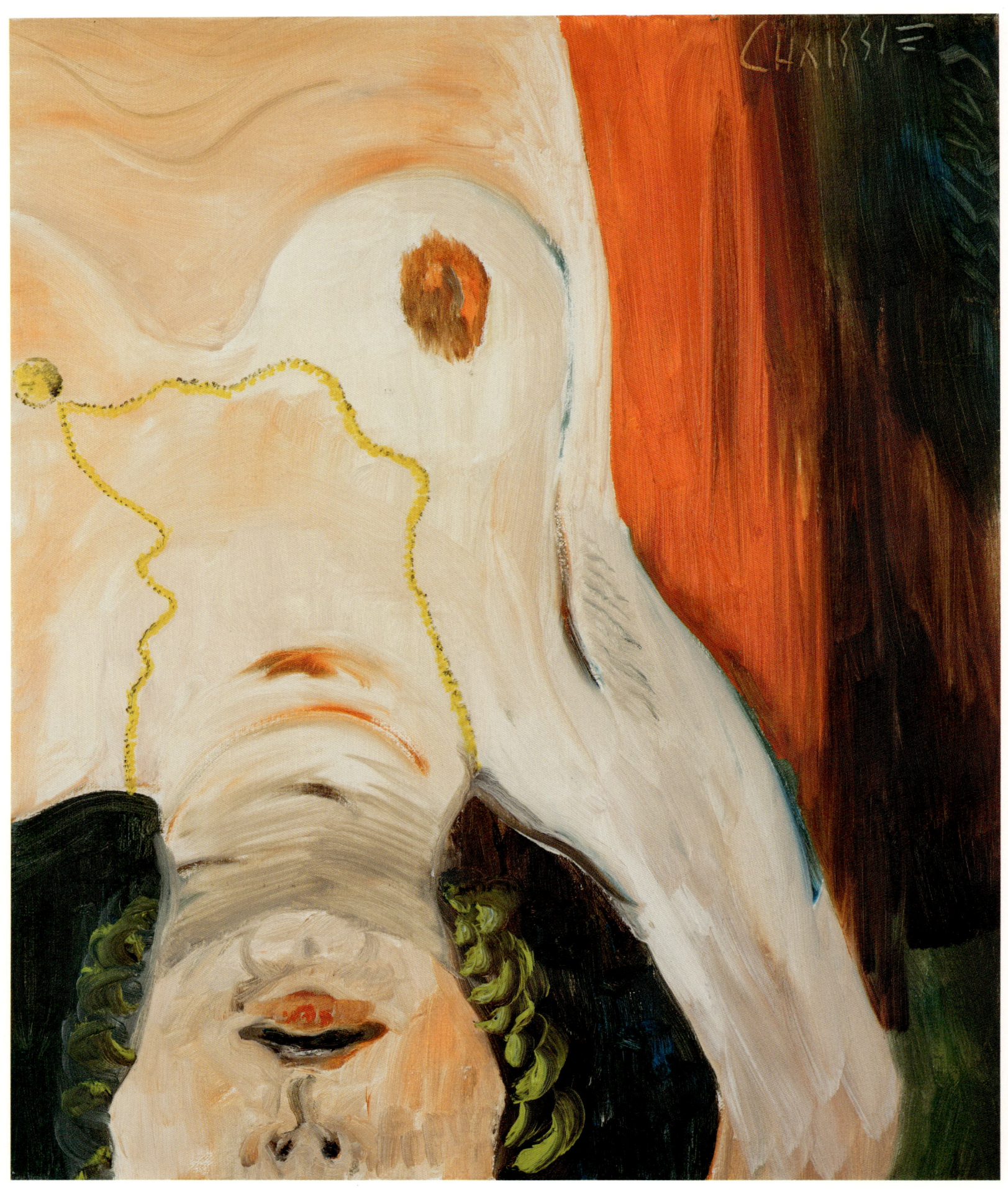

WOMAN SUNBATHING
Oil on canvas
60 x 50 cm
(23⁵⁄₂ x 19³⁄⁴ in)
27 July 2016

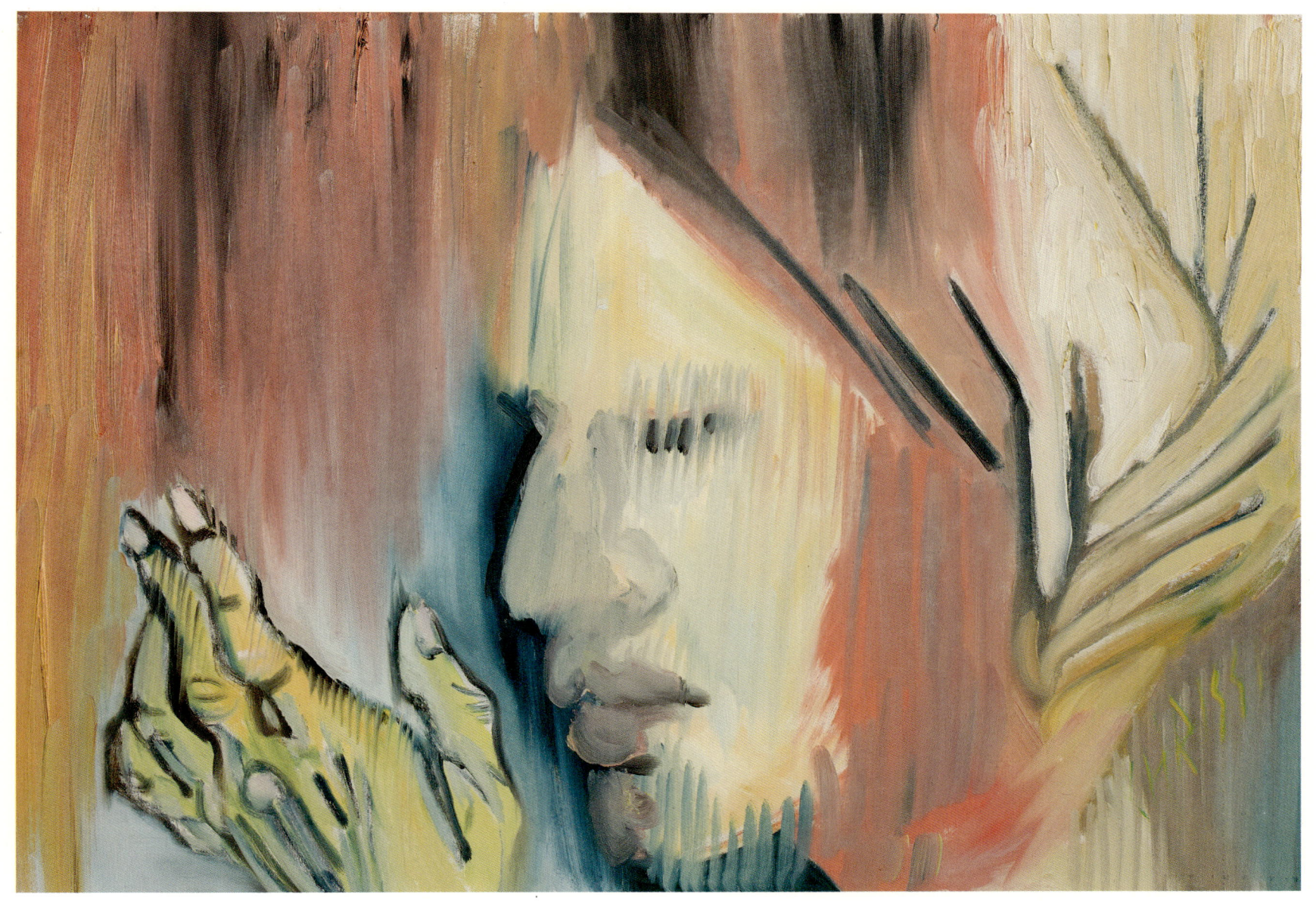

Giving yourself over to painting is easier if you don't live with anyone. Get a cat instead. Having said that, I don't have a cat. If I did, there'd be a hundred paintings of it by now.

TUESDAY SKETCH
Oil on canvas
50 x 70 cm
(19³⁄₄ x 27¹⁄₂ in)
16 May 2017

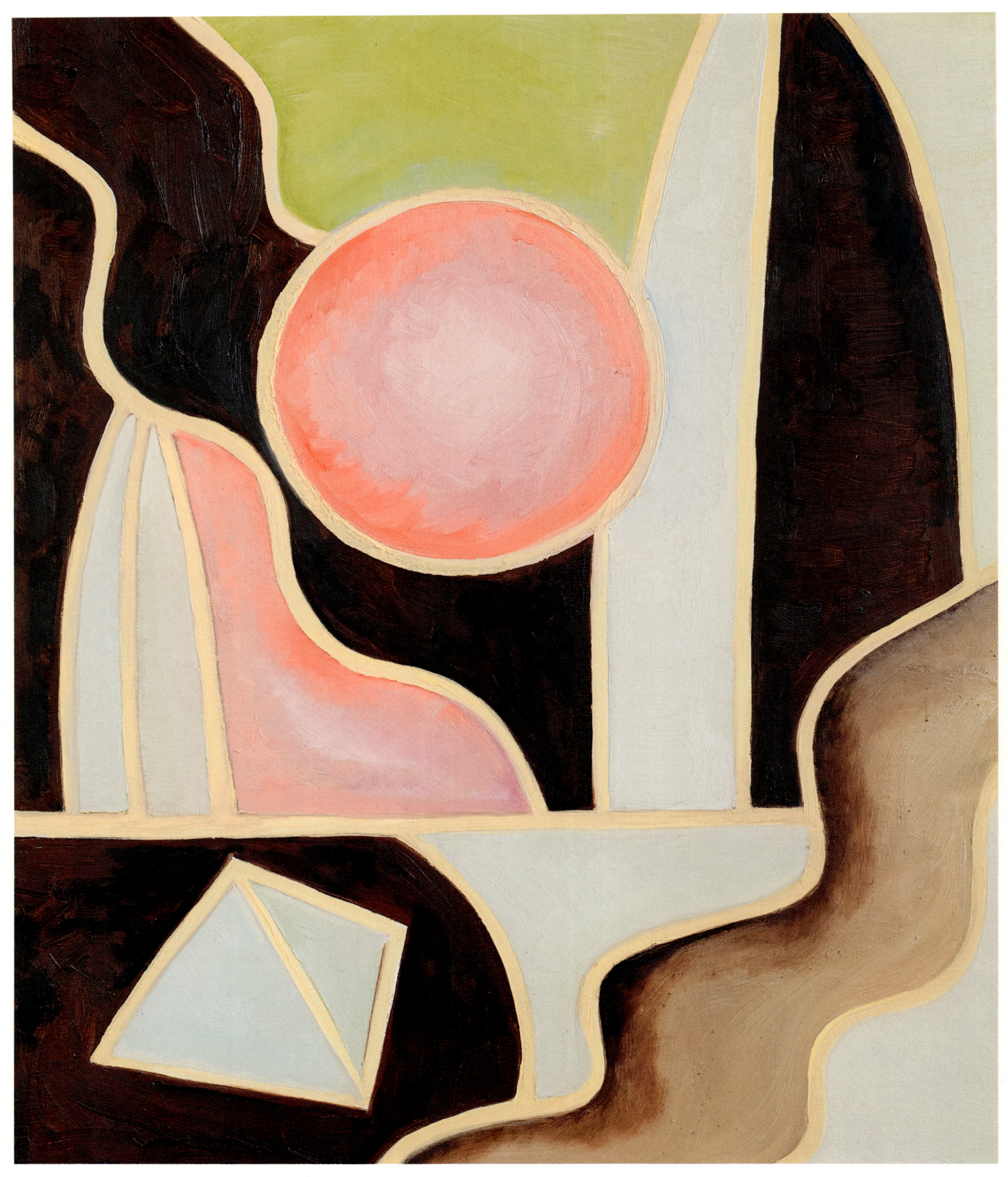

PINK AND BROWN
MONDAY
Oil on canvas
60 x 50 cm
(23¹/₂ x 19²/₃ in)
29 August 2016

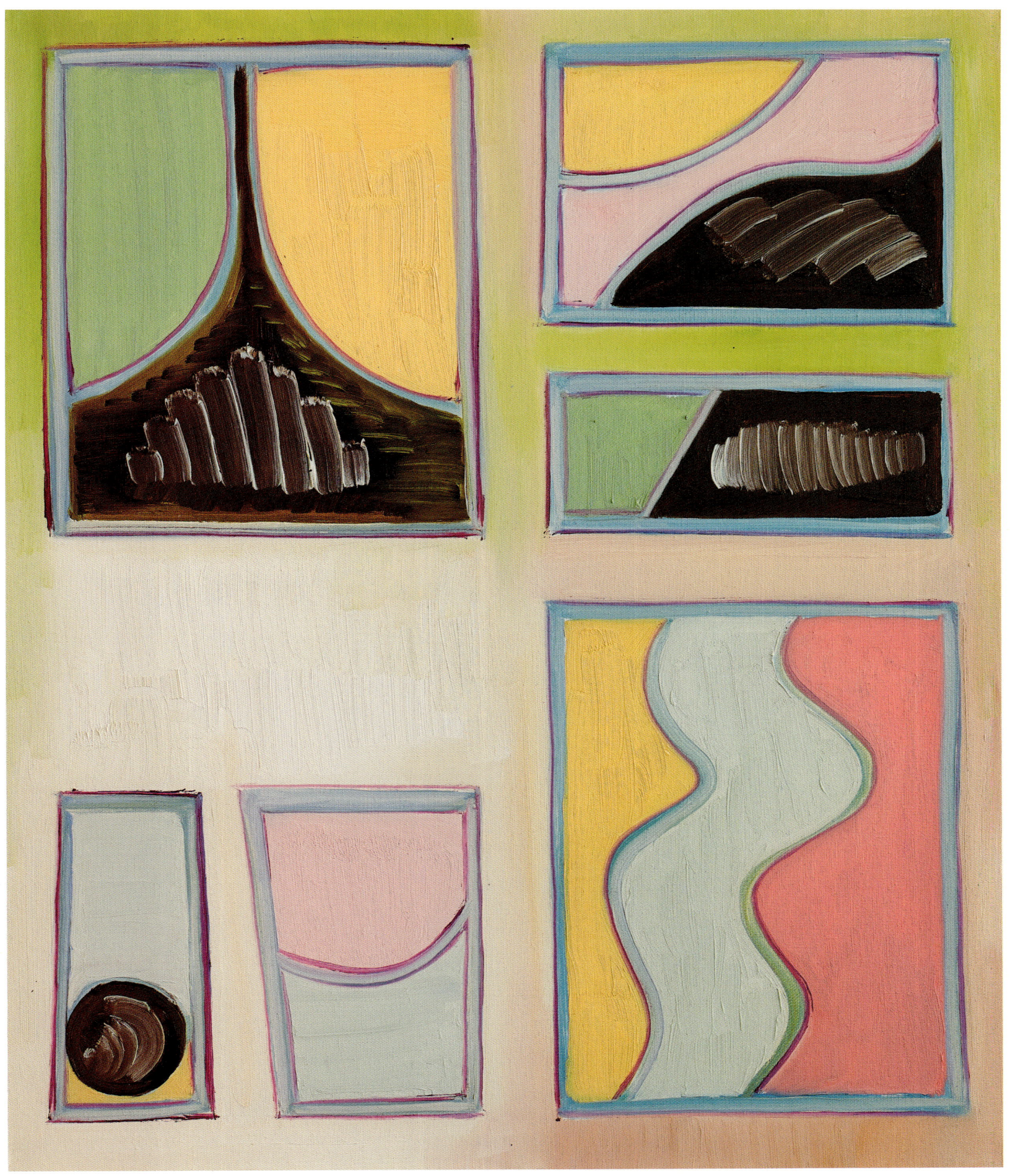

PINK AND BROWN
TUESDAY
Oil on canvas
60 x 50 cm
(23¹⁄₂ x 19³⁄₄ in)
29 August 2016

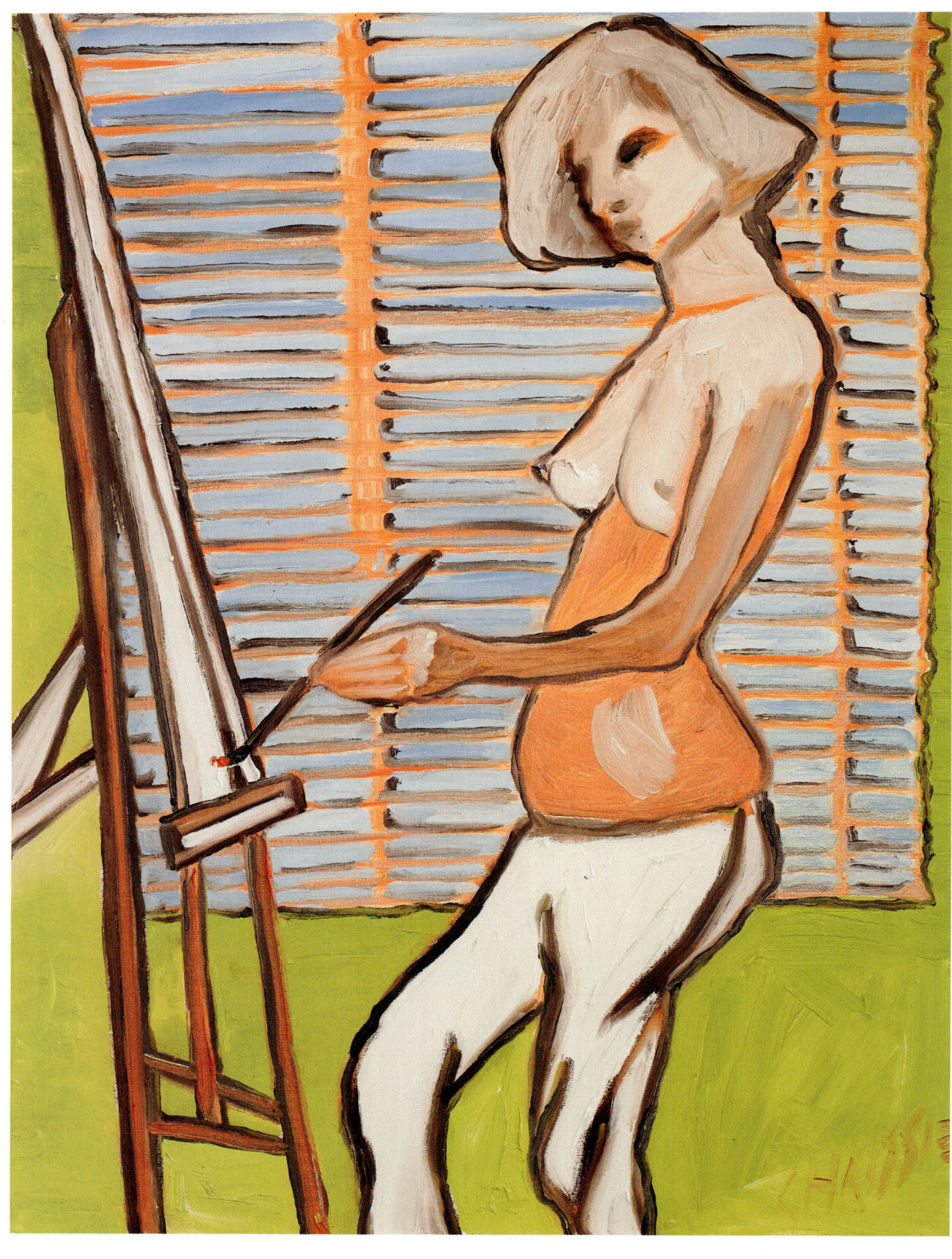

SATURDAY PAINTER
Oil on canvas
80 x 60 cm
(31¹/² x 23¹/² in)
27 August 2016

Another dreaded self-portrait. Sometimes it's just too easy…

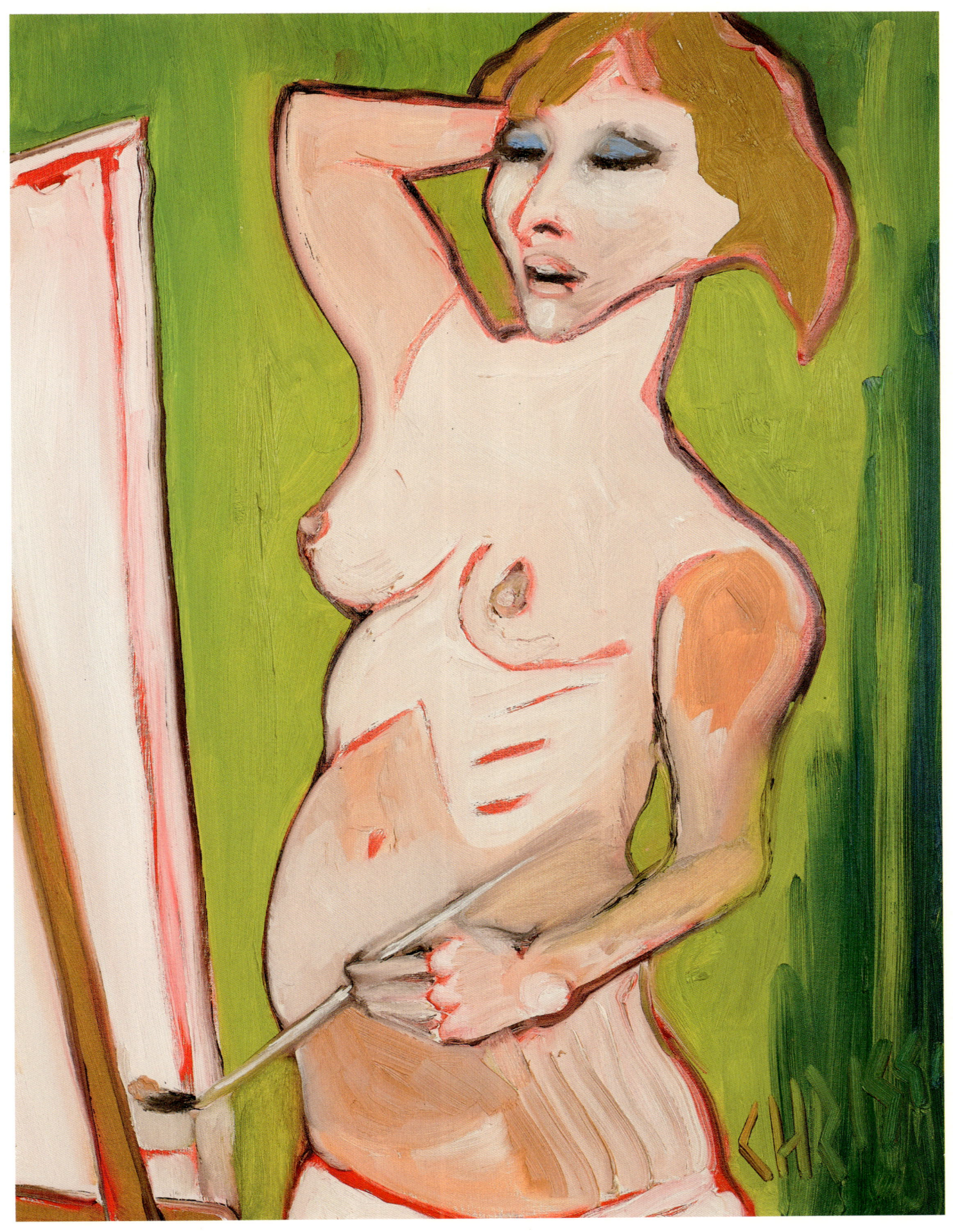

SHE LIKES TO PAINT
Oil on canvas
80 x 60 cm
(31¹′² x 23¹′² in)
30 August 2016

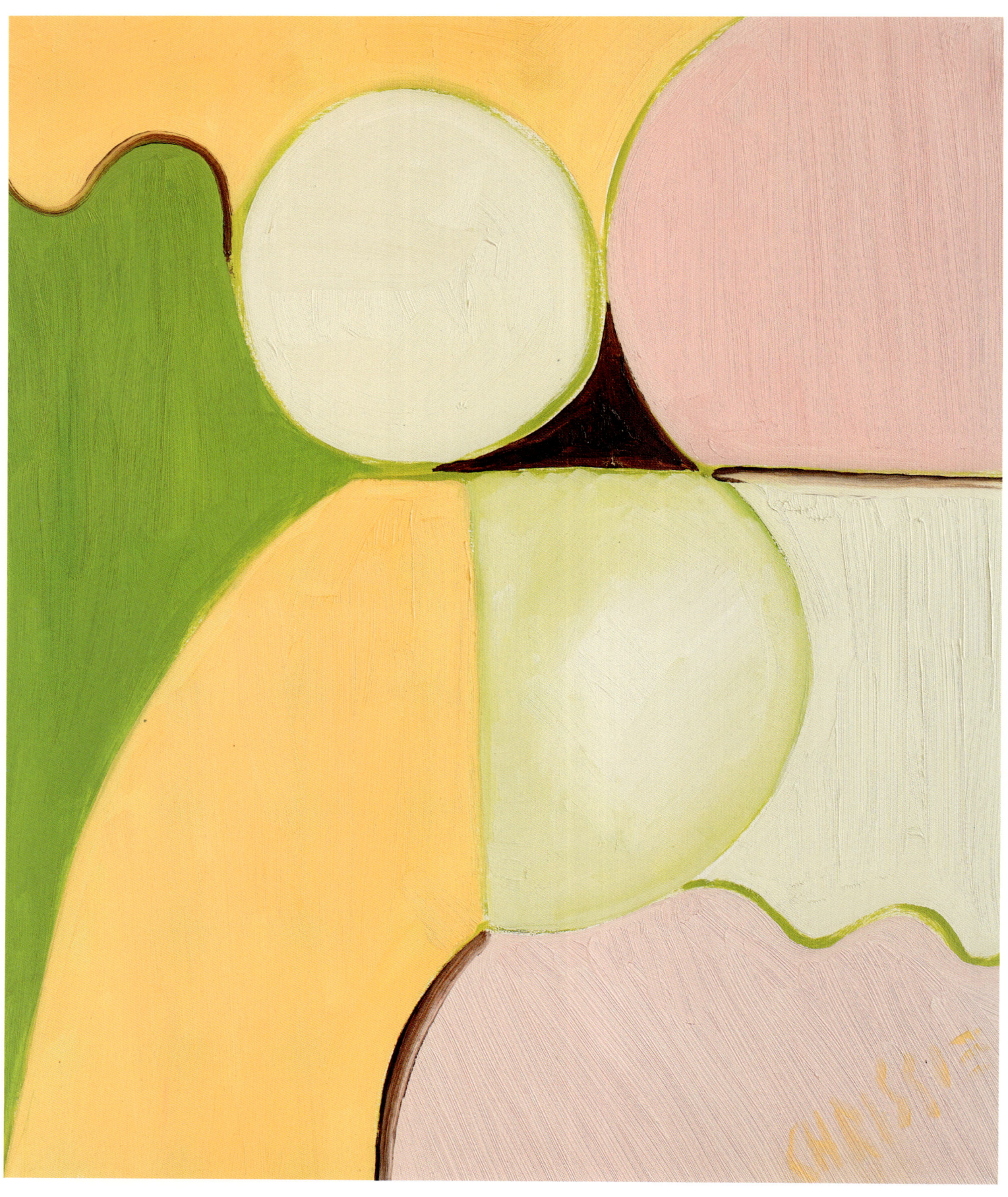

WEDNESDAY SHAPES I
Oil on canvas
60 x 50 cm
(23¹⁄² x 19³⁄⁴ in)
31 August 2016

WEDNESDAY SHAPES II
Oil on canvas
60 x 50 cm
(23¹⁄² x 19³⁄⁴ in)
31 August 2016

These are two of my favourites.

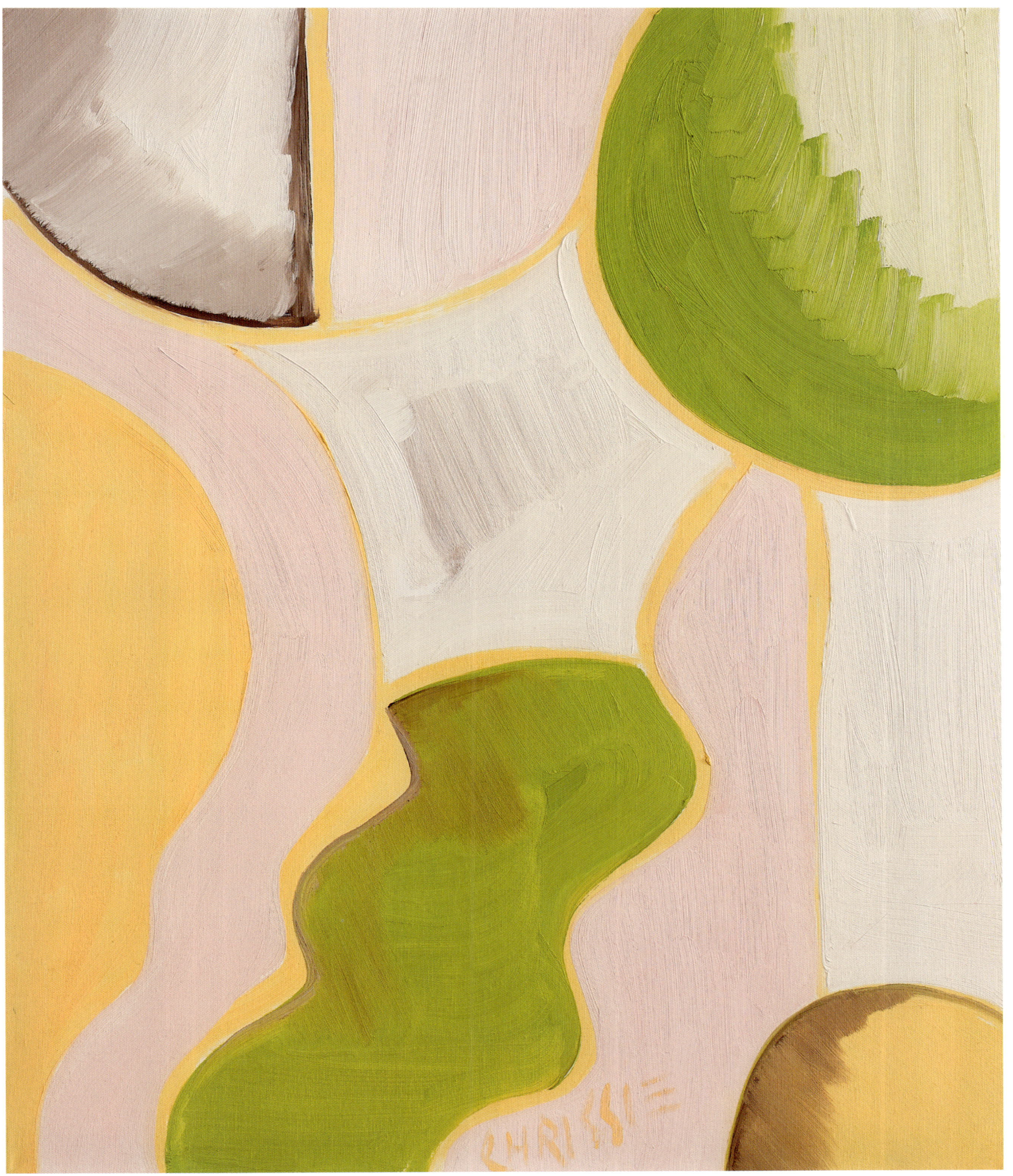

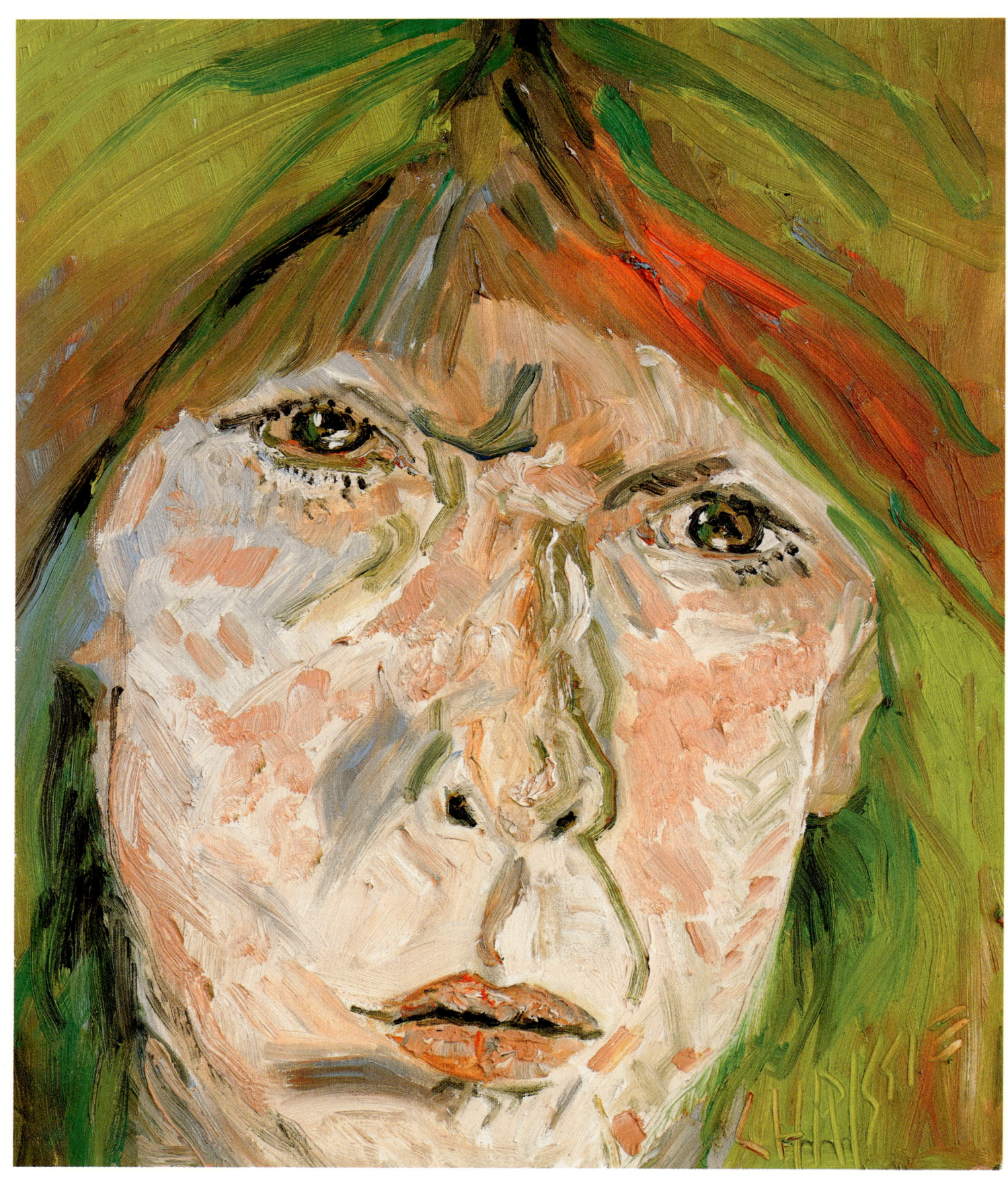

SELF – MORE AND THEN
Oil on canvas
60 x 50 cm
(23¹/² x 19³/⁴ in)
13 August 2016

SELF GLASSES
Oil on canvas
60 x 50 cm
(23¹/² x 19³/⁴ in)
13 September 2016

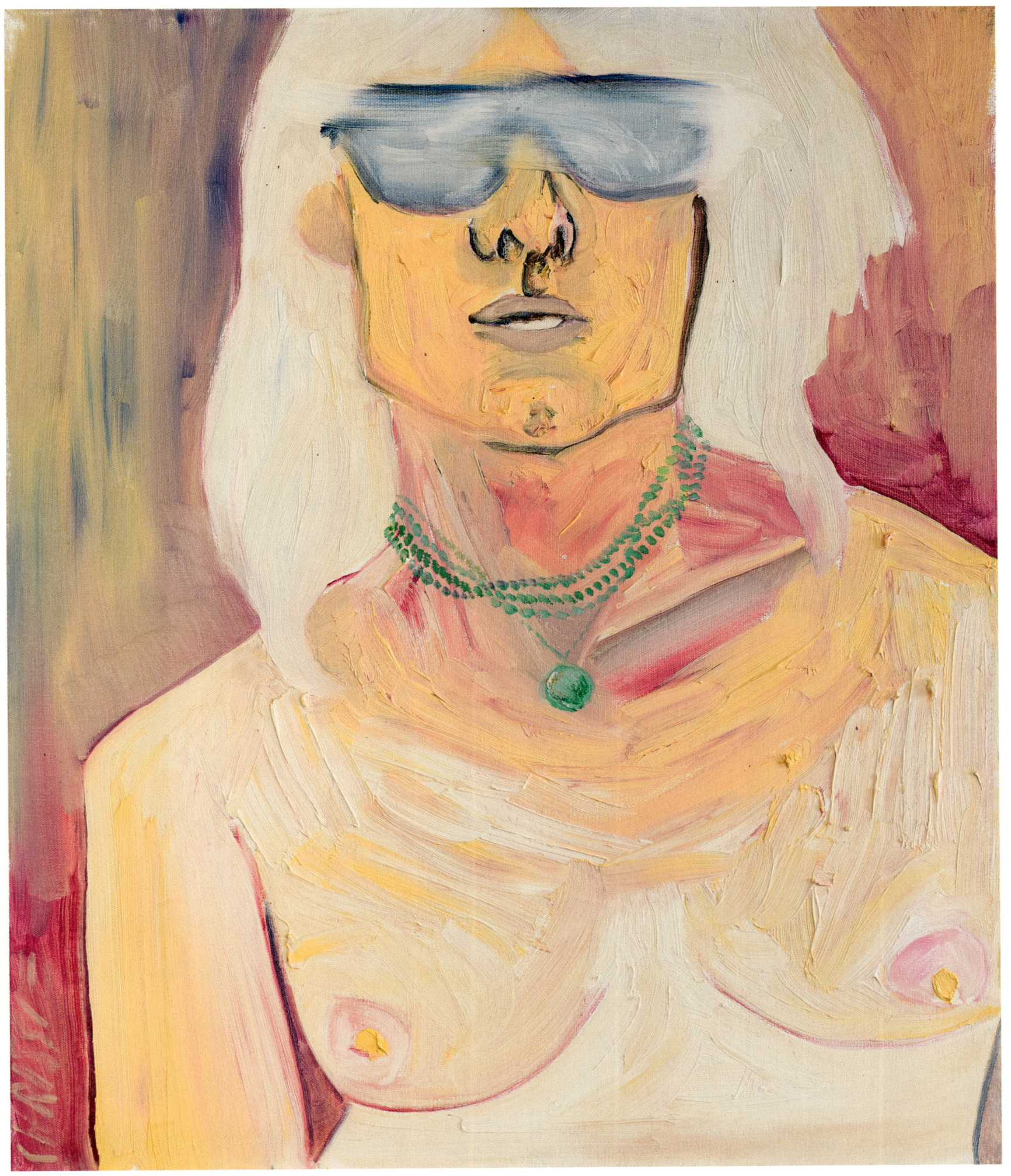

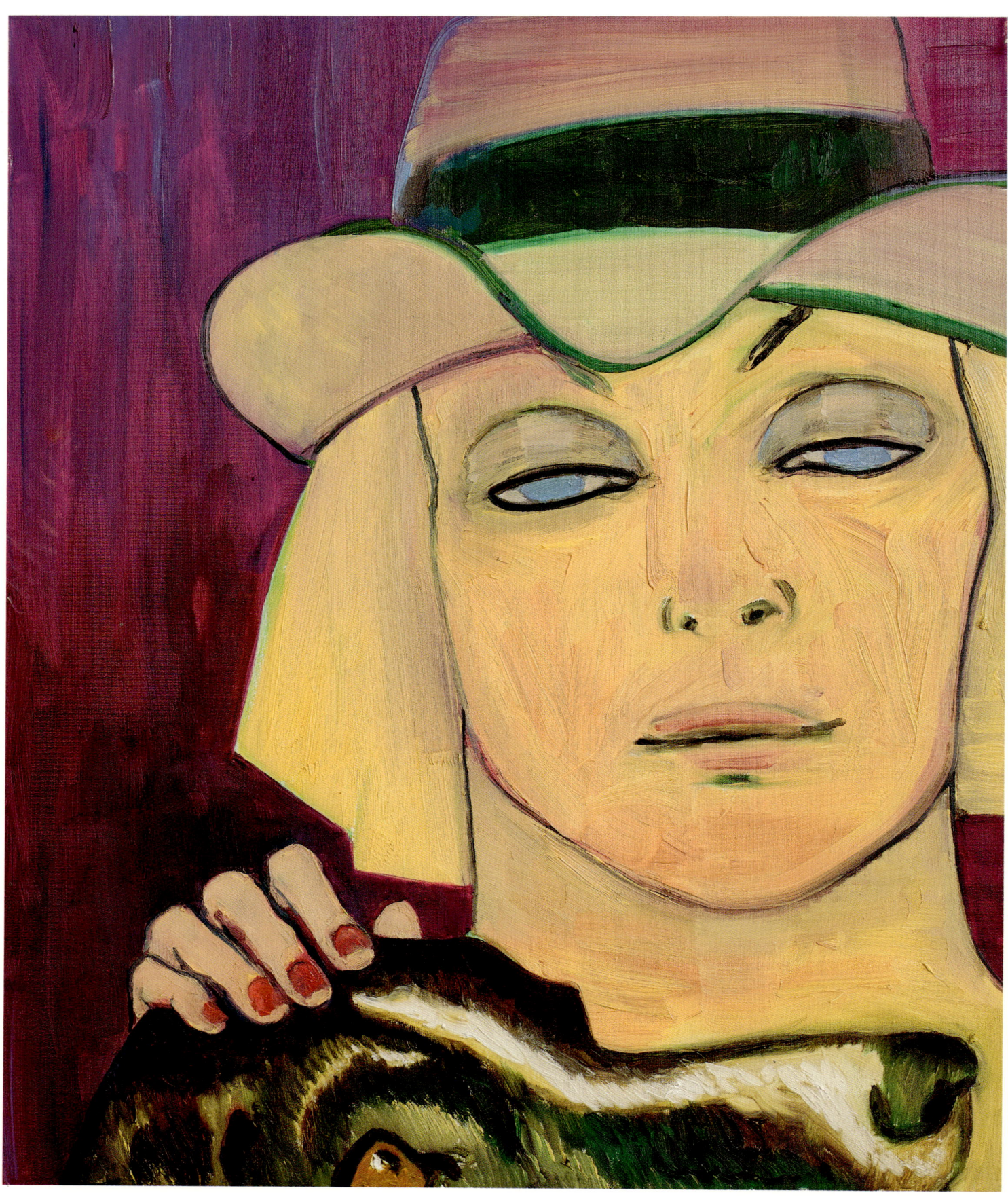

MIRANDA I
Oil on canvas
60 x 50 cm
(23¹⁄₂ x 19³⁄₄ in)
13 September 2016

MIRANDA II
Oil on canvas
50 x 40 cm
(19³⁄₄ x 15³⁄₄ in)
13 September 2016

The thing about Miranda Richardson is she has perfect features. In some ways, from a painter's point of view, she's too pretty to paint. Who would believe such perfect features? I'd have to really move them around a lot. Miranda loves her dog, so I put the dog in there — even though it wasn't actually there.

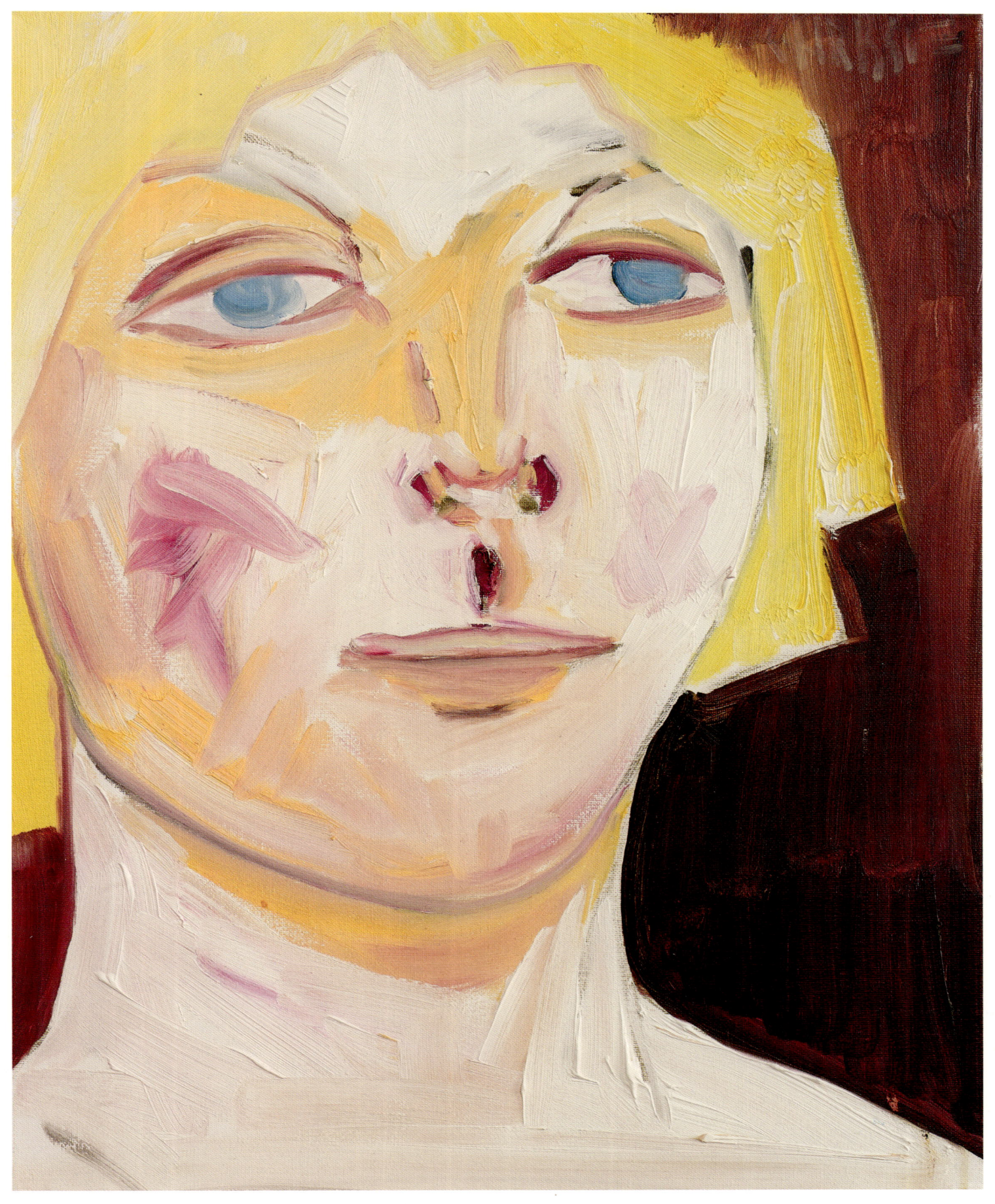

This was Miranda after she left. I tried to distort her in her absence.

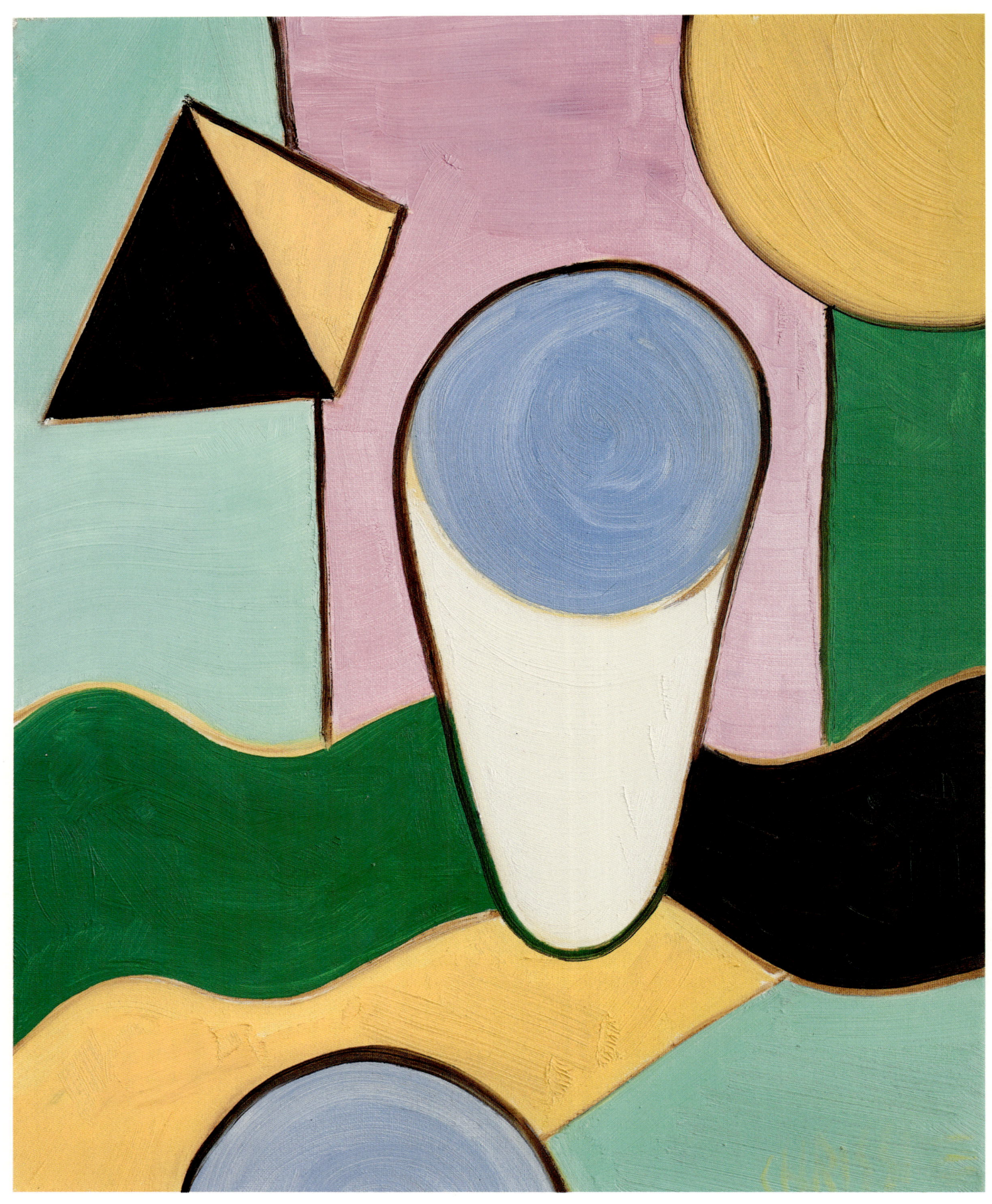

'WHY NOT' SHAPES I
Oil on canvas
50 x 40 cm
(19¾ x 15¾ in)
20 September 2016

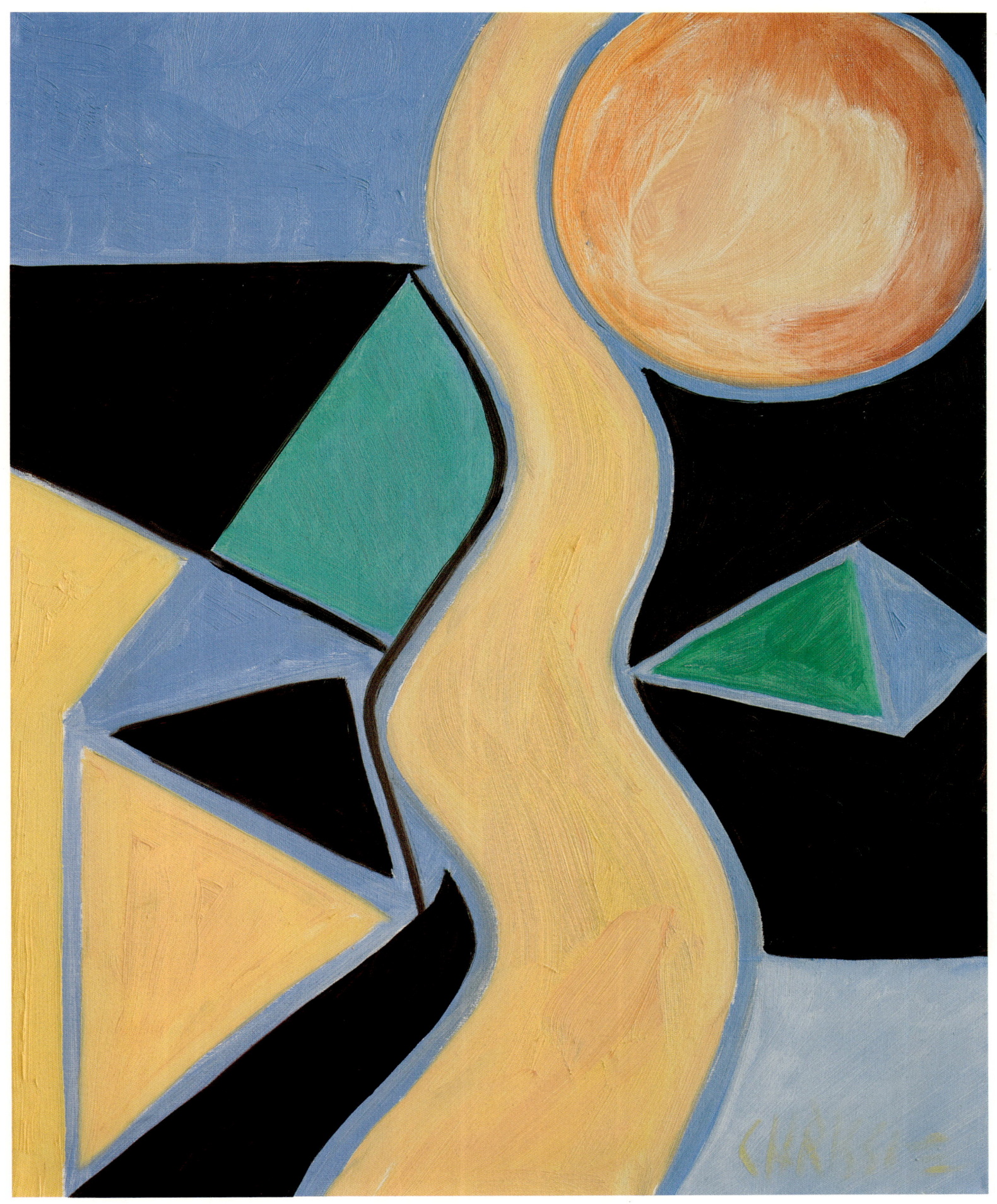

'WHY NOT' SHAPES II
Oil on canvas
50 x 40 cm
(19¾ x 15¾ in)
20 September 2016

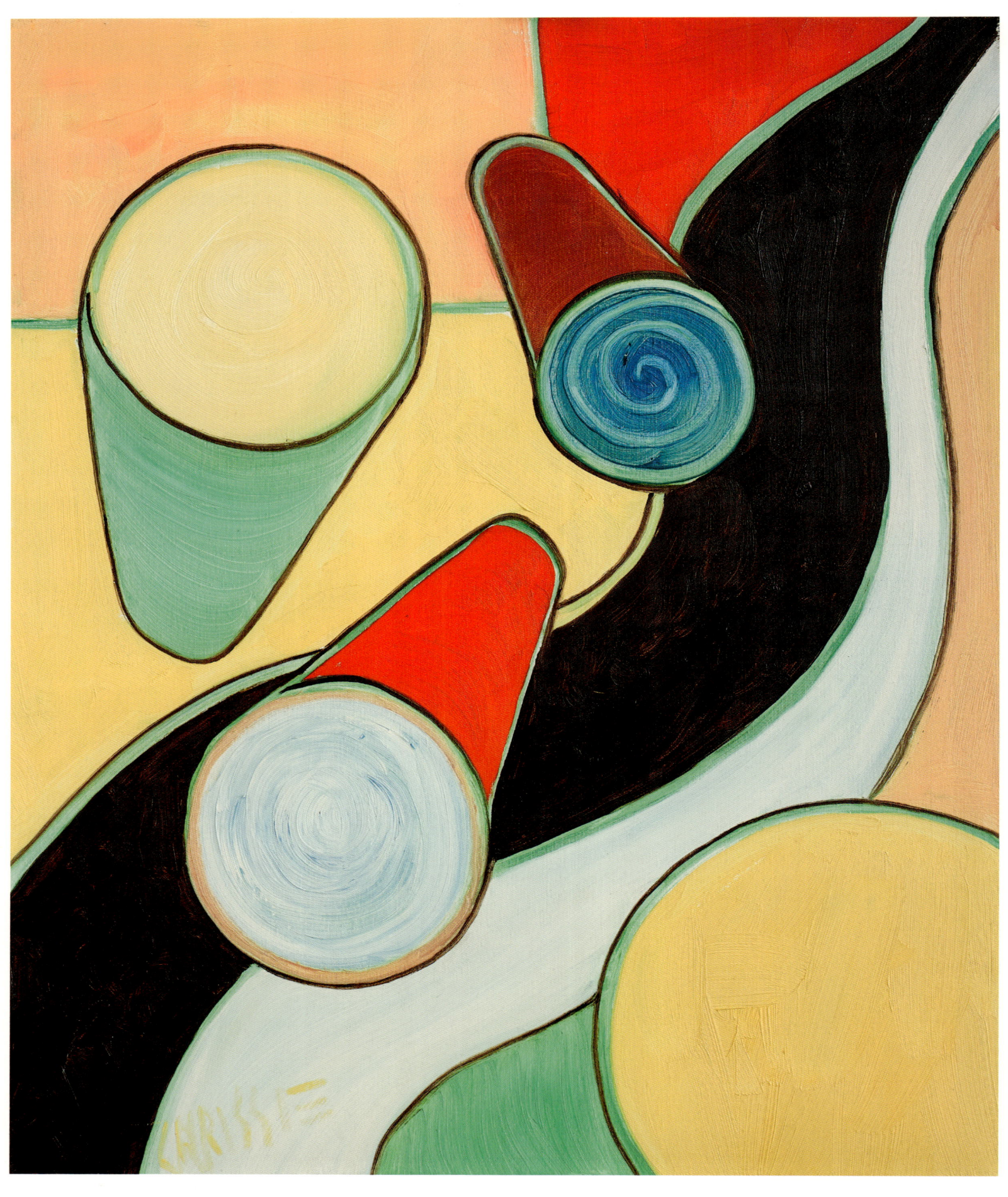

SEPTEMBER SHAPES I
Oil on canvas
60 x 50 cm
(23¹⁄² x 19³⁄⁴ in)
20 September 2016

I got into this cone theme. I started putting cones in everything.
What would Freud say?

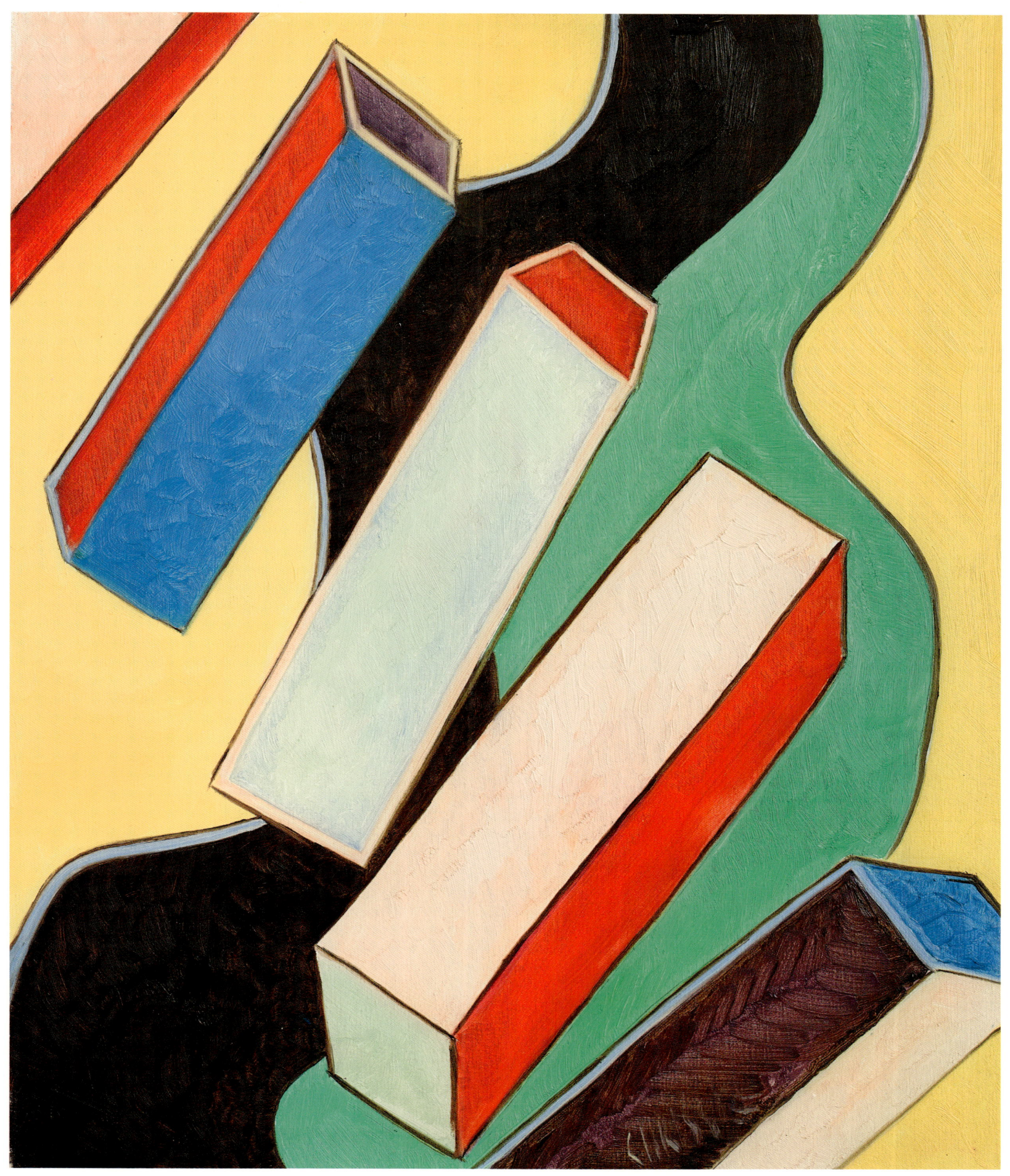

SEPTEMBER SHAPES II
Oil on canvas
60 x 50 cm
(23¹ᐟ² x 19³ᐟ⁴ in)
20 September 2016

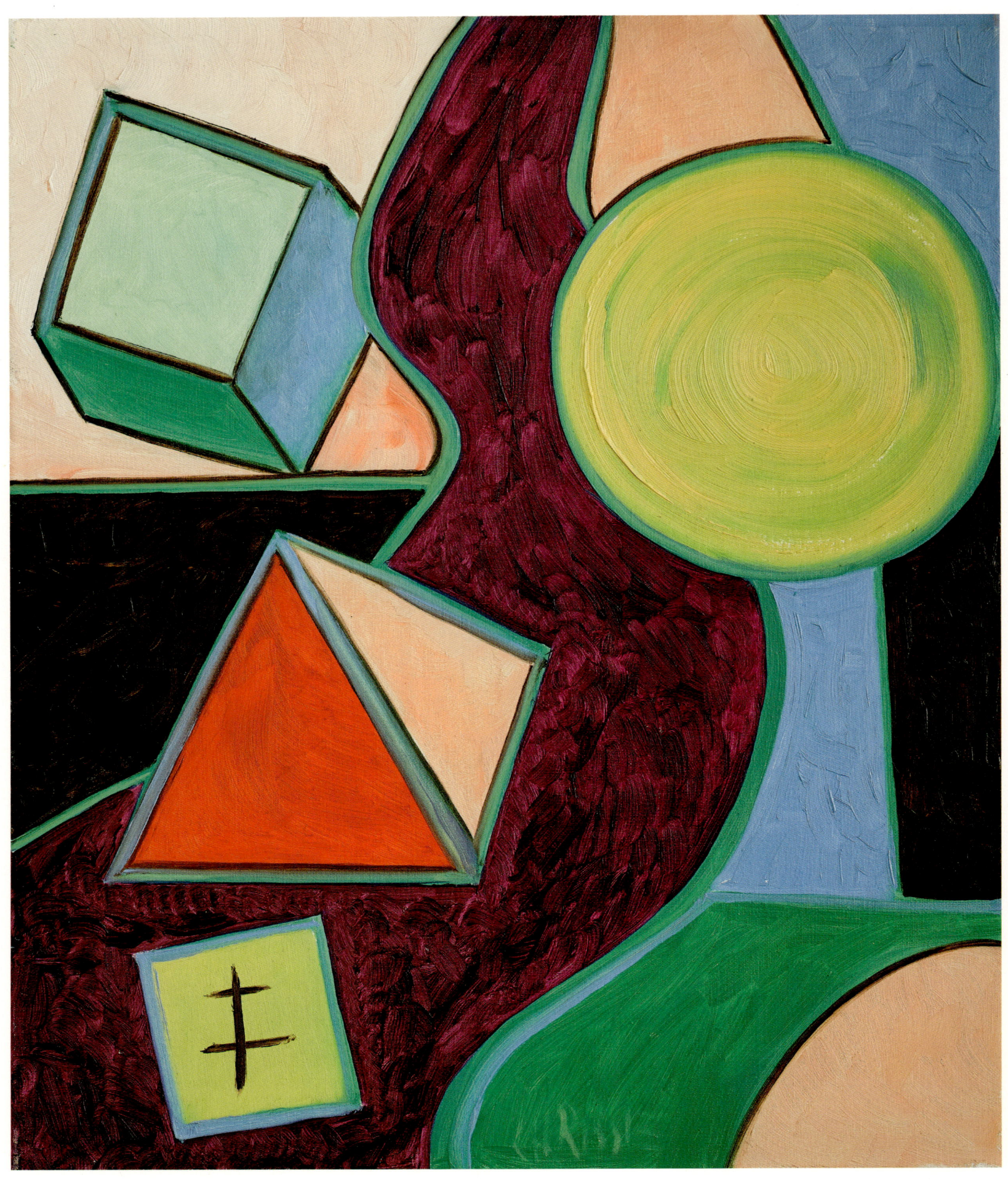

SEPTEMBER TUMBLING I
Oil on canvas
60 x 50 cm
(23¹/² x 19³/⁴ in)
20 September 2016

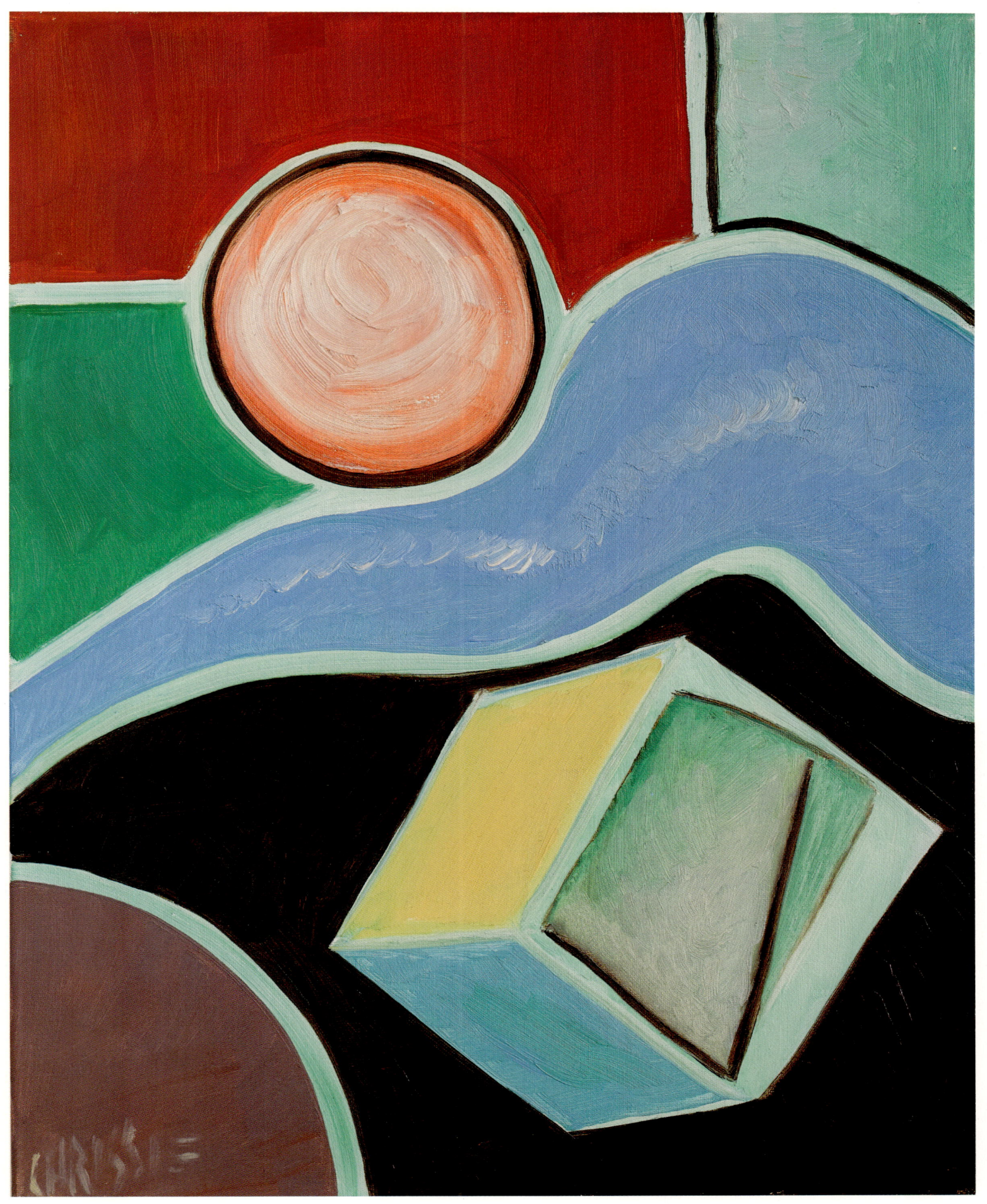

SEPTEMBER TUMBLING II
Oil on canvas
50 x 40 cm
(19³/⁴ x 15³/⁴ in)
20 September 2016

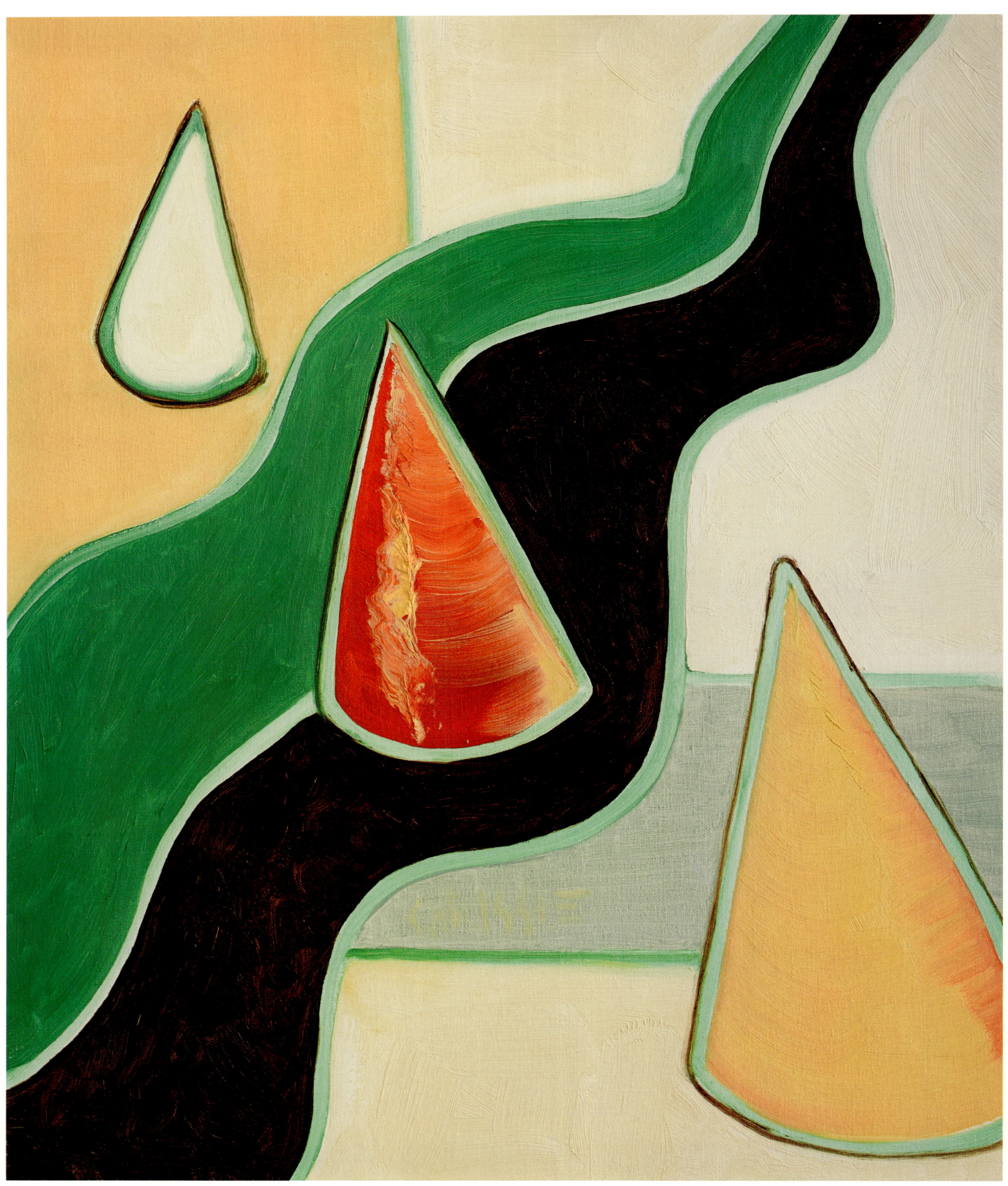

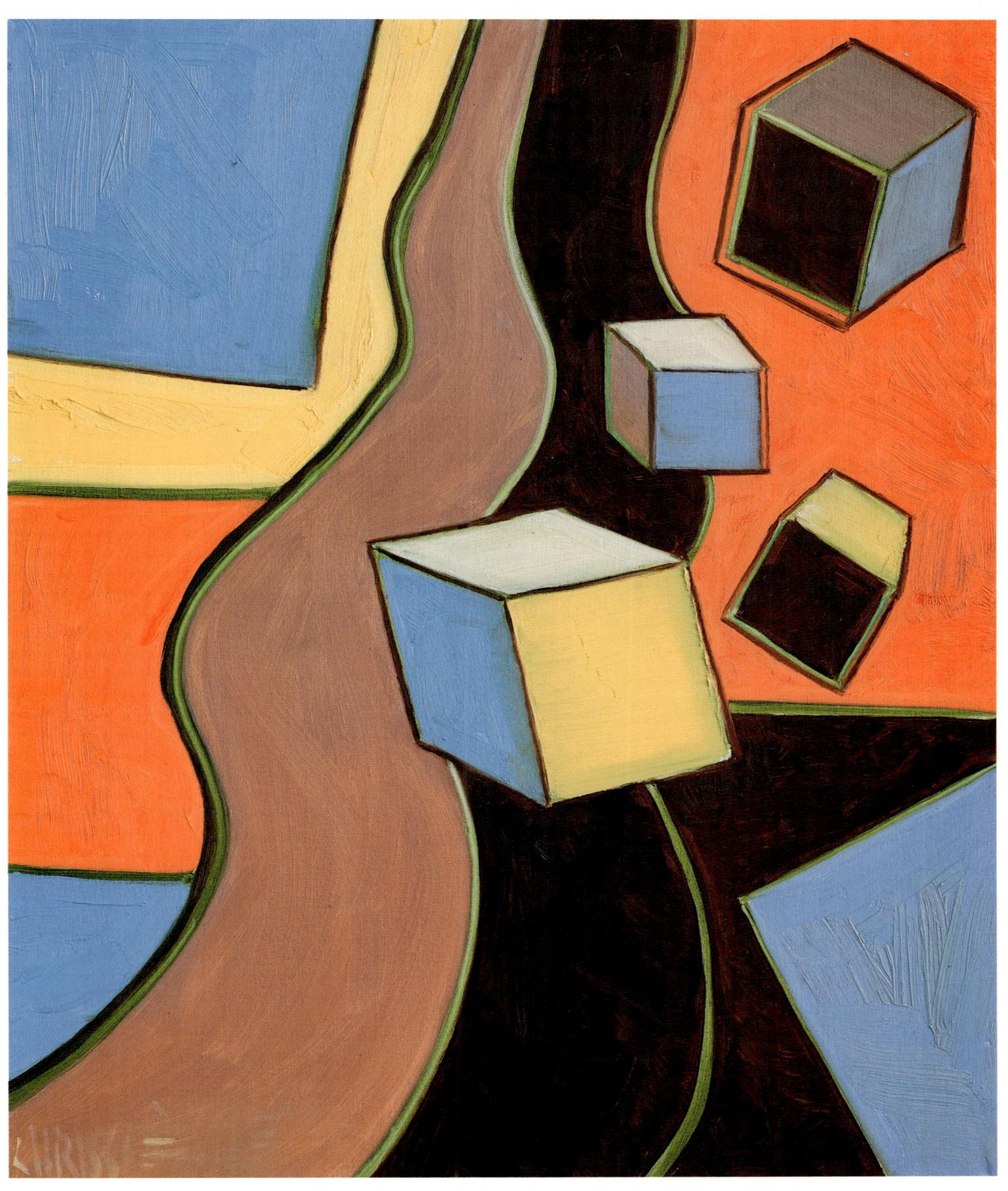

WEDNESDAY SHAPES I
Oil on canvas
60 x 50 cm
(23¹ᐟ² x 19³ᐟ⁴ in)
21 September 2016

WEDNESDAY SHAPES II
Oil on canvas
60 x 50 cm
(23¹ᐟ² x 19³ᐟ⁴ in)
21 September 2016

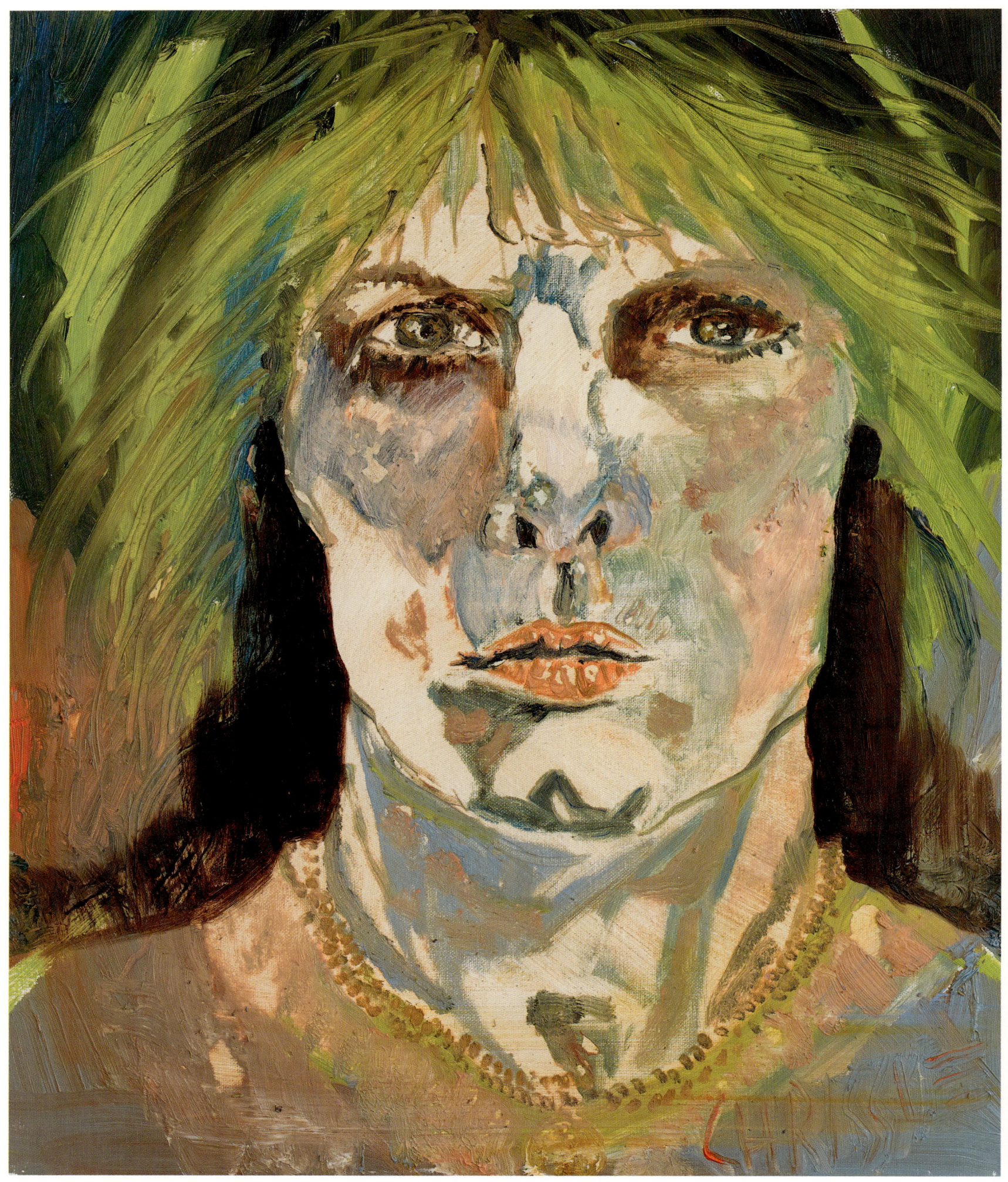

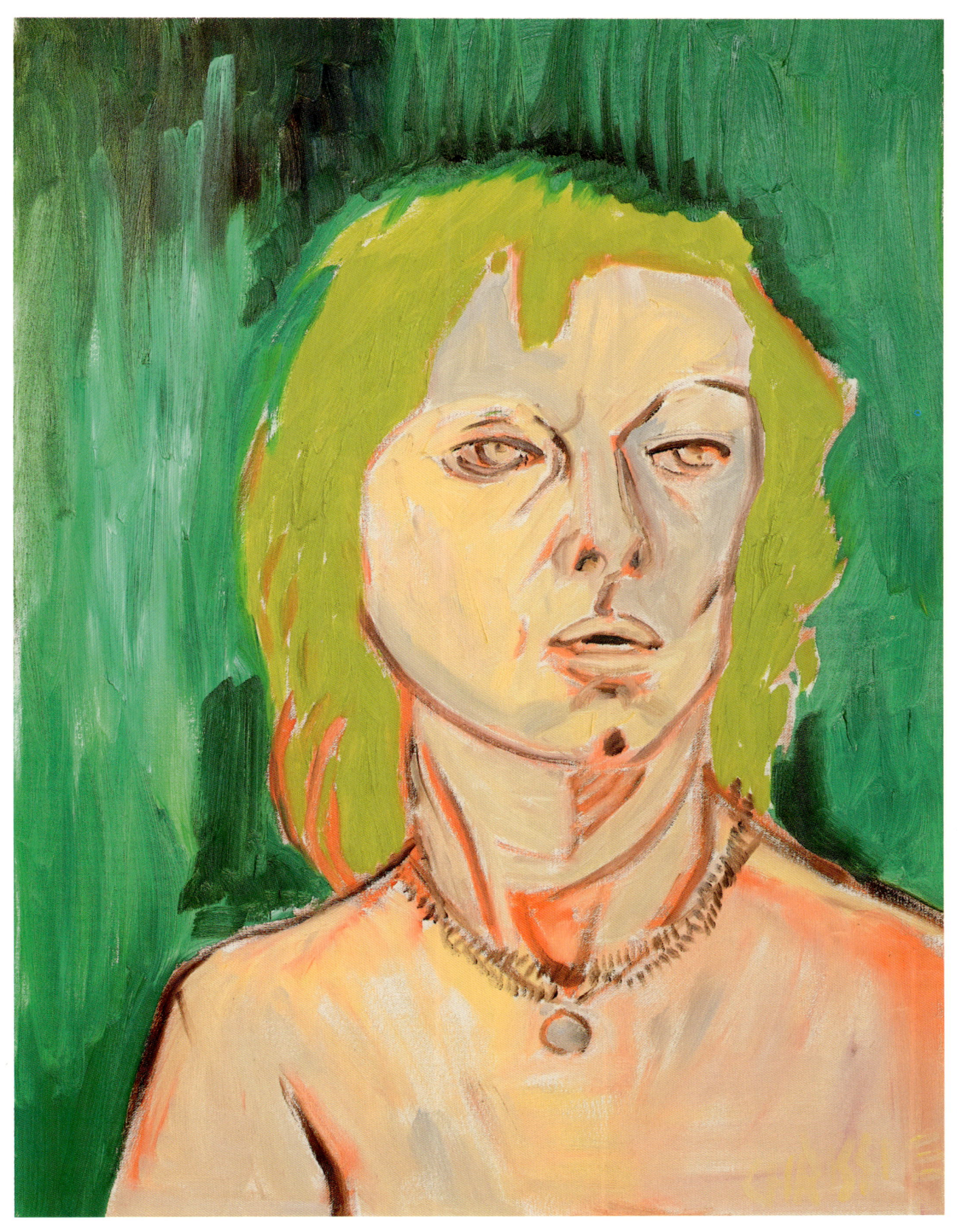

WASHED-OUT SELF
Oil on canvas
60 x 50 cm
(23¹ᐟ² x 19³ᐟ⁴ in)
15 August 2016

GREEN SEPTEMBER
Oil on canvas
80 x 60 cm
(31¹ᐟ² x 23¹ᐟ² in)
24 September 2016

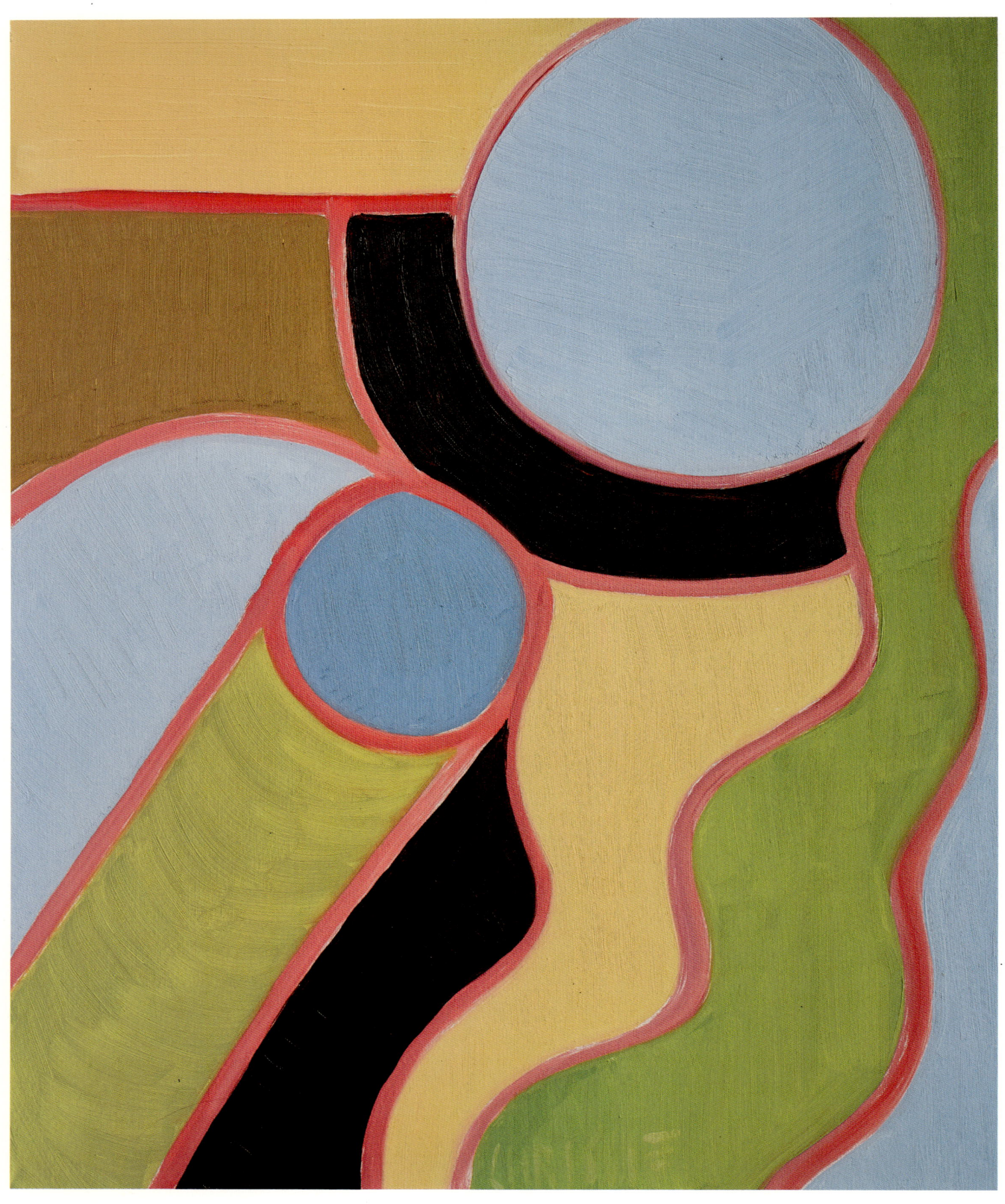

SHOOTING STAR
Oil on canvas
60 x 50 cm
(23¹/² x 19³/⁴ in)
2 October 2016

SUNDAY PAINTER
Oil on canvas
80 x 60 cm
(31¹/² x 23¹/² in)
2 October 2016

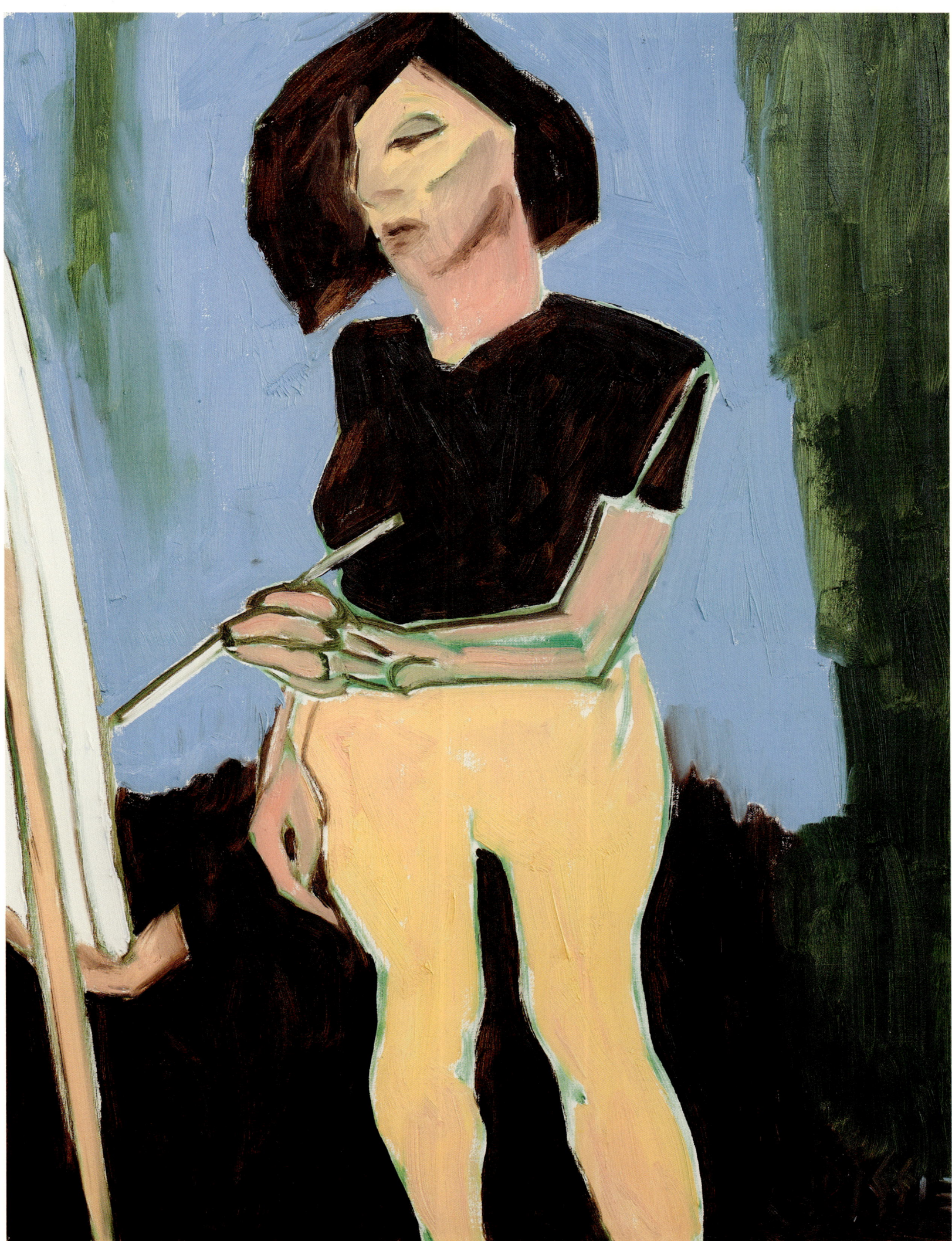

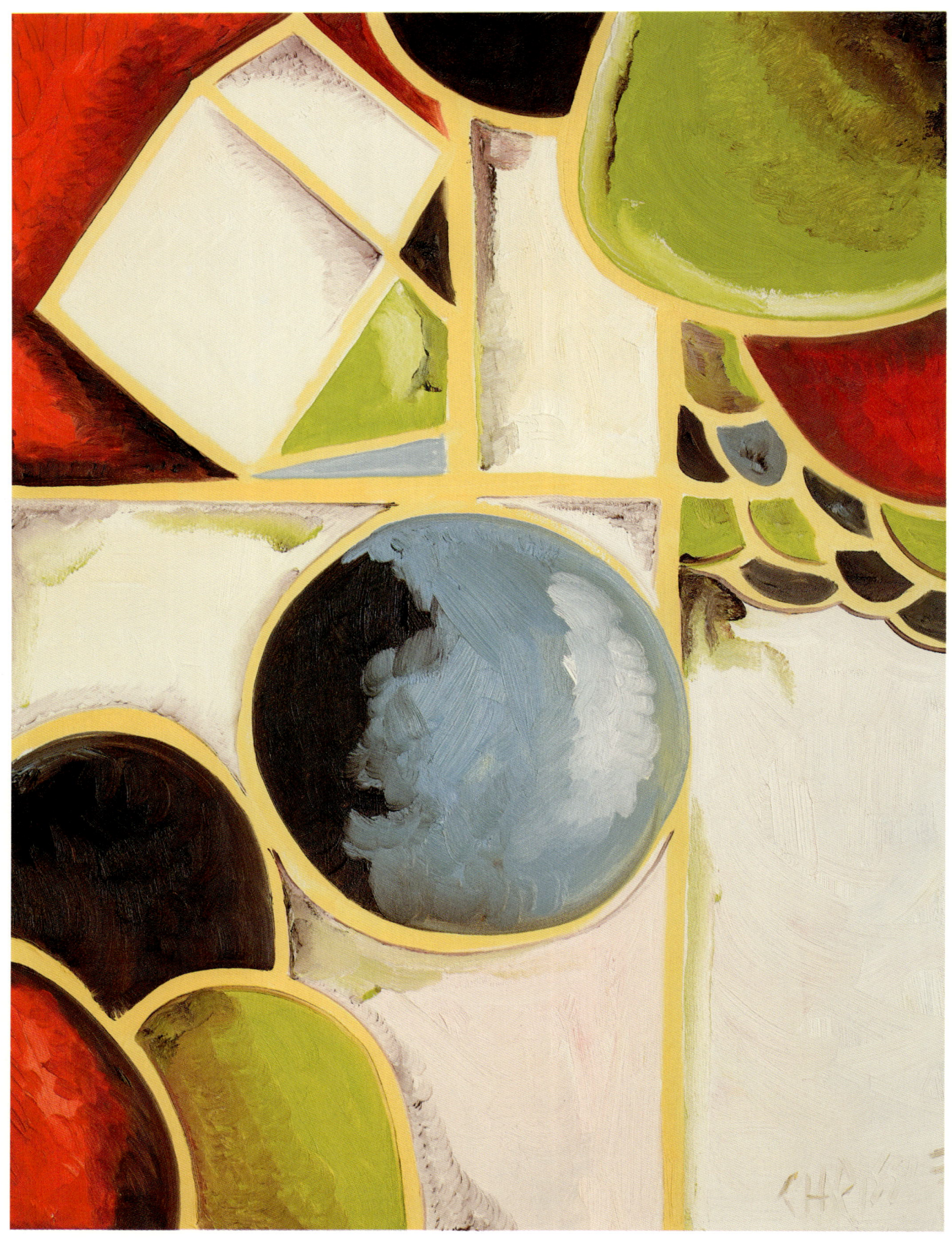

SHAPES BEGIN '17
Oil on canvas
80 x 60 cm
(31$^{1/2}$ x 23$^{1/2}$ in)
17 January 2017

SHAPES '17
Oil on canvas
80 x 60 cm
(31$^{1/2}$ x 23$^{1/2}$ in)
17 January 2017

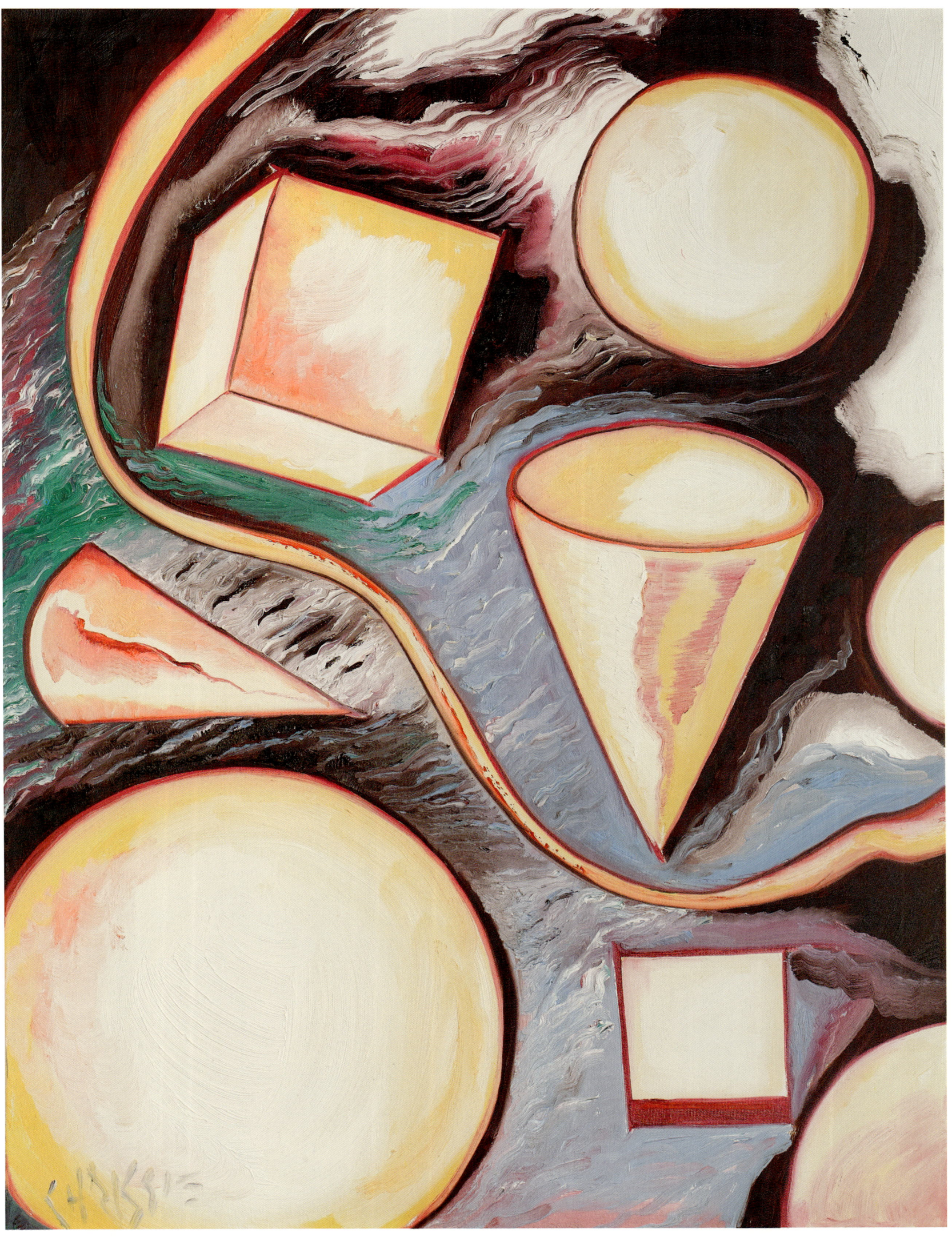

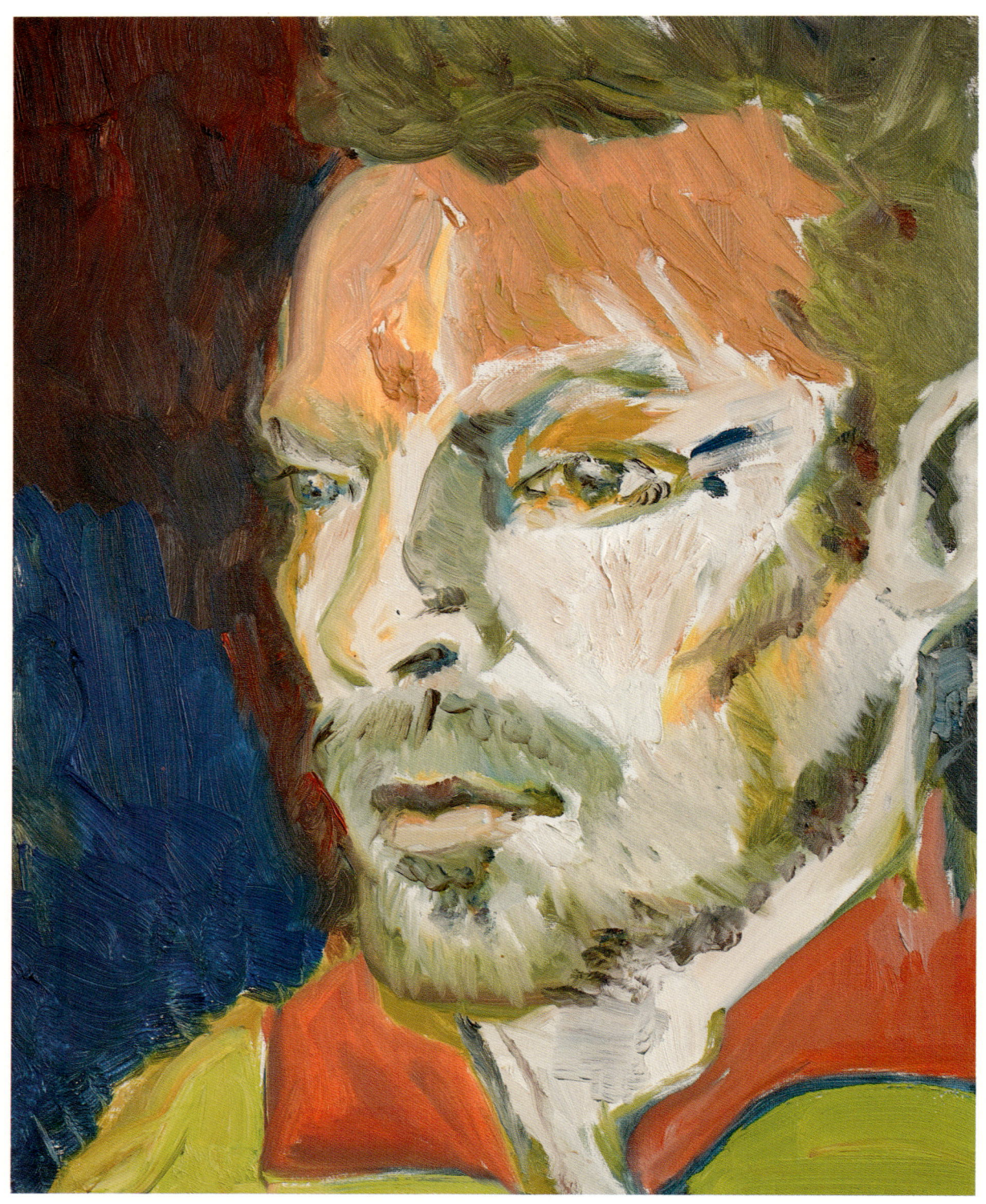

I went to the Chelsea Flower Show with Helen Terry and some friends, for her birthday. She took us into the kiosk of the artist James Gillick, as she already had one of his paintings (he does magnificent still lifes). When we got talking to him, I said that I'd been painting and he offered to give me a lesson. So he came over one day, and we ended up just walking to the park and having a pizza. Then when we came back I painted him — in about 20 minutes — and that's as far as we got with the lesson. I didn't really learn any techniques from him, although he did show me how to roll the last bit of paint out of the tube.

JAMES GILLICK
TUESDAY
Oil on canvas
50 x 40 cm
(19³/₄ x 15³/₄ in)
17 January 2017

MARIE
Oil on canvas
80 x 60 cm
(31¹/₂ x 23¹/₂ in)
18 January 2017

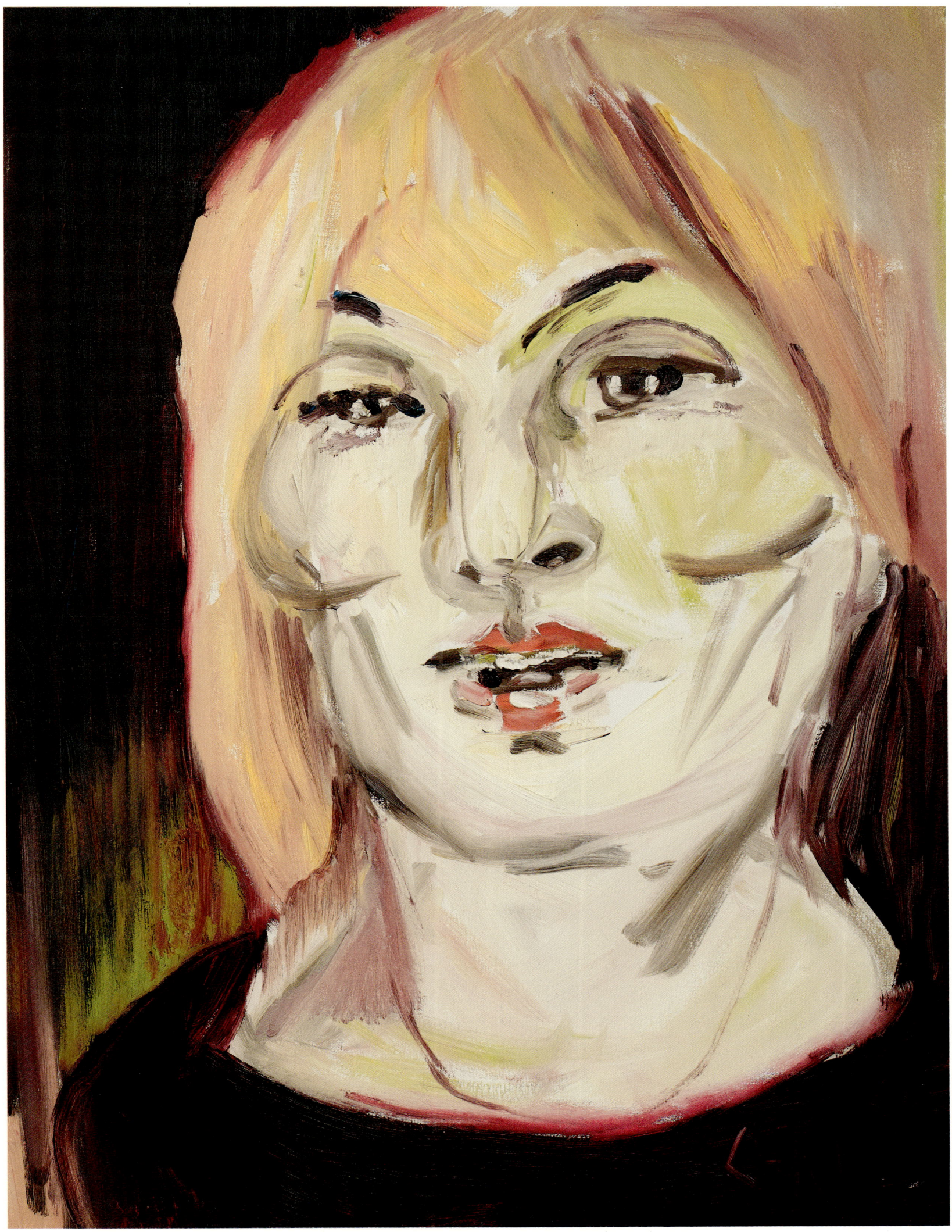

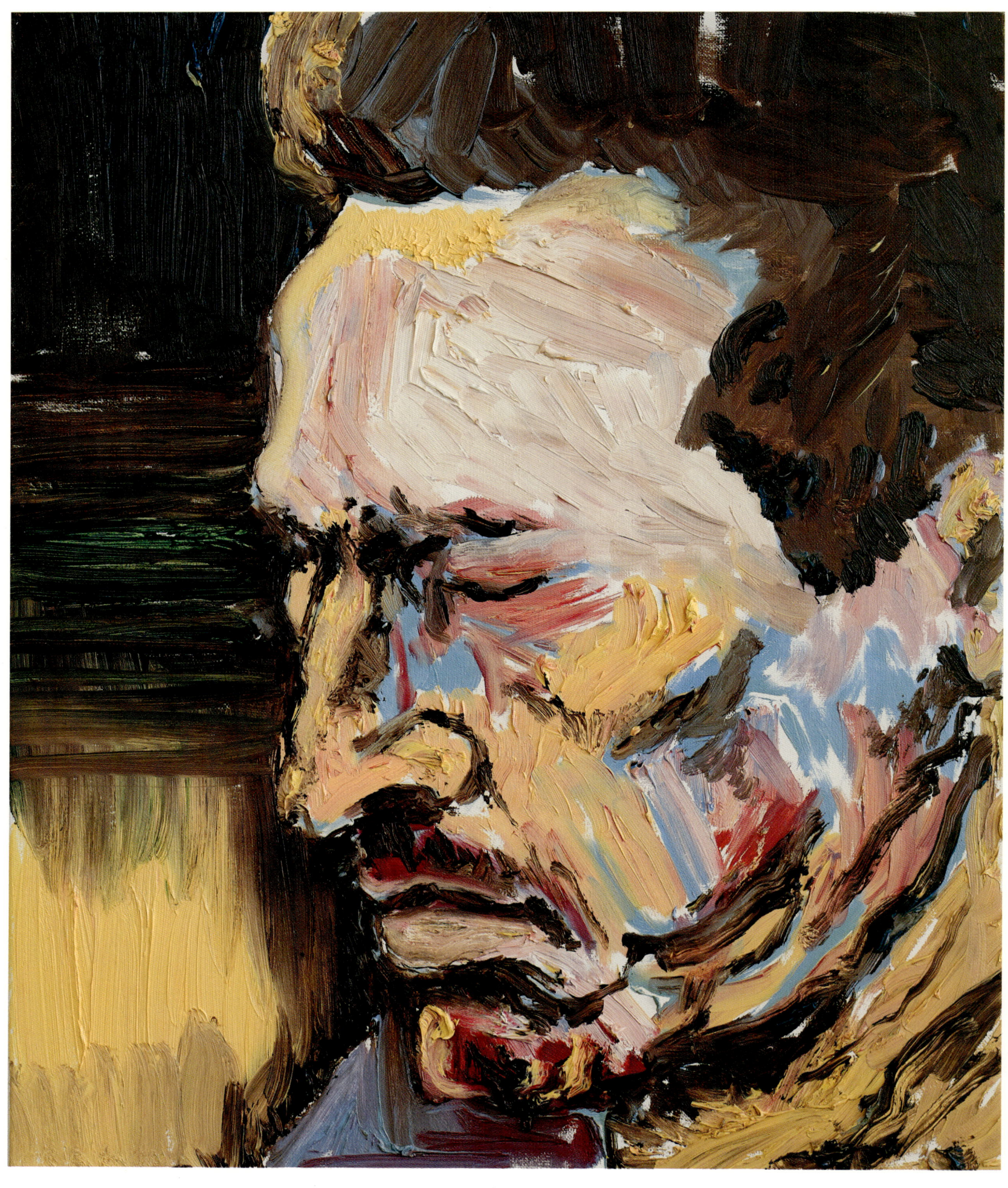

MICHAEL W. I
Oil on canvas
60 x 50 cm
(23¹/² x 19³/⁴ in)
19 January 2017

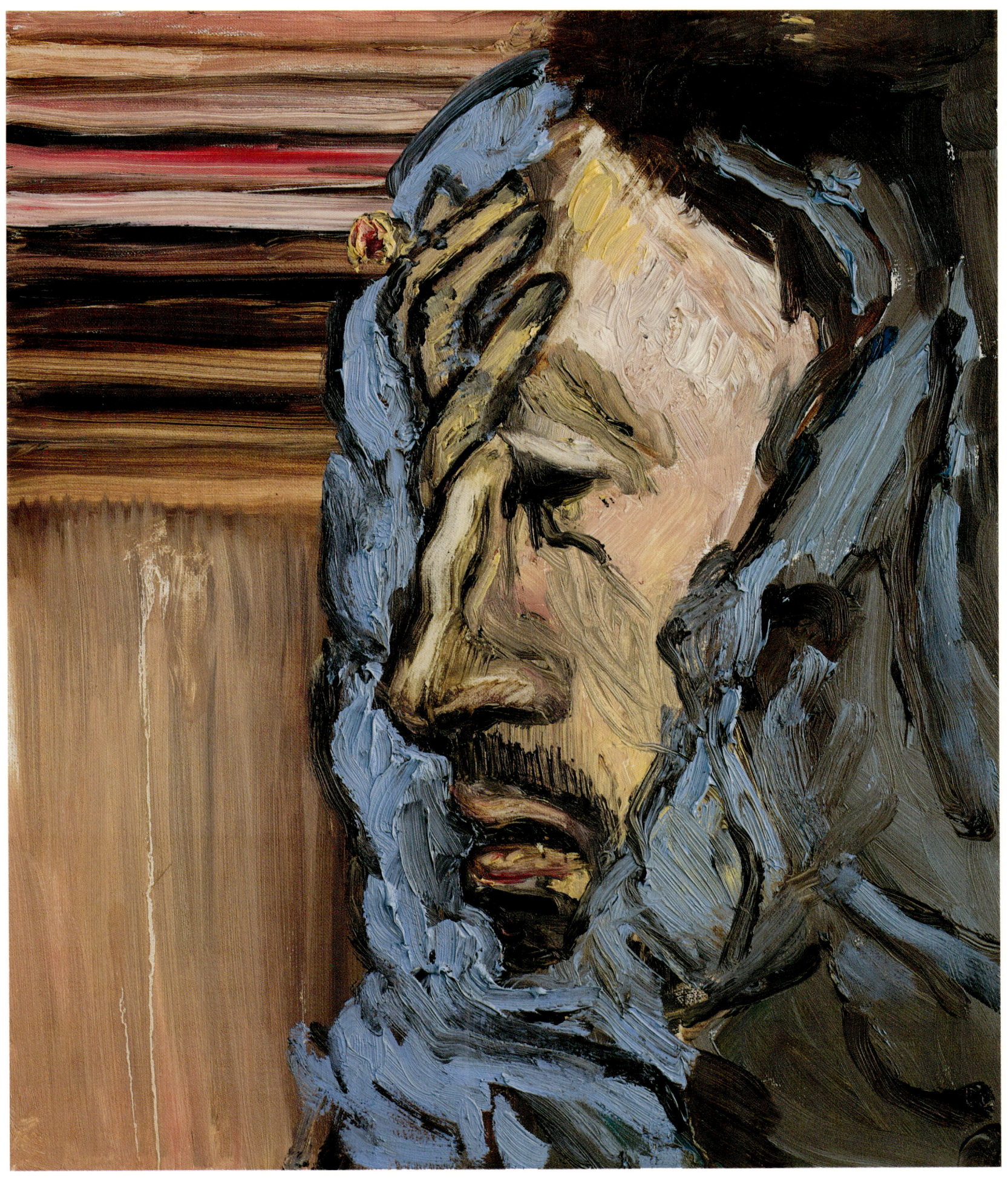

MICHAEL W. II
Oil on canvas
60 x 50 cm
($23^{1/2}$ x $19^{3/4}$ in)
19 January 2017

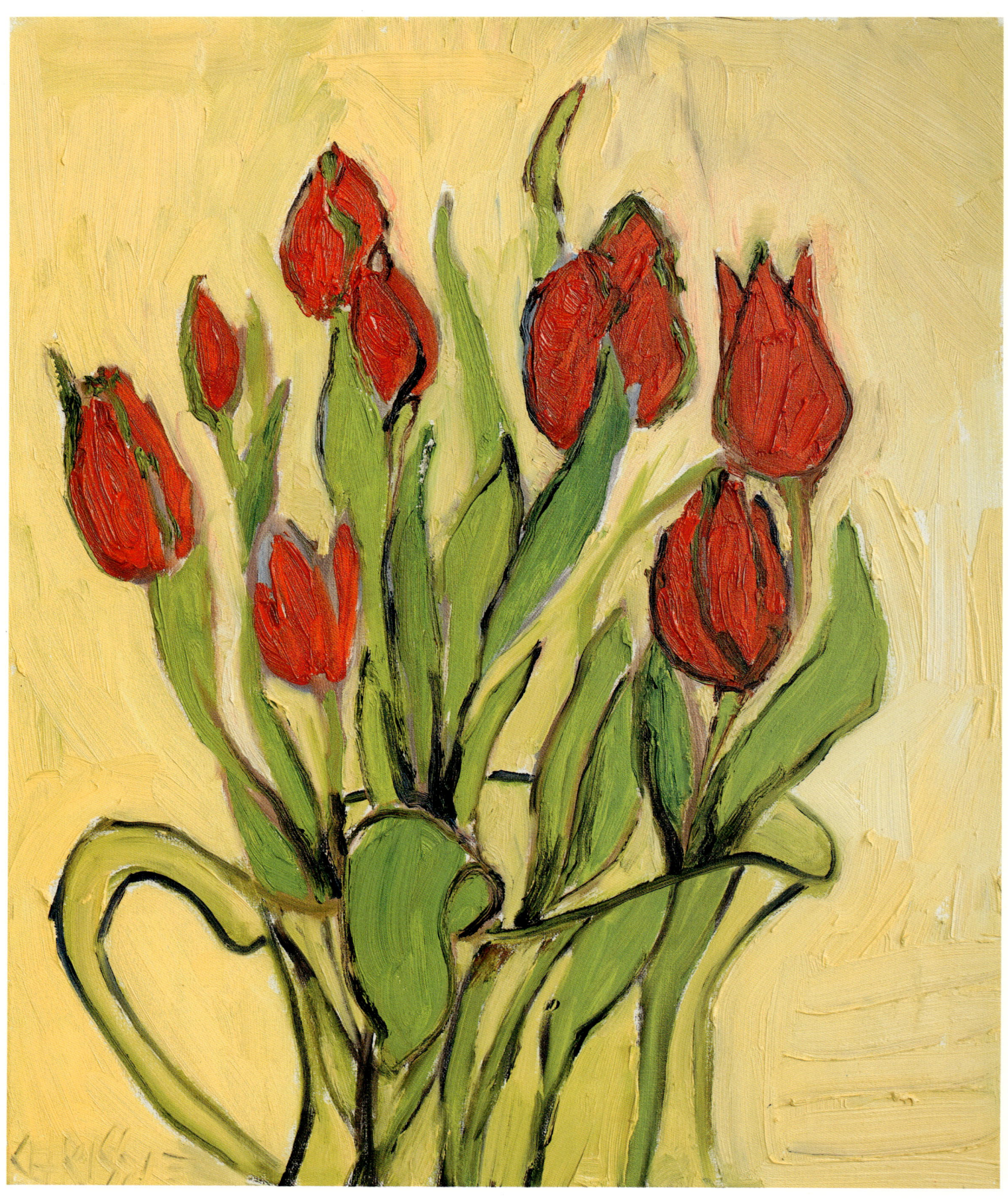

GLASS PITCHER TULIPS
Oil on canvas
60 x 50 cm
(23¹⁄₂ x 19³⁄₄ in)
29 January 2017

RED WEDNESDAY TULIPS
Oil on canvas
80 x 60 cm
(31¹⁄₂ x 23¹⁄₂ in)
1 February 2017

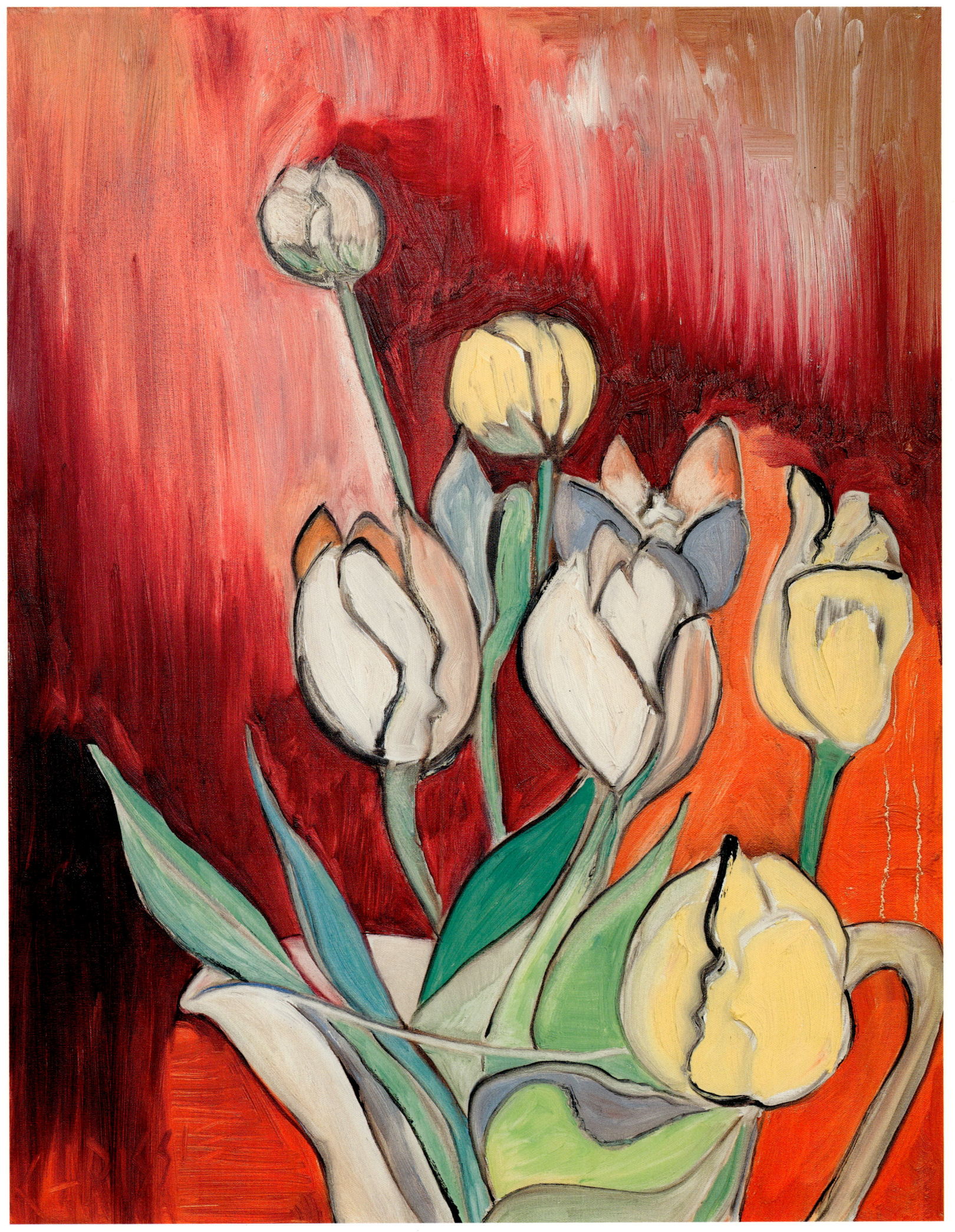

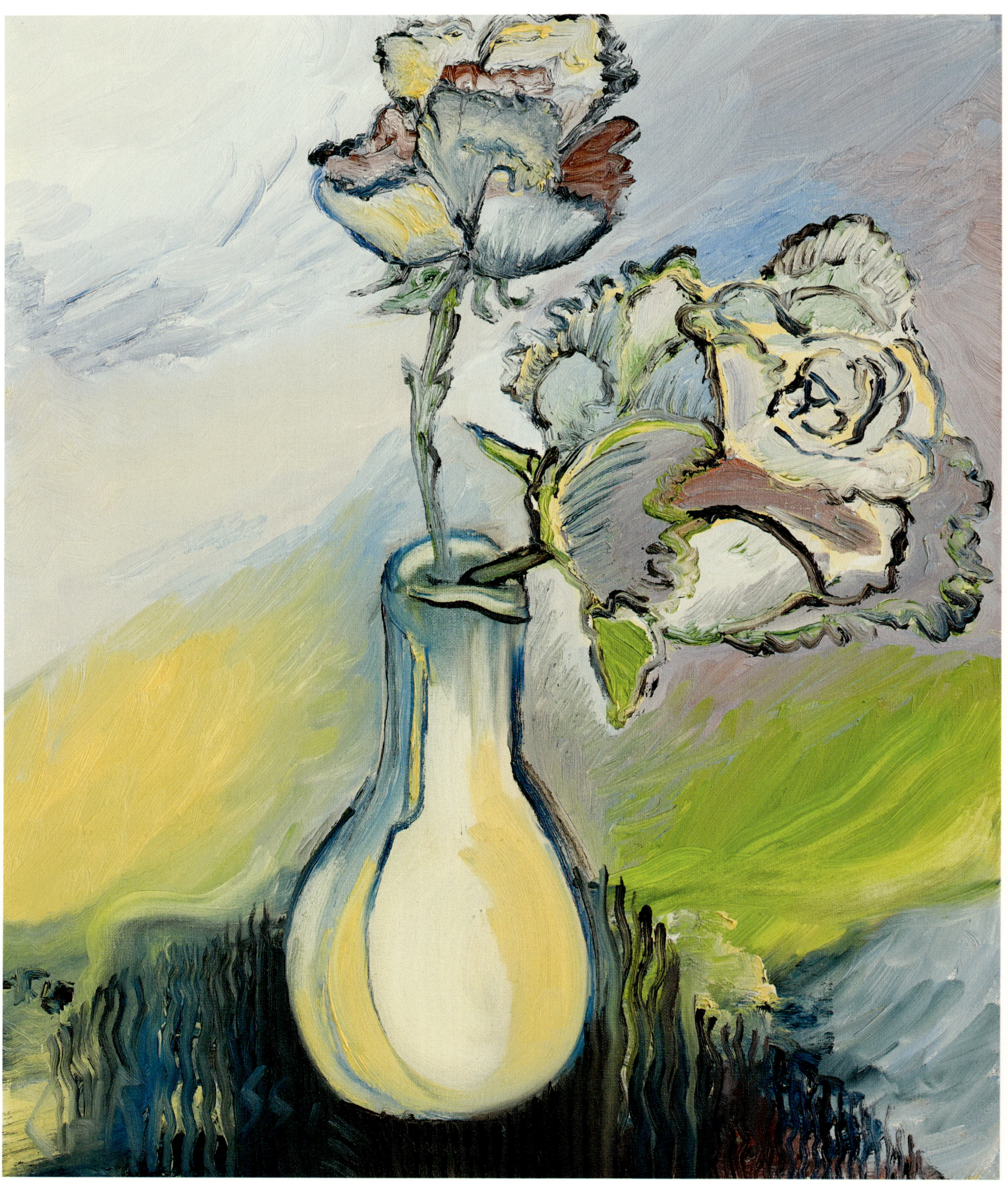

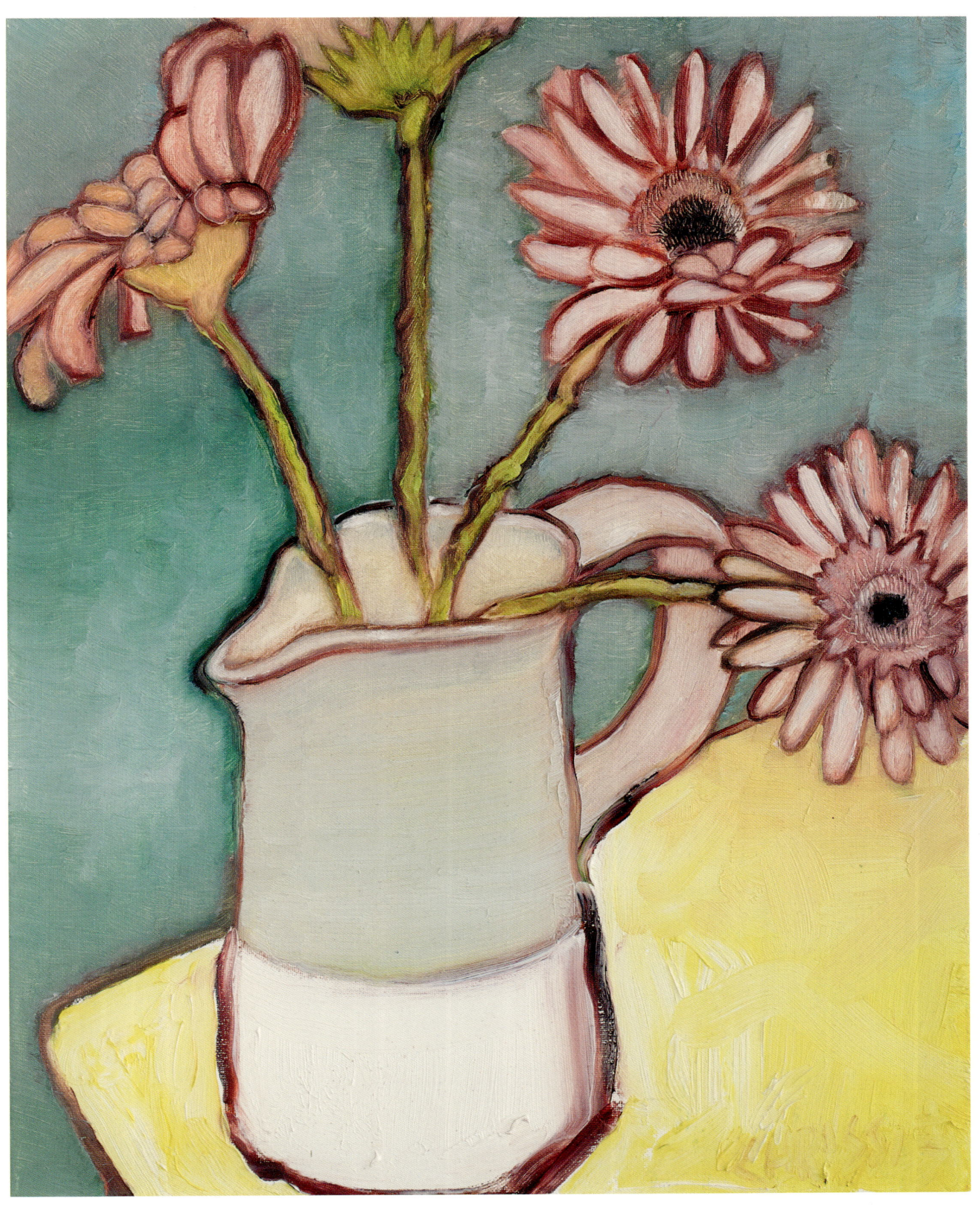

EVENING ROSES
Oil on canvas
60 x 50 cm
(23¹ᐟ² x 19³ᐟ⁴ in)
6 February 2017

EVENING GERBERAS
Oil on canvas
50 x 40 cm
(19³ᐟ⁴ x 15³ᐟ⁴ in)
20 March 2016

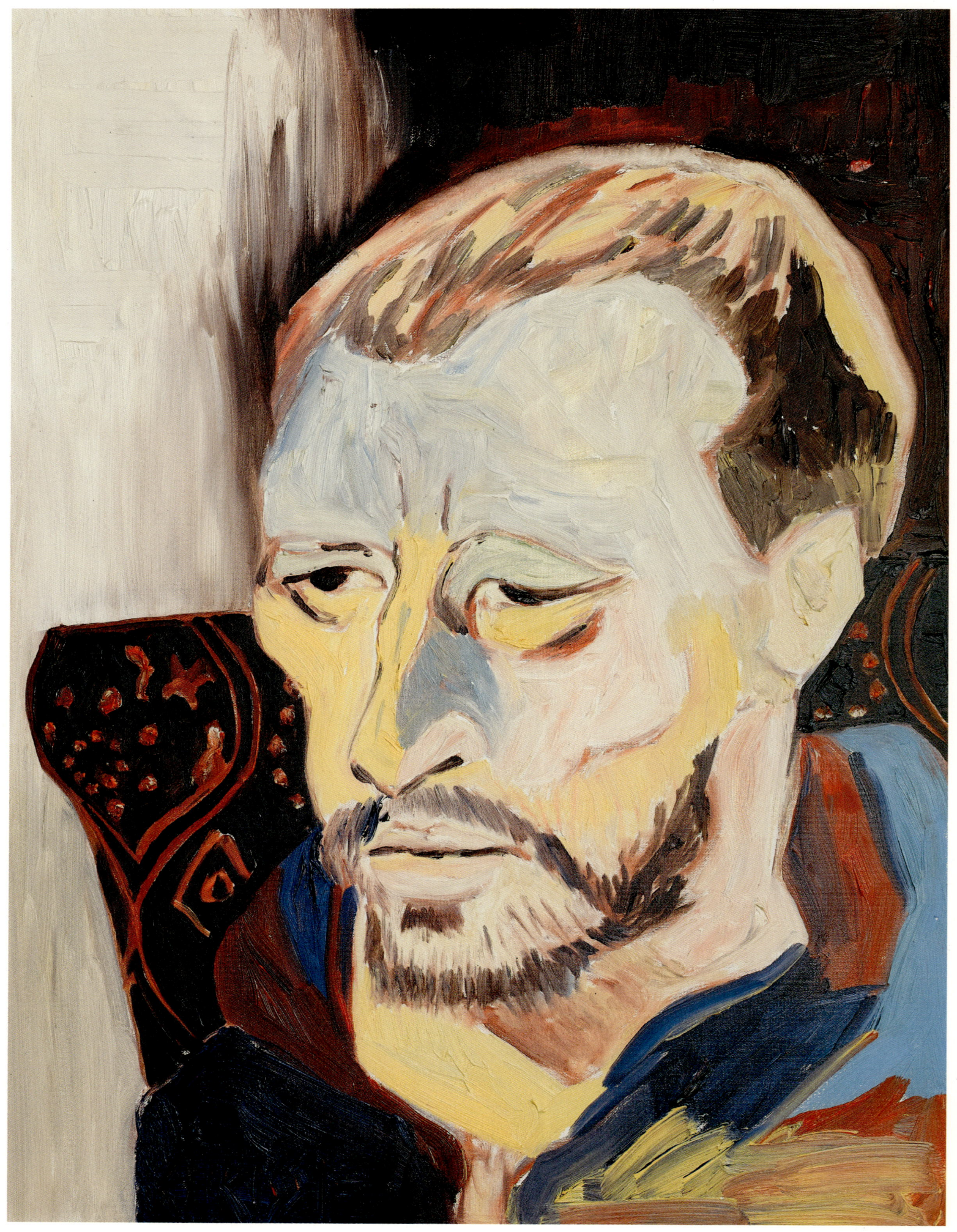

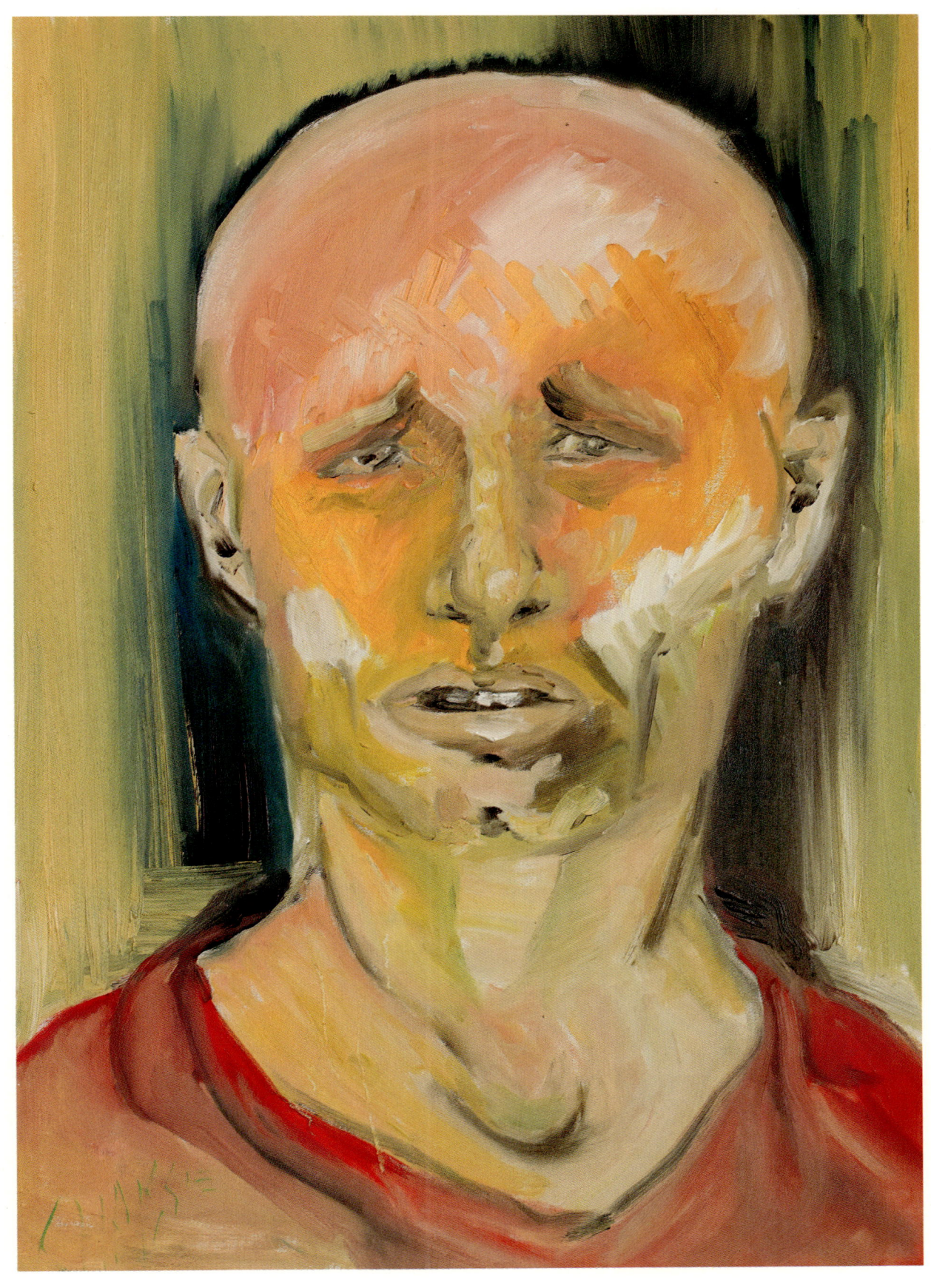

Michael Clark, esteemed punk, dancer and choreographer, came over recently.
It was rainy and he seemed a bit anguished. We spent an hour or two together
talking about a project. I painted this after he left. So, although this actually
doesn't look anything like him — he's much more beautiful than this — I think
it captured his mood.

MICHAEL W.
SATURDAY TODAY
Oil on canvas
80 x 60 cm
(31¹⁄₂ x 23¹⁄₂ in)
4 February 2017

MAN PERPLEXED
Oil on canvas
70 x 50 cm
(27³⁄₄ x 19³⁄₄ in)
17 May 2017

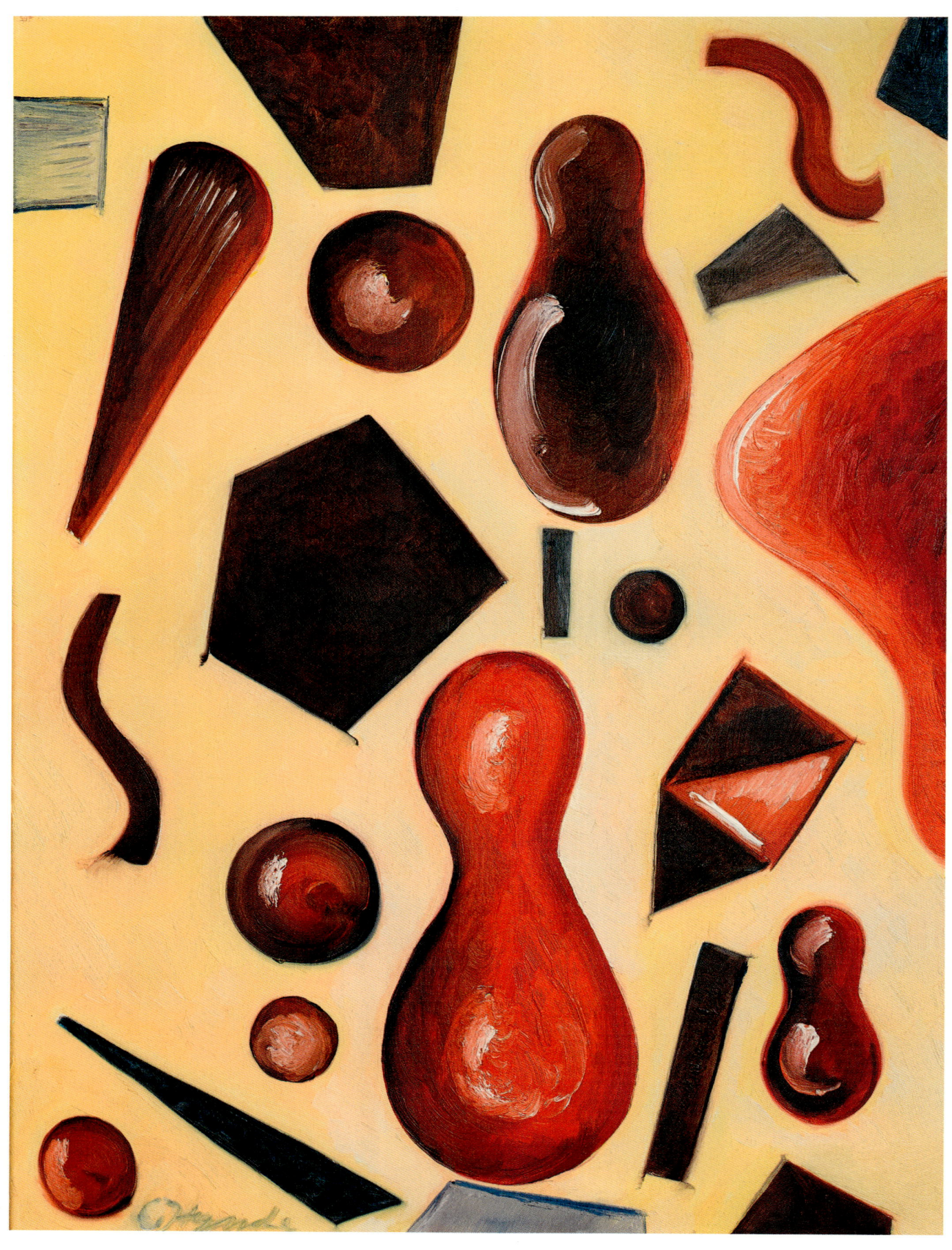

I think this painting signals a turning point. This was when I started doing these floating shapes. I'll find one thing, and I'll carry on doing it as long as it stays interesting and keeps me away from flowers and self-portraits.

EASTER '17
Oil on canvas
80 x 60 cm
(31$^{1/2}$ x 23$^{1/2}$ in)
17 April 2017

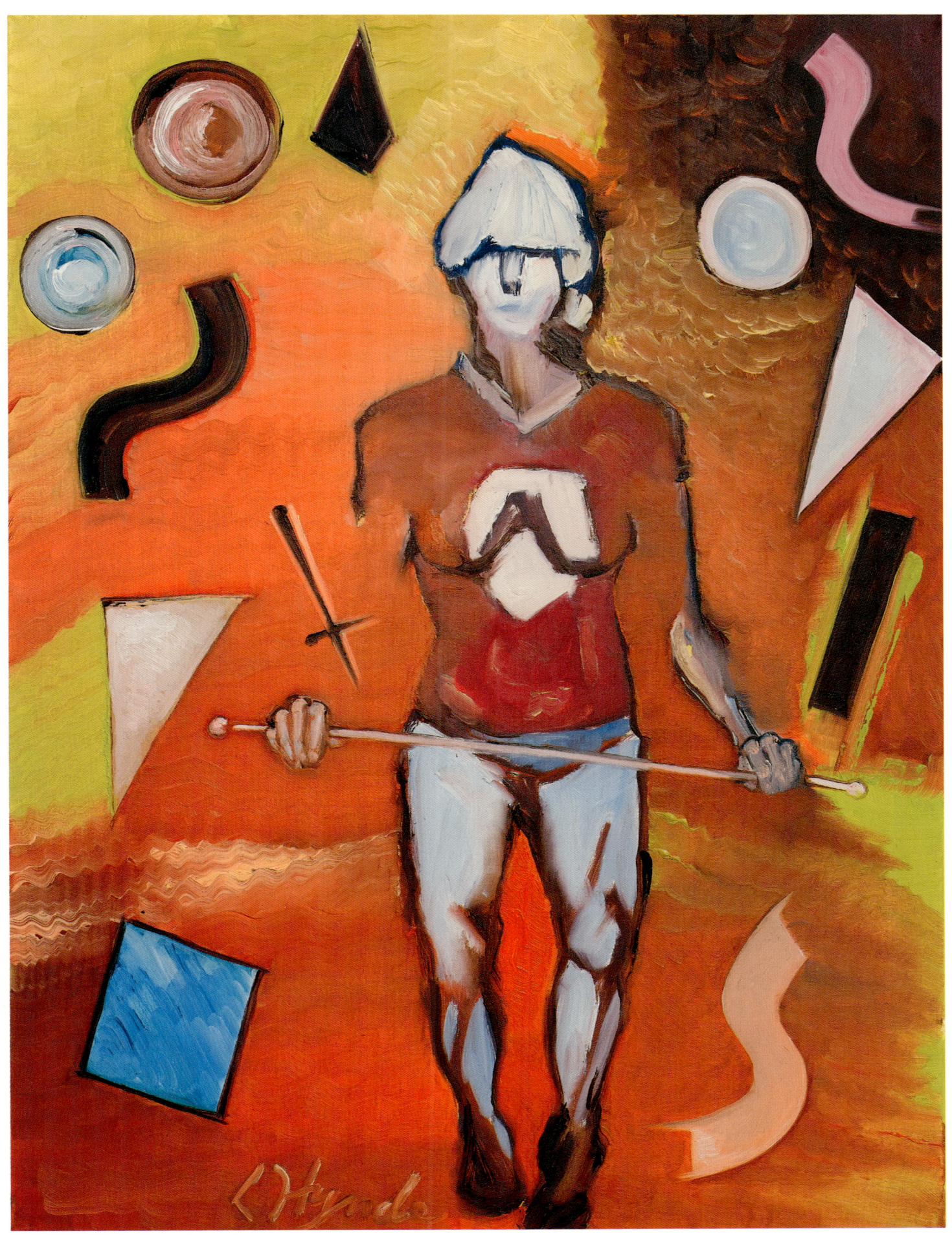

THIS IS IT MONDAY
Oil on canvas
80 x 60 cm
(31$^{1/2}$ x 23$^{1/2}$ in)
17 April 2017

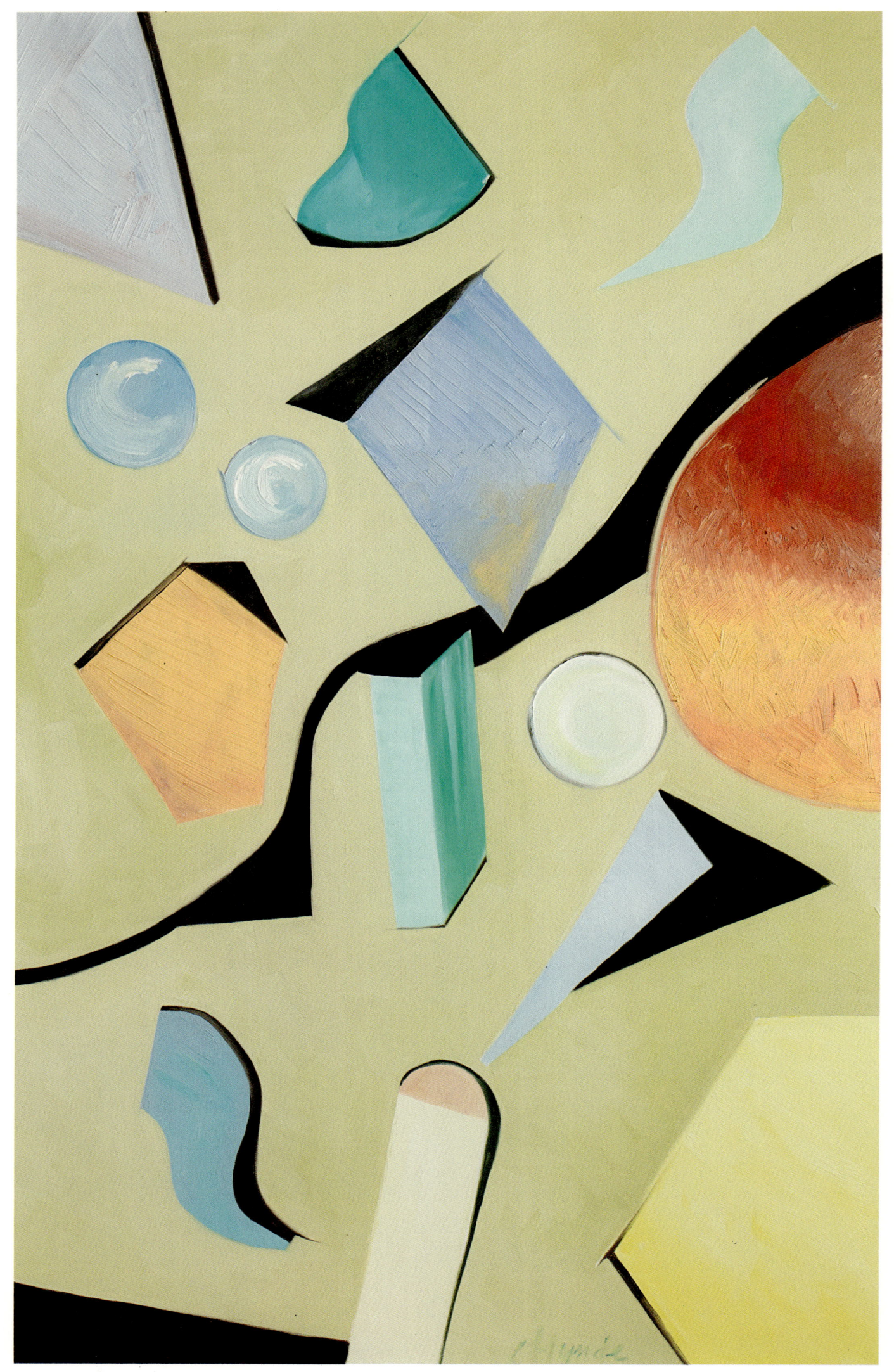

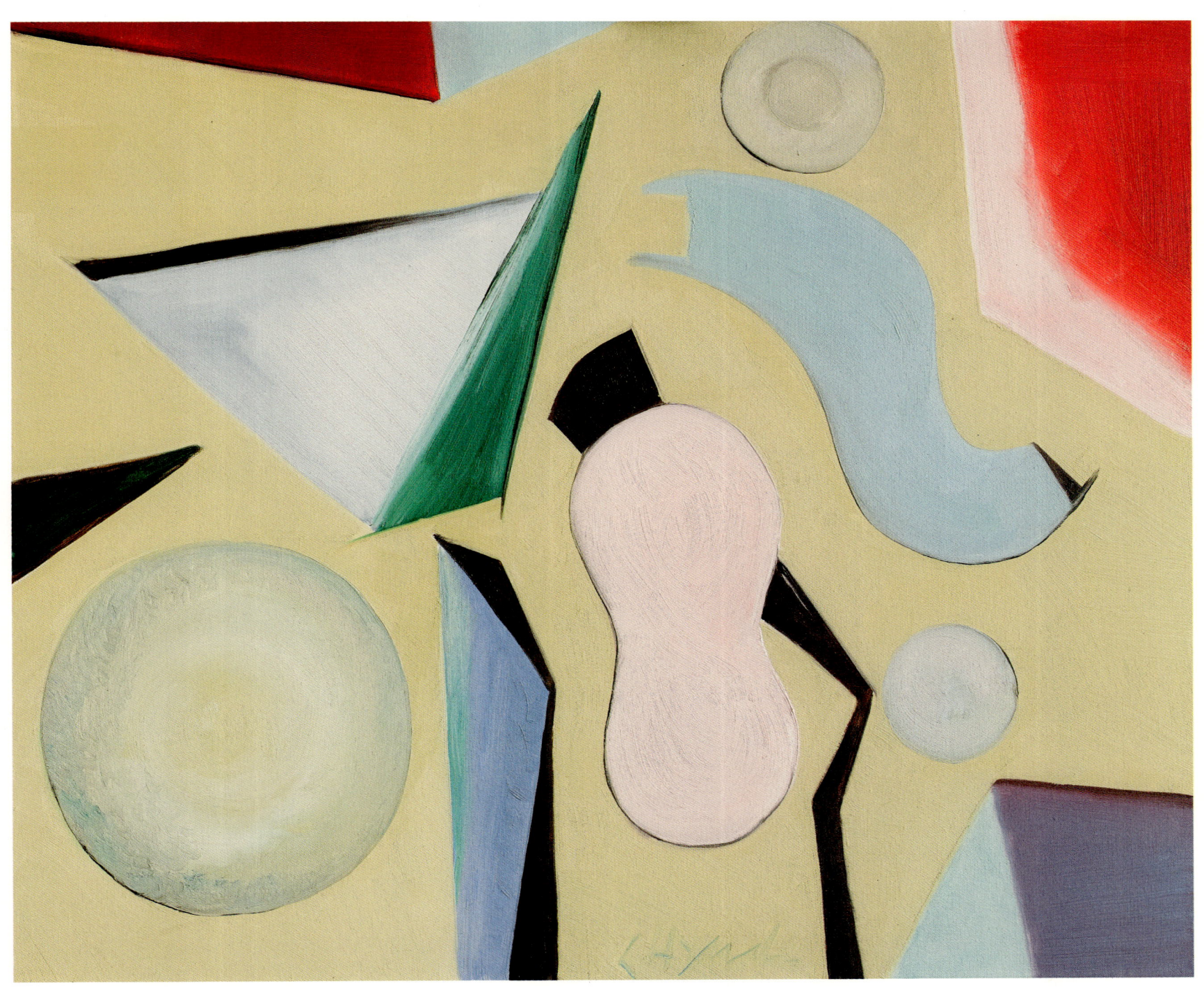

*Colour is the fun part about painting. In nature you see it most vividly
in flowers, birds and fish.*

APRIL SHOWERS I
Oil on canvas
120 x 75 cm
(47$^{1/4}$ x 29$^{1/2}$ in)
19 May 2017

APRIL SHOWERS II
Oil on canvas
50 x 60 cm
(19$^{3/4}$ x 23$^{1/2}$ in)
19 May 2017

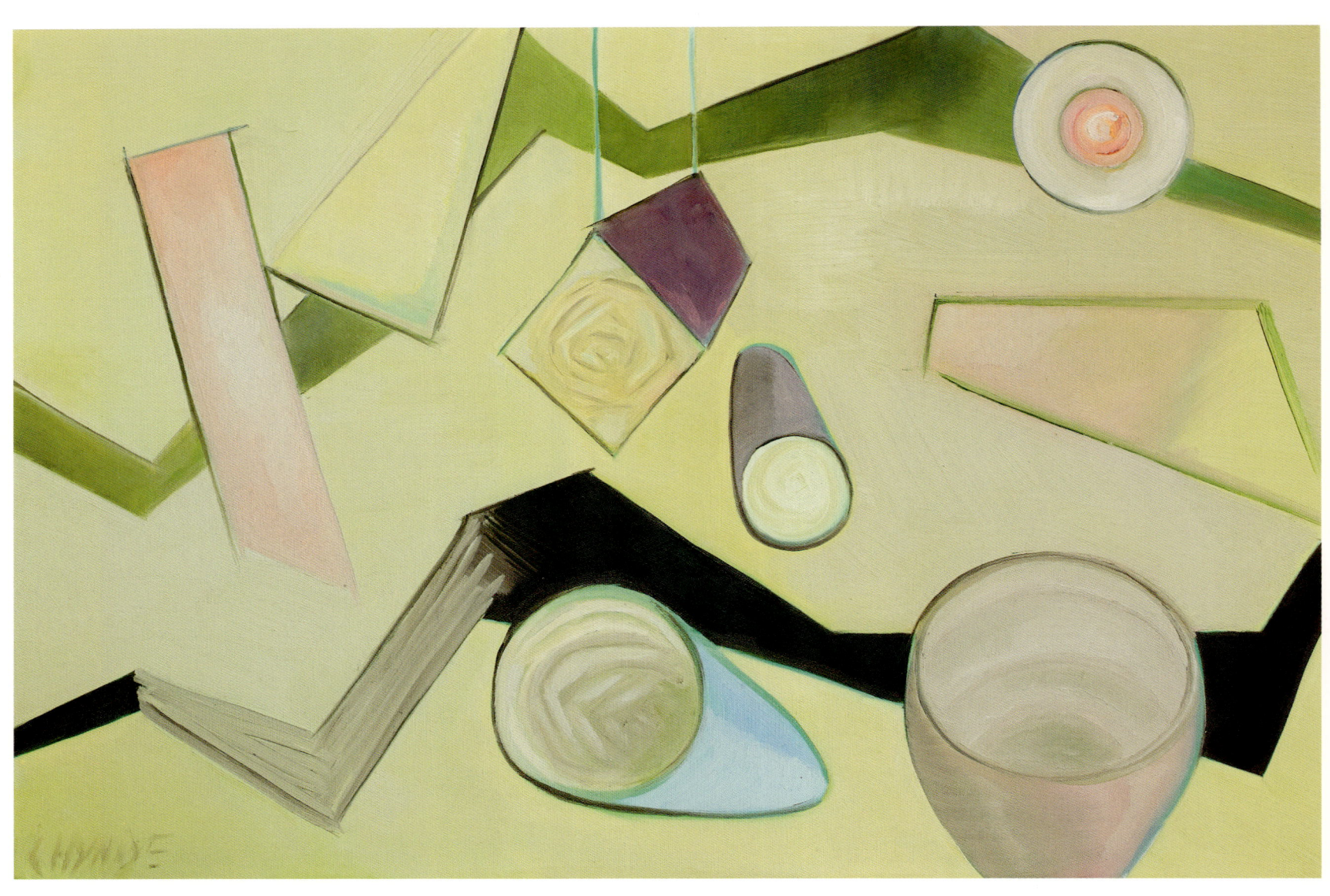

I want to use this painting as the cover art of Valve Bone Woe, *the album I've been making with Marius de Vries.*

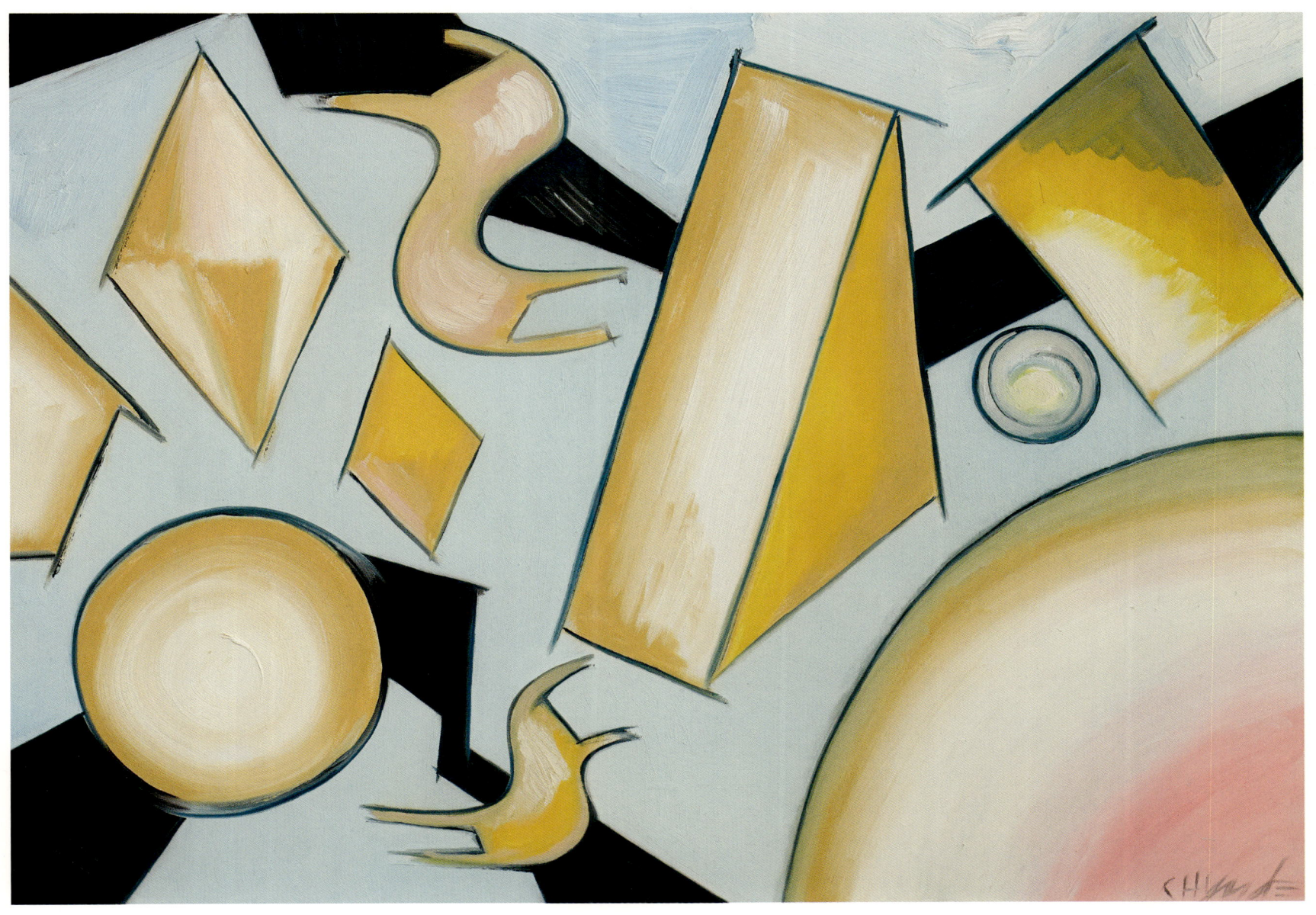

Colour therapy is a very interesting thing. I'm hyper-aware of how certain colours can alter your mood. On an overcast day, if you wear pink or yellow sunglasses it can really lift you. I have a psychedelic mindset from when I was younger. Colour affects you in a psychedelic way.

VALVE BONE WOE
Oil on canvas
50 x 75 cm
(19³/⁴ x 29¹/² in)
16 May 2017

TUESDAY BLUE YELLOW
AFTERNOON
Oil on canvas
60 x 85 cm
(23¹/² x 33¹/² in)
16 May 2017

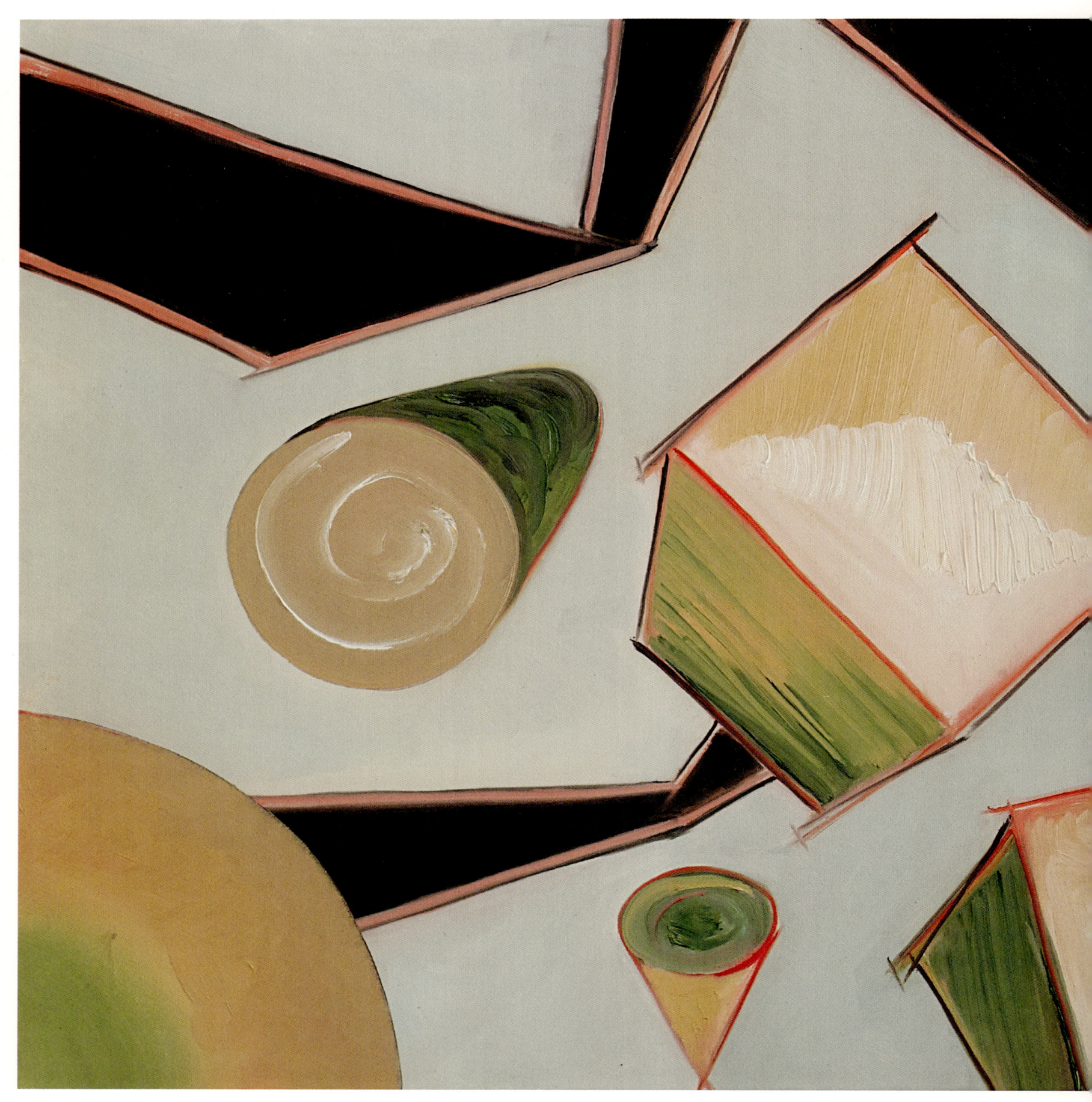

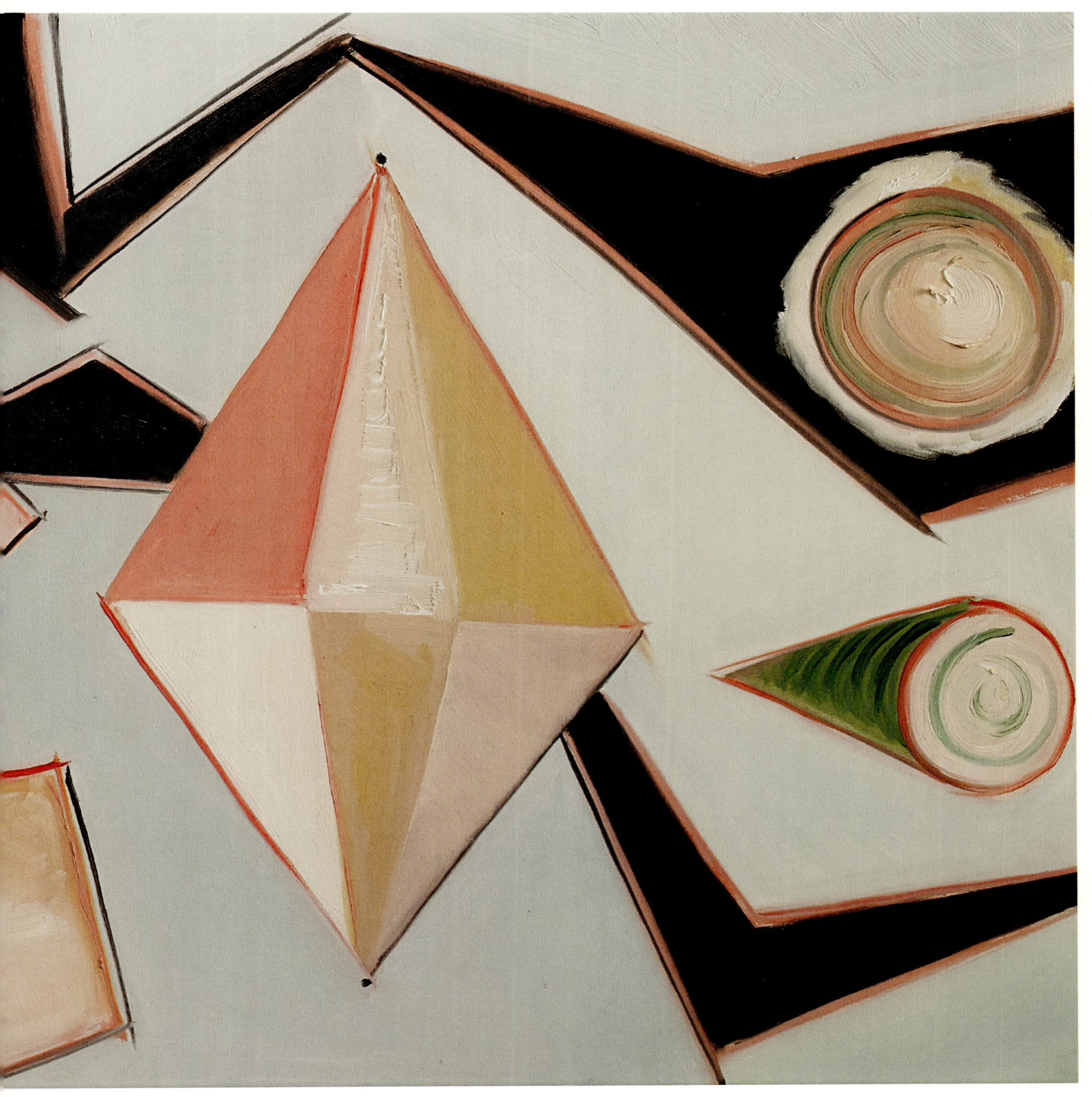

WEDNESDAY
DANCER SHAPES
Oil on canvas
50 x 100 cm
(19³/₄ x 39¹/₂ in)
17 May 2017

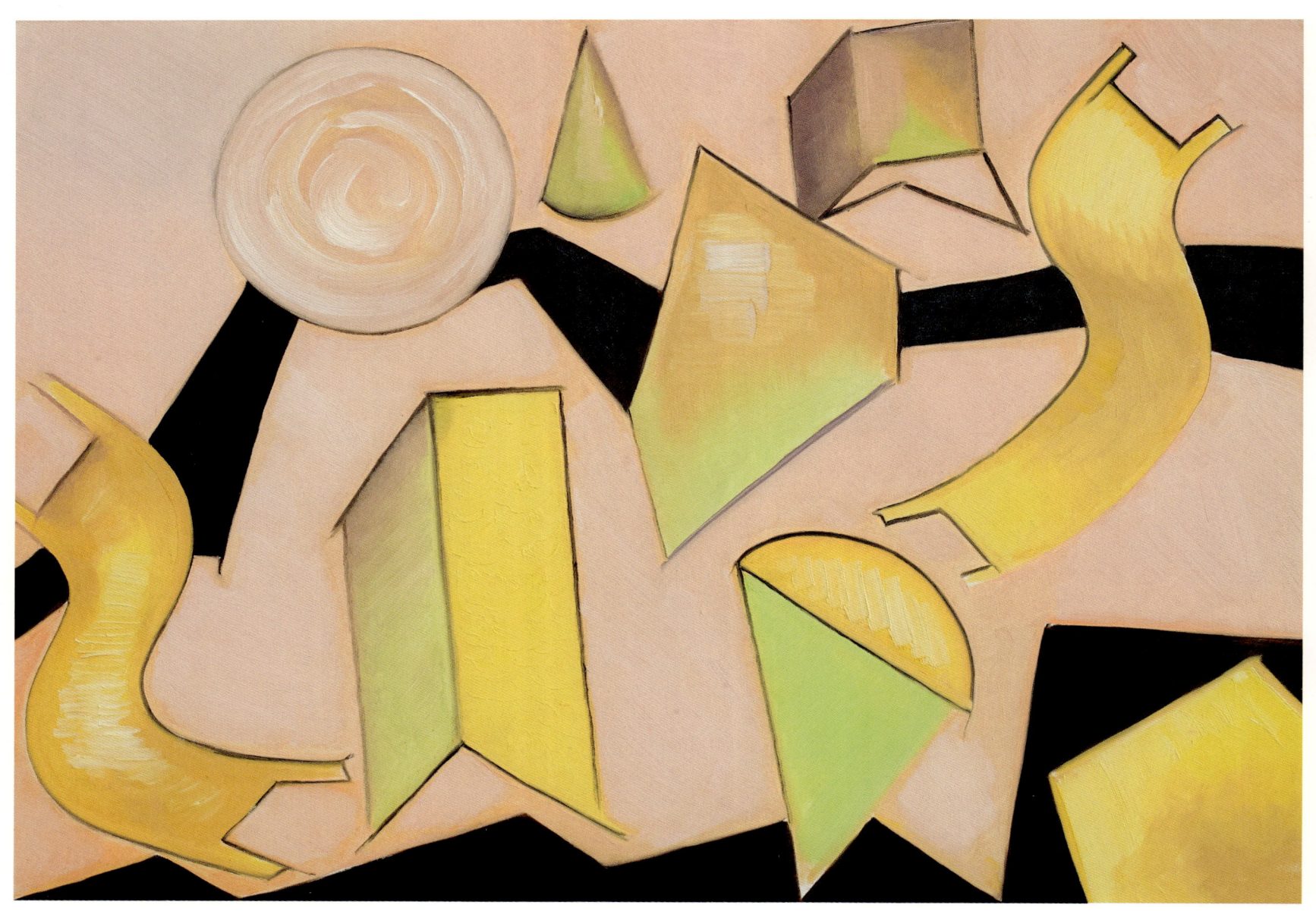

The art world is always moving and changing. The world is moving and changing. Which makes for an interesting exchange of impressions and ideas within a community of artists. I'm not in on those conversations with artists because I'm mainly in the music world.

If I'm at a party, I've found one way to clear the room is to say, 'I don't like art.' Everyone is appalled. You get the drinks table all to yourself. Of course, that's ridiculous. Everyone loves art.

SHAPES OF MAY II
Oil on canvas
60 x 85 cm
(23$^{1/2}$ x 33$^{1/2}$ in)
19 May 2017

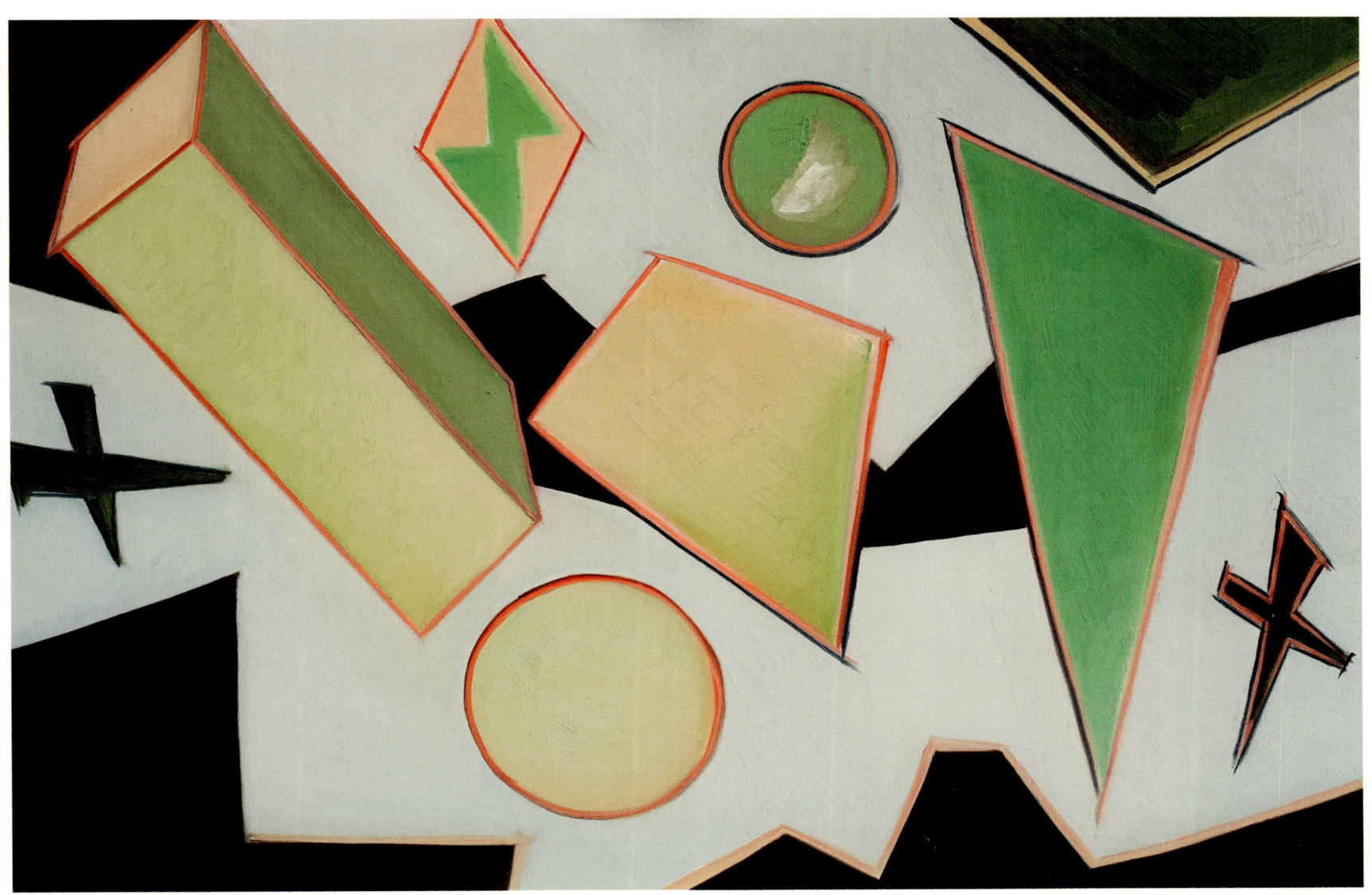

Art is difficult to judge. Unless it's really about the experience you have when you're standing in front of something looking at it. It's only your feelings that can judge it.

Collectors have become secondary artists. Their collection defines who they are — their form of expression is what they've collected and what they deem as worthy and valuable. And they are welcome to collect and invest in my paintings. It's the audience that keeps the artist alive — without a beholder, art is meaningless. It's the yin and yang of everything.

WEDNESDAY
FALLING SHAPES
Oil on canvas
50 x 70 cm
(19³/⁴ x 27¹/² in)
24 May 2017

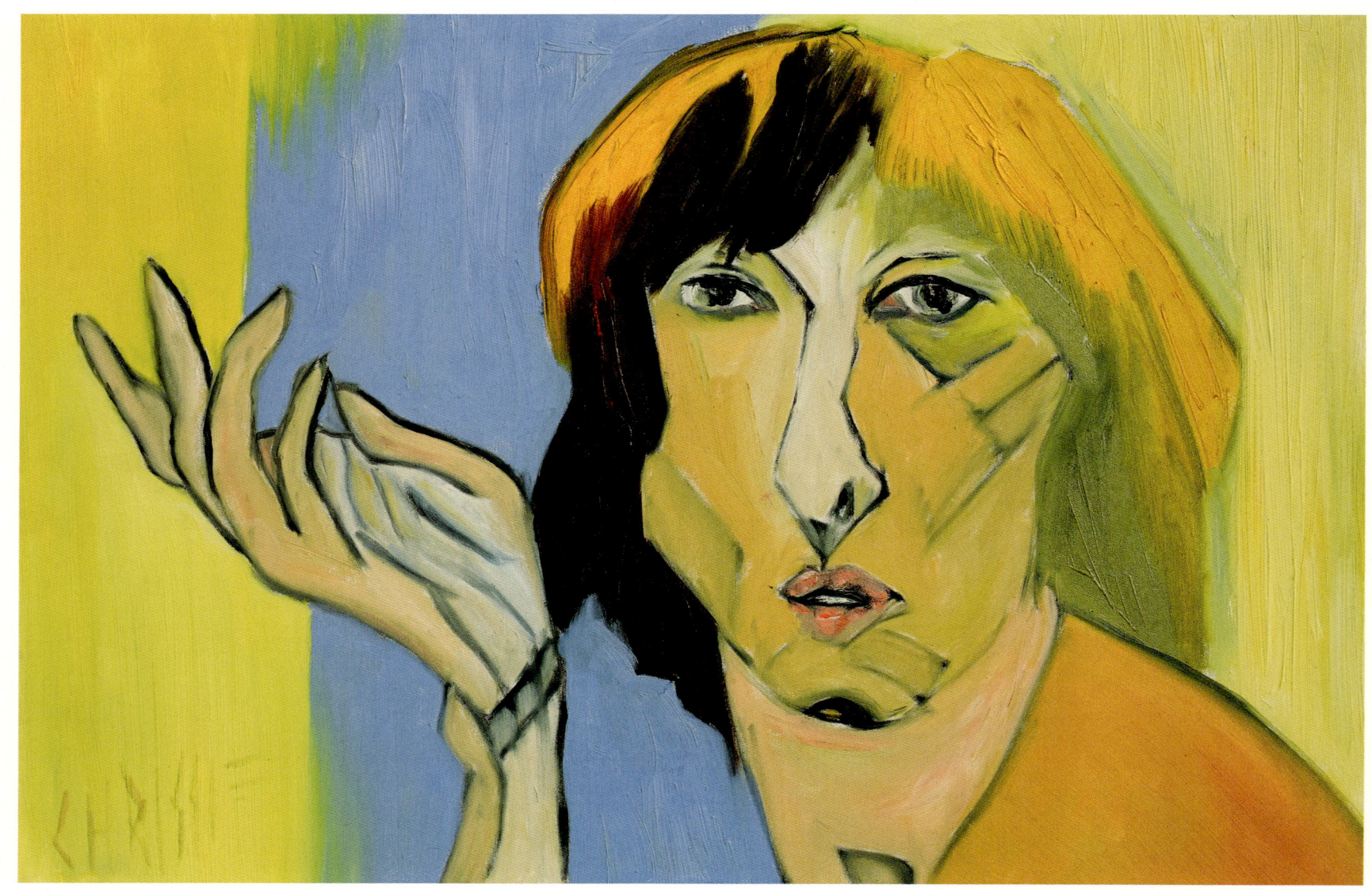

In former times, you wouldn't know how anyone looked unless someone had done a portrait of them for posterity. Then photography kind of ruined it, and I suppose I've harboured a resentment towards photography because of that, as would anyone who naturally prefers portraiture.

Pre-photography, it must have been so thrilling to paint a very faithful image of someone. Now you can either take a picture or paint from a photograph.

THURSDAY SELF I
Oil on canvas
40 x 60 cm
(15³/⁴ x 23¹/² in)
25 May 2017

THURSDAY SELF II
Oil on canvas
75 x 60 cm
(29¹/² x 23¹/² in)
25 May 2017

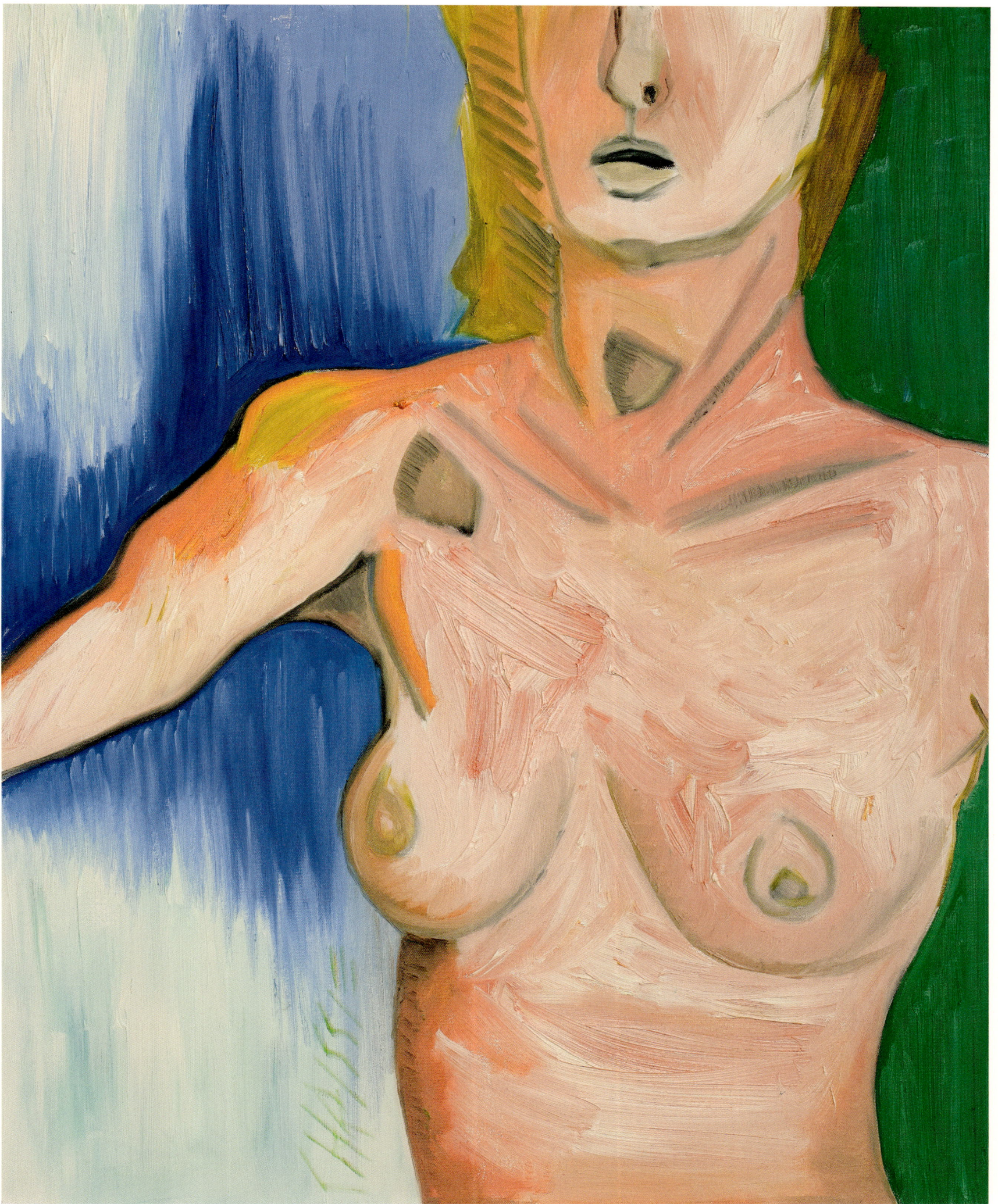

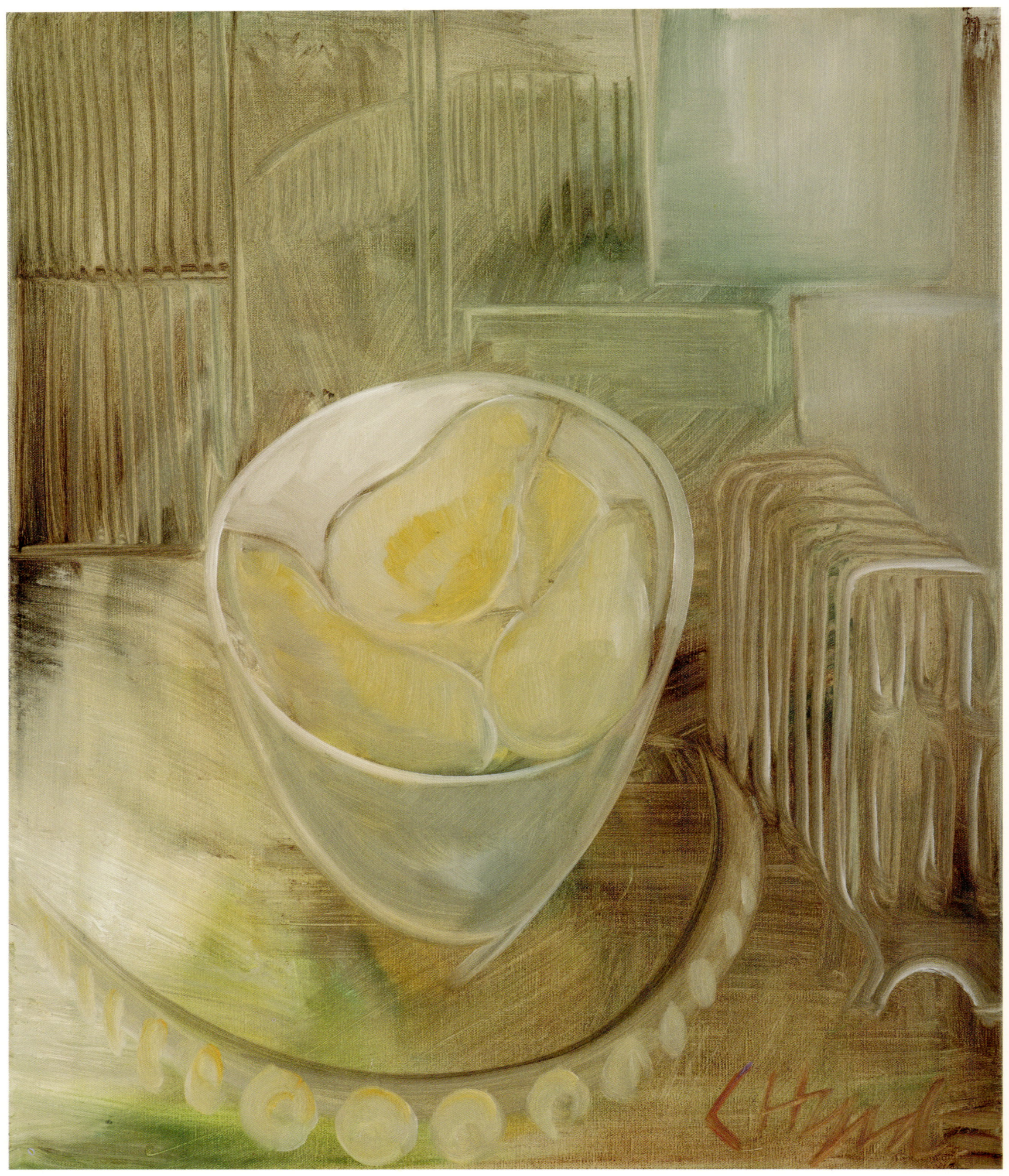

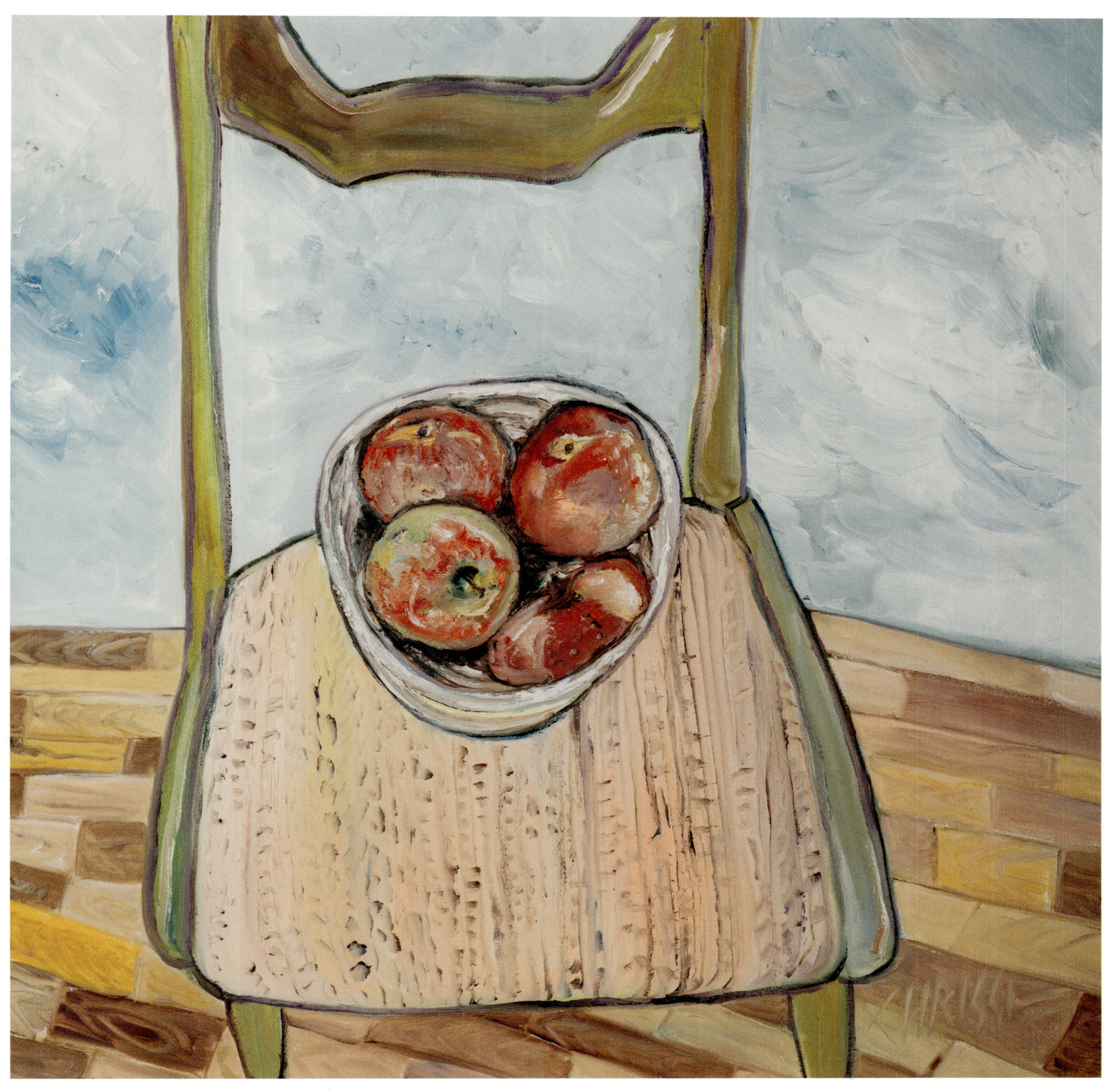

GHOST PEARS
Oil on canvas
65 x 54 cm
($25^{1/2}$ x $21^{1/4}$ in)
7 May 2017

APPLE PEACHES
CHAIR SÈTE
Oil on canvas
60 x 60 cm
($23^{1/2}$ x $23^{1/2}$ in)
26 August 2017

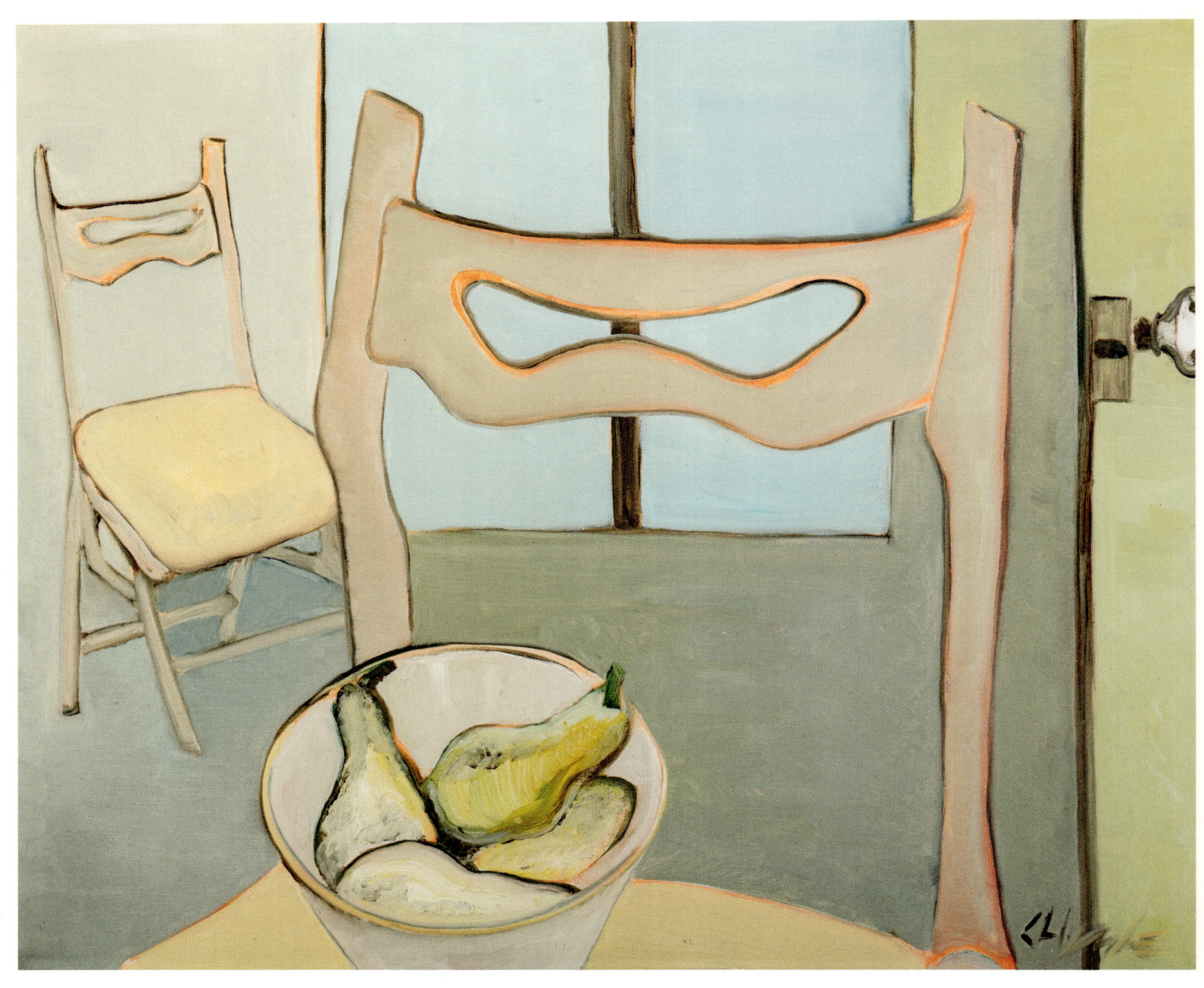

*At my home studio in Sète, southern France, there's a stillness
compared to life in London. I'd like to meet other painters but so far
I feel like I'm a rogue faction. I've gone off on my own, I do this and
I have no real conversation about it.*

SÈTE PEARS I
Oil on canvas
54 x 65 cm
(21¹ᐟ⁴ x 25¹ᐟ² in)
25 May 2017

SÈTE PEARS II
Oil on canvas
80 x 60 cm
(31¹ᐟ² x 23¹ᐟ² in)
25 May 2017

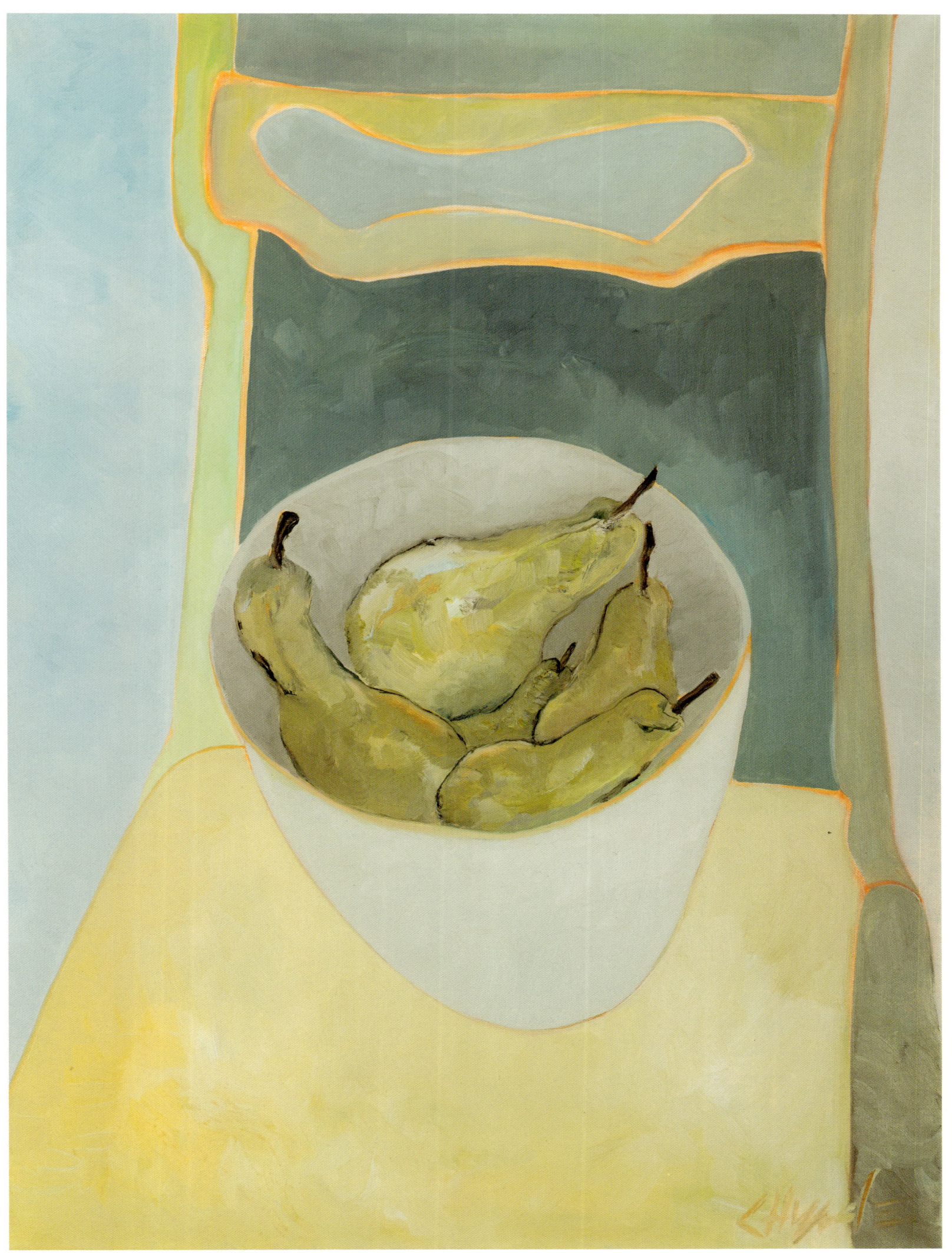

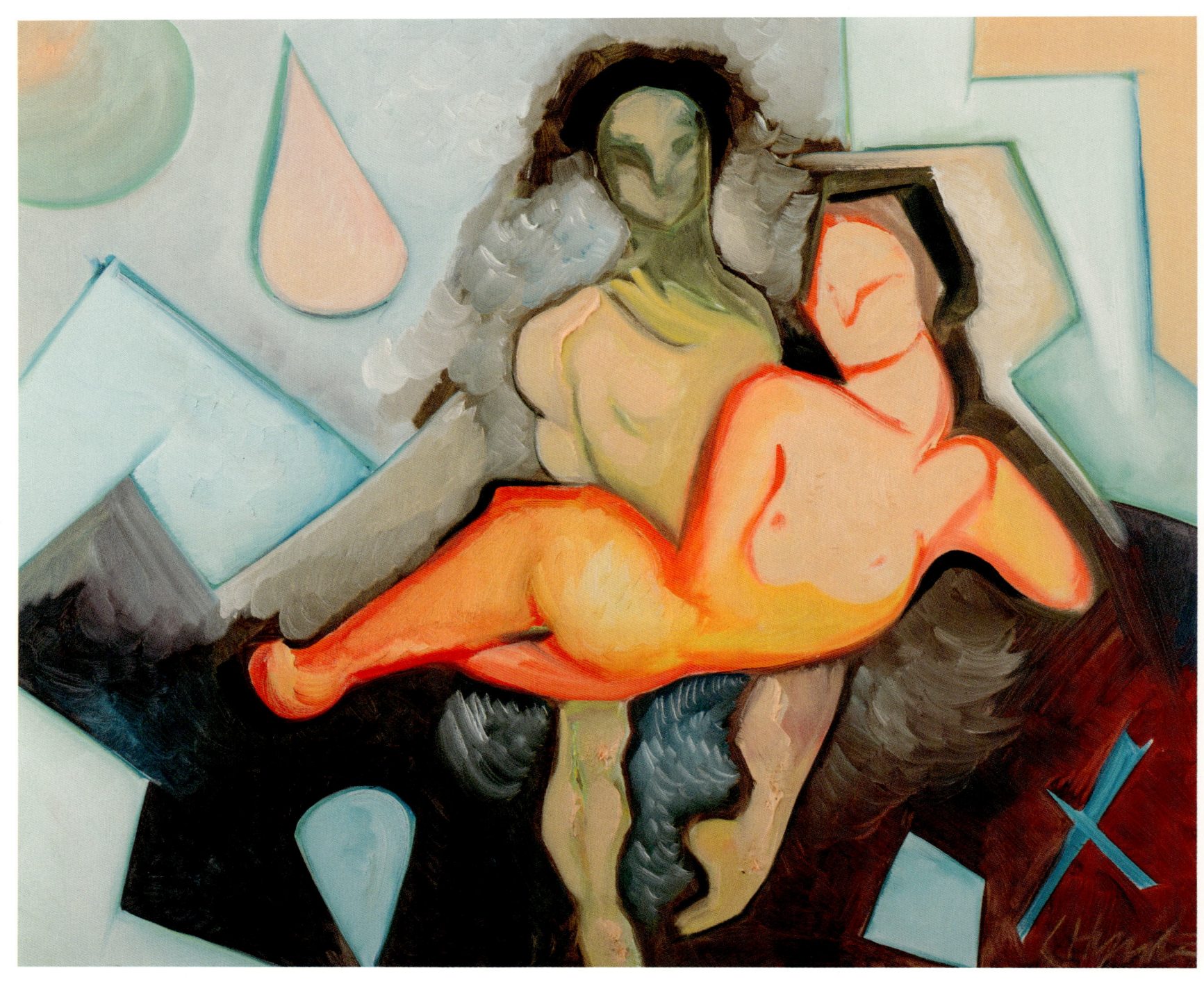

For a few days I obsessively watched clips of Sergei Polunin and Natalia Osipova.

BALLET
Oil on canvas
54 x 65 cm
(21$^{1/4}$ x 25$^{1/2}$ in)
26 May 2017

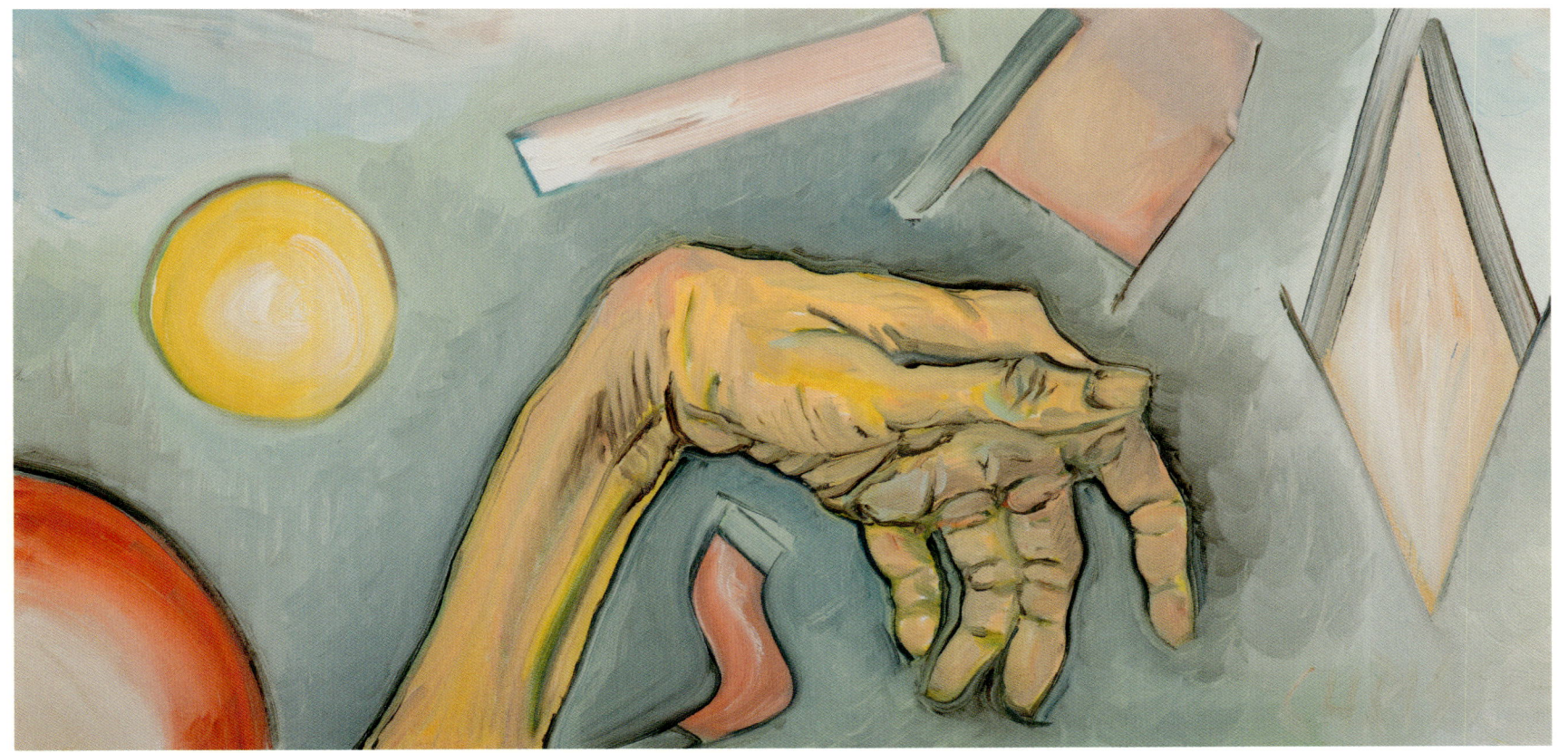

I like working with my hands. When I was a kid I liked to sew, whittle, make tree forts, anything. Sometimes I'll write with both hands and then try writing backwards with both hands. Watching television and films, you stop doing a lot of that, because you're otherwise engaged. Screens are putting hands out of business, but I've found it's good to keep your hands busy.

SÈTE HAND
Oil on canvas
30 x 60 cm
(11³/⁴ x 23¹/² in)
26 May 2017

It's fantastic painting in Sète. My man, Van Gogh, was just down the road.
There's definitely something about the light and how it affects the paint.
Obviously the light in Sète is fantastic. I have yet to paint outdoors there,
but I open up the windows. I think the quality of the air is just as important.

Some people, like James Gillick, mix their pigments. I tried stretching
canvases, which for me took longer than the actual painting. Snatching time
in between tours is frustrating. Maybe one day, if I make painting my main
pursuit, I can concentrate on the details better.

SÈTE SHAPES
Oil on canvas
60 x 60 cm
(23$^{1/2}$ x 23$^{1/2}$ in)
27 May 2017

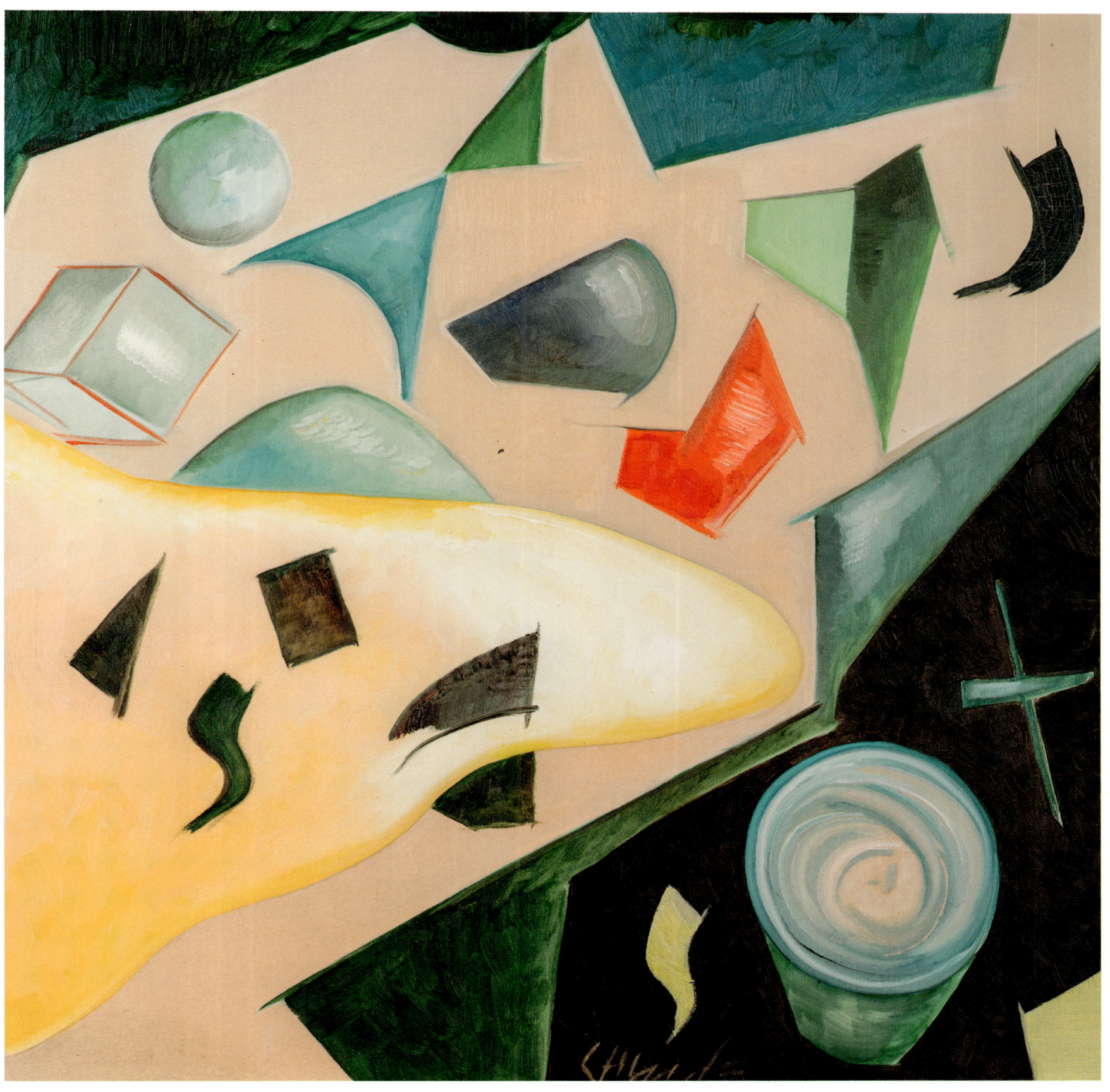

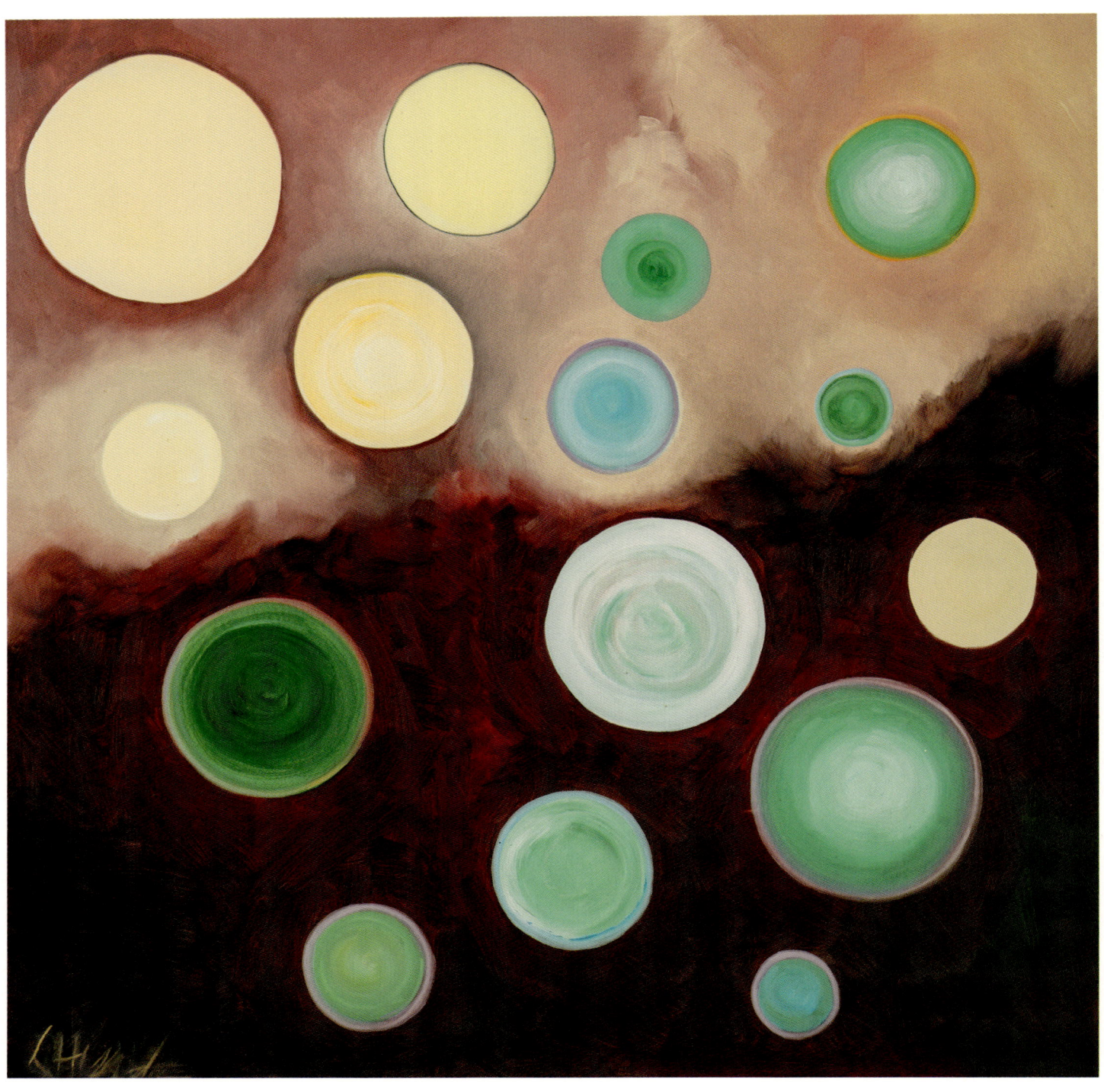

I was very driven when I did this painting, and I don't know why, but it's one of
the few that I thought about in advance. I had circles in my mind for days even
though it's a very simple painting.

There's a similarity between drawing circles and straight lines, and singing.
A certain element of breath control. I wonder if anyone watching a show
and hearing me sing thinks, 'It sounds as if she's drawing a circle.'

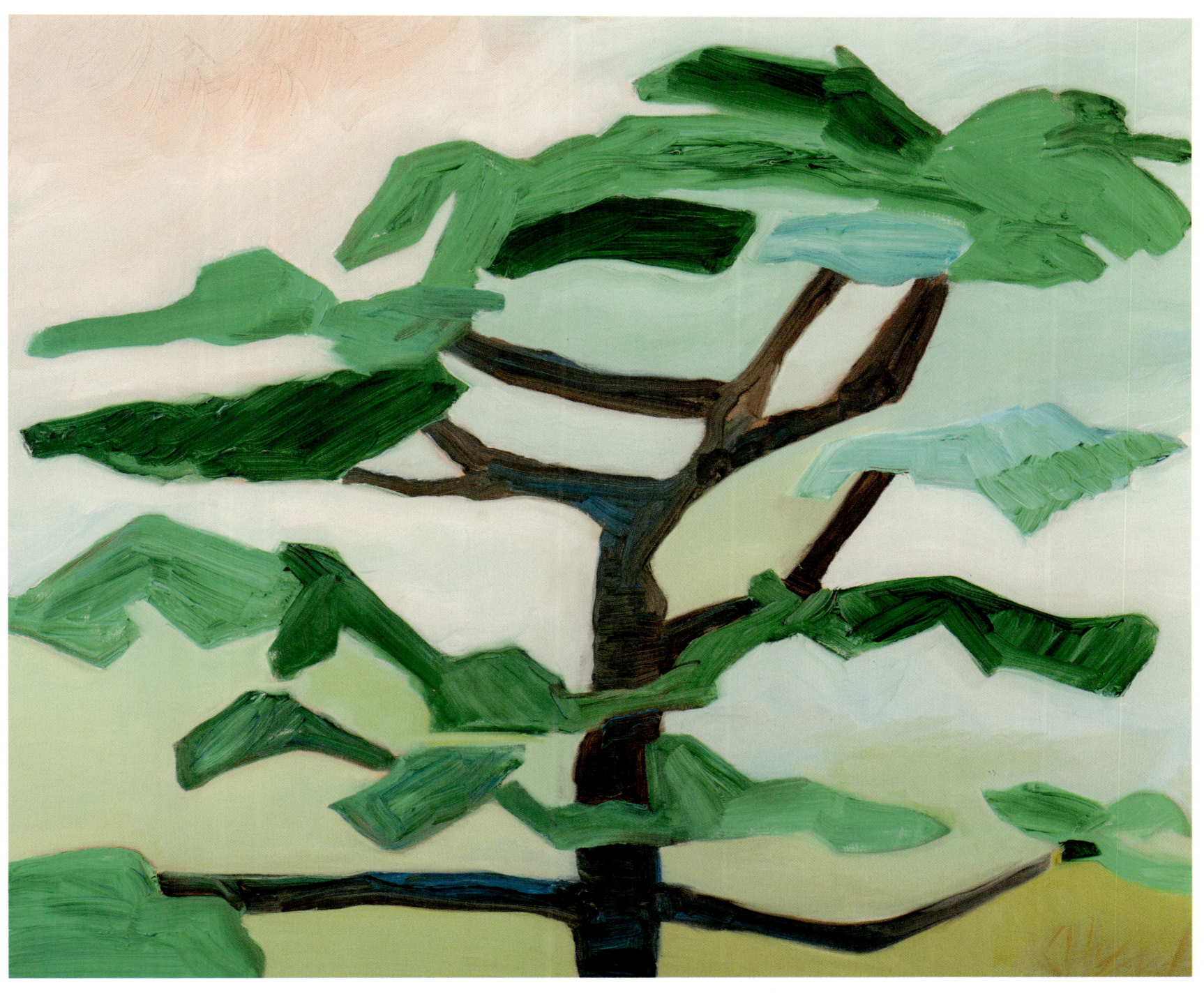

For me, art is a way of connecting to the divine — taking elements from the things that are around us that otherwise we take for granted. You actually don't create anything, do you? It's already there.

SÈTE CIRCLES
Oil on canvas
80 x 80 cm
(31$^{1/2}$ x 31$^{1/2}$ in)
27 May 2017

SÈTE TREE
Oil on canvas
54 x 65 cm
(21$^{1/4}$ x 25$^{1/2}$ in)
27 May 2017

I started this in the morning, but then I had to leave to go to Noel Gallagher's 50th birthday party. All the time I was there, I was thinking I had to get home and finish the painting. I called it 'Dancing Noels', because I like to put something in there to remind me what was going on that day. In fact, Noel Gallagher never dances.

DANCING NOELS
Oil on canvas
100 x 70 cm
(39$^{1/2}$ x 27$^{1/2}$ in)
28 May 2017

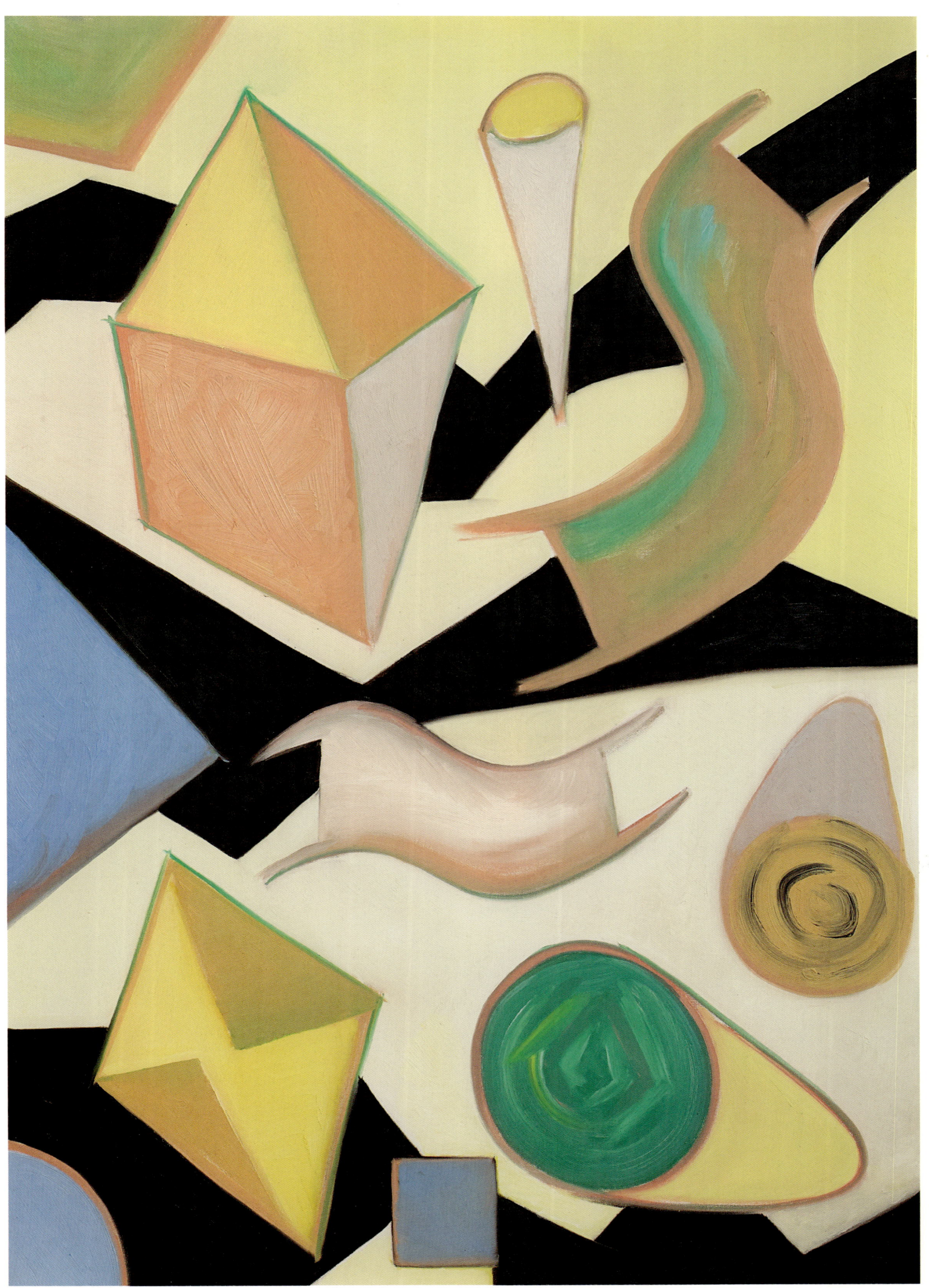

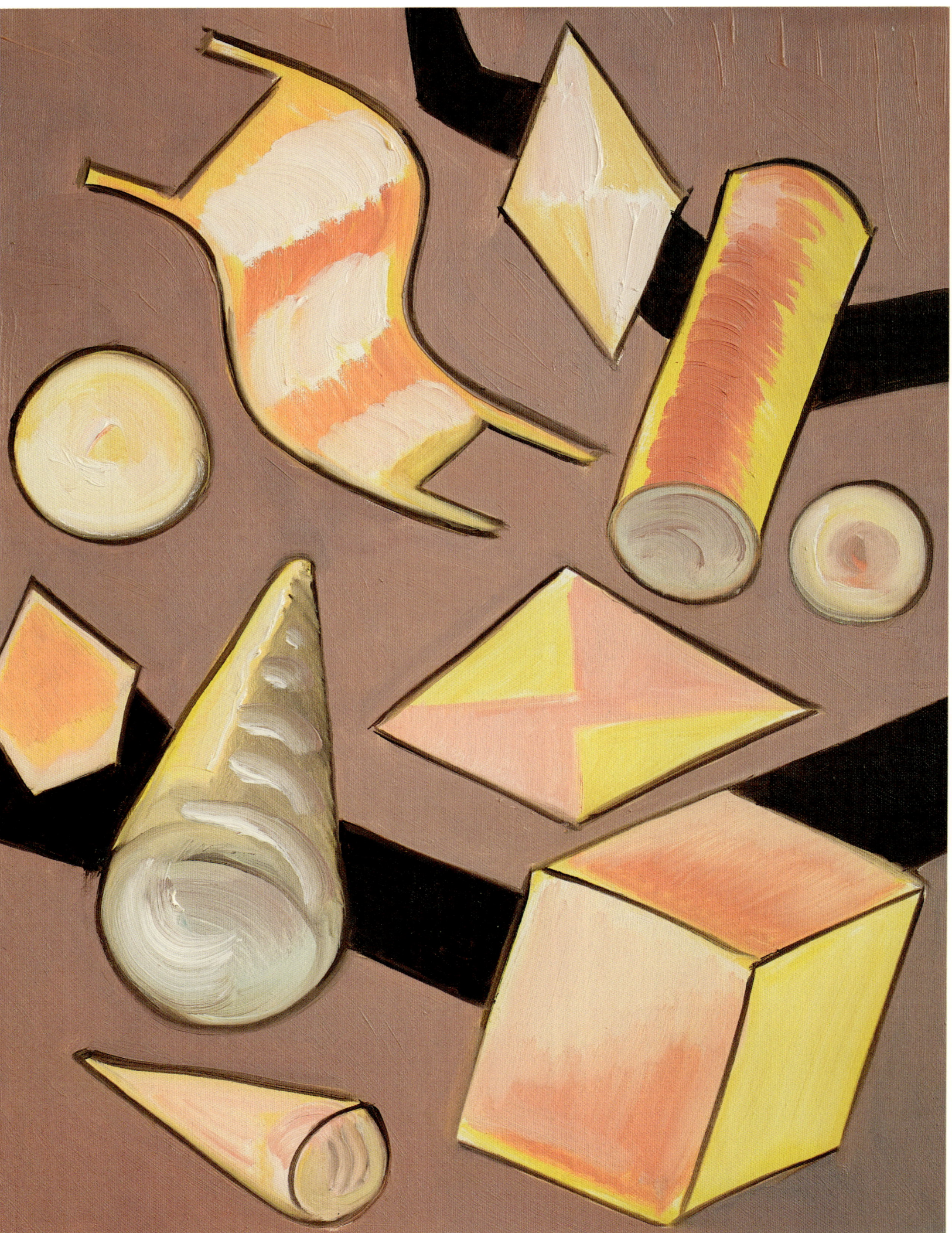

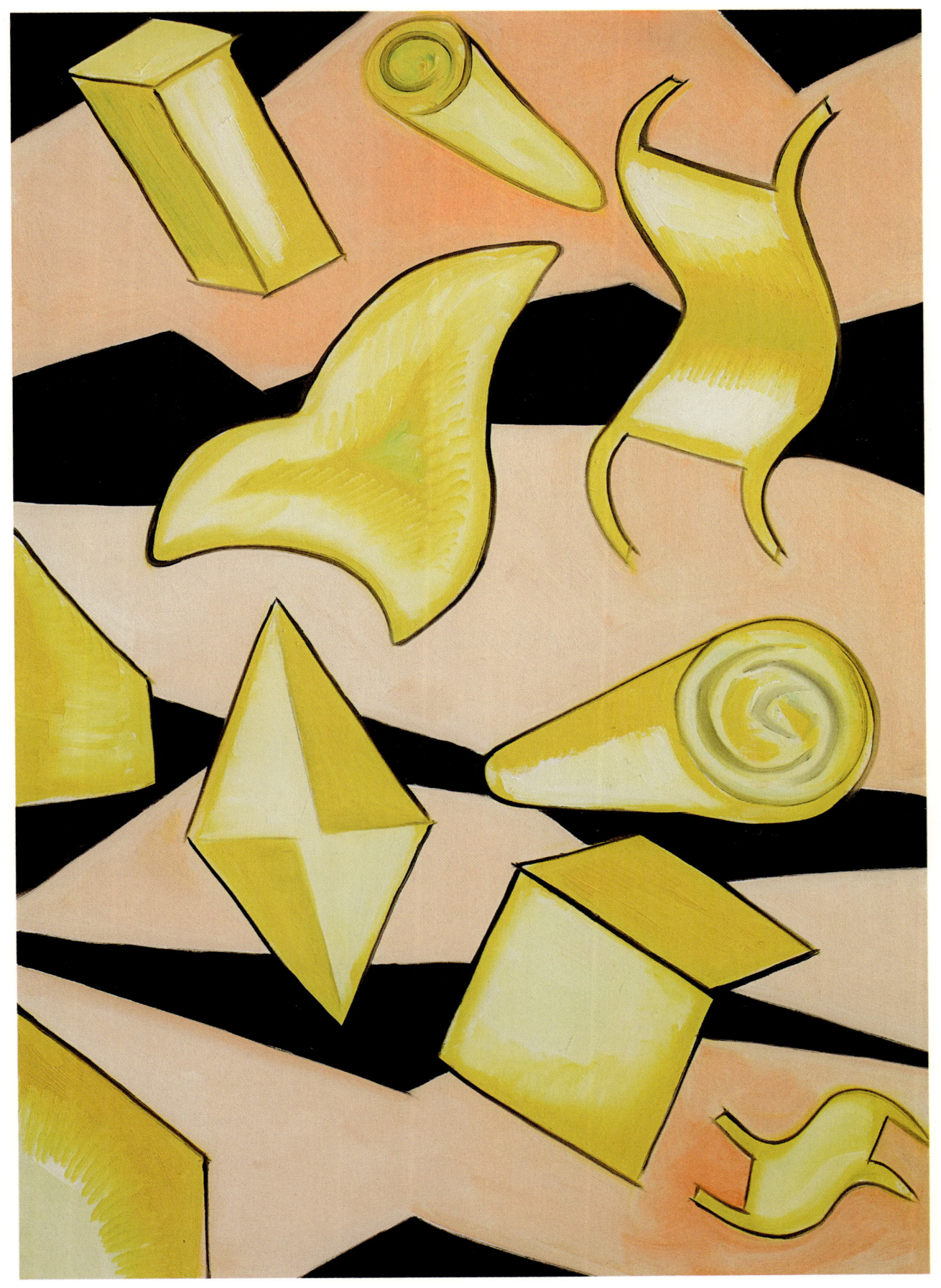

JUNE SHAPES
Oil on canvas
60 x 45 cm
(23$^{1/2}$ x 17$^{3/4}$ in)
8 June 2017

SHAPES OF THINGS
Oil on canvas
100 x 70 cm
(39$^{1/2}$ x 27$^{1/2}$ in)
16 June 2017

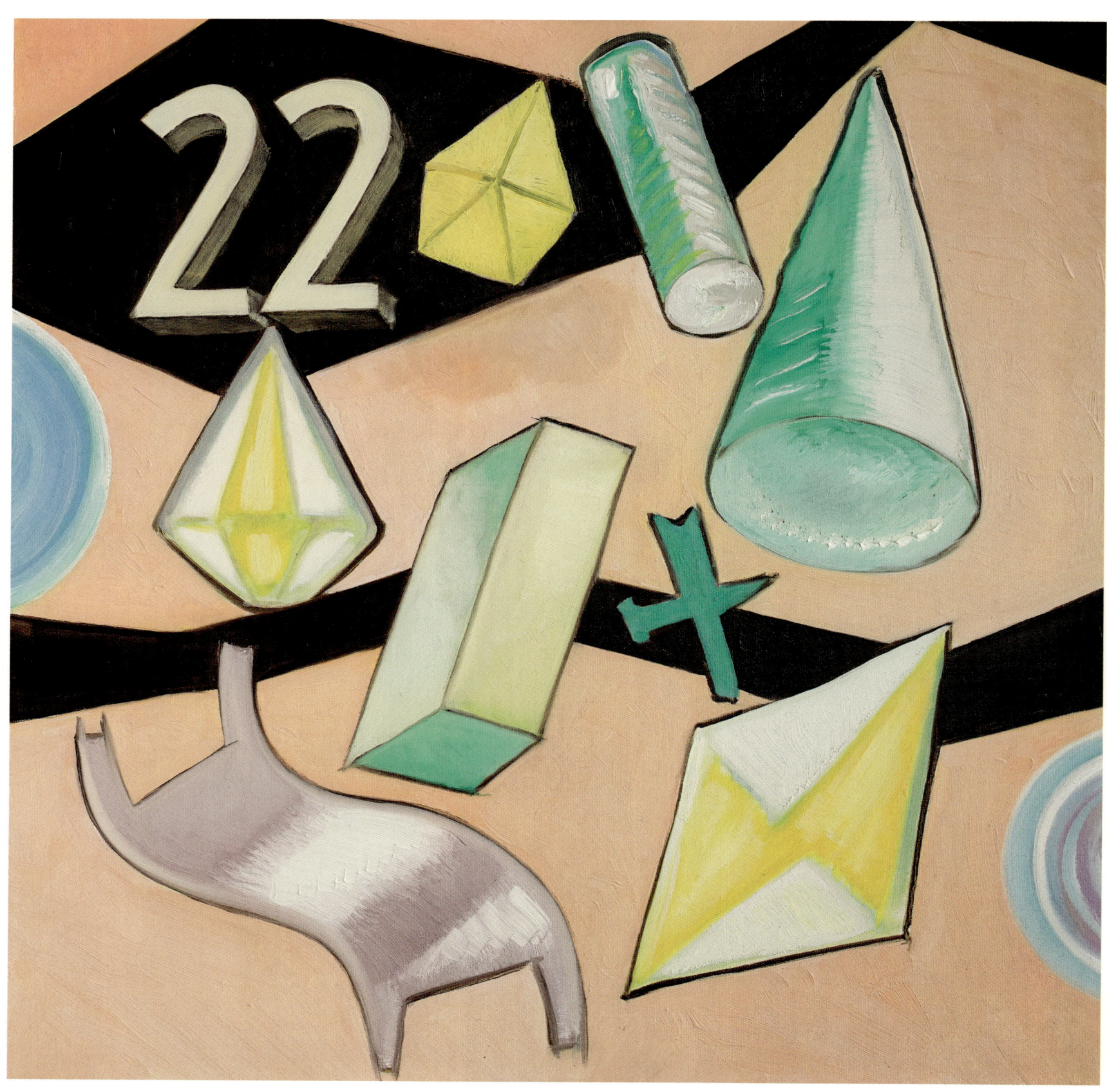

JUNE'S SHAPING
Oil on canvas
60 x 60 cm
(23$^{1/2}$ x 23$^{1/2}$ in)
16 June 2017

JUNE SHAPES II
Oil on canvas
100 x 80 cm
(39$^{1/2}$ x 31$^{1/2}$ in)
8 June 2017

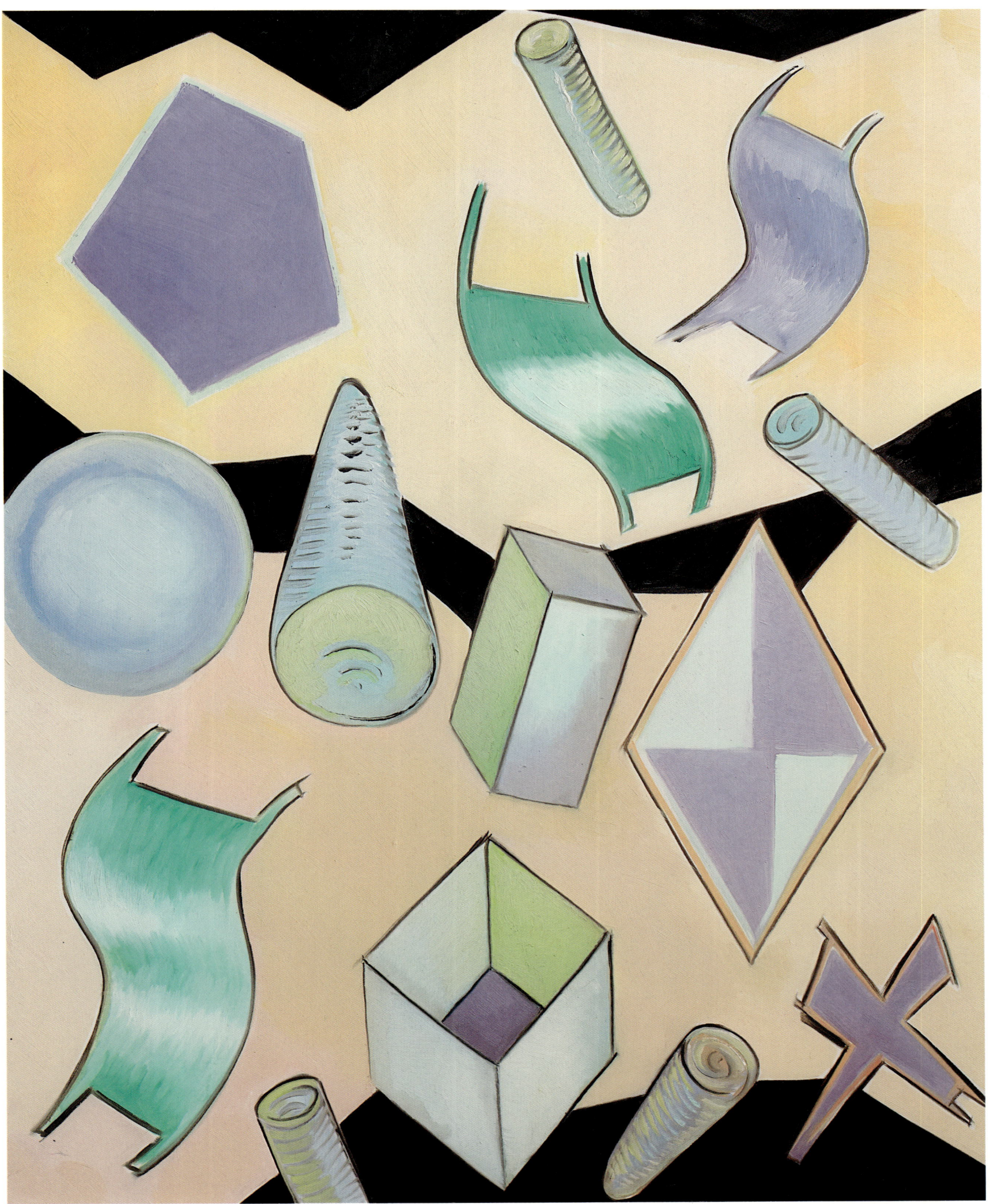

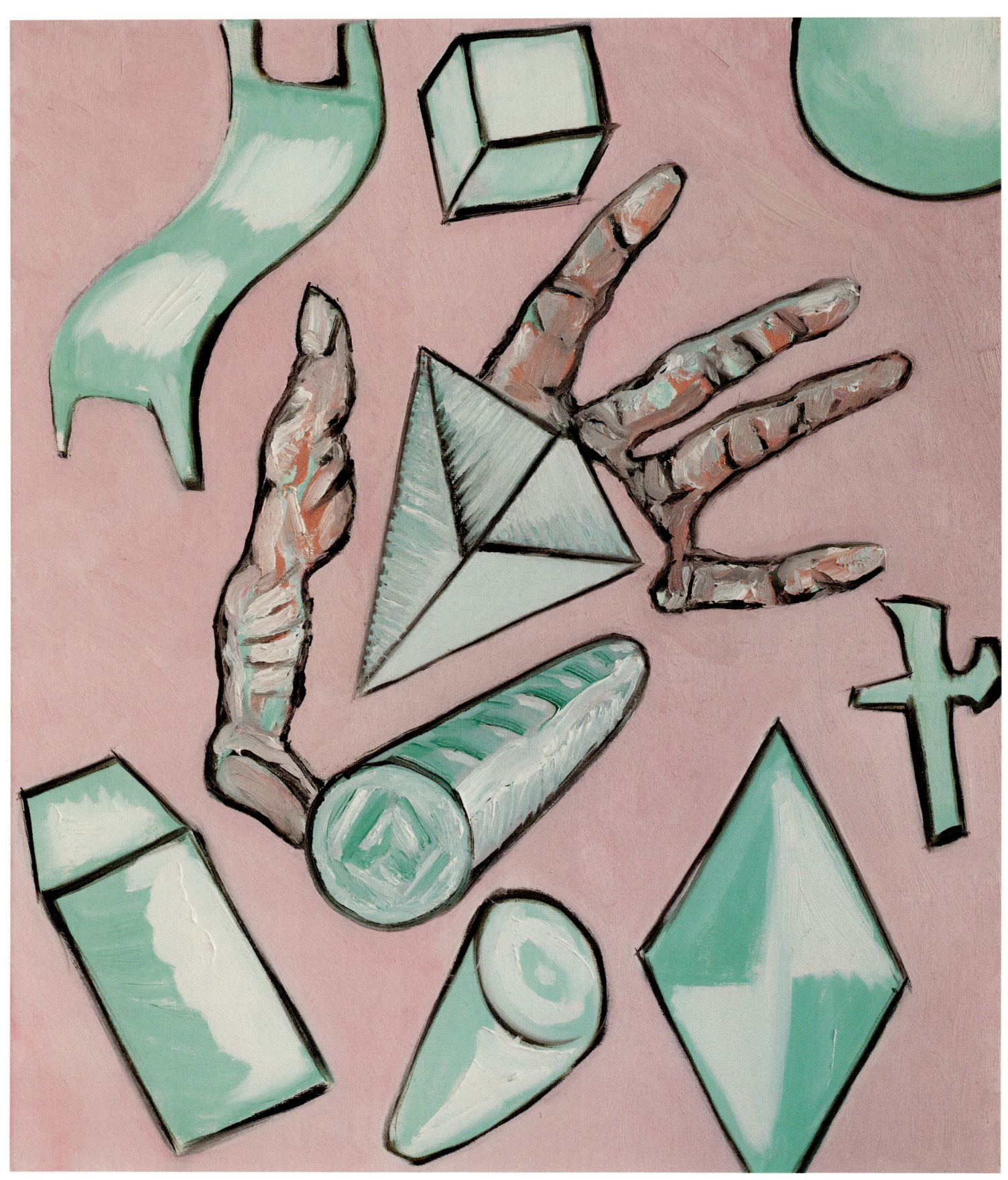

JUNE HAND SHAPES
Oil on canvas
60 x 50 cm
(23¹ᐟ² x 19³ᐟ⁴ in)
16 June 2017

HANDS AND SHAPES
Oil on canvas
100 x 100 cm
(39¹ᐟ² x 39¹ᐟ² in)
22 June 2017

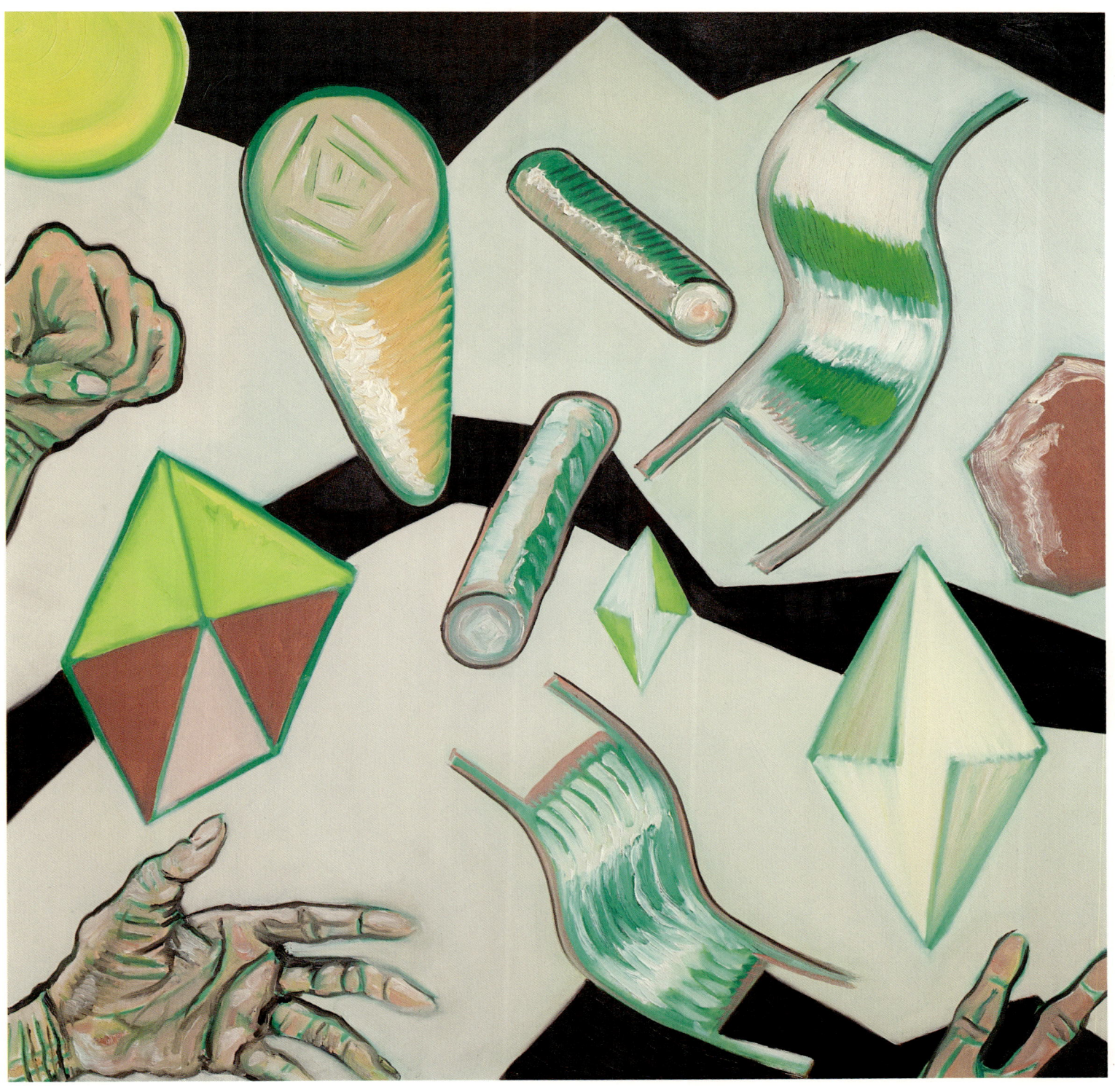

I love having someone sit so I can really paint their hands and their features and their veins and everything, but I haven't had much success getting people to pose. I heard that Lucien Freud would have people pose for weeks. Coincidentally, they were usually naked women. I think he had Kate Moss in there for a year.

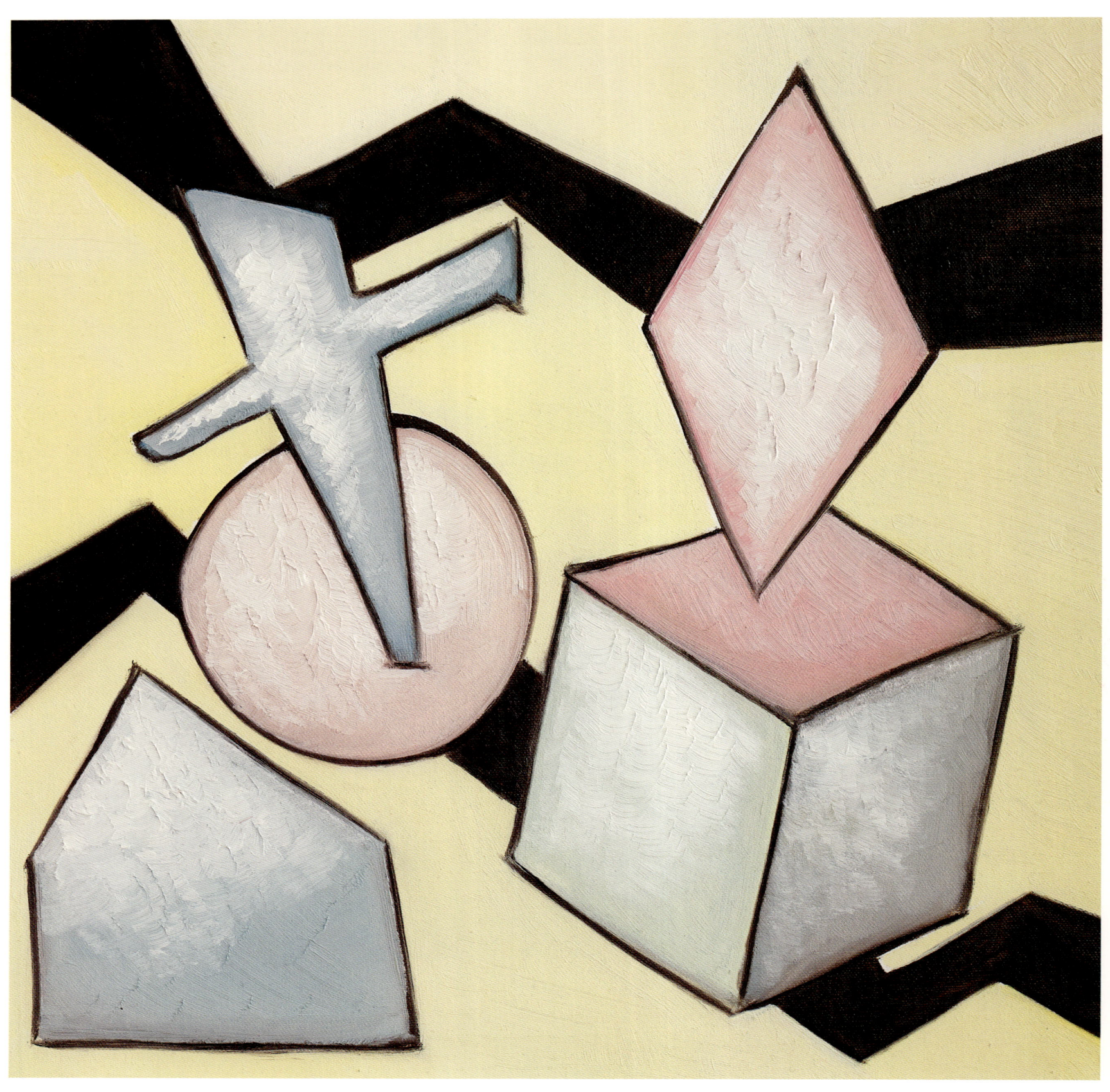

MAY JUNE SHAPES 11
Oil on canvas
40 x 40 cm
(15³/⁴ x 15³/⁴ in)
22 June 2017

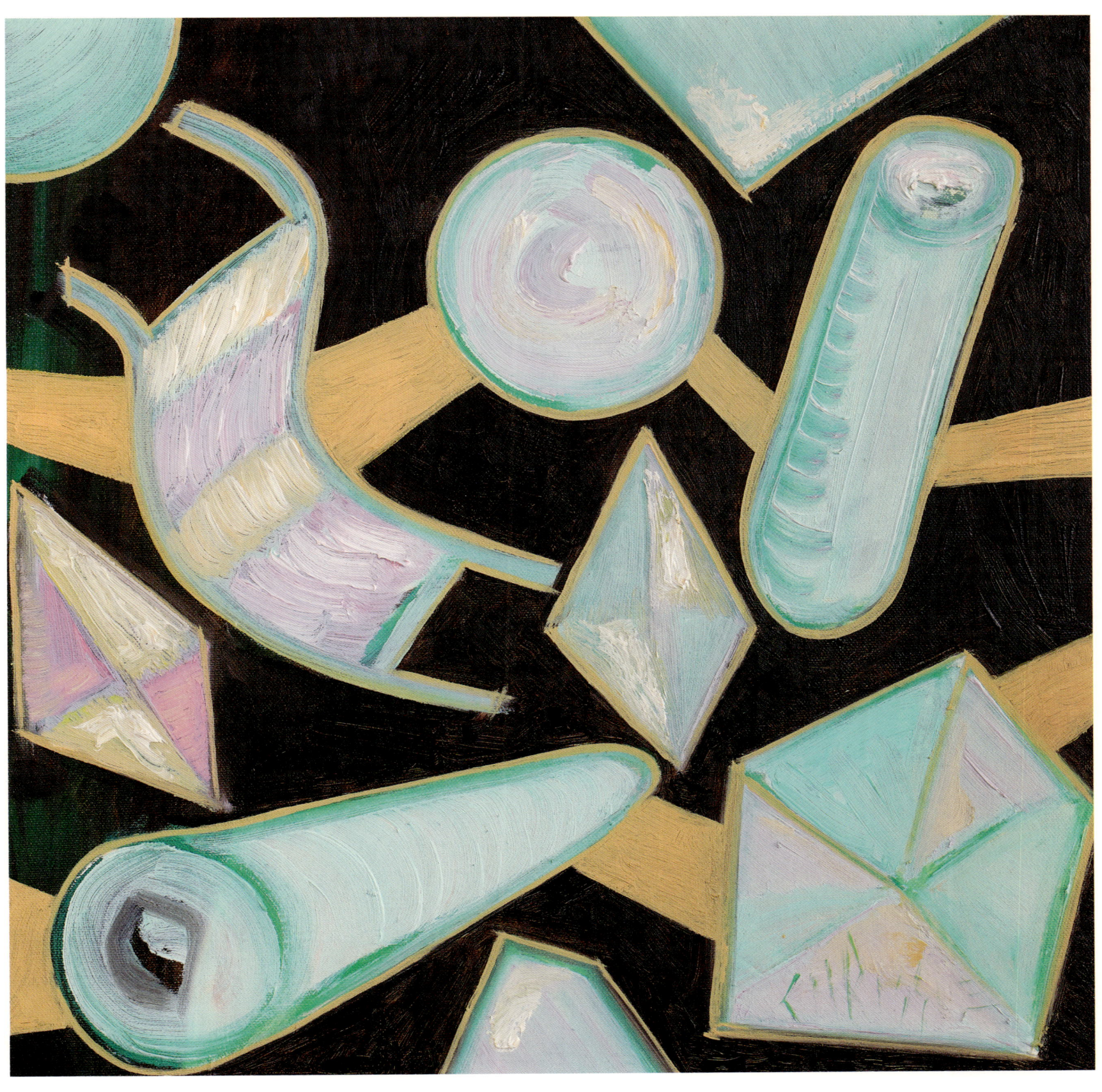

MAY JUNE
SHAPES NIGHT
Oil on canvas
40 x 40 cm
(15³⁄₄ x 15³⁄₄ in)
6 August 2017

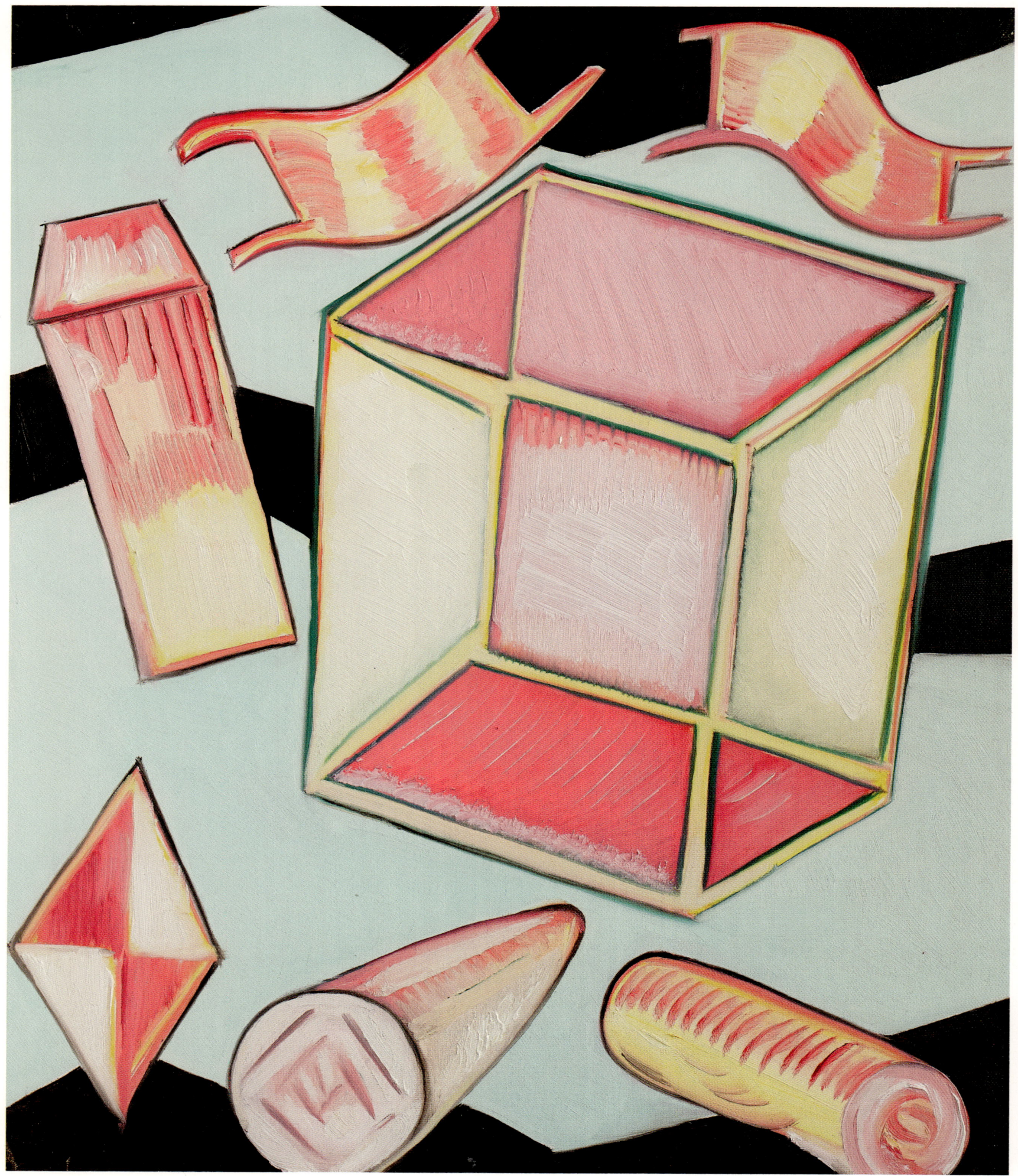

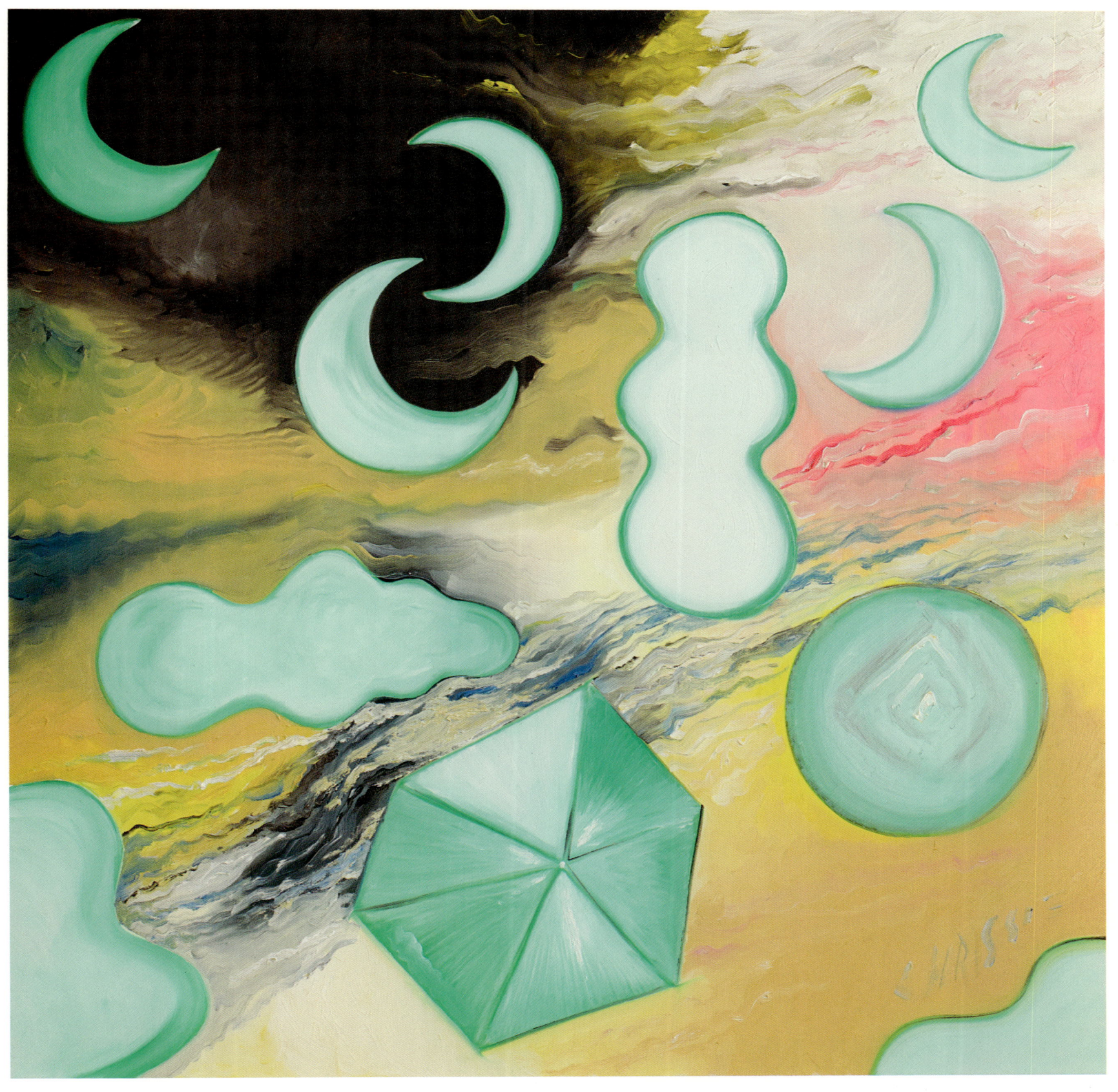

We'd just played a festival in Inverness, and there had been some storms surrounding that show, a lot of turbulence. This is what came out of it.

CANDY SHAPES
Oil on canvas
60 x 50 cm
(23$^{1/2}$ x 19$^{3/4}$ in)
22 June 2017

TURBULENCE
INVERNESS
Oil on canvas
100 x 100 cm
(39$^{1/2}$ x 39$^{1/2}$ in)
6 August 2017

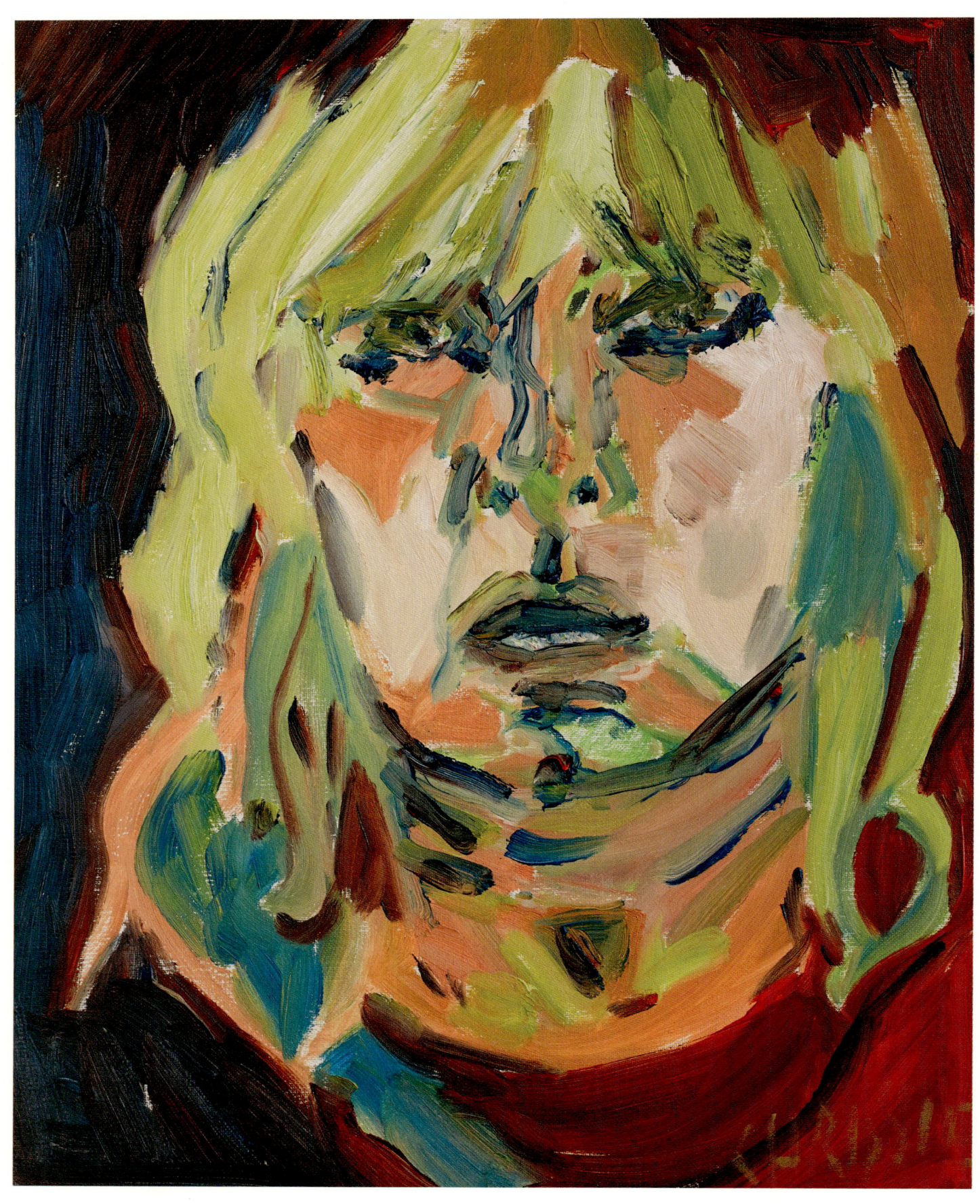

SÈTE SELF
Oil on canvas
50 x 40 cm
(19³/⁴ x 15³/⁴ in)
2 June 2016

TOUCHING CANVAS
Oil on canvas
80 x 60 cm
(31¹/² x 23¹/² in)
3 July 2016

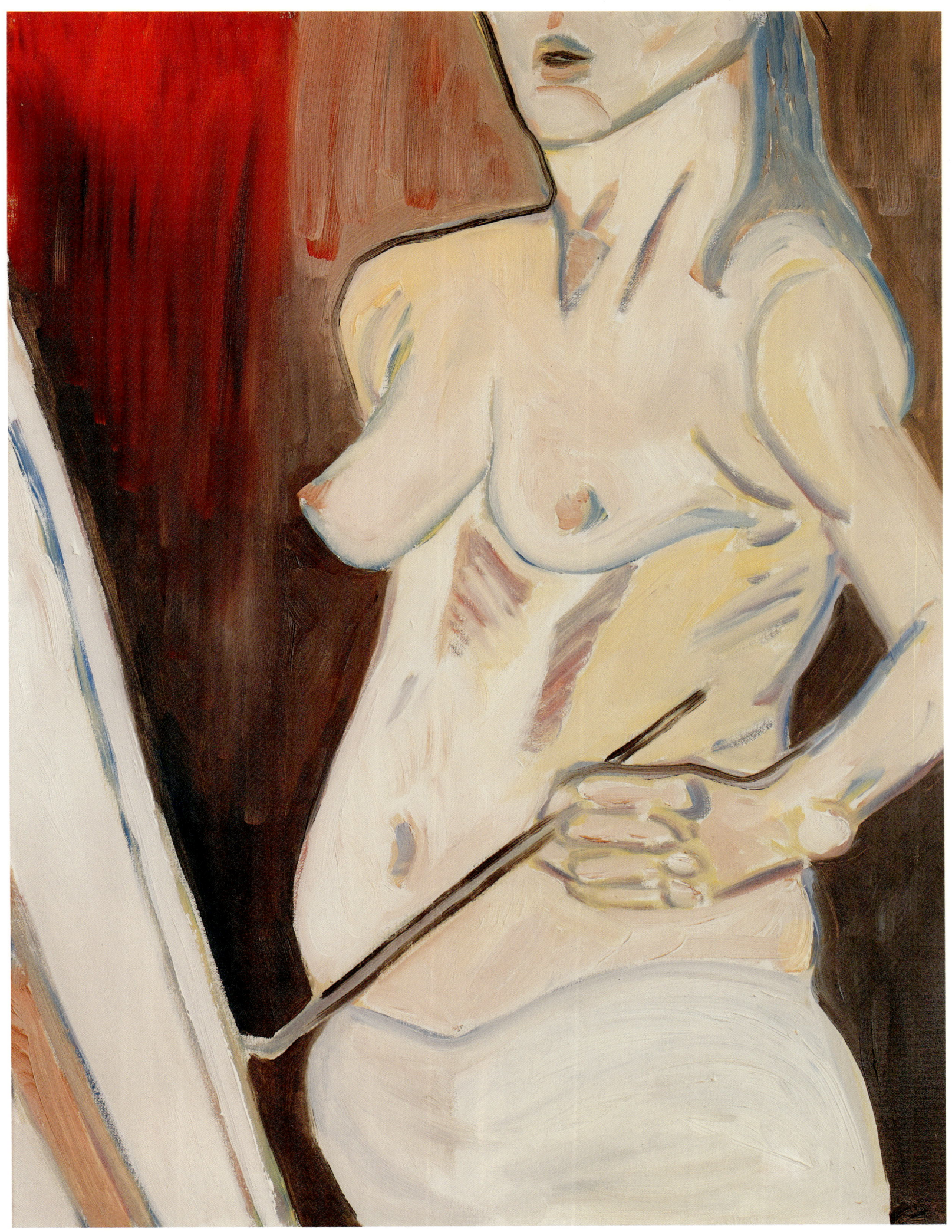

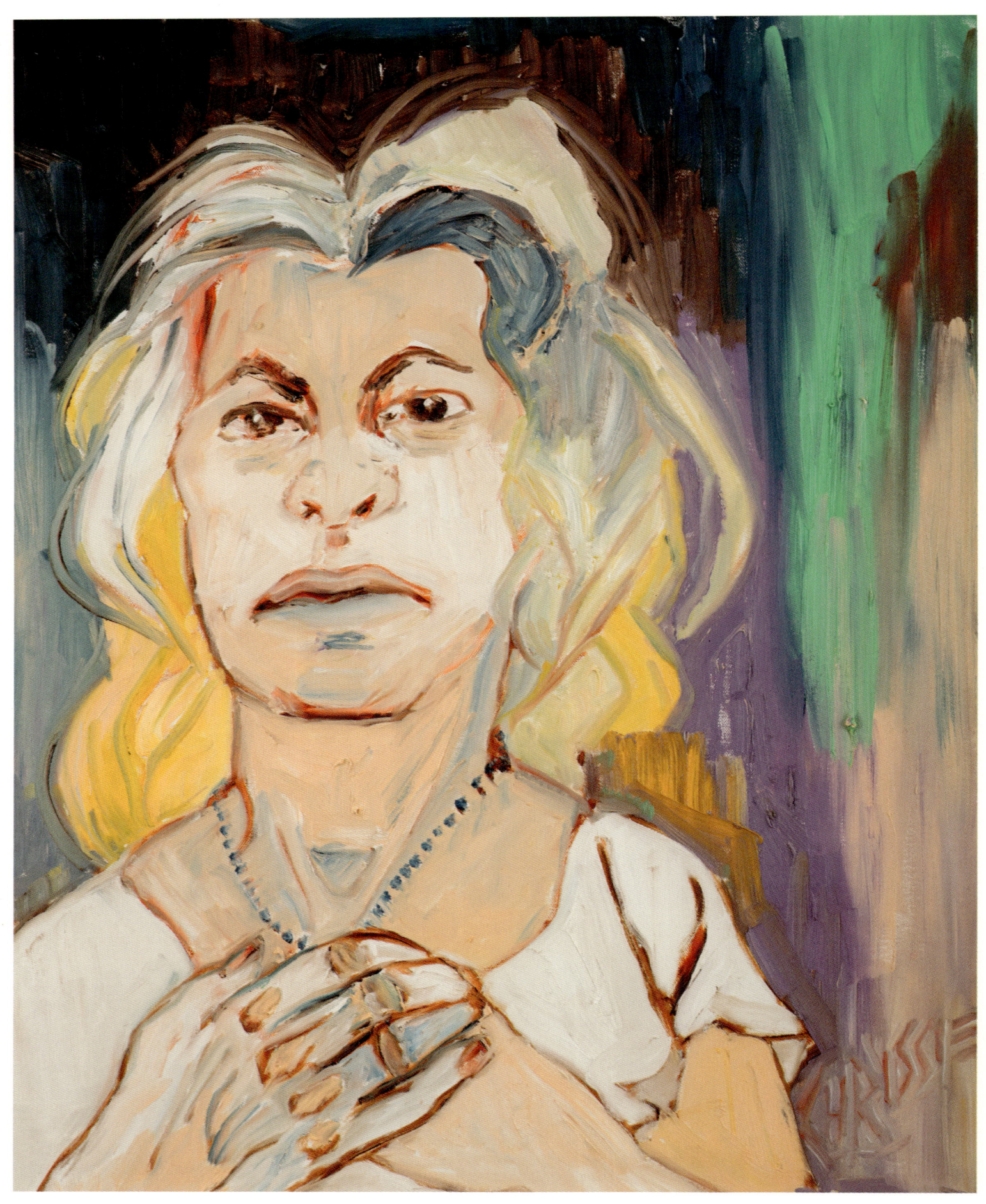

Sandra Bernhard sat for me in France. She's got an amazing face to paint.
I also painted her daughter, Cicely, but from memory.

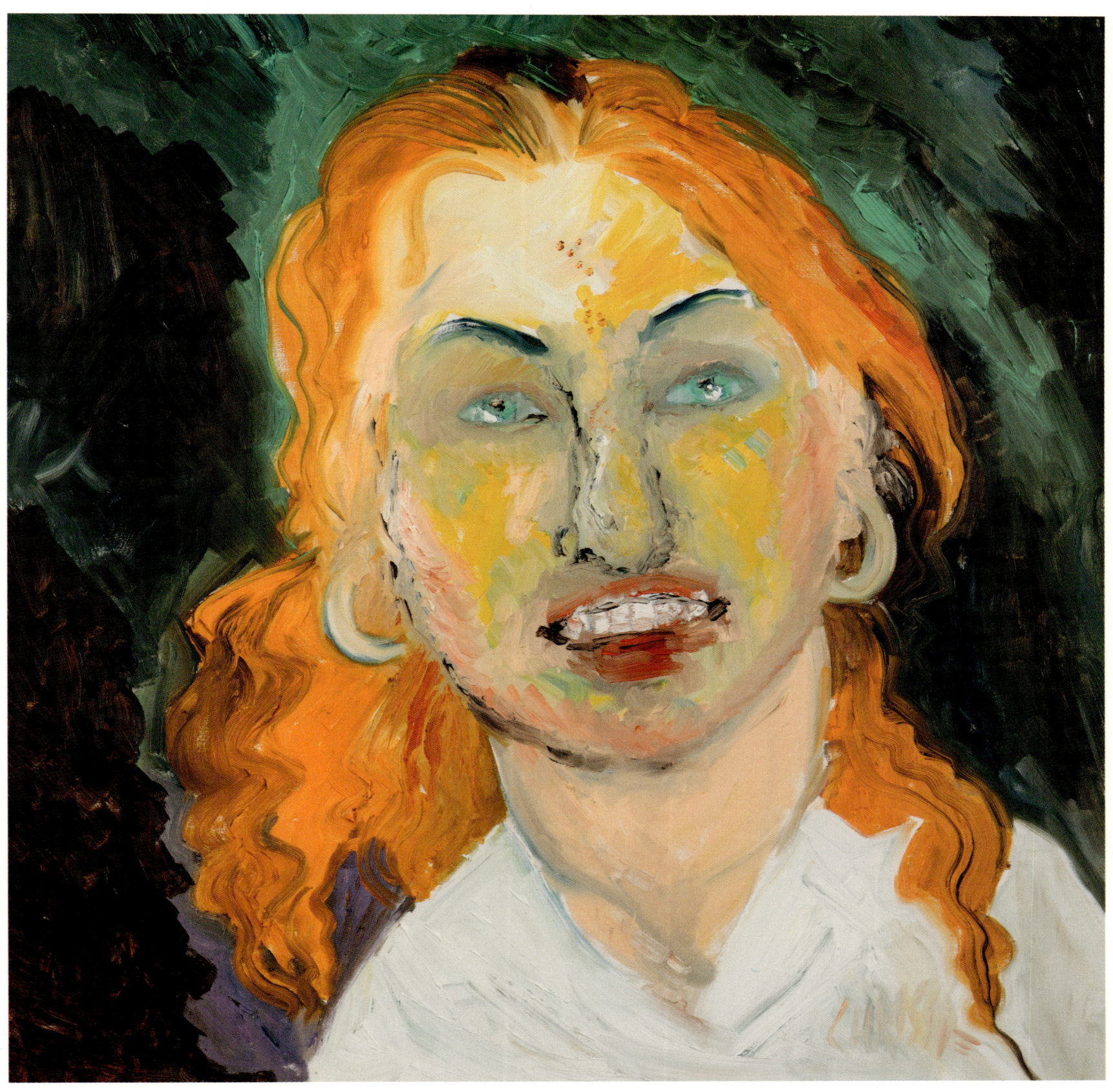

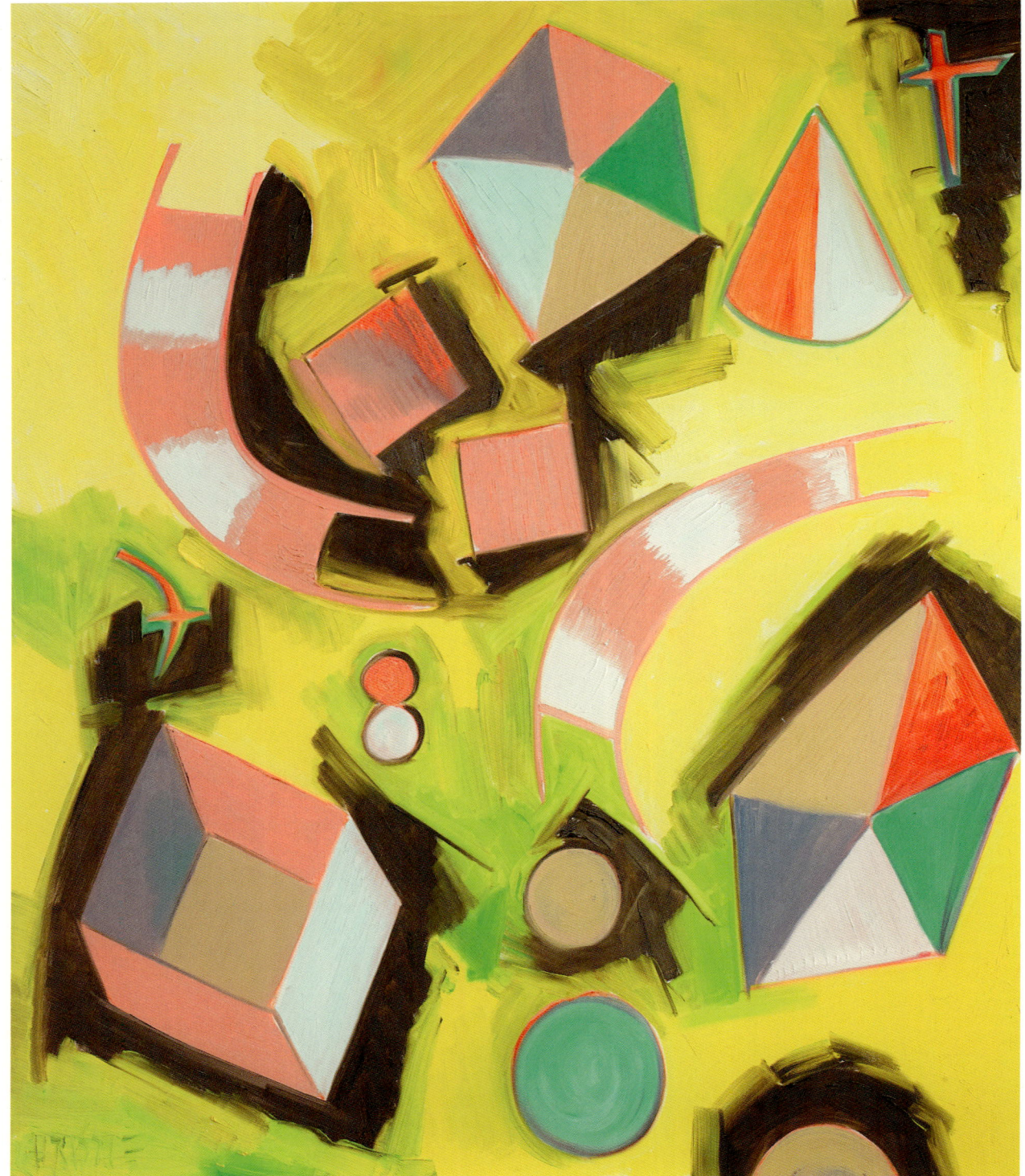

These were painted before and after a Floyd Mayweather fight. The turbulence was I suppose from the pre-fight build-up or maybe it was my own turbulence. As sports go, I like the stripped-down nature of boxing. It's a very difficult sport to talk about, and often hard to defend, because it can be brutal and people get hurt. It's very raw.

Some people think boxing is all about trying to hit someone, but it's equally about trying not to get hit. Yin and yang — it's called the sweet science. The training and knowledge, and dedication and sacrifice that goes into it commands respect, whether you like the game or not. Hearing the fighters recount every move of every round after a fight is awe-inspiring for me, knowing that any ordinary person would have been carried out on a stretcher within three minutes.

PRE-MAYWEATHER
TURBULENCE
Oil on canvas
120 x 100 cm
(47¹/⁴ x 39¹/² in)
26 August 2017

POST-MAYWEATHER
TURBULENCE
Oil on canvas
120 x 100 cm
(47¹/⁴ x 39¹/² in)
27 August 2017

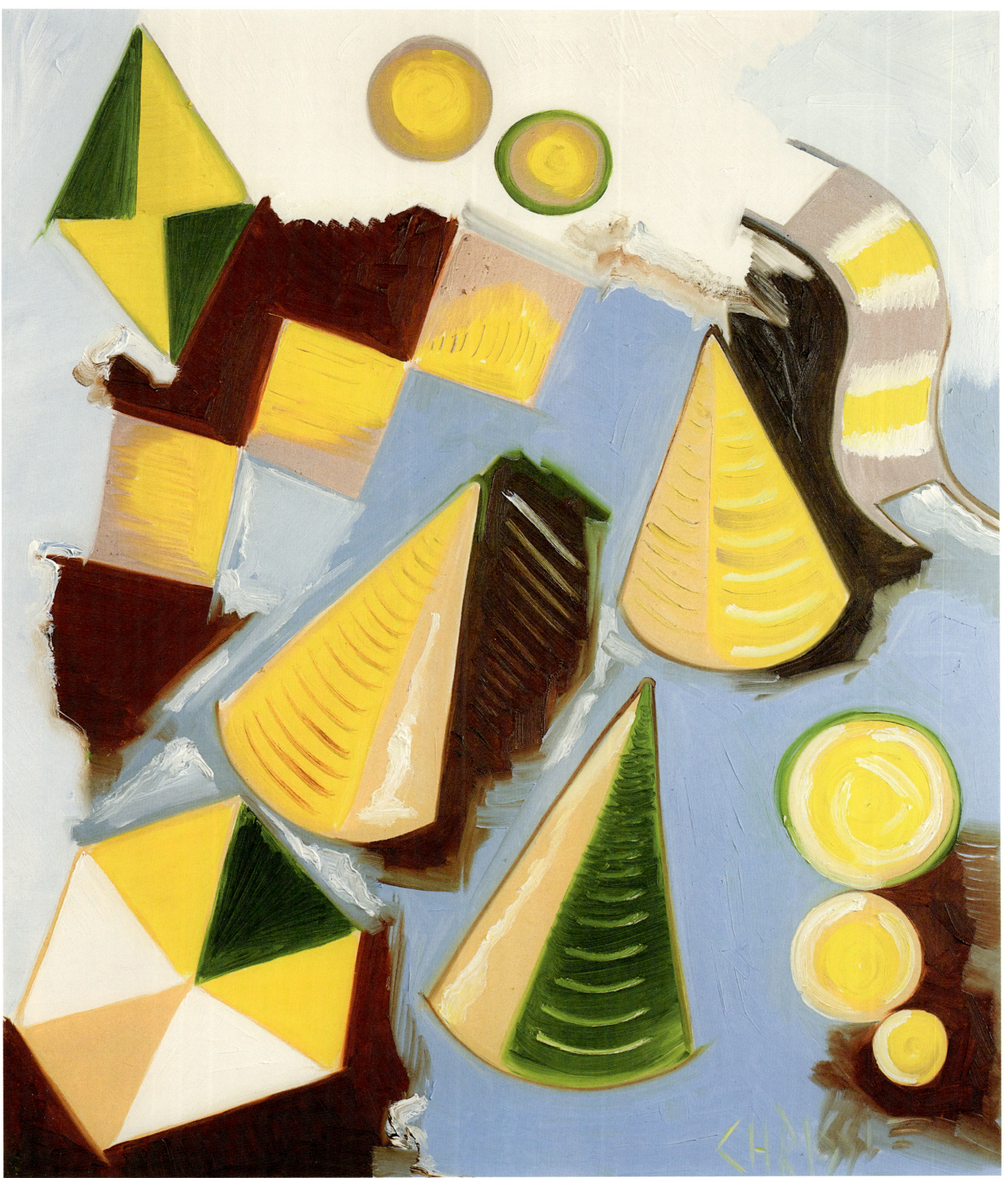

If I put as much energy into the guitar as I put into these paintings, I'd be a much better player. You have to put the hours in. That's what I say to guitar players when I'm teaching them the basics — my C.H. guide to rock 'n' roll guitar. If someone's frustrated, I say, 'Yeah, remember that Jeff Beck started exactly where you are right now.' I don't know if that makes an impression on them, but it works for me.

BLIND HANDS
Oil on canvas
80 x 60 cm
(31$^{1/2}$ x 23$^{1/2}$ in)
5 September 2016

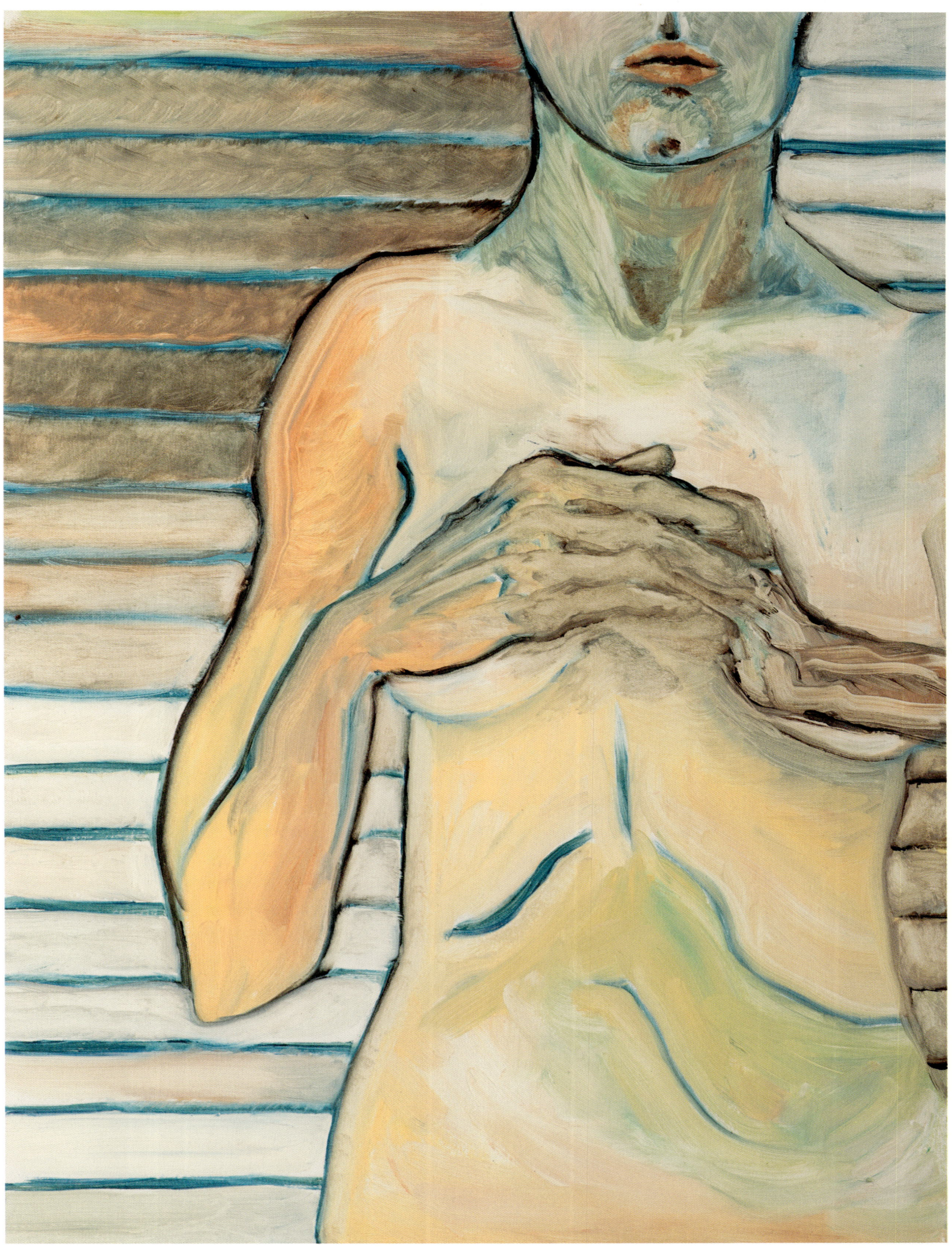

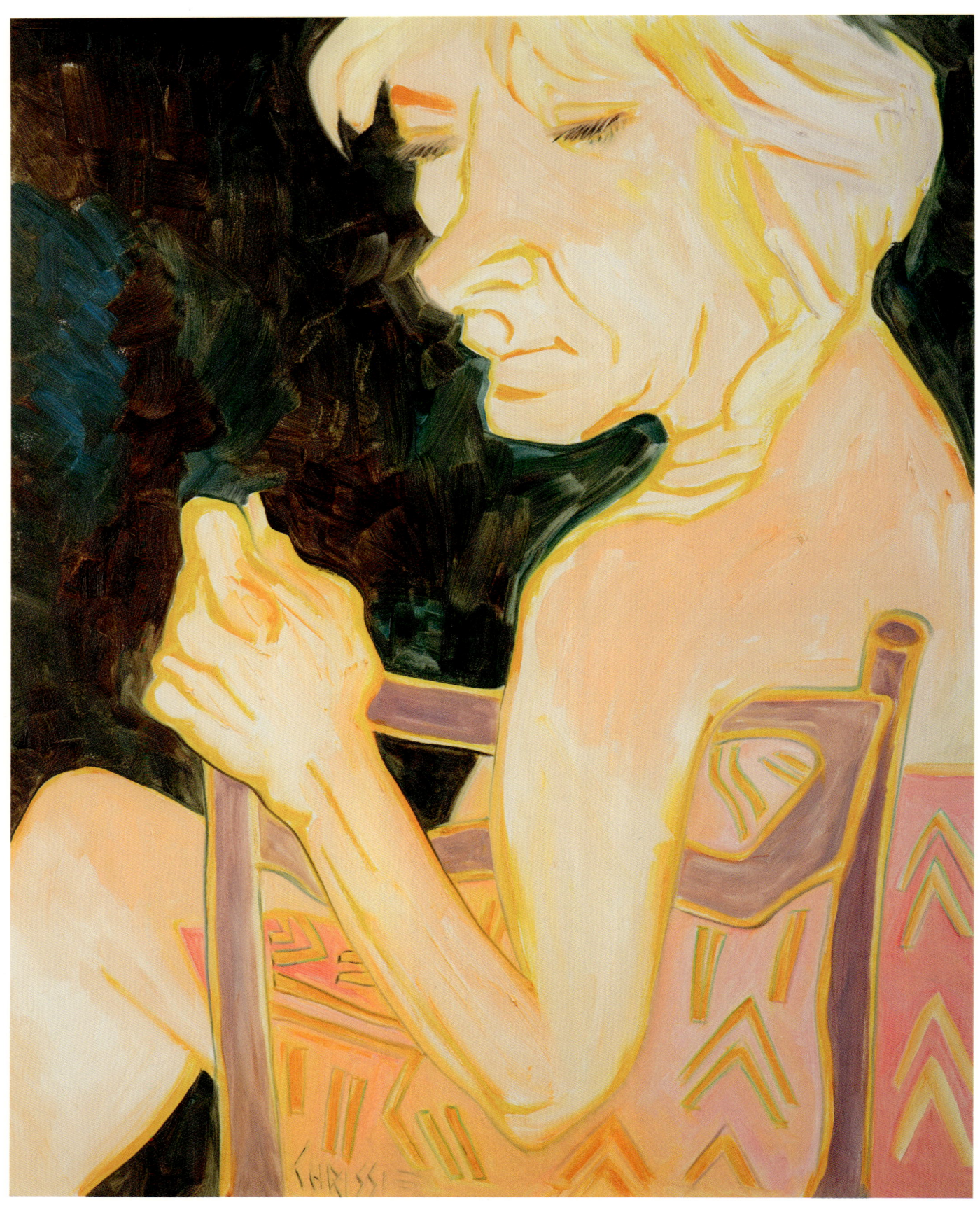

This is my friend Dianne Athey, also a painter, who came to see me in France.
We've been drawing each other since we were ten.

DIANNE SÈTE REPOSE
Oil on canvas
92 x 73 cm
(36¹⁄⁴ x 28³⁄⁴ in)
17 September 2017

DIANNE SÈTE
Oil on canvas
73 x 60 cm
(28³⁄⁴ x 23¹⁄² in)
17 September 2017

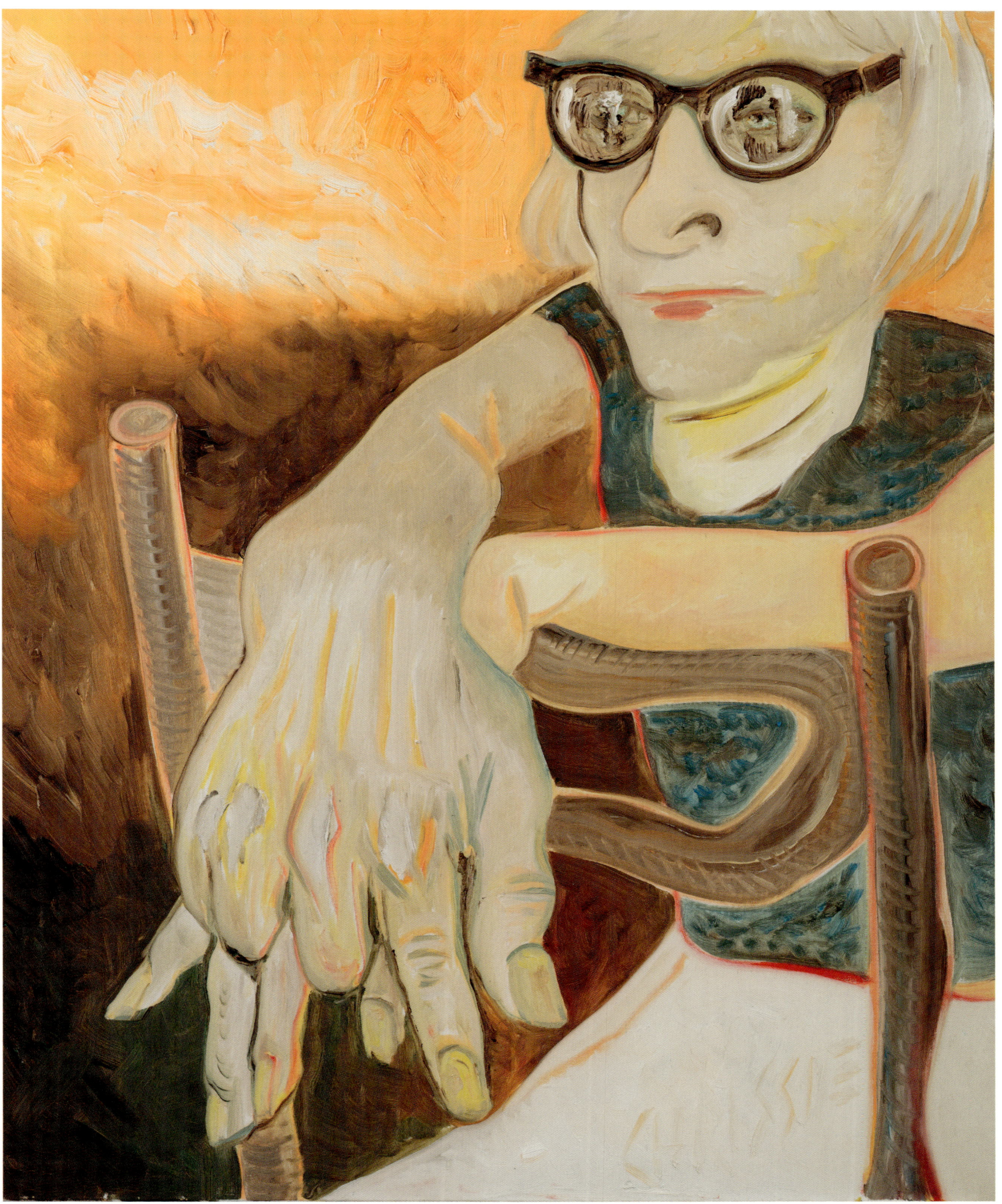

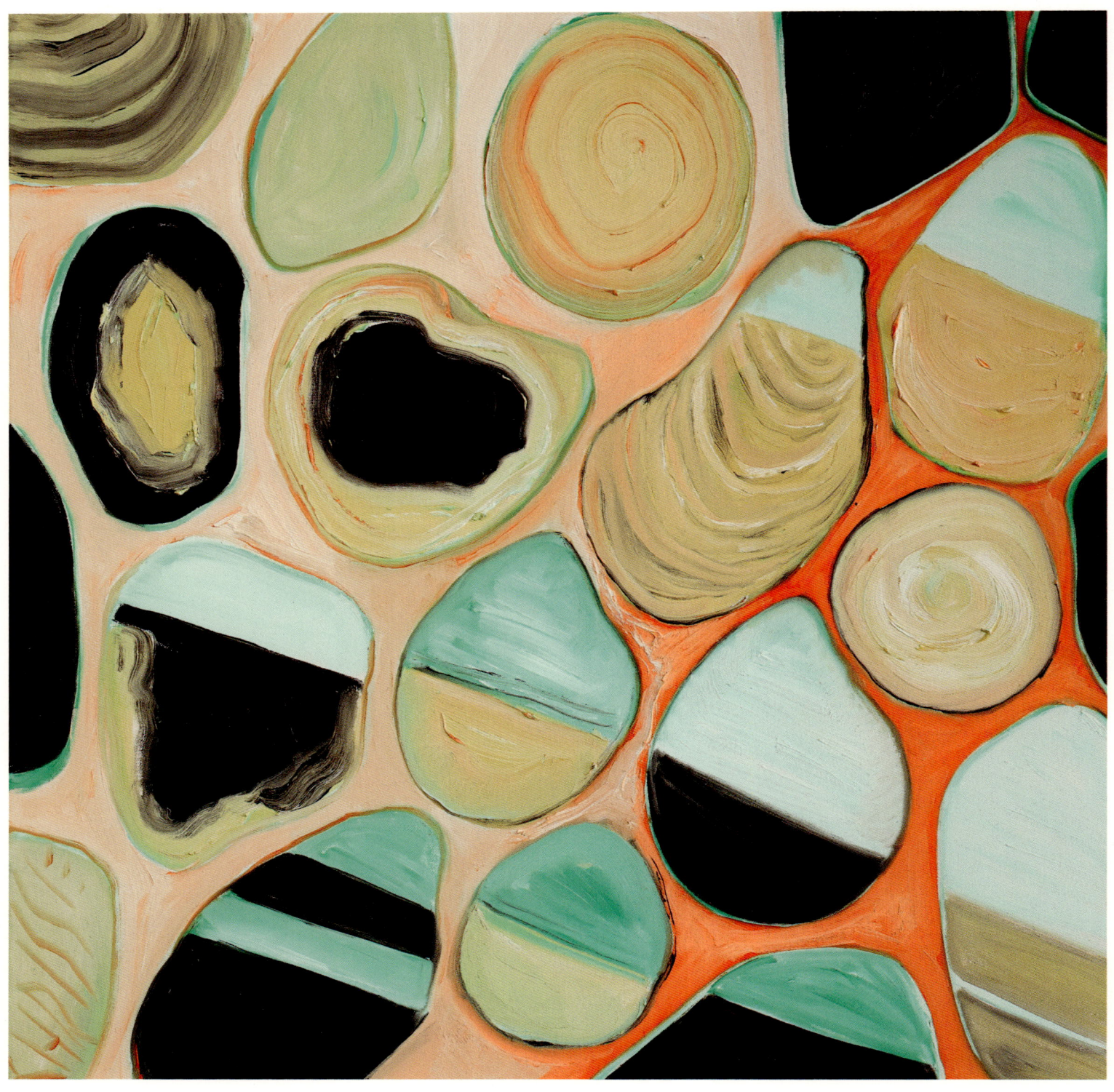

There can be a kind of snobbery about being defined by what you collect, watch or wear. I have a very hippie/punk mentality about stuff. Joseph Corré (son of Vivienne Westwood and Malcolm McLaren) got criticised for burning his collection of punk memorabilia. I cheered. That's punk.

FRIDAY ROCKS
Oil on canvas
60 x 60 cm
(23$^{1/2}$ x 23$^{1/2}$ in)
1 December 2017

NATALIE DECEMBER SUNDAY
Oil on canvas
90 x 70 cm
(35$^{1/2}$ x 27$^{1/2}$ in)
10 December 2017

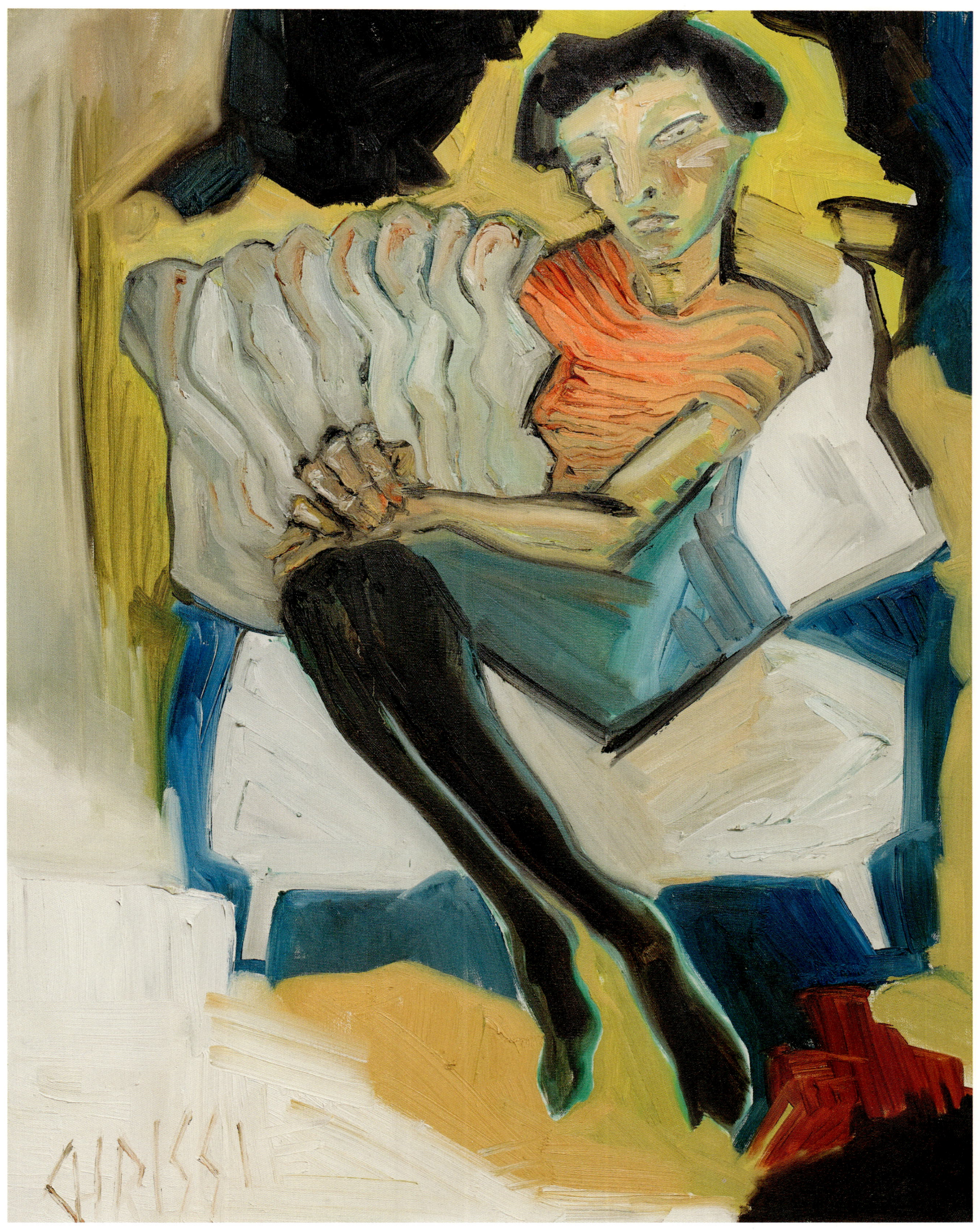

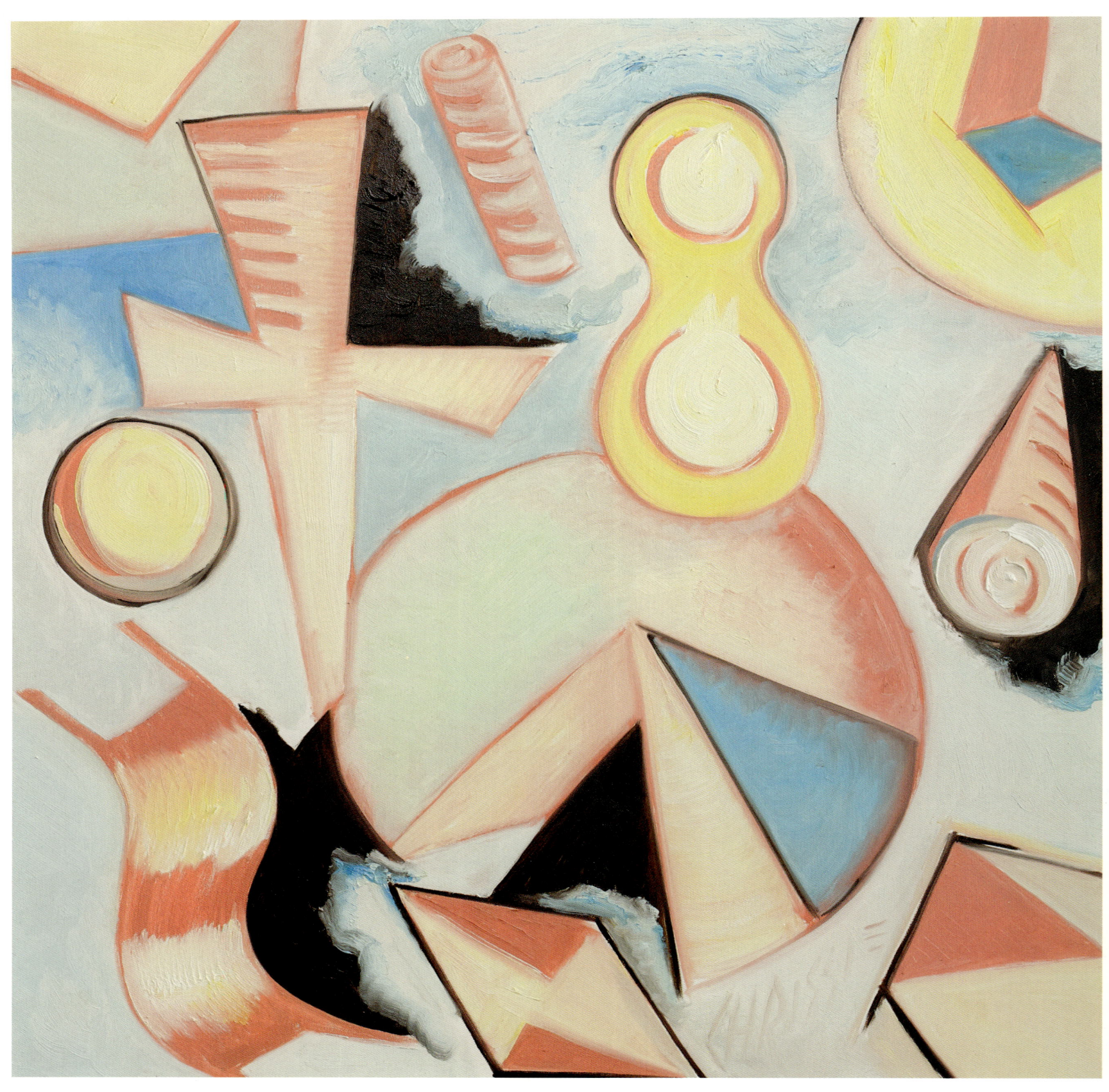

DECEMBER SUNDAY
SHOWERS
Oil on canvas
80 x 80 cm
(31¹ᐟ² x 31¹ᐟ² in)
10 December 2017

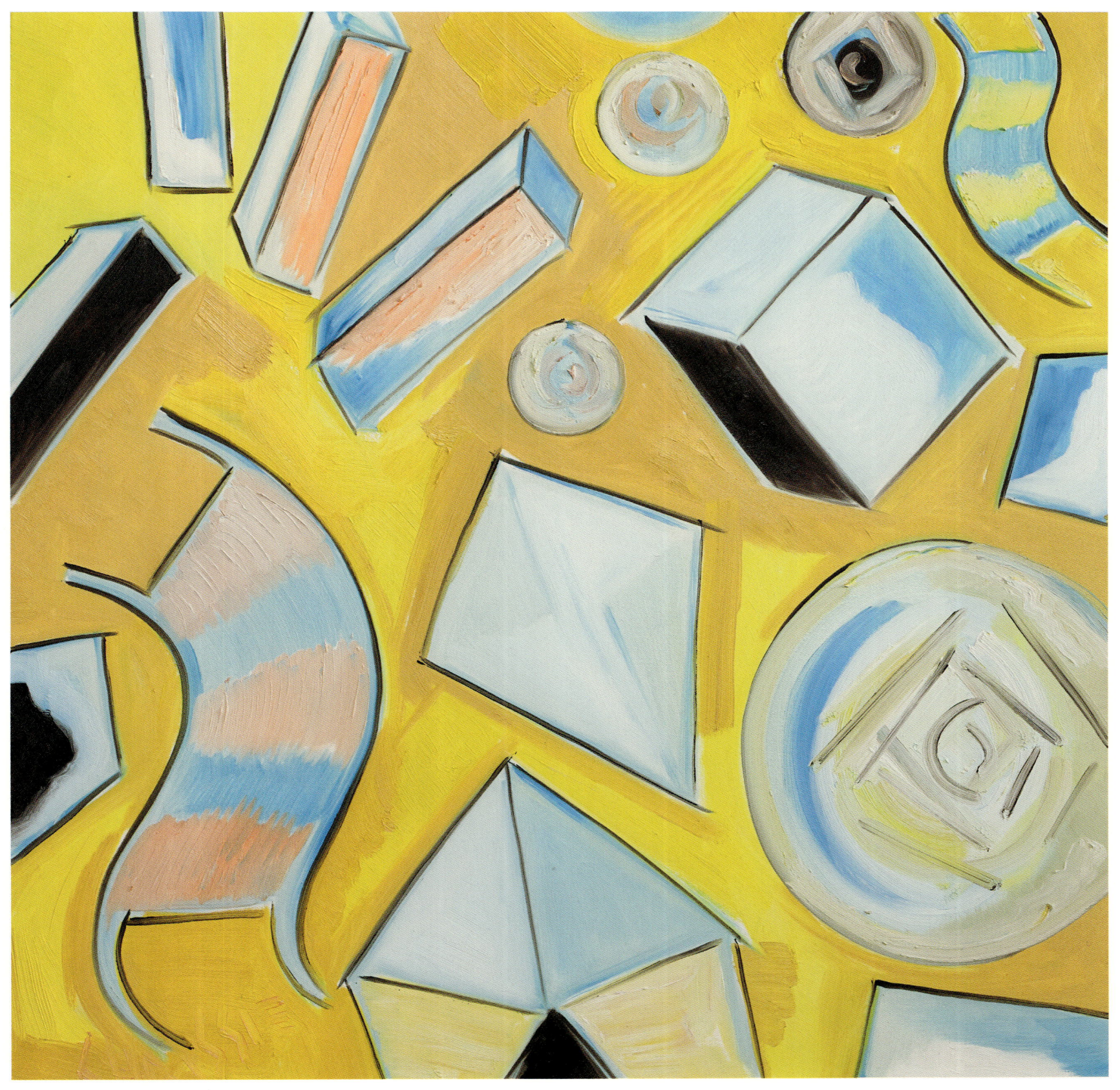

These are two of my favourites. They were done on the same day.

DECEMBER SUNDAY
SHAPES
Oil on canvas
80 x 80 cm
(31$^{1/2}$ x 31$^{1/2}$ in)
10 December 2017

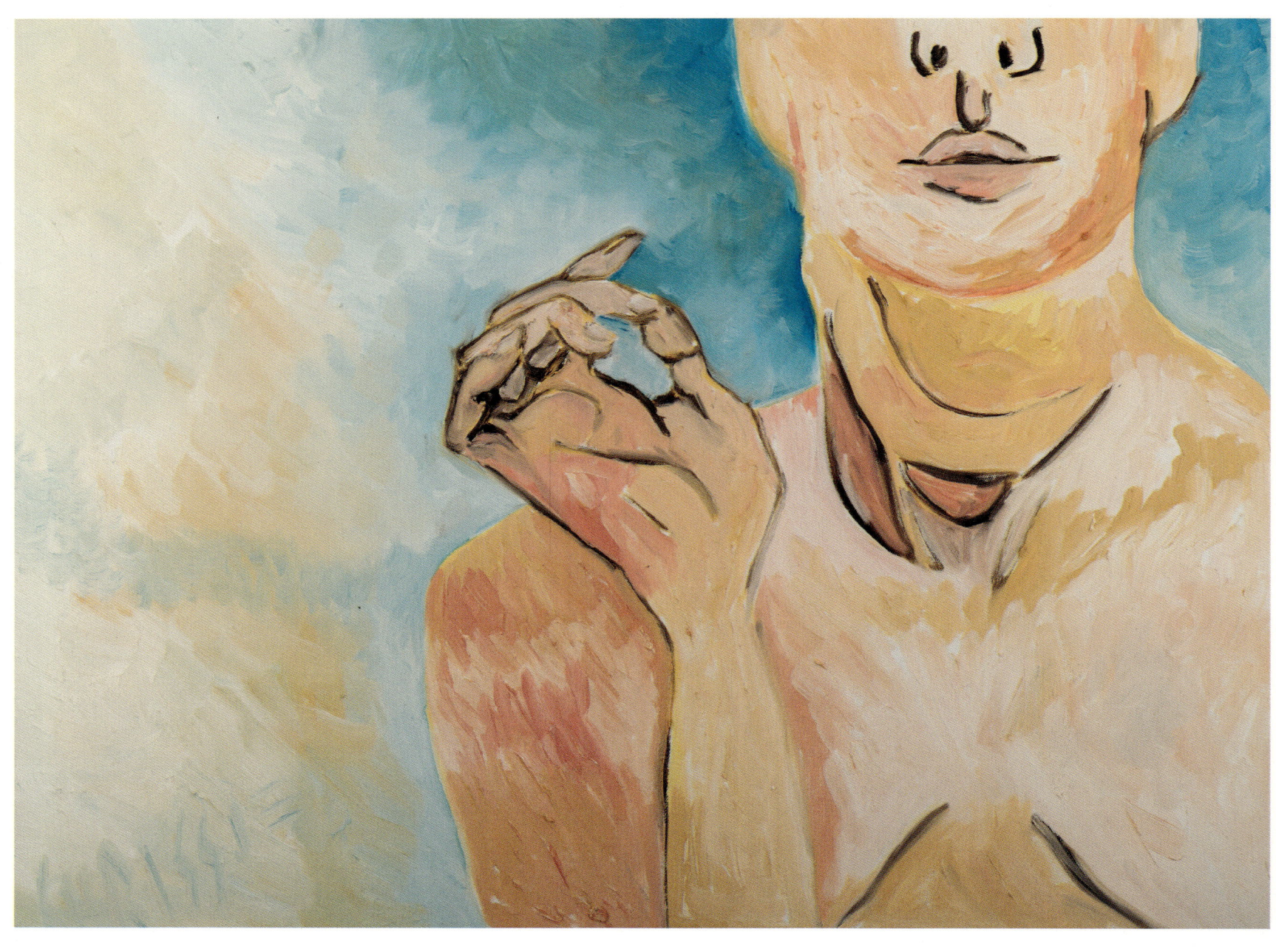

SELF OF THE PARTY
Oil on canvas
60 x 80 cm
(23¹ᐟ² x 31¹ᐟ² in)
1 January 2018

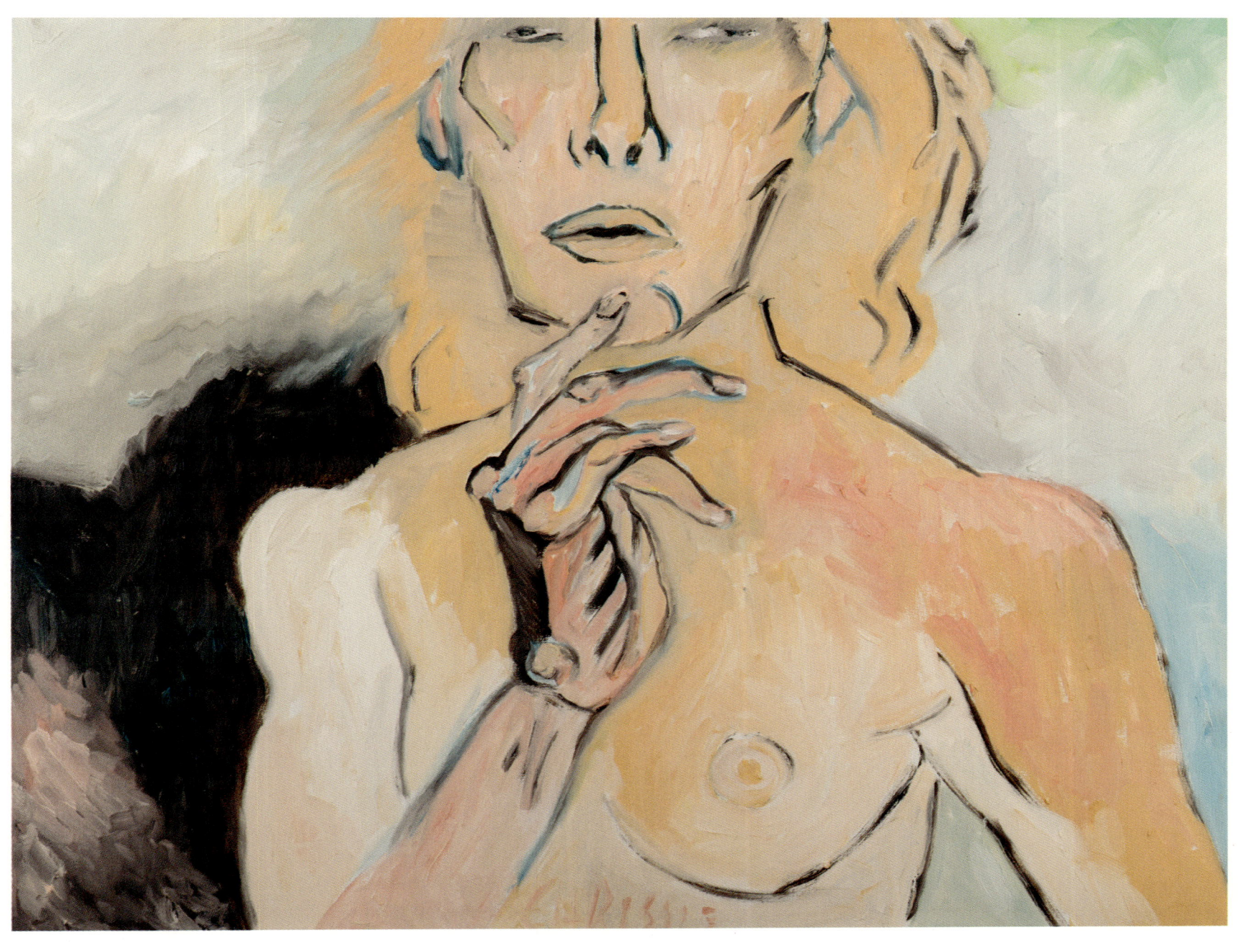

BLONDE FRIDAY
Oil on canvas
70 x 90 cm
(27¹/² x 35¹/² in)
5 January 2018

179

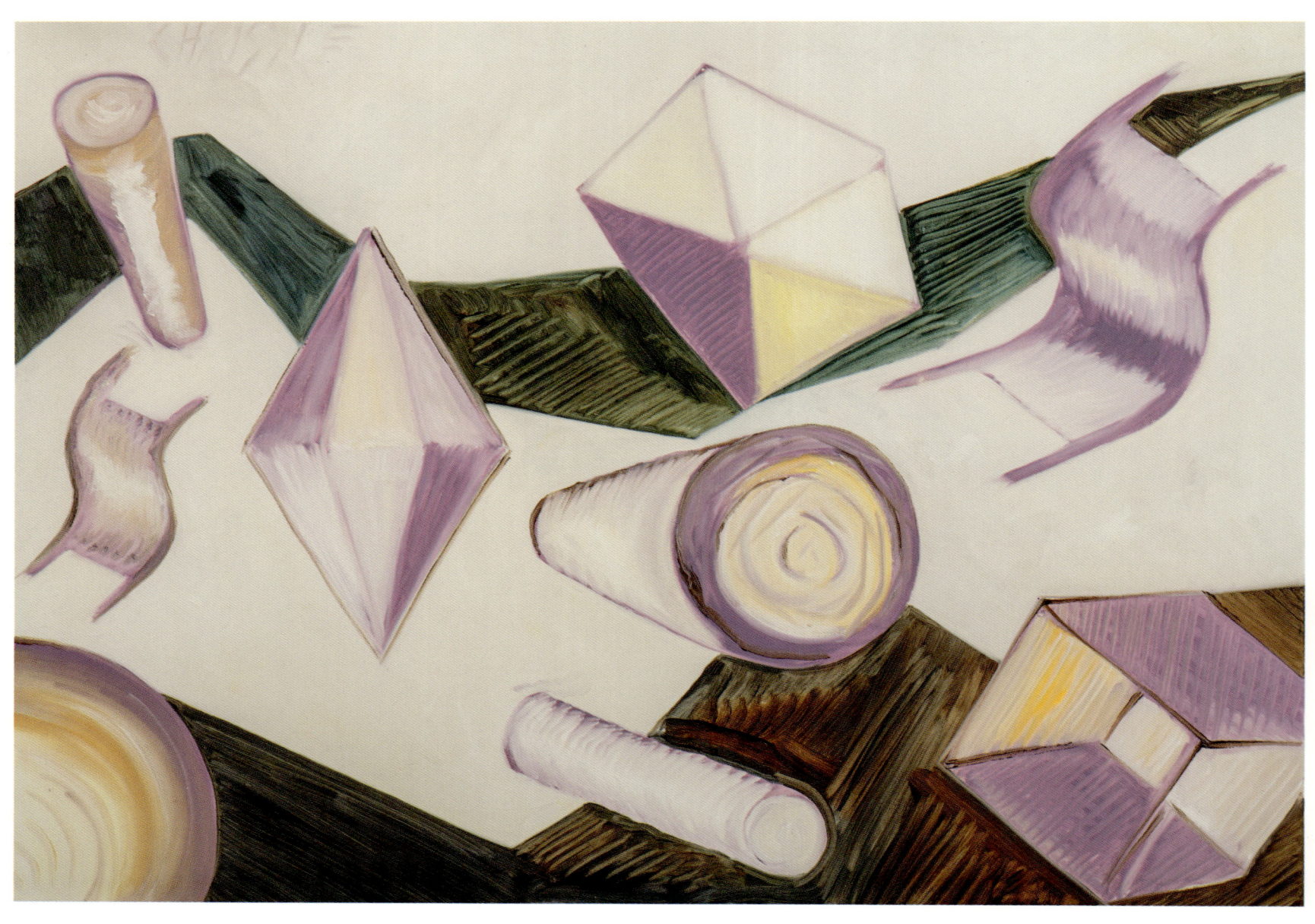

SÈTE SUMMER I
Oil on canvas
64 x 92 cm
(25¹/₄ x 36¹/₄ in)
14 January 2018

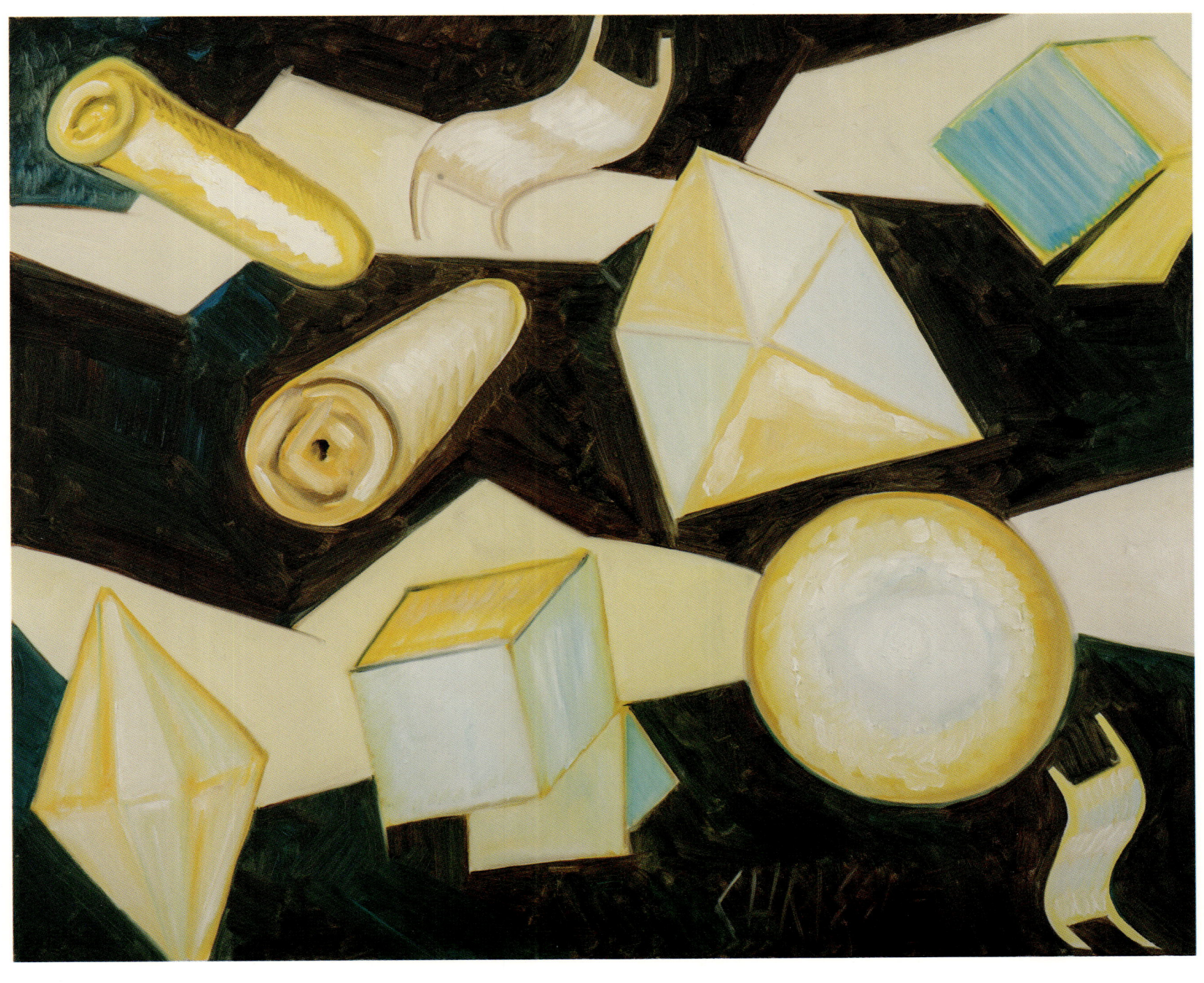

SÈTE SUMMER II
Oil on canvas
60 x 73 cm
(23¹⁄₂ x 28³⁄₄ in)
14 January 2018

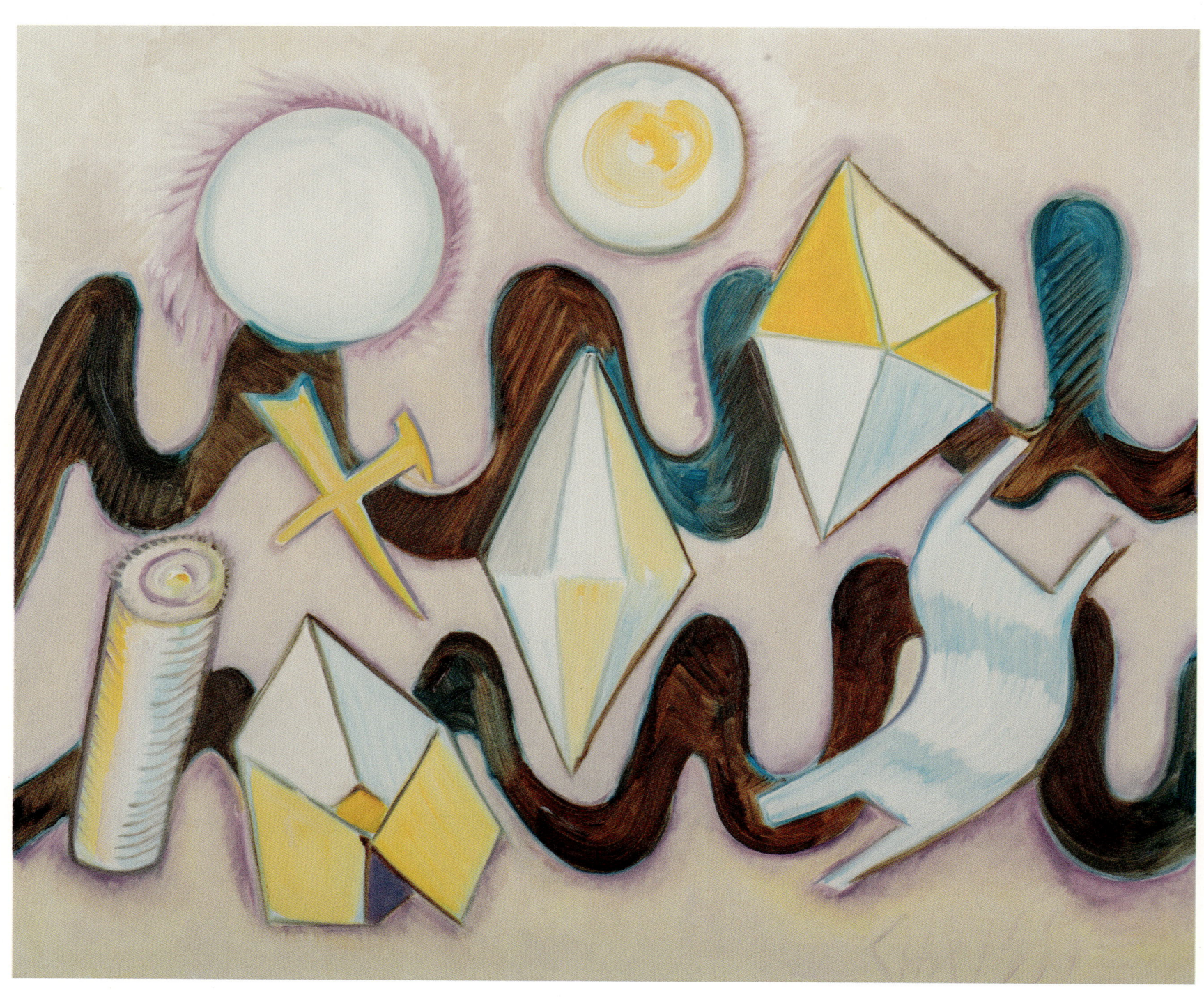

The other kind of painting I love is wall painting. I love having a brush and getting all around the light fittings and the sockets, and I don't tape anything off. You have to hold your breath, outline it all, then you fill it all in, and you stand back, and think, 'Ahhhh.'

I did one the other day. Twice, in a closet. I painted half of it this bright acid green, and the other half a psychedelic purple. When I woke up the next morning I belted down to have a look at it. I was so excited but got a horrible shock. I went over the whole thing with a muted cactus green.

I definitely missed my calling as a painter decorator because I take no prisoners and I won't stop. I went off on tour once and I was standing on tiptoe on a ladder to get in the last corner of a corridor. Someone shouted, 'The cab's waiting!' When I got back some builders had come in to repair something and repainted the whole wall. I risked my life to get up to that corner!

SÈTE SUMMER III
Oil on canvas
50 x 60 cm
(19³⁄⁴ x 23¹⁄² in)
14 January 2018

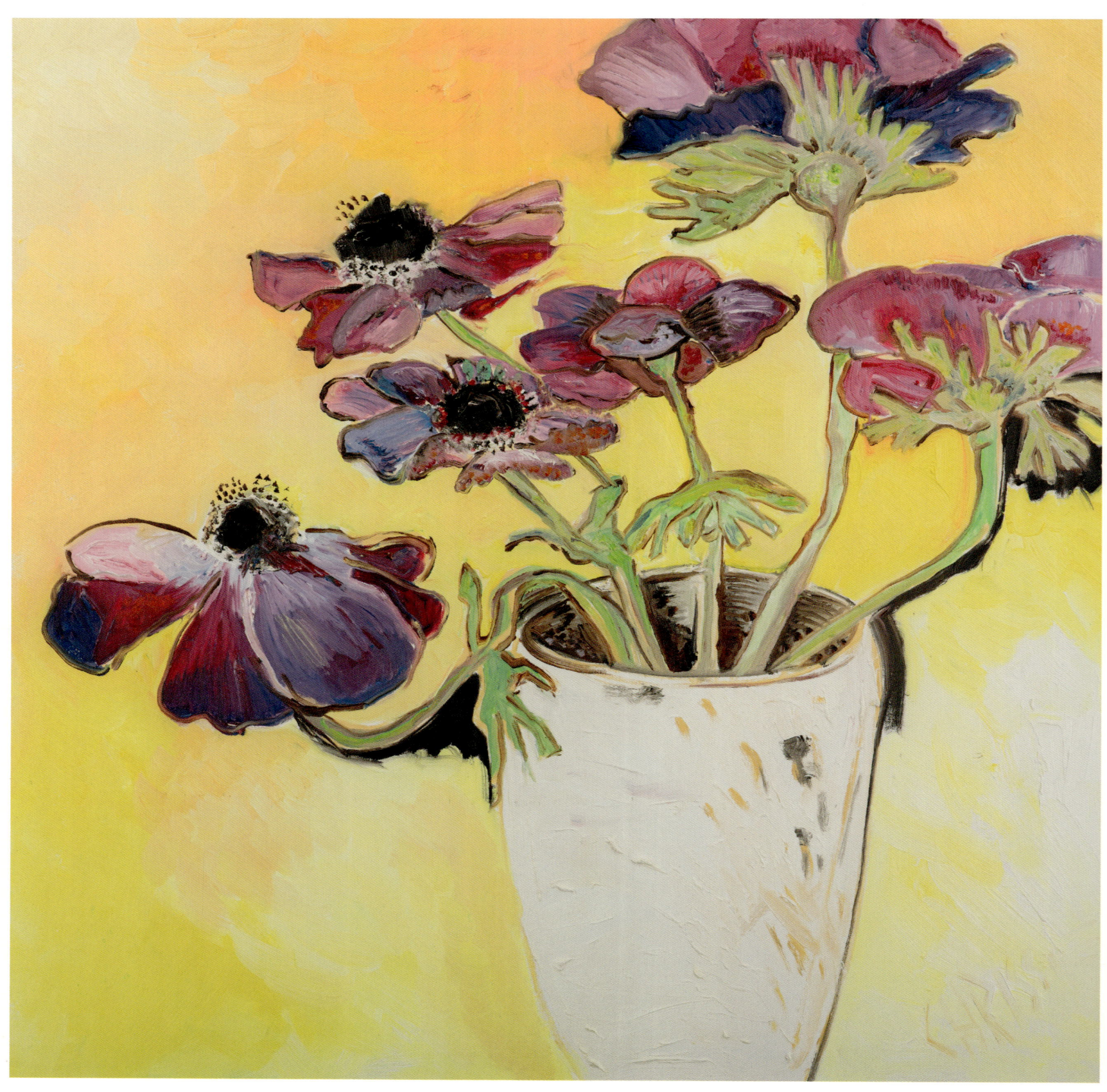

I've been told that in Chinese the words for 'opportunity' and 'crisis' are the same. Whether that's the case or not, when there's a crisis I always look for the opportunity. When my kids left home it created an emotional crisis, but it was an opportunity for me to go on the road and to paint.

Astrologically, in terms of the Saturn return, every 28 years there's a period of four or five years in your life when your clock goes back to zero and you rethink everything. The second return is in your late fifties. It's a huge transition, and even if you don't realise that it's happening at the time, a person feels very unsettled. It's only looking back that you recognise a transition.

I really got into painting after my second Saturn return.

IAN FLOWERS APRIL
Oil on canvas
80 x 80 cm
(31$^{1/2}$ x 31$^{1/2}$ in)
7 April 2018

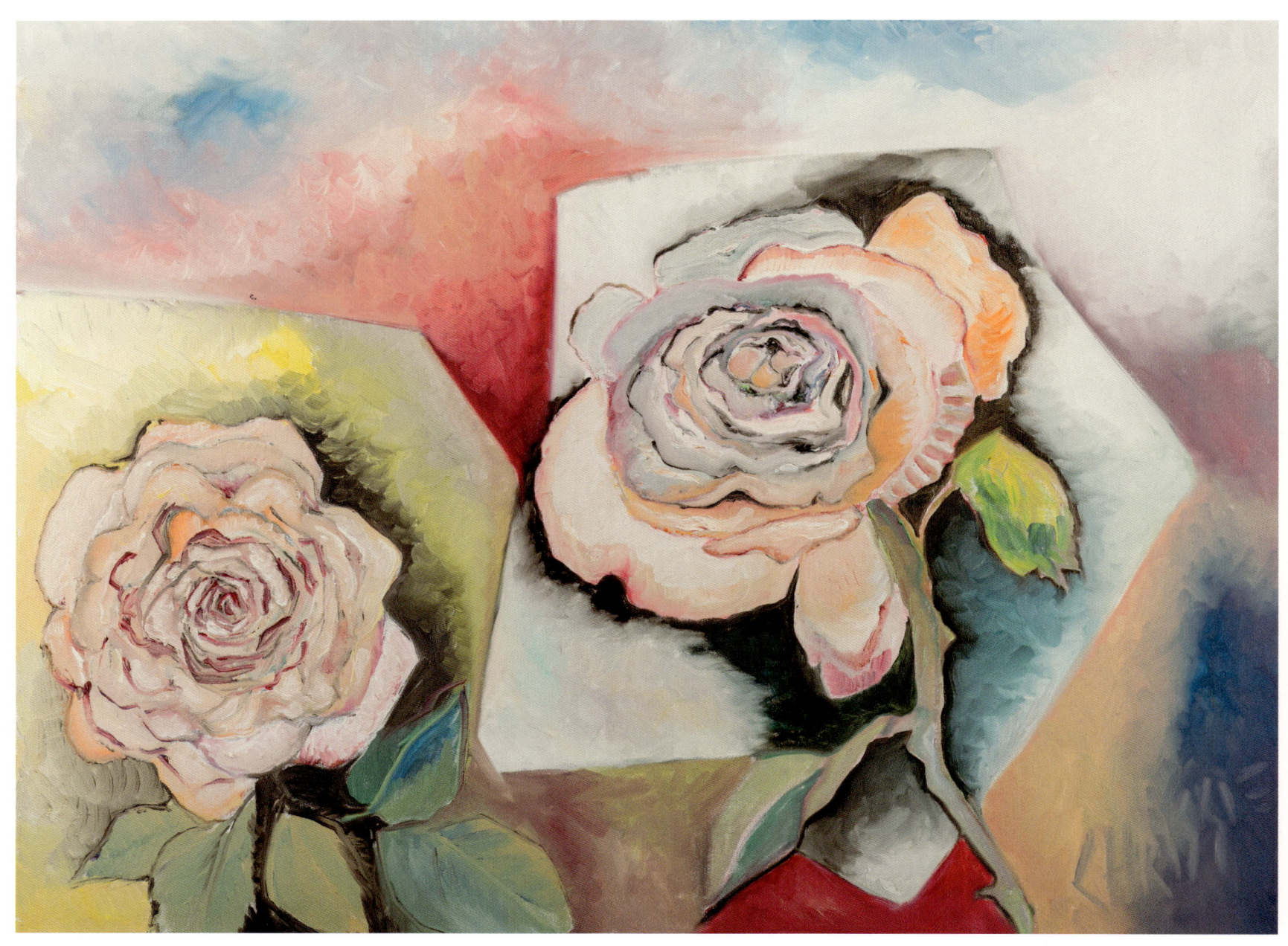

*While I was painting this, I got an unexpected email from Morrissey. I don't
know if he likes painting or my paintings, but I know he likes flowers.*

MORRISSEY FLOWERS
Oil on canvas
76 x 100 cm
(30 x 39¹ᐟ² in)
9 April 2018

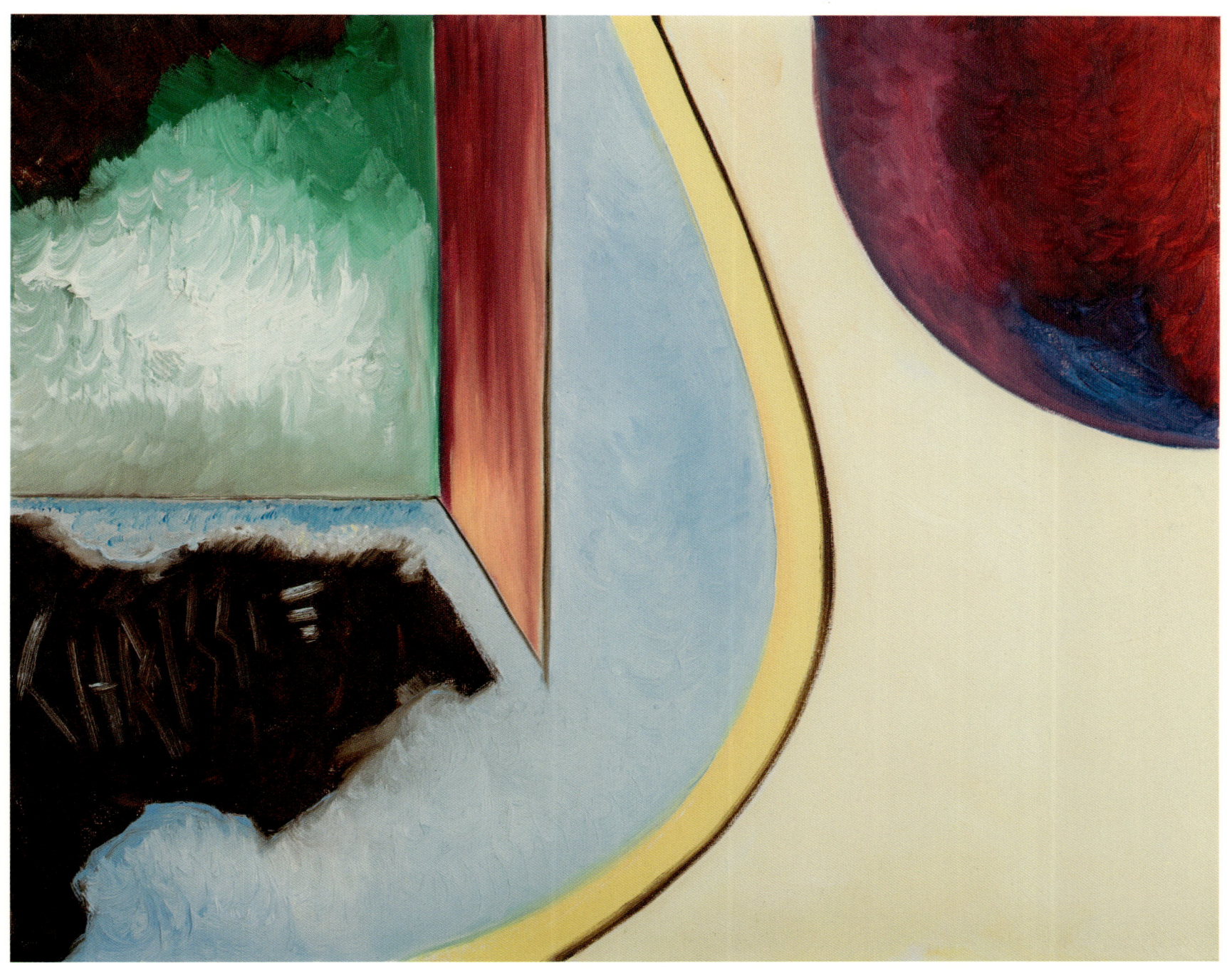

LEFT BEHIND
Oil on canvas
40 x 50 cm
(15³/₄ x 19³/₄ in)
9 April 2018

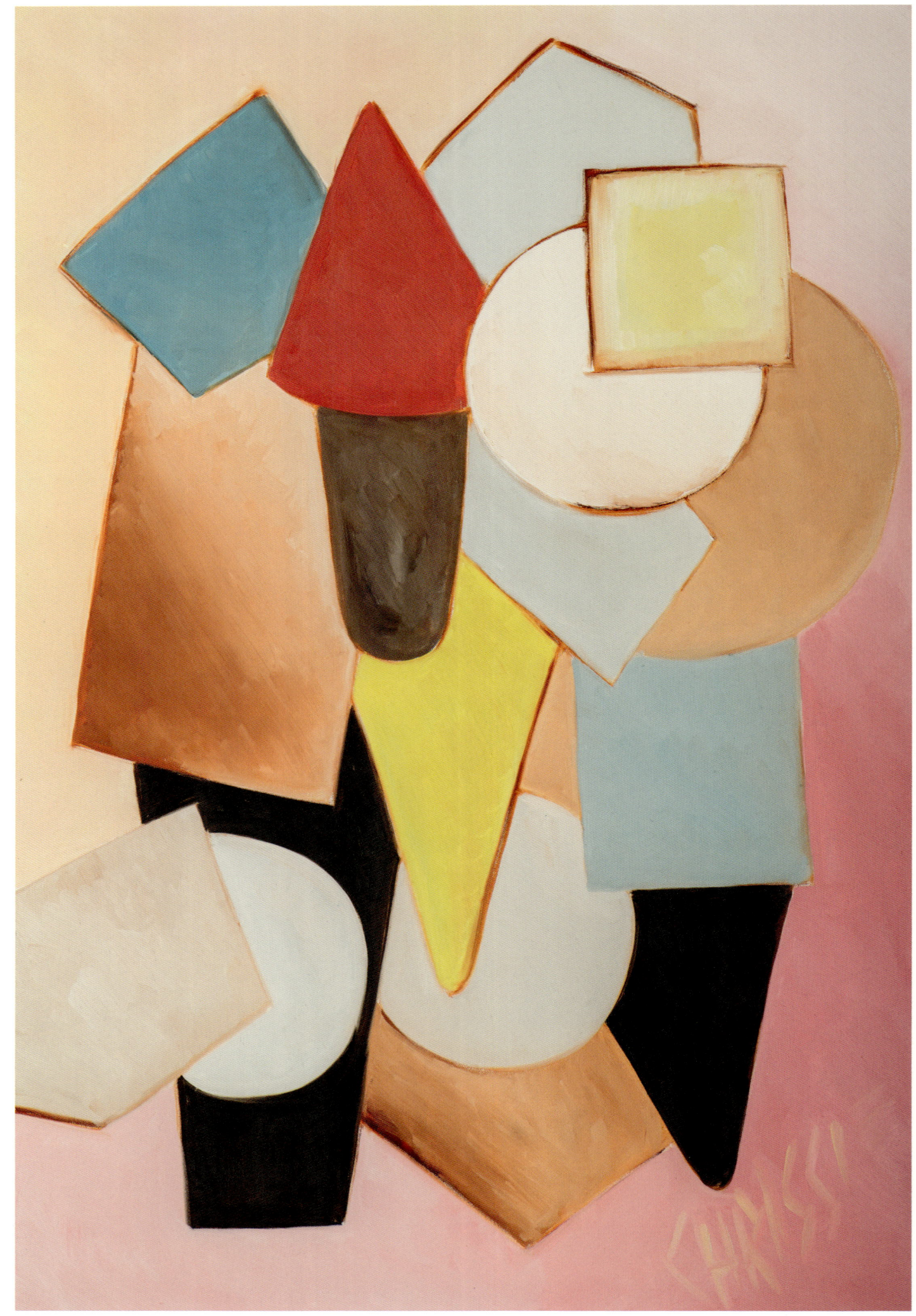

APRIL SHOWERS I
Oil on canvas
91 x 61 cm
(36 x 24 in)
10 April 2018

APRIL SHOWERS II
Oil on canvas
91 x 61 cm
(36 x 24 in)
10 April 2018

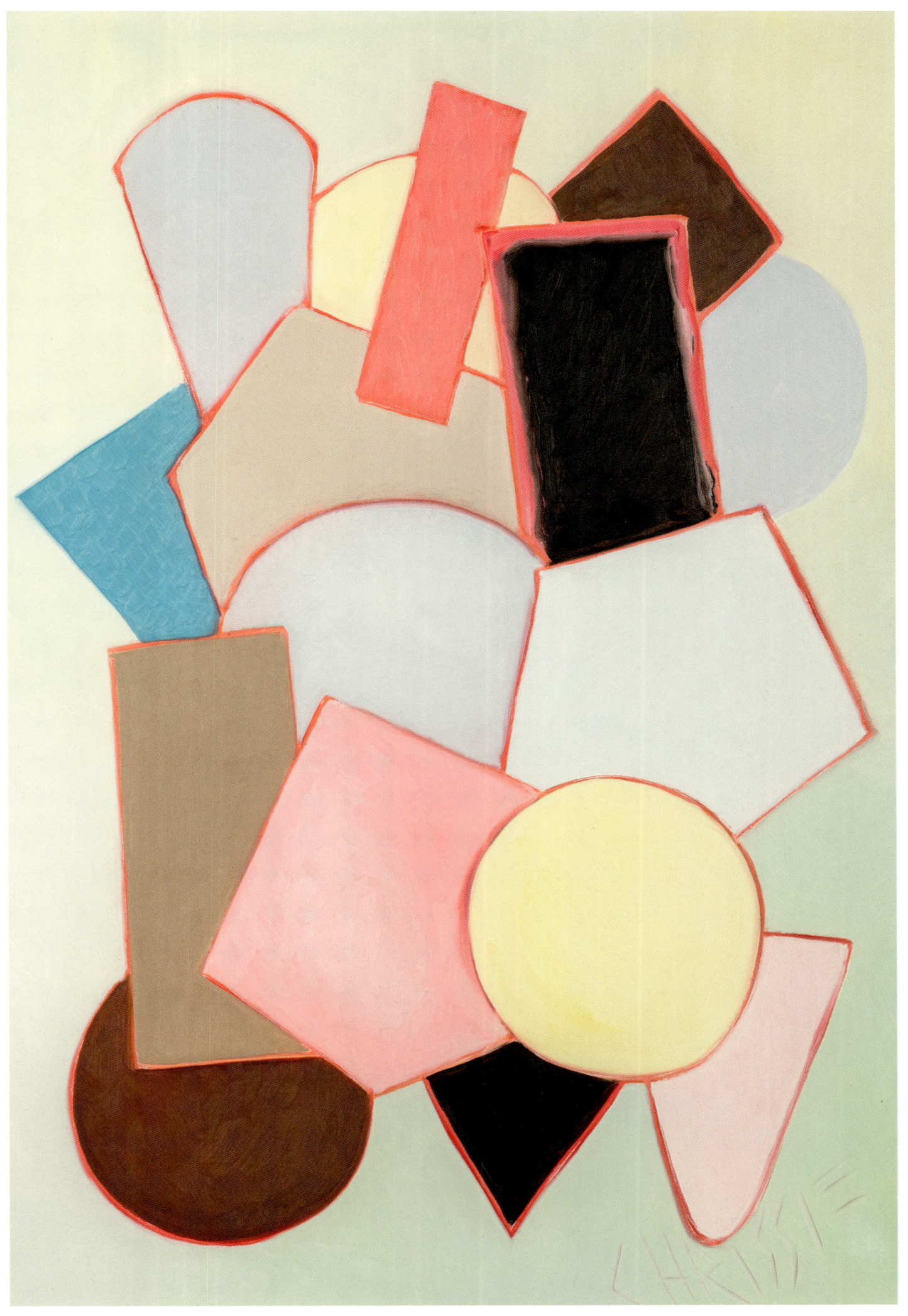

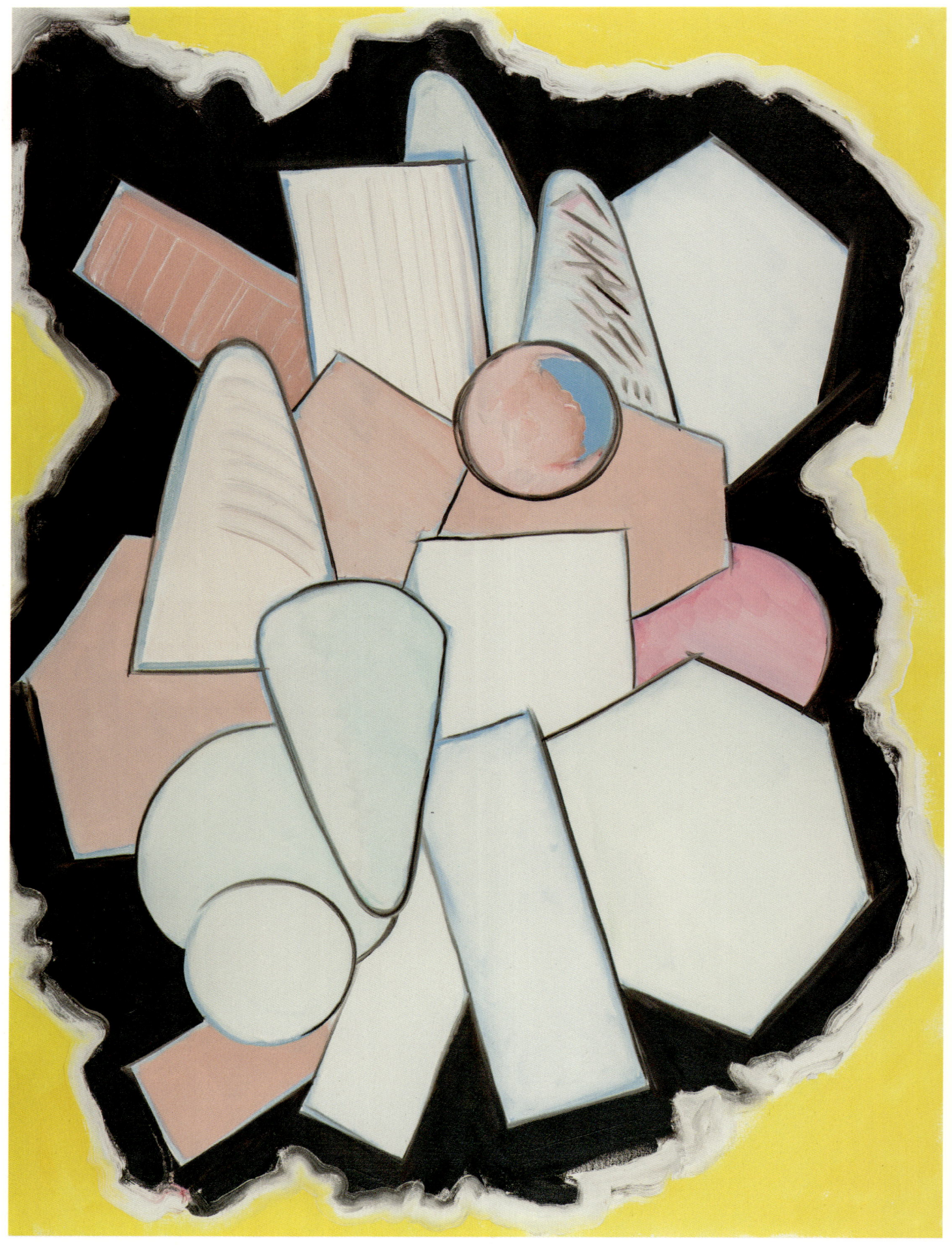

YELLOW SHAPES
Oil on canvas
100 x 76 cm
(39¹ᐟ² x 30 in)
14 April 2018

BLUE SKY SHAPES
Oil on canvas
100 x 80 cm
(39¹ᐟ² x 31¹ᐟ² in)
14 April 2018

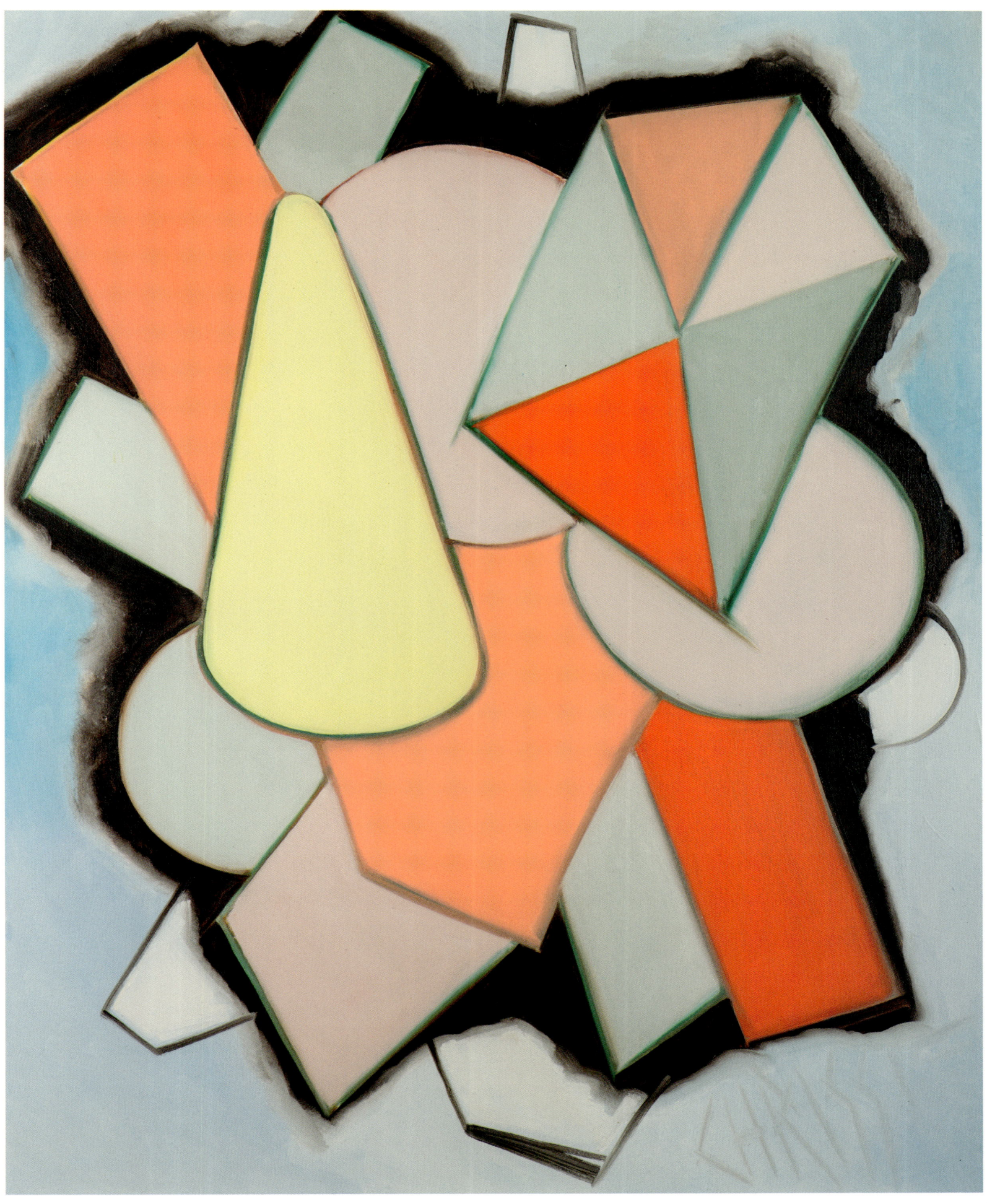

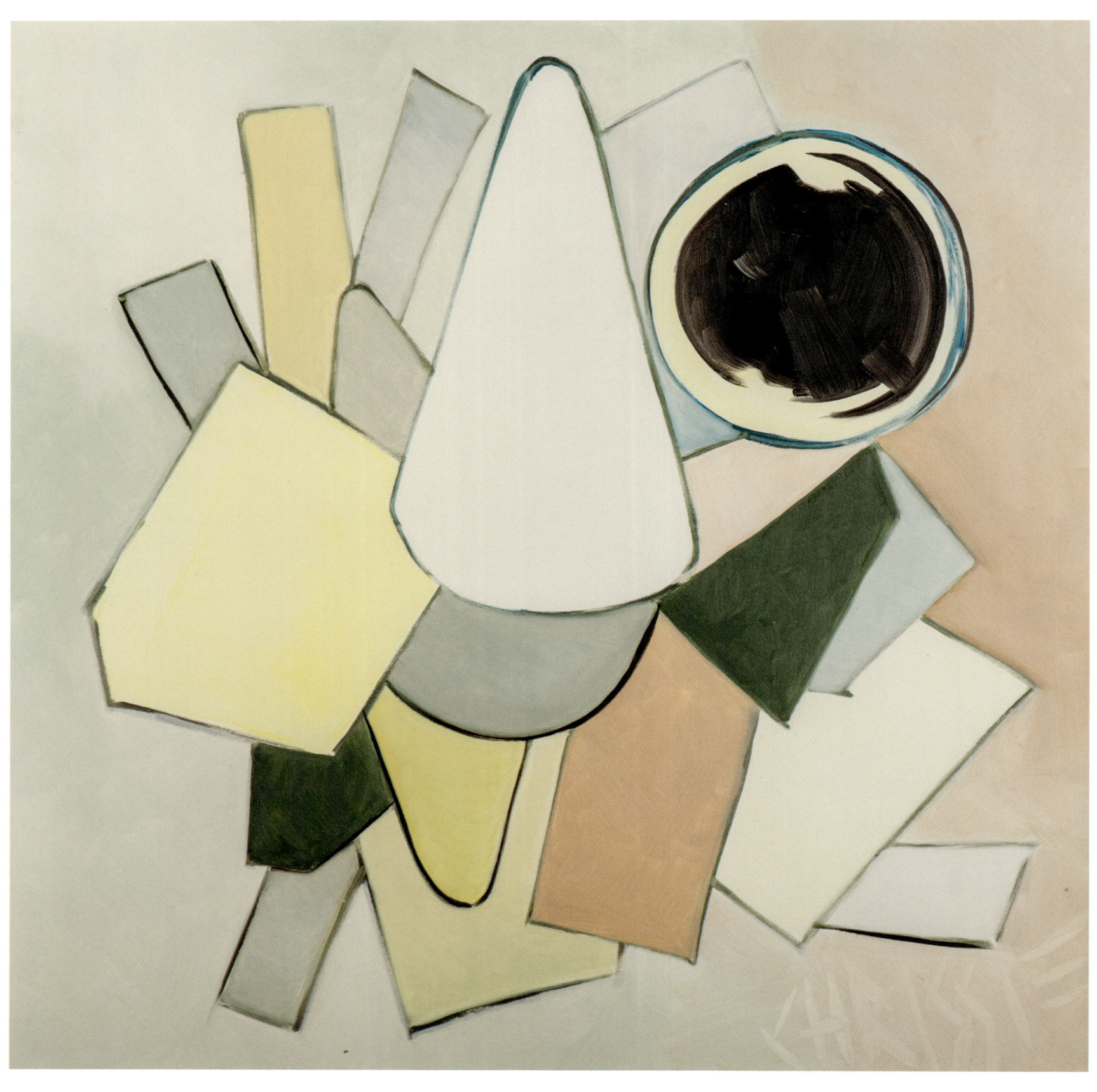

SHAPES EVENING
Oil on canvas
80 x 80 cm
(31$^{1/2}$ x 31$^{1/2}$ in)
14 April 2018

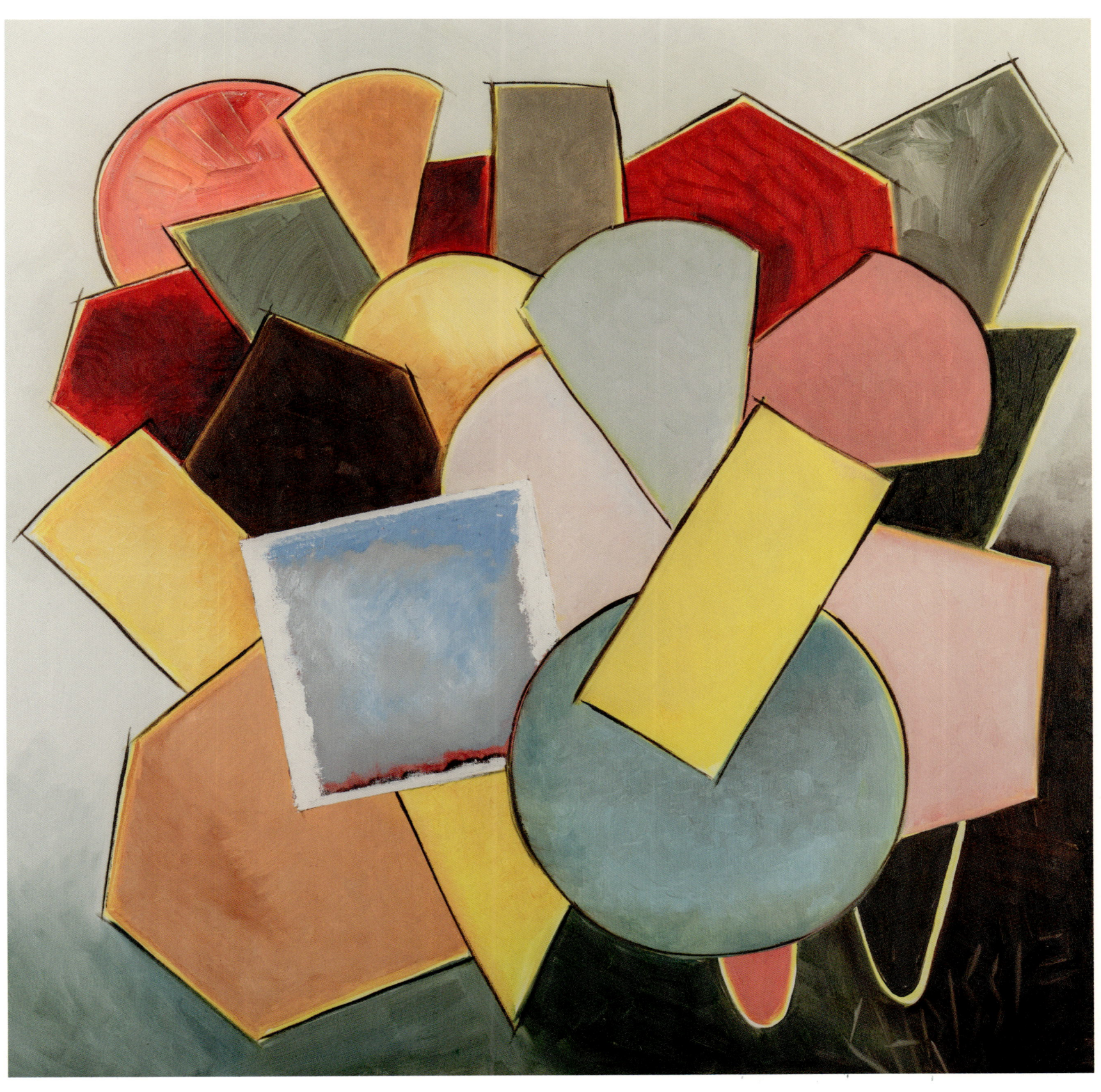

REVISITED COLOURS
Oil on canvas
80 x 80 cm
(31$^{1/2}$ x 31$^{1/2}$ in)
18 April 2018

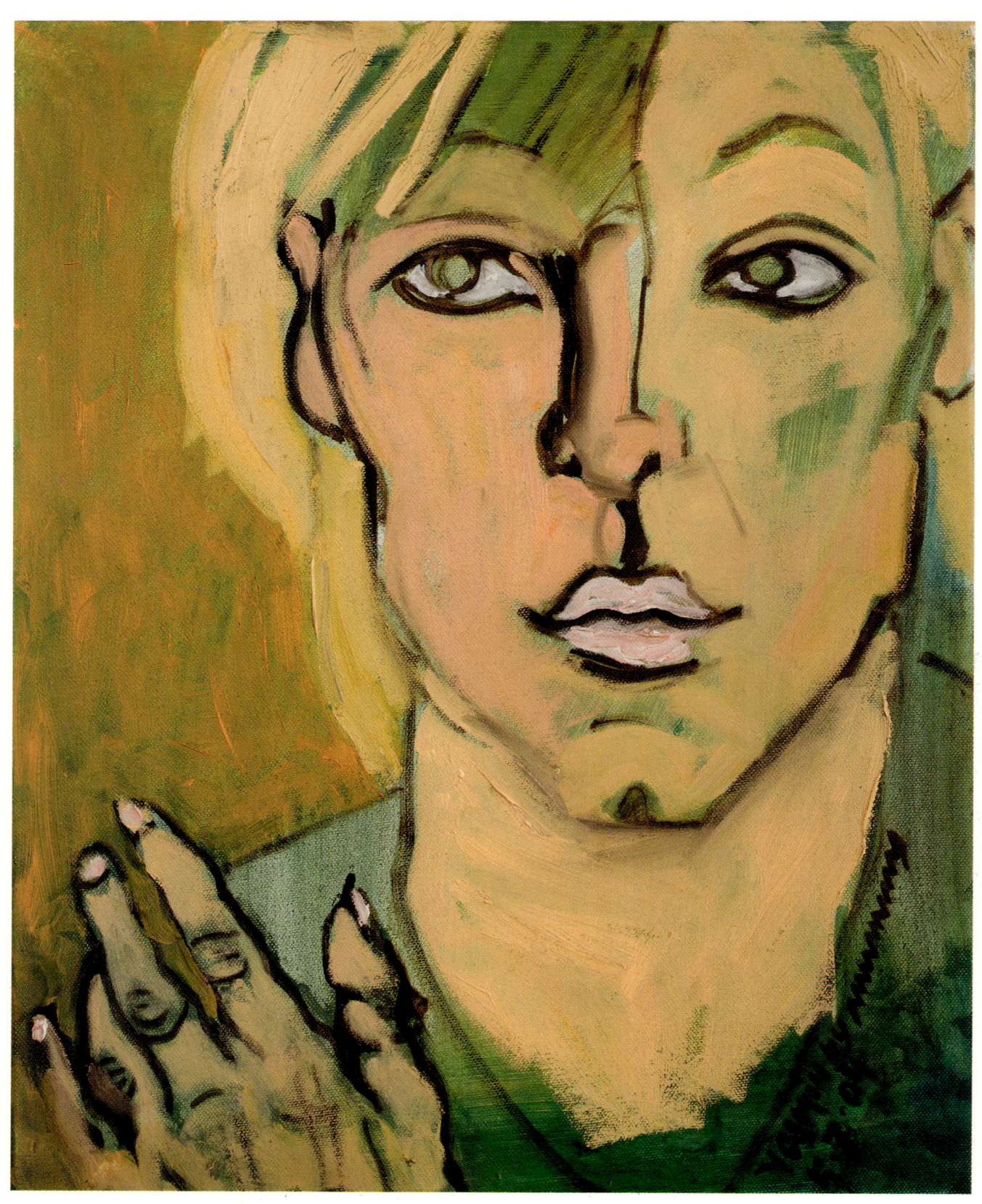

Here's my younger daughter, Yasmin. It's another early painting. Except, that's my hand. She has beautiful unlined hands, not like mine. Young face, old hand.

YASMIN I
Oil on canvas
50 x 40 cm
(19³/₄ x 15³/₄ in)
5 July 2004

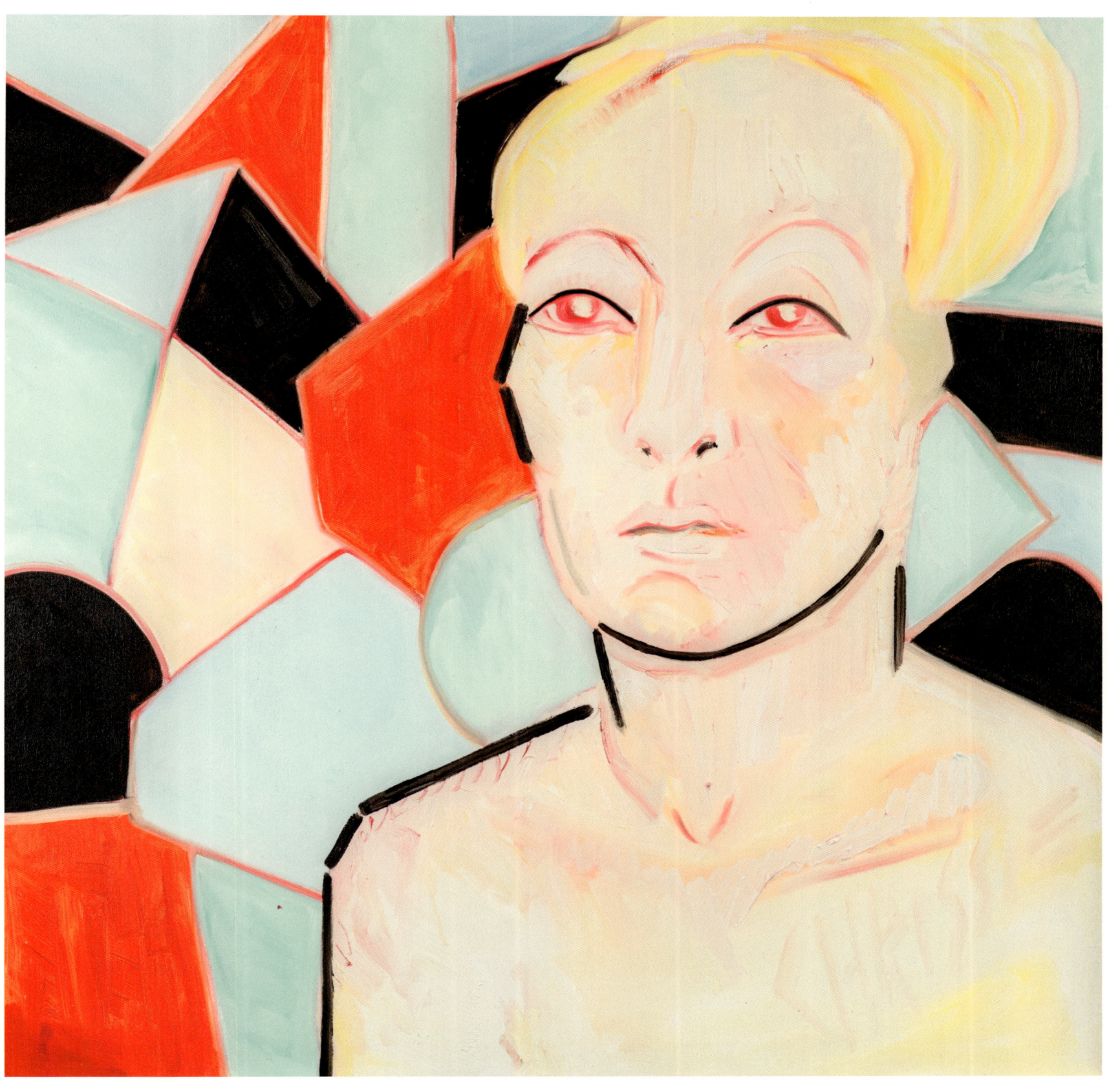

YASMIN
Oil on canvas
80 x 80 cm
(31¹⁄² x 31¹⁄² in)
18 April 2018

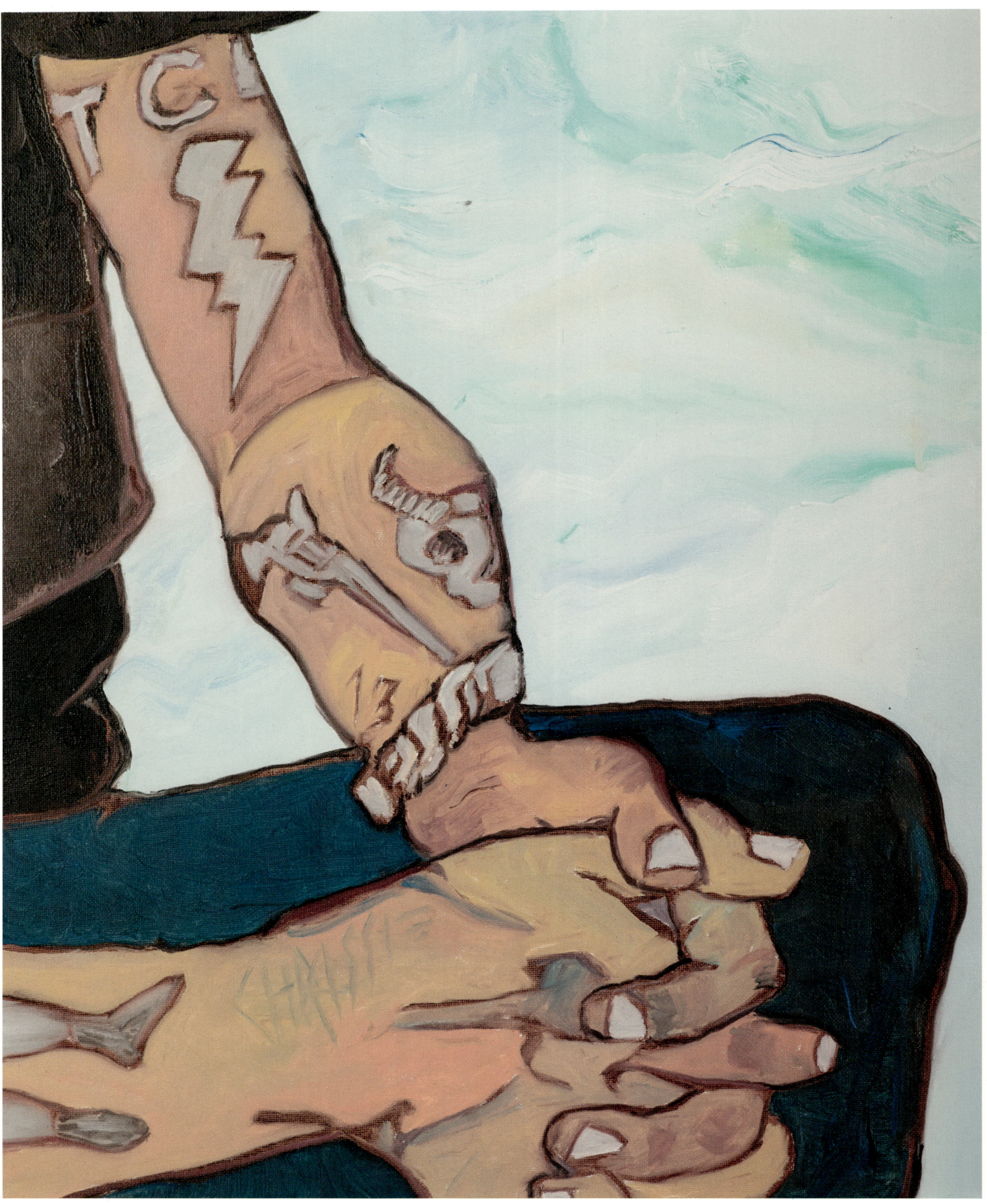

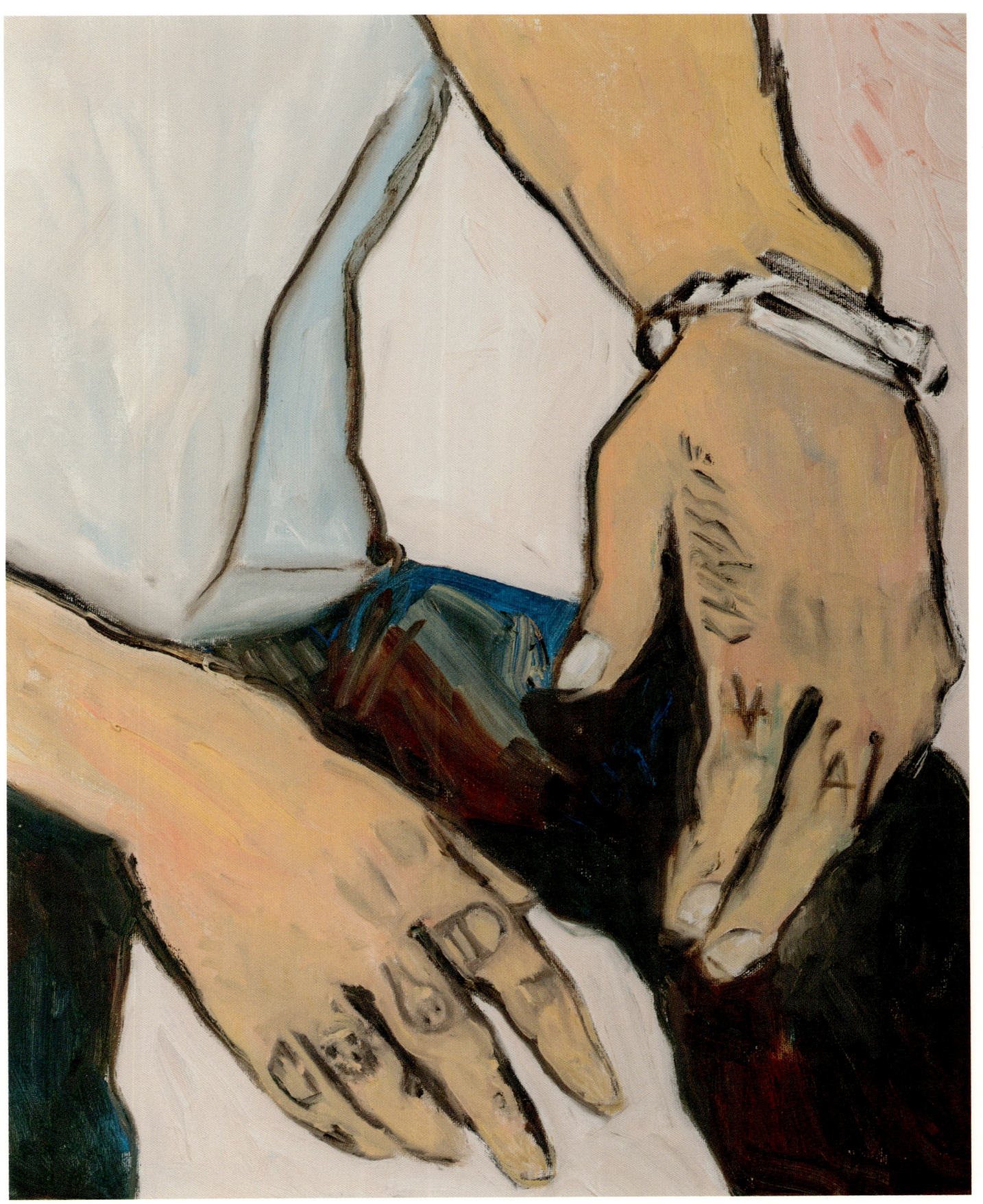

*David, my guitar tech, was downstairs in the little home studio, when I said,
'Quick, come up.' Thinking I wanted him to carry something downstairs, he
asked, 'Do you need a hand?' I said, 'I do, actually. Just sit there and hold still
for a minute.'*

DAVID
Oil on canvas
50 x 40 cm
(19³/₄ x 15³/₄ in)
18 April 2018

APRIL 30 HANDS
Oil on canvas
50 x 40 cm
(19³/₄ x 15³/₄ in)
30 April 2018

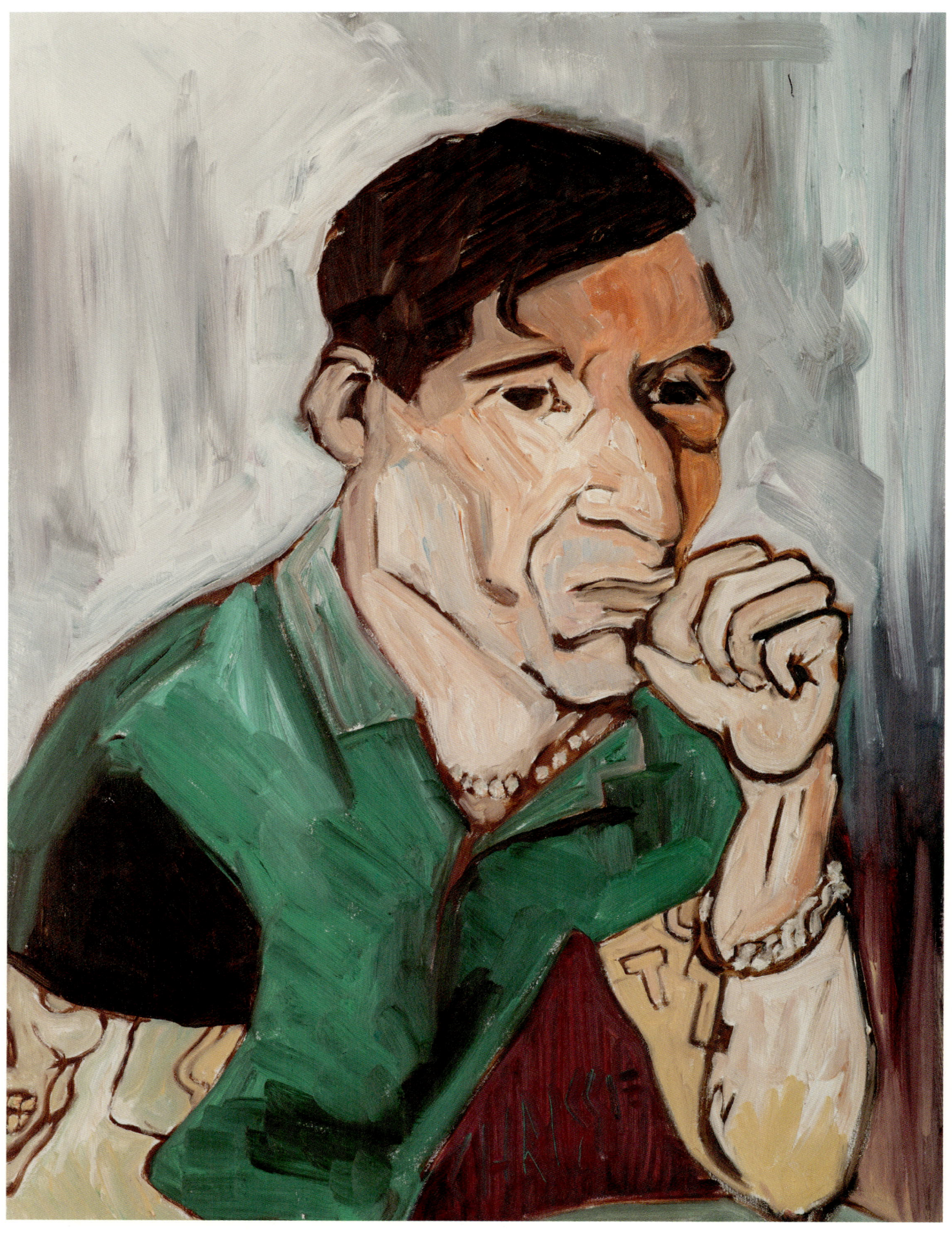

DAVID IN REPOSE
Oil on canvas
80 x 60 cm
(31$^{1/2}$ x 23$^{1/2}$ in)
27 May 2018

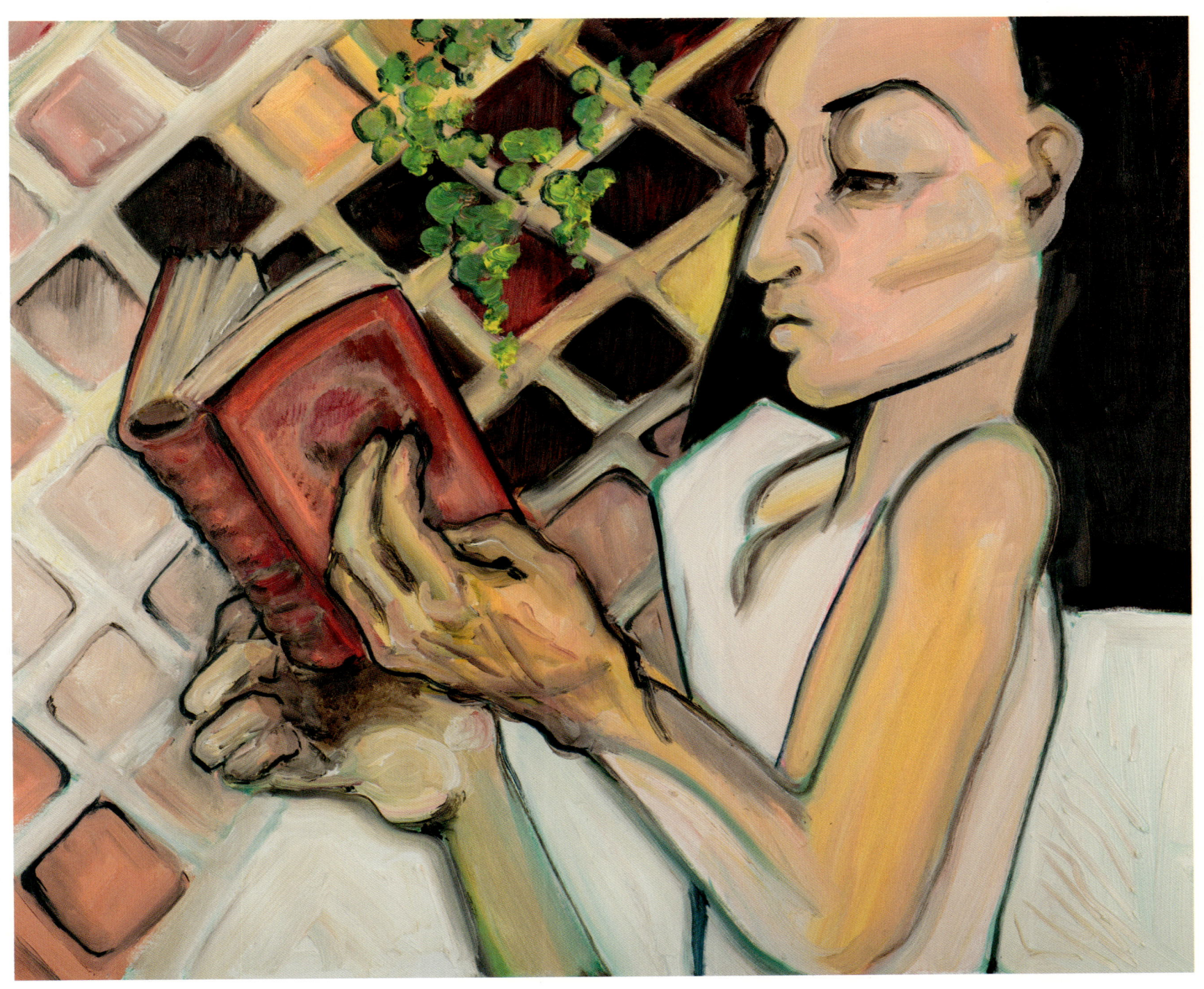

MAKI READING
MONDAY
Oil on canvas
50 x 60 cm
(19³/⁴ x 23¹/² in)
4 June 2018

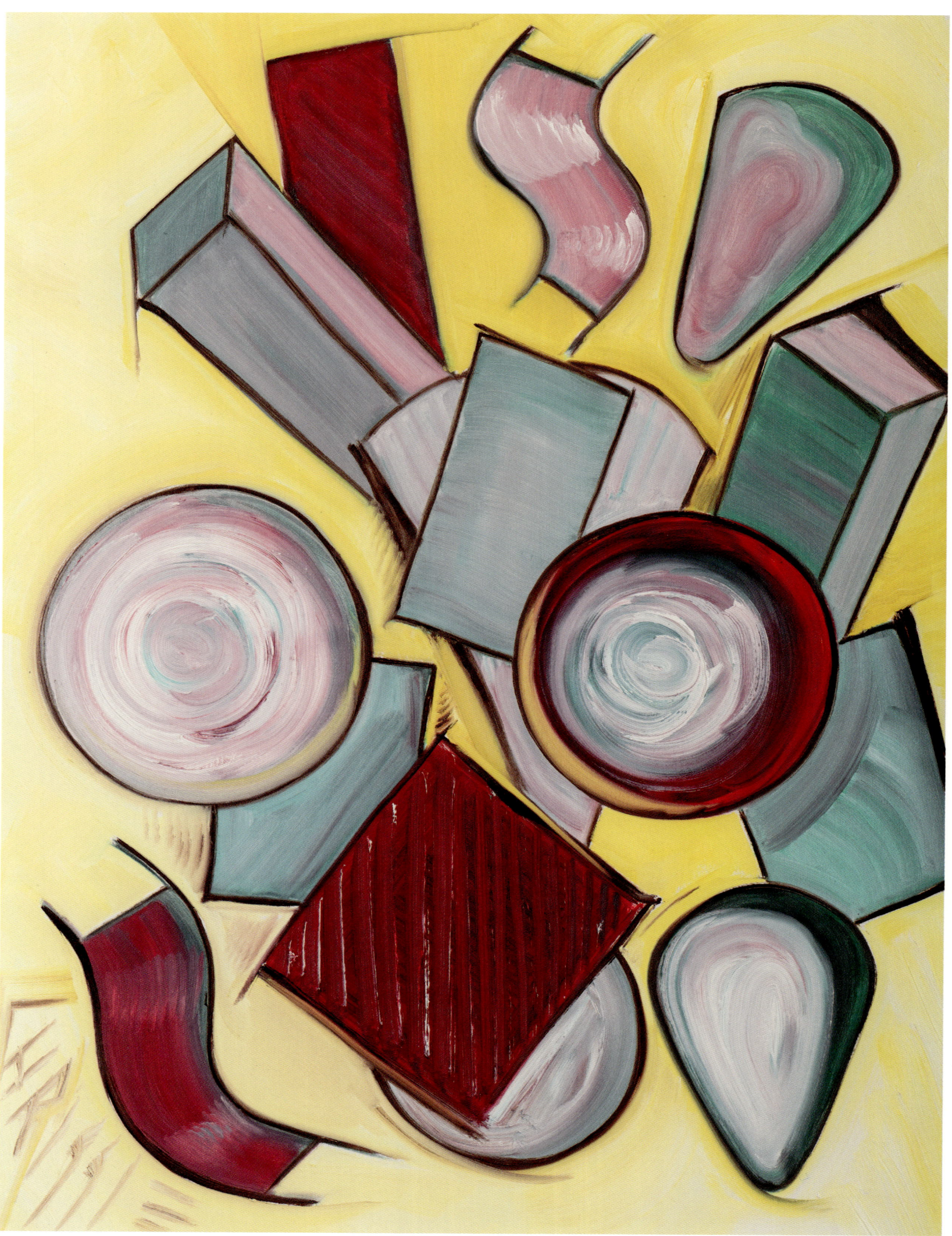

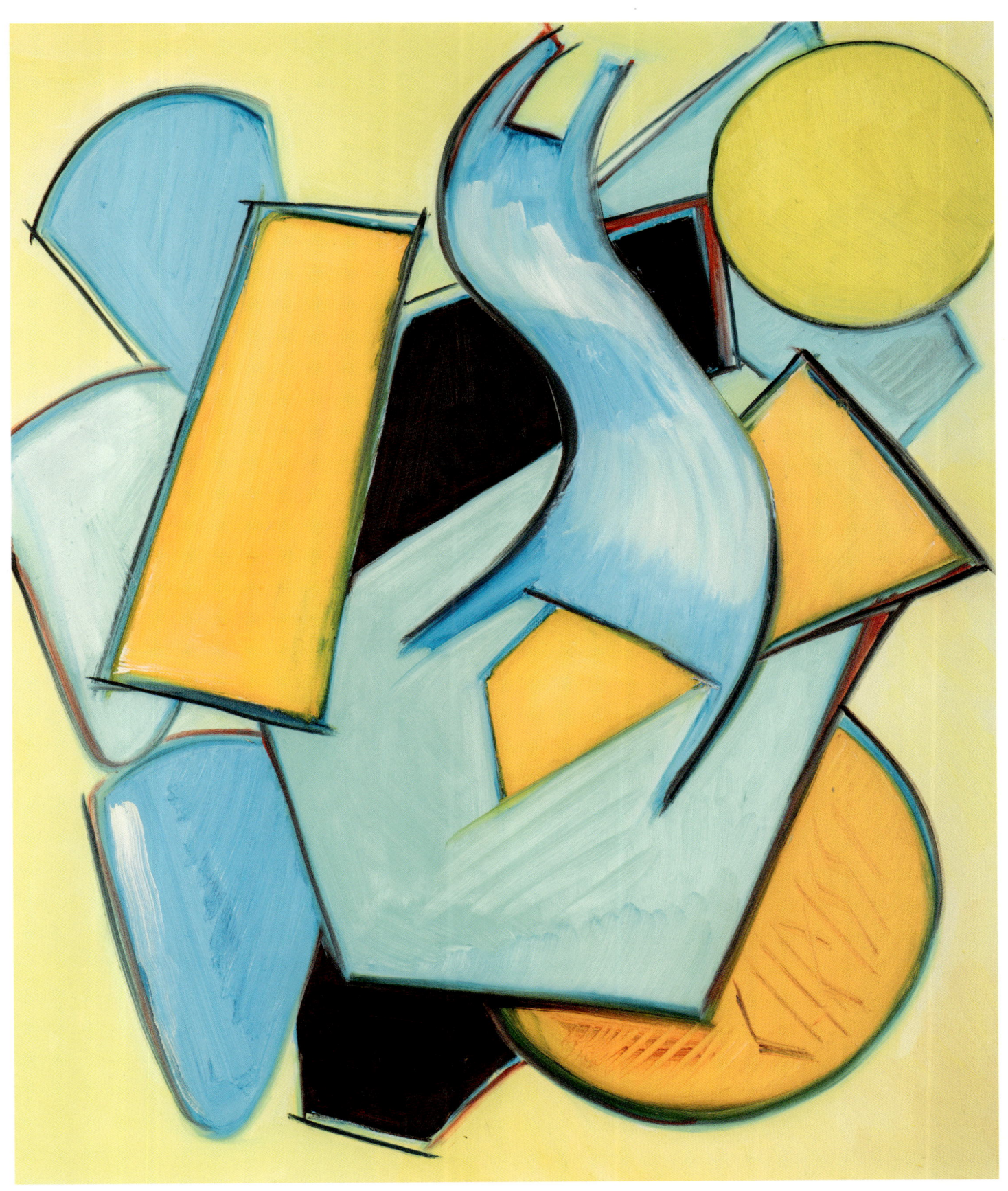

YELLOW SKY
Oil on canvas
80 x 60 cm
(31$^{1/2}$ x 23$^{1/2}$ in)
3 May 2018

MAY YELLOW
SHAPES I
Oil on canvas
60 x 50 cm
(23$^{1/2}$ x 19$^{3/4}$ in)
3 May 2018

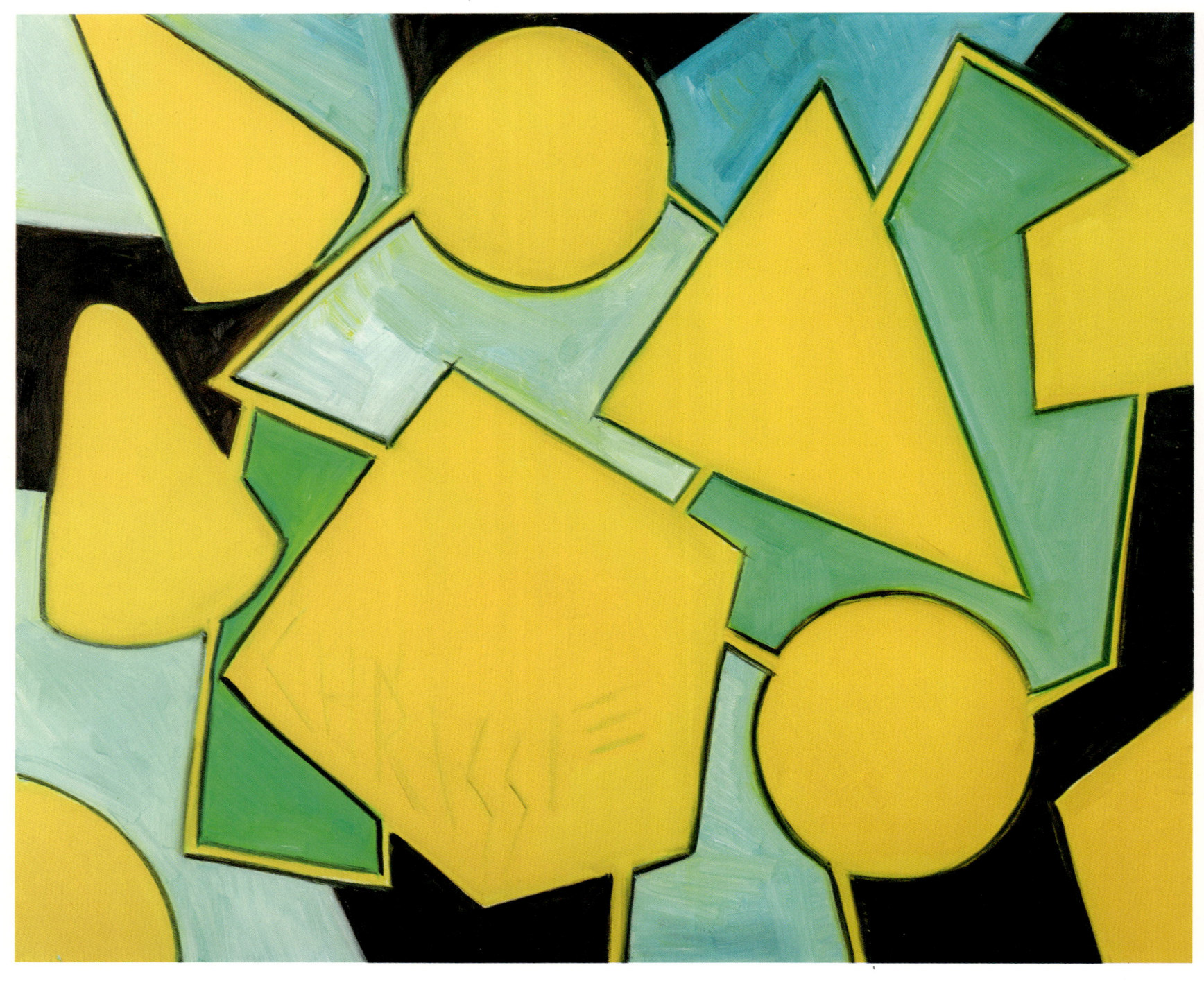

I'm just starting to see how my painting voice is emerging. I need more time, time is always running out.

MAY YELLOW
SHAPES II
Oil on canvas
50 x 60 cm
(19³/⁴ x 23¹/² in)
12 May 2018

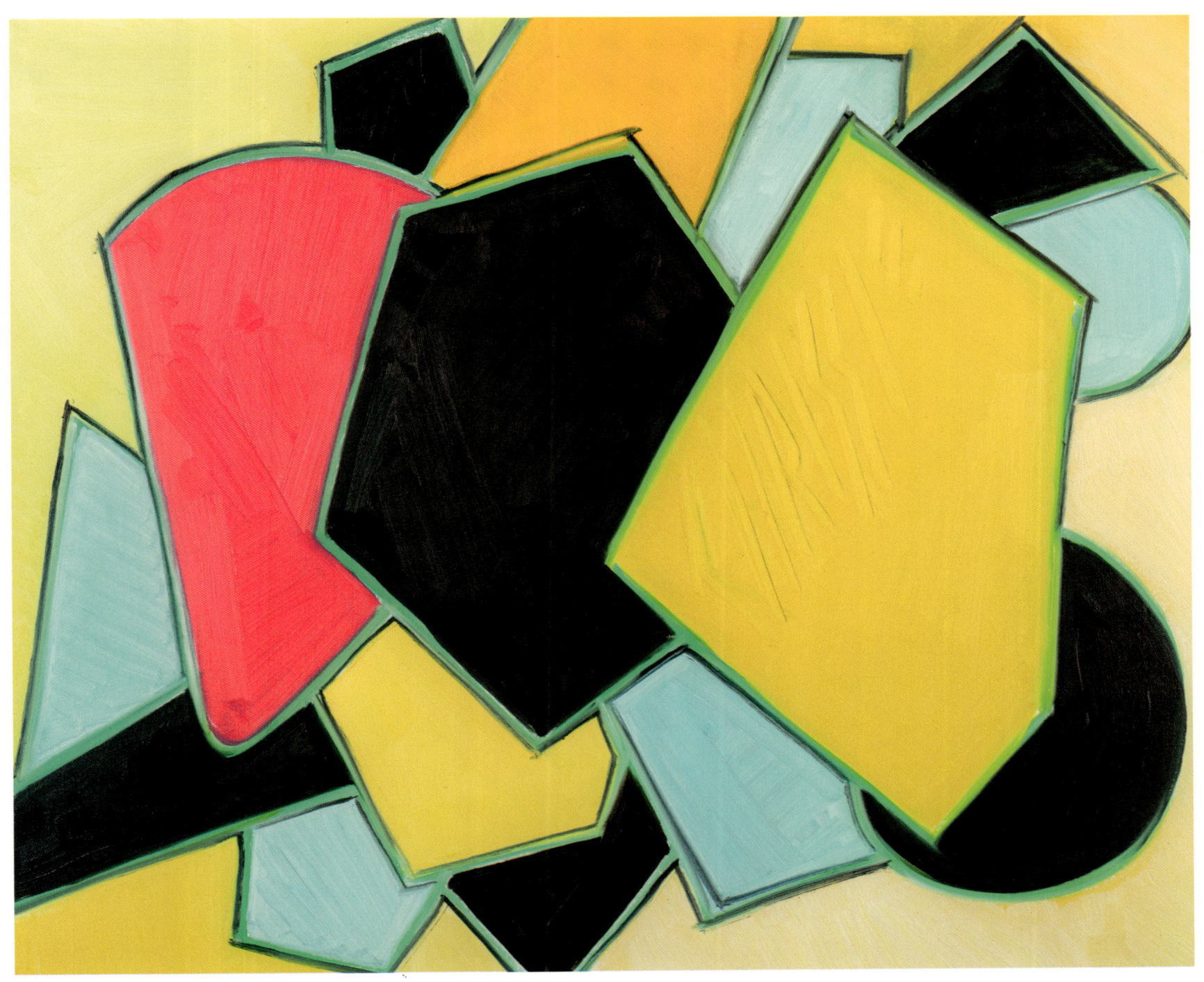

Experience of working menial jobs has certainly been very useful in my life,
because I always have that to compare things to. For example, I'm nervous
to go on stage but then I'm not cleaning a house. I appreciate what a
privilege it is to have time to paint.

SUNDAY SHAPES
Oil on canvas
50 x 60 cm
(19³⁄₄ x 23¹⁄₂ in)
12 May 2018

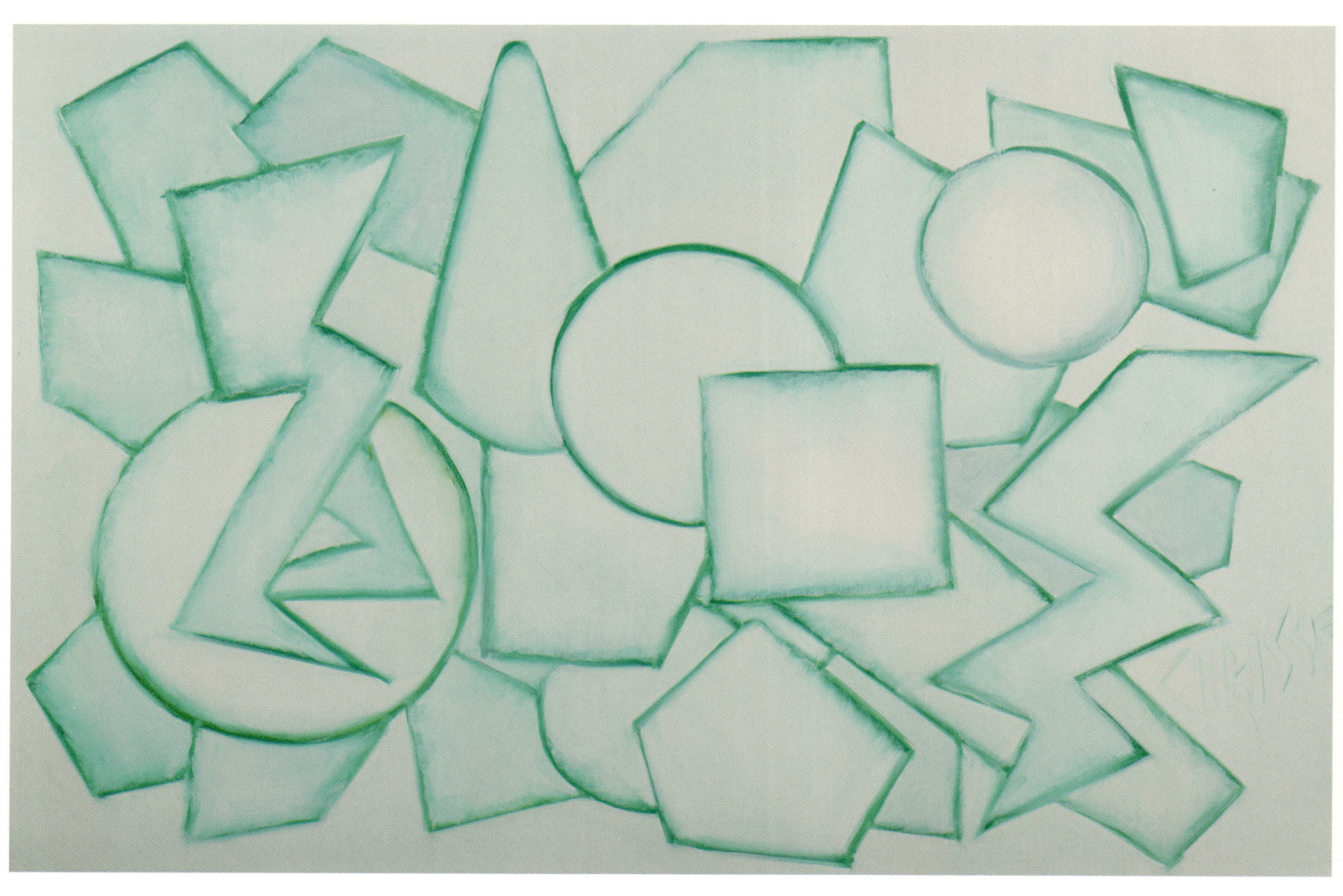

ONE BRUSH GREEN I
Oil on canvas
50 x 76 cm
(19³/⁴ x 30 in)
12 May 2018

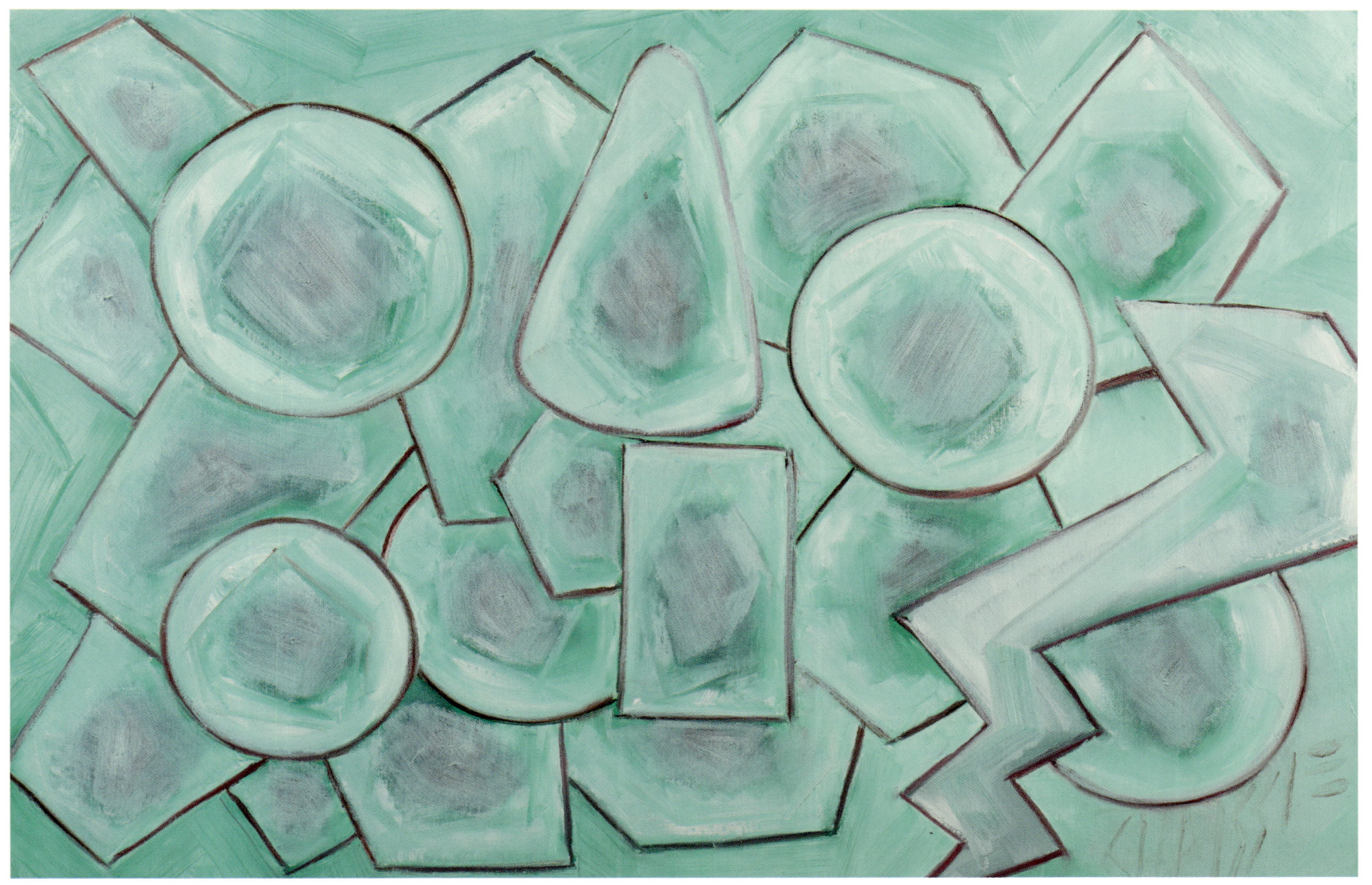

Painting is like making a new record. I can have 10 or 11 songs in my head for a long time, but once I record them and release them, then I can move on. It's hard to move on when there's a backlog of stuff. It holds you back. I'm a big believer in keeping things moving all the time.

Take these paintings and release me.

ONE BRUSH GREEN II
Oil on canvas
50 x 76 cm
(19³/₄ x 30 in)
24 May 2018

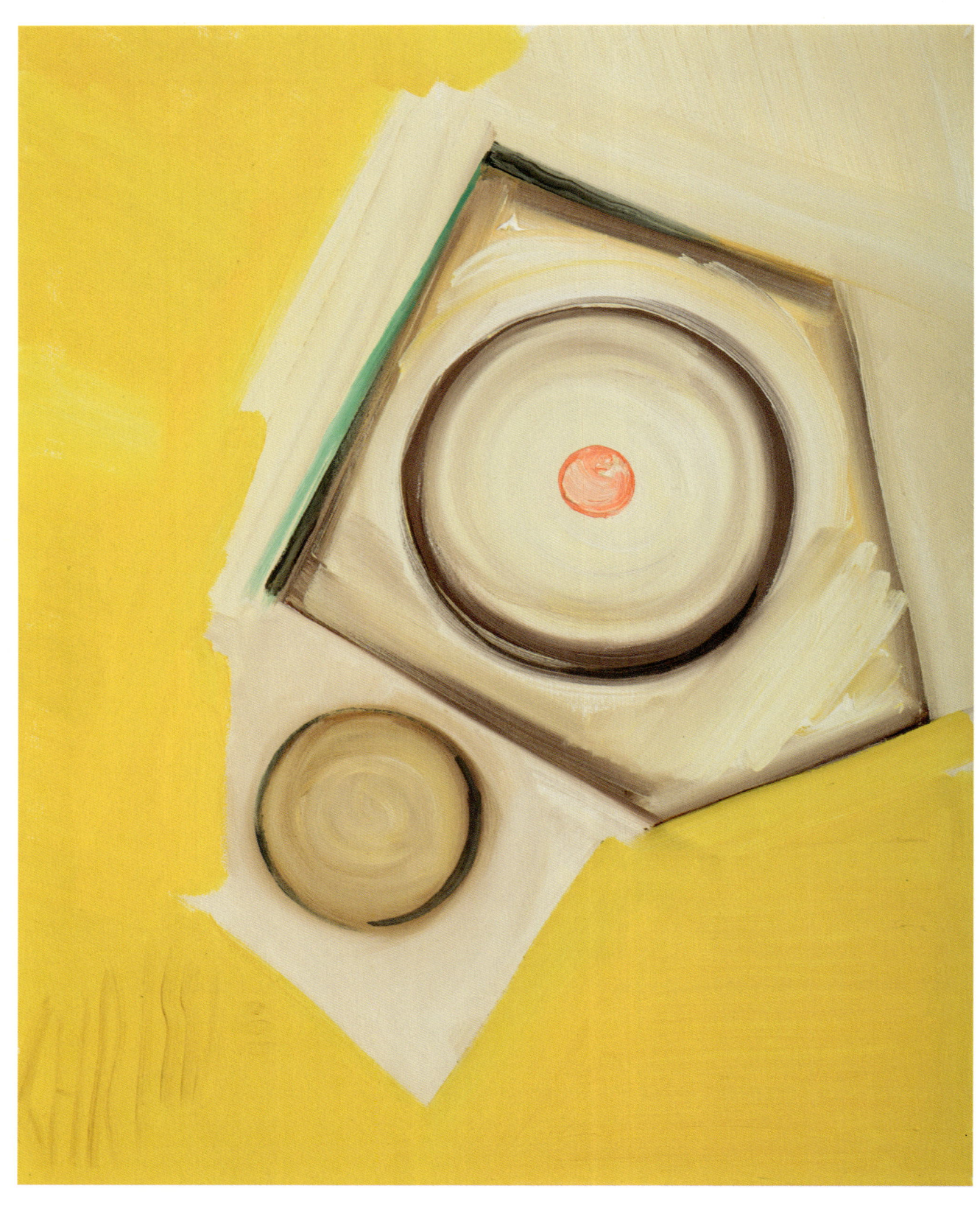

YELLOW AFTERNOON I
Oil on canvas
50 x 40 cm
(19¾ x 15¾ in)
21 May 2018

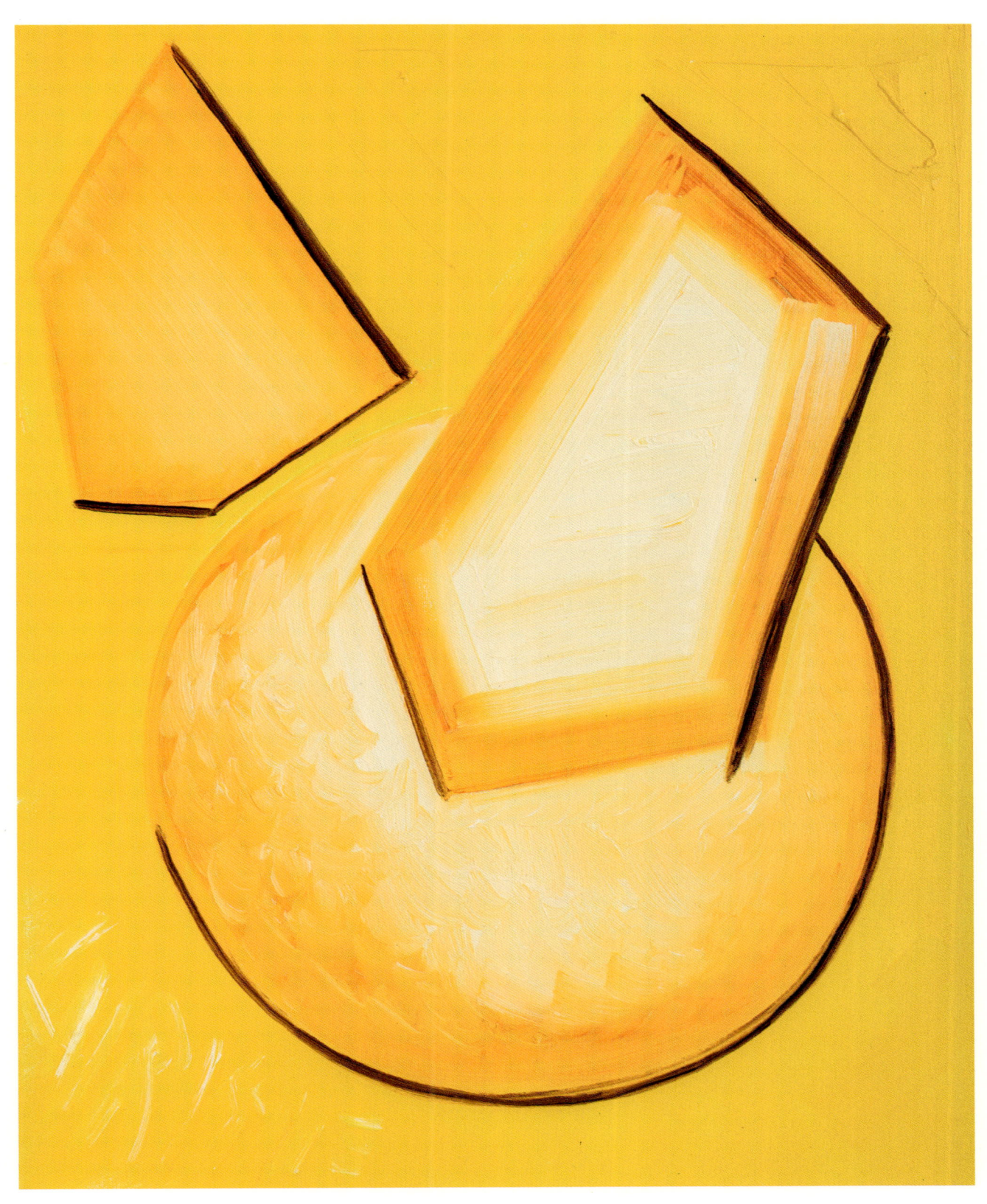

YELLOW AFTERNOON II
Oil on canvas
50 x 40 cm
(19³/₄ x 15³/₄ in)
21 May 2018

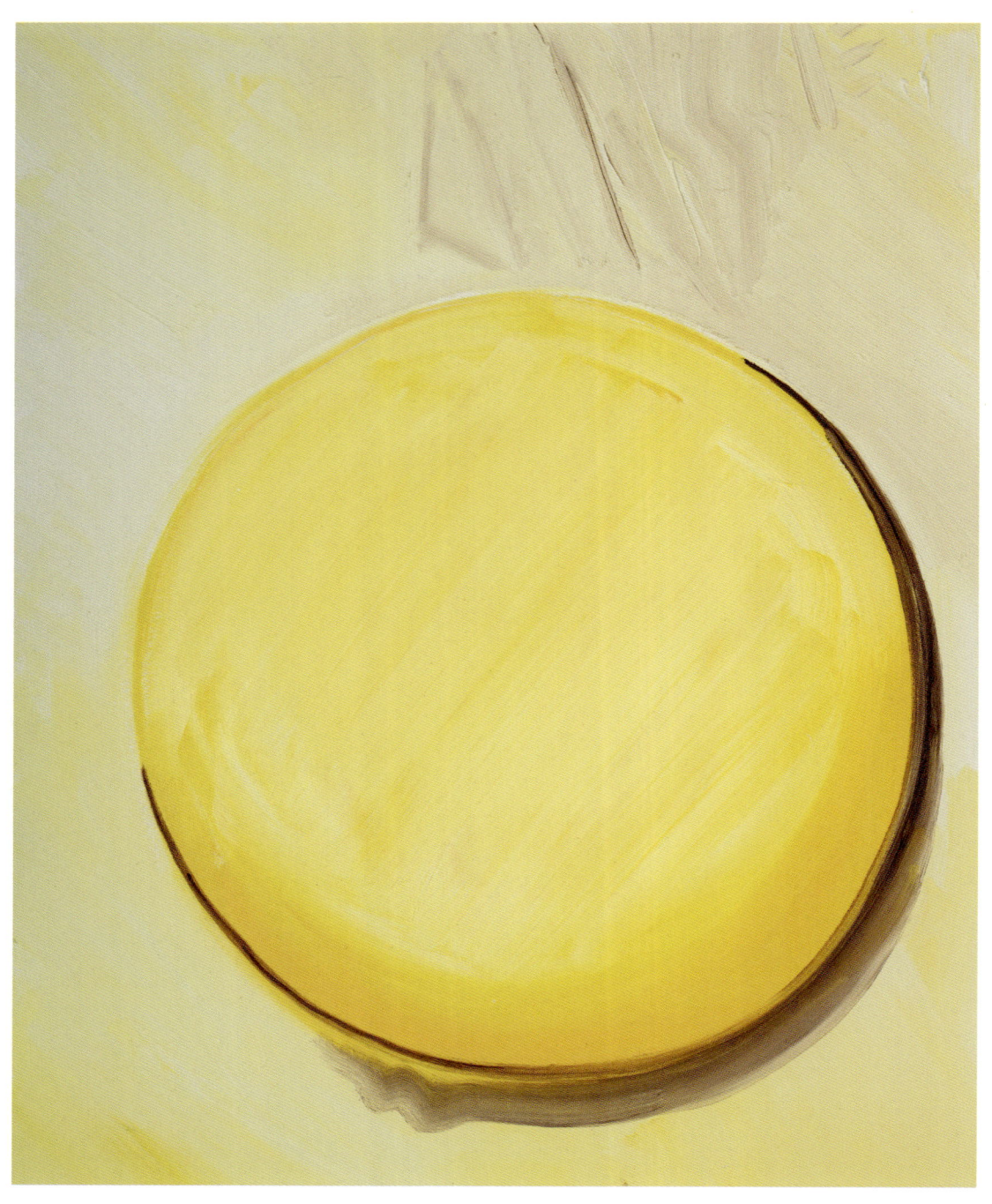

YELLOW AFTERNOON III
Oil on canvas
50 x 40 cm
(19¾ x 15¾ in)
21 May 2018

Everybody's asking where did you go?
This was gonna be my masterpiece
The paint's not even dry yet — oh no
I could trace the outline of a shadow
but I need blood and breath
To mix my colours

I know I'm not Monet or Van Gogh
I can't draw like S. Clay Wilson
You're inside this brush that drips with red
I can't paint from memories or photos
I need blood and breath
But you left me nothing

Where did you go?
After you promised me a portrait
Took off your clothes
Held a pose
Drawing your arms,
and your hands and veins and fingers,
and your lips
and your broken nose
…on your eyes,
So just stare into the distance
Please don't move
Whatever you do
While I'm adding the blue

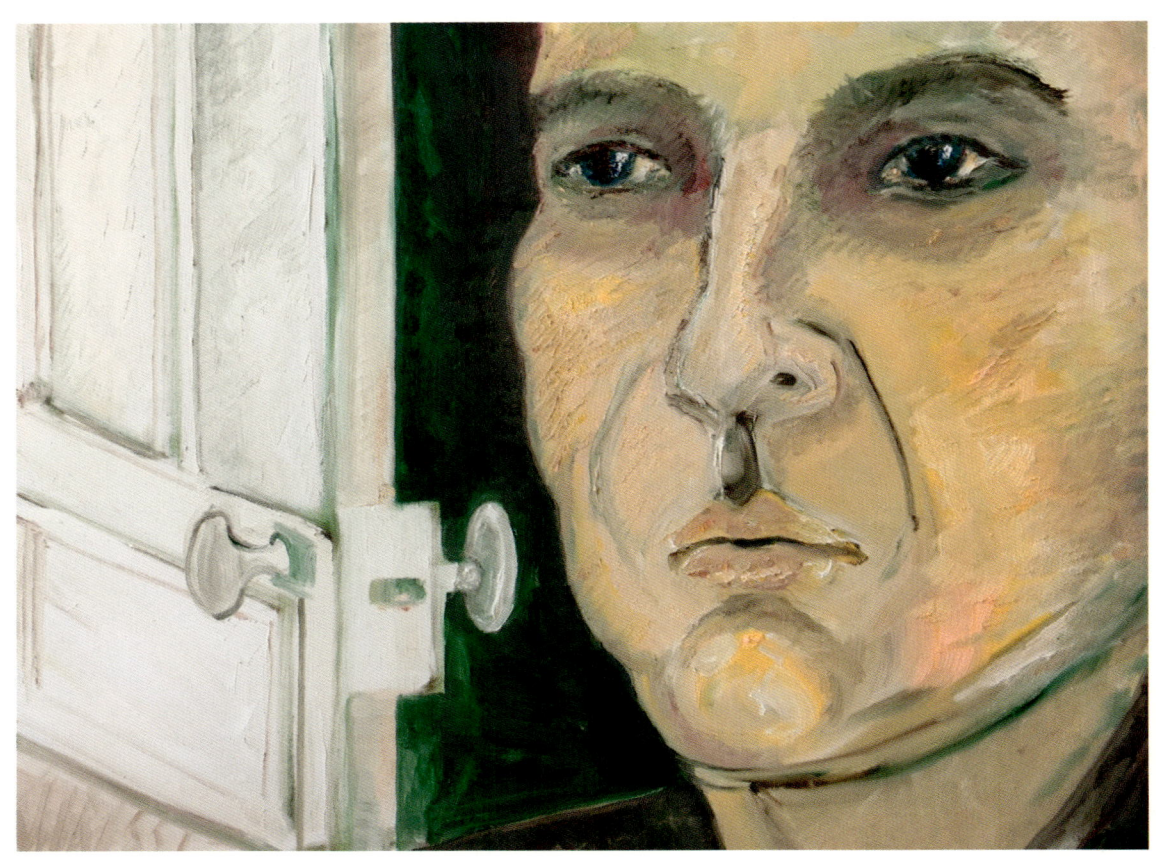

AUTHOR ACKNOWLEDGEMENTS

Special thanks to Catherine and Nick Roylance for their enthusiasm, and as the children of Brian Roylance for keeping the Genesis vision alive.

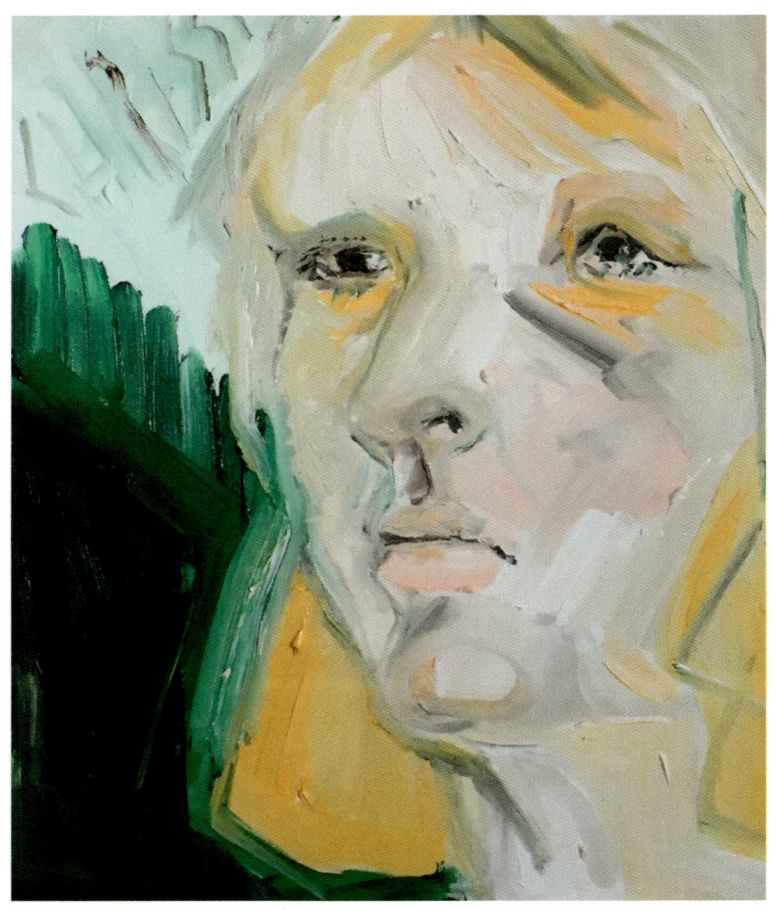

NICHOLAS SÈTE
Oil on canvas
30 x 40 cm
(11³⁄⁴ x 15³⁄⁴ in)
25 May 2018

CATHERINE SÈTE
Oil on canvas
40 x 30 cm
(15³⁄⁴ x 11³⁄⁴ in)
25 May 2018

PUBLISHER'S NOTE

Our thanks to Chrissie Hynde for giving us the keys to her studio and allowing us to present her paintings to Genesis readers and the world for the very first time. Working with Chrissie has been an exciting creative collaboration and we are incredibly grateful for the energy and insight she gave to every stage of the project.

To Chrissie's team at Quietus Management, with thanks to: Ian Grenfell, Didz Hammond and Clementine de Banzie Lampard.

Thank you to Brian Eno and Tim Marlow for their words and enthusiasm.

Special thanks to Jill Furmanovsky for her superb photography and support.

Lastly, thanks to our photographers and editorial team: Richard Pereira, Paul Stead, Teresa Fernandez, Alexandra Rigby-Wild and James Hodgson.

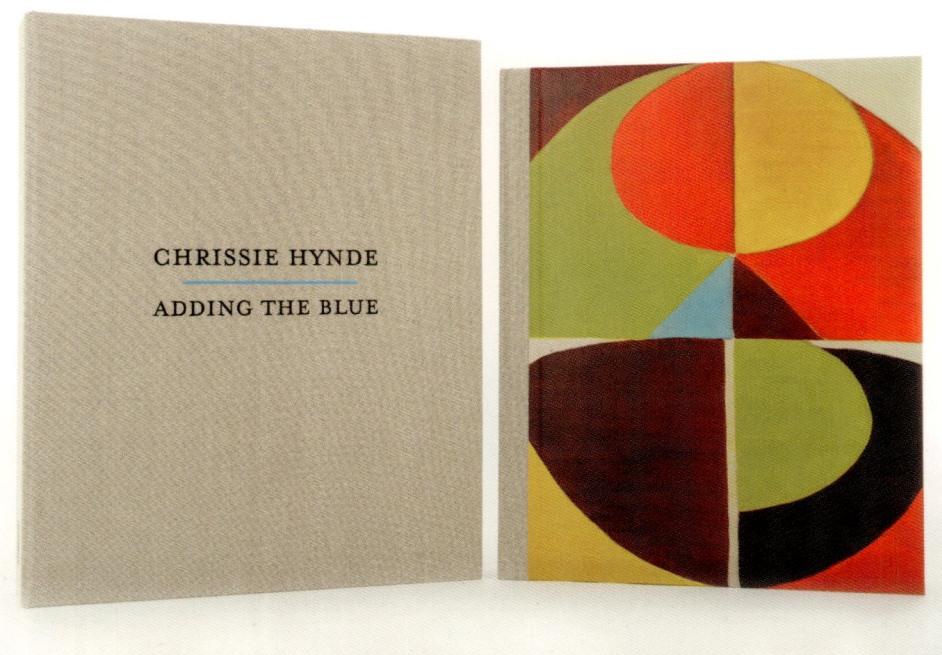

ADDING THE BLUE BY CHRISSIE HYNDE
Limited Edition Book & Fine Art Print Collection

Chrissie Hynde's Adding The Blue *is available as an artist-signed and numbered book limited to 1,000 copies worldwide.*

Since 1974, Genesis Publications has created over 100 titles with renowned authors, as varied as they are many, including Sir Peter Blake, David Bowie, Jimmy Page, Ringo Starr, Eric Clapton and Ronnie Wood.

Each cloth-bound copy of Adding The Blue *is signed by Chrissie Hynde, presented in a solander case and accompanied by a special art print. A selection of Chrissie's paintings are also available as limited edition prints.*

To order a limited edition book, or a fine art print, please visit our website:

addingtheblue.com | genesis-publications.com

THIS EDITION FIRST PUBLISHED
IN 2018 BY GENESIS PUBLICATIONS

COPYRIGHT © 2018
GENESIS PUBLICATIONS LTD

ALL TEXT AND PAINTINGS
COPYRIGHT © 2018 CHRISSIE HYNDE

PAGE 2 AND BACK COVER:
PHOTOGRAPHS COPYRIGHT © 2018
JILL FURMANOVSKY

ISBN: 978-1-905662-54-8

PRINTED AND BOUND BY IMAGO
PUBLISHING LTD

THIS BOOK FIRST APPEARED
AS A LIMITED EDITION OF 1,000
NUMBERED COPIES, SIGNED
BY CHRISSIE HYNDE

GENESIS PUBLICATIONS LTD
GENESIS HOUSE, 2 JENNER ROAD
GUILDFORD, ENGLAND, GU1 3PL

FINE BOOKS AND PRINTS SINCE 1974
GENESIS-PUBLICATIONS.COM